THE ANGELS

THE ANGELS

A History of
the 11th Airborne Division

Lt. Gen. E. M. Flanagan, Jr. USA (Ret.)

Foreword by Lt. Gen. William B. Yarborough, USA (Ret.)

PRESIDIO

940.54127

Published by Presidio Press
31 Pamaron Way, Novato, CA 94949

Library of Congress Cataloging-in-Publication Data

Flanagan, E. M., 1921- *8-90 BT 2200*
   The Angels: a history of the 11th Airborne Division/E. M. Flanagan, Jr.
      p.   cm.
   ISBN 0-89141-358-8
      1. United States. Army. Airborne Division, 11th—History.
2. World War, 1939-1945—Regimental histories—United States.
3. World War, 1939-1945—Campaigns—Pacific Area. I. Title.
D769.346 11th.F58 1989
940.54'1273—dc20   89-34470
                                                               CIP

Photographs 2, 4, and 8-16 courtesy National Archives
Printed in the United States of America

To Joseph May Swing, 1894–1984
Lieutenant General, U.S. Army

The first history of the 11th Airborne Division was dedicated to "the combat dead and wounded of the 11th Airborne Division." It seems only proper and right that this book should be dedicated to the man whose superior training standards, exacting disciplinary demands, and sincere concern for his men made those combat dead and wounded numbers as low as possible, given the rigors of combat and the extraordinary battle missions expected of and executed by the lightweight, half-sized 11th Airborne Division.

A draftee, not of the 11th, wrote that "those guys of the 11th Airborne Division bounced when they walked." And as Maj. "Ripcord" Walker so accurately and warmly put it: "That bounce evidenced our pride of service and was stamped into us by that arrogant, irascible, exacting but thoroughly wonderful commander —General Joseph M. Swing." No matter—whether it was in training, in a division review, on a prolonged road march, on the baseball diamond, on the football field, on the basketball court, but primarily in combat—we simply wanted "Uncle Joe" to be proud of us.

CONTENTS

FOREWORD

Perhaps the most lasting impression this magnificent history of the 11th Airborne Division has left with me is a deep sense of gratitude for having known, served with, and shared experiences with so many of the great airborne soldiers who march through its pages.

Although my wartime airborne service was half a world away from the operational area of the 11th Airborne Division, reading its history is for me almost like looking through a family album.

All of the sites at which the Angels engaged in military operations in the Philippines are well known to me. Fort McKinley on Luzon was my first duty station upon graduation from the United States Military Academy in 1936. Assigned to Fort McKinley at the same time were two officers whose names were destined to become household words within the airborne community: William T. Ryder and James M. Gavin.

In nearby Manila, a corporal in the 31st Infantry named Hobart Wade would become platoon sergeant of the Parachute Test Platoon, would ultimately win a commission, return to the Philippines with the 11th Airborne Division and jump on Tagaytay Ridge as a member of the 511th Parachute Infantry Regiment.

From the essence distilled by Bill Ryder's Parachute Test Platoon in the early 1940s, a tradition for extraordinary daring, leadership and accomplishment spread to the fledging American parachute battalions, then to the regiments which received cadres linking them to a common origin. From the regiments the genes were passed to divisions, corps and even to an Allied airborne army. Their numbers were different, but each American airborne unit was and remained a blood brother of the others. The triumphs of one were celebrated by all without jealousy or envy.

When the first Medal of Honor for an American paratrooper was won at Anzio by Paul B. Huff of the 509th Parachute Infantry Battalion, the entire airborne brotherhood rejoiced. After all, the 509th Parachute Battalion had formerly been the 2d Battalion 503d Parachute Infantry and the 501st Parachute Battalion, mother of them all, had been scooped up from Panama, redesignated 2d Battalion 503d Parachute Infantry and shipped to the Pacific Theater to join its parent regiment.

Along with Orin (Hardrock) Haugen who would, as the gallant commander of the 511th Parachute Infantry Regiment die of wounds received during the siege of Manila, I had been a company commander in the newly-formed 501st Parachute Infantry Battalion. I was later to command the 509th Parachute Infantry Battalion in the Italian and Southern France Campaigns.

In the early airborne days at Fort Benning, I had "prop blasted" with a young paratroop captain by the name of John J. Tolson 3d. Jack Tolson would rise to the rank of lieutenant colonel and command the 3d Battalion, 503d Parachute Infantry which participated in the seizure of Nadjab Airfield in New Guinea in September of 1943. Jack was destined to become an army aviator, and I rode with him in his helicopter in Vietnam where he, as a major general, commanded the 1st Cavalry Division and where he won the Distinguished Service Cross, the Distinguished Flying Cross and forty-four Air Medals, among other awards. Jack was later to be promoted to three star rank and given command of America's top airborne unit, the XVIII Airborne Corps.

In the brilliant action marked by the same professionalism, imagination and daring as the classical German airborne assault on Fort Eben Emael, Colonel George M. Jones's 503d Parachute Infantry Regiment returned the American flag to Japanese-held Corregidor Island. The same George Jones would later take command of the Green Berets at Fort Bragg. After four years spent in laying the foundations for an exponential surge in Special Forces' growth, George turned the Green Beret command over to me in 1961 in exchange for the 66th Counterintelligence Corps Group in Germany which I relinquished to him.

The rescue of 2147 American Prisoners of War who had been interned by the Japanese in a camp at Los Banos on the Laguna de Bay
forty miles south of Manila was executed with textbook precision by
a combined parachute and ground assault in which the 1st Bn 511th
Parachute Infantry, the 1st Bn 188th Glider Infantry and D Battery of
the 457th Parachute Field Artillery Bn played the major roles. This operation will remain in military history as a classical example of the use
of airborne troops to achieve tactical surprise.

The 11th Airborne veterans with whom I had rubbed elbows
represented no inconsiderable pool of military virtue. It was not difficult to account for the success and reputation of a division which had
been blessed in wartime with such talent. My only problem with them
was that the nickname "Angel" was a misnomer or, at least, was a rather
loose interpretation.

Reading the saga of the Angels brings to mind once again the
excitement which marked my first serious encounter with the third
dimension—the curiosity and fascination I felt upon seeing a light
airplane fumbling and bouncing across the tarmac of a country airfield
before struggling unsteadily into the air.

I remember the smell of the airplane varnishes, the grease and oil,
and the smell of the engine exhausts which were peculiarly intriguing,
somehow different, even pleasing. Then, too, there is the recollection
of wonder mixed with some uneasiness upon being belted into the seat
of an apparatus which carried me aloft for the first time to see below
a world which appeared more vast and different than I had ever dreamed
it would be.

To contemplate stepping from the relative security of a flying vehicle into thin air while depending completely upon a parachute system
which was far from "idiot-proof" aroused an emotion that few of us
ever took lightly. It tested enzymes and hormones which would later
be identified as important assets for producing a superior breed of warrior. These are facts which are well known to all airborne soldiers.

The challenge of jumping from an airplane in flight or descending
onto a hostile landing zone in an aircraft without an engine would be
paralleled later by life or death situations for which airborne soldiers
had already prepared themselves by identifying and strengthening their
own psychological assets.

The collective discipline inside the aircraft would be translated into
personal discipline, courage and staying power on the battlefield.

The history of the 11th Airborne Division in itself constitutes a comprehensive and eloquent definition of the true meaning of "American Airborne Soldier."

The inclusion of the 11th Airborne division in General Douglas MacArthur's order of battle constituted a quantum leap in the tactical and strategic options open to him. This was an outfit which could operate amphibiously, by parachute, with gliders and as elite ground combat teams with equal enthusiasm and skill.

It was most appropriate for the Angels to have been given the honor of being the first American force to enter defeated Japan in an occupation role.

It is certain that wherever Veterans of World War II airborne operations gather, as with the Infantry's "Ballad of Roger Young," tales of airborne action at Manarawat, Tagaytay Ridge, Los Banos, and Camalaniugan will be told with forgivable exaggeration, heartfelt nostalgia, and much reverence.

The author of this history, Edward Michael Flanagan, Jr., had been a wartime commander of the 11th Division's Battery of the 457th Parachute Field Artillery Battalion. From 1968 to 1971 this same "Fly" Flanagan, who in the interim had added army aviation to his many skills, took command of the U.S. Army's Special Warfare assets adding his battle experience, innovation and leadership to the command with which both George Jones and I had been privileged to serve in succession previously. Fly would rise to three star rank and retire after having commanded the U.S. Sixth Army. I am grateful to Fly for having written this book.

William P. Yarborough
Lieutenant General, U.S. Army (Retired)
Southern Pines, North Carolina
February, 1989

ACKNOWLEDGMENTS

Writing a history of a combat unit requires a great deal of research of official records and the study of informal input from the men who participated in the actions. The bibliography contains some 150 entries—attesting to the volume of mail and records available to the author. The official records help to verify the remembrances. I am deeply indebted to all those members of the old 11th who took the time and the effort to write to me. Some of the men and women who contributed so much to my efforts deserve special attention.

Major General Albert E. Pierson wrote more than thirty letters, answering in detail my many questions about all phases of the division's operations. He has a remarkable ability to recall events, names, and places.

Colonel Glenn McGowan sent me many photos and letters answering my questions and telling me facts about the division and its men that I had never known before. From his positions, initially as XO of the 511th and then as G-1 on the division staff, he had been able to keep abreast of many of the personnel actions about which most of us knew little.

Henry Burgess contributed a manuscript recounting his personal reminiscences about many phases of the division's operations, particularly the Los Banos raid, the Aparri operation, and the rapid move of the division from Lipa to Okinawa to Atsugi.

Colonel Art Lombardi, "the godfather" and my first sergeant in B Battery of the 457th, dug into files and sent me copies of records and his own memories.

Mrs. Cecil Fullilove (Mary Anne Swing) sent me copies of her father's letters to his father-in-law, Gen. Peyton C. March, the chief of staff of the army in World War I, and gave me permission to quote them.

Colonel Robert E. Kennington helped enormously with his letters, records, and recollections.

Brigadier General Henry Muller gave me great assistance, especially in reconstructing the early days of airborne and the 511th in particular.

John Conable, a stalwart both in the 457th and on the division staff, wrote and gave me his outstanding autobiography from which I quote liberally.

And finally, as usual, Adele Horwitz, the experienced and superb editor in chief of Presidio Press, gave me sound and specific advice on the makeup, arrangement, and content of the book.

CHAPTER 1

BACKGROUND

For the World War II belligerents, January and February 1943 were months of historically significant dates and momentous events. The scattered arenas of the war, its worldwide prevalence and dominance, the beginnings of the tide turning in the Allies' favor, and the further tightening of U.S. belts are evident from some of the headlines of those months:

18 January—Russians relieve Leningrad at last
24 January—Roosevelt, Churchill, and de Gaulle hold war council in Casablanca
31 January—German Army gives in at Stalingrad
3 February—War Department bans hard liquor in the U.S. Army
3 February—Finland begins talks with the USSR
5 February—Mussolini ousts twelve from government, including son-in-law, Ciano
8 February—U.S. bombers smash at Naples, causing heavy damage at harbor installations
8 February—Burma: British General Wingate leads guerrilla forces, "Chindits," against Japanese
9 February—Japan quits the Solomons
9 February—Russians head west, take back Kursk
15 February—North Africa: Germans break U.S. lines at Faid-Sened Sector in central Tunisia

16 February—Yankee star Joe DiMaggio joins U.S. Army as a voluntary inductee
18 February—Rommel takes three towns in Tunisia
18 February—Madame Chiang Kai-shek asks for defeat of Japan in address to Congress
21 February—Canned food, shoes rationed in U.S.
21 February—North Africa: German tanks and two infantry battalions crack Allied line and occupy Kasserine Pass
22 February—Outnumbered seven to one, German General Manstein launches counterattack in Caucasus
26 February—Yanks in tough fight for Kasserine Pass
26 February—U.S. Flying Fortresses and Liberators pound Reich docks and U-boat lairs at Wilhelmshaven

There was one other date in February 1943 that was not particularly earthshaking or significantly memorable except to a few thousand soldiers, many of whom had recently been inducted into the Army of the United States and were learning the rites and rights (and restrictions) at a number of hastily built World War II training centers. Others for whom that date was important were the cadre men who would later fuse, mold, train, and coerce those recruits into a formidable, fighting airborne division. The date was 25 February 1943; the division, the 11th Airborne.

Camp Mackall, North Carolina, a training center hacked out of the pine trees and built with that same unseasoned pine on the sand dunes of south central North Carolina, was forty miles west of Fort Bragg near the small town of Hoffman, North Carolina, and not far from the plush golfing resorts of Southern Pines and Pinehurst. Camp Mackall was the first home of the 11th Airborne Division. It was a home only in the loosest, generic sense of the word.

Camp Mackall came into being because of the rapid growth of airborne units in late 1942 and early 1943. The facilities at Fort Benning, where airborne units had initially been activated and trained, were becoming crowded and overtaxed. Some airborne units then moved to Fort Bragg. Shortly, Fort Bragg reached its maximum capacity. The chief of engineers then decided to build a new camp, almost exclusively for airborne units, among them, eventually, the Airborne Command, the 11th and 17th Airborne Divisions, the 541st Parachute Infantry Regiment, and a number of smaller parachute outfits. That new camp was originally called Camp Hoffman.

No particular fuss or furor marked the activation day of the 11th at Camp Mackall. Major General Joseph M. Swing, the recently appointed division commander, whose forty-ninth birthday was three days after the activation date of the 11th Airborne, had, as his luncheon guest, Maj. Gen. E. G. Chapman, Jr., the commanding general of the Airborne Command, whose Headquarters was also located at Camp Mackall. The day was cool and the sky overcast, not unusual weather for North Carolina in February. After lunch, the two generals went on a jeep tour of the 11th Airborne's sector of Mackall. The troops of the 11th Airborne Division would shortly learn that General Swing demanded from higher headquarters everything that he could get for "his men"; in turn, he demanded a maximum effort from his soldiers according to the historically proven thesis that the harder men trained, the better they would fight and the lower their casualties would be. The troops may not have thought that the rigors they were about to go through were for their own good; tough combat would later prove that they were.

There is an old saying in the army that one's last post is the best and the current post is the worst. For once, at least, Camp Mackall proved valid that old army adage. What Generals Swing and Chapman saw that afternoon must have given them considerable pause and raised numerous doubts in their minds that the camp would ever be ready for the thousands of men who would shortly be pouring into it from Forts Benning and Toccoa, Georgia; Fort Benjamin Harrison, Indiana; Camp Wolters, Texas; Fort Sill, Oklahoma; Fort Lewis, Washington; Fort Dix, New Jersey; Fort Meade, Maryland; and Camp Upton, New York.

On that cold February afternoon when Generals Swing and Chapman rode through the camp, Camp Mackall was a dreary, ugly collection of partially completed tar paper–covered buildings, unfinished roads, and swarming, noisy construction crews. A pall of dust hung over the entire area. The pine knolls of the North Carolina sand hill country (beautiful and, before the war, pristine and conducive to the leisurely development of country clubs and golf courses) were beginning to show the results of the engineers' feverish work. But bulldozers still wallowed along the ditches of the unpaved roads. In some areas, the building crews had moved on, leaving behind them a collection of squat, black, one-story barracks, mess halls, supply rooms, separate latrines—that is, not inside the barracks or the bachelor officers' quarters (BOQs)—warehouses, orderly rooms, and other structures. The troops would shortly refer to the whole collection as tar-paper shacks, particularly when the wintery North Carolina winds whistled through the cracks in the floors and walls. The airborne Yankees who thought that North Carolina was just a mile or so north of Florida and who were anticipating balmy southern weather after the rigors of the northern winters were in for a miserable surprise: The outside training areas of North Carolina in the winter were almost as windy and blustery as the Catskills, even though a snowstorm was a rare happening.

Most of the U.S. training centers built at the beginning of World War II were constructed at least to last out the war. The barracks were two stories, with latrines and showers inside, some sort of central heat, and separate NCO rooms at the ends of the open bays, which housed the bulk of the troops. The other buildings in such camps were also solidly constructed, given the circumstances of their hasty fabrication and erection. All these buildings had, on their exteriors, overlapping, horizontal siding and were painted white. These buildings, some of which are still in use today on some permanent military posts almost fifty years after their construction, were laid out with some military precision, were reasonably comfortable, and were designed with some thought to their function and utility.

Not so Camp Mackall. By 1943, the armed forces were expanding so rapidly and men and women were flowing into the services at such an accelerated rate that the construction crews could not keep pace with the growth of the army. In the very early days of the war, the War Department planners estimated that full mobilization of the army would result in a force about equal to the size of the ground forces in World War I. In actuality, the final size of the World War II army was twice that of the World War I army. As a result, the construction of camps could not keep pace with the vast numbers of men inducted in World War II. In addition, the chief of engineers of the army found that constructing the fairly solid camps that the army had been building in the early stages of the war was far too costly. Therefore, to save money and to speed up construction, the army planners went to a new type of construction known as "theater of operations."

Camp Mackall, one of the last training camps to be built in the United States during World War II, fell under this modified and frugal plan. The troops were unaware of and did not care about the technical name of the plan under which Mackall was hastily hammered together; they knew only that they had not been blessed with even minimum-standard living quarters. But that feeling would pass, submerged as it would soon become under the intensity of the training they were about to undergo, training so rigorous that eventually the troops felt that combat would be a relief.

On 8 November 1942, just a few weeks after the chief of engineers had selected the Hoffman site for the construction of a new camp, work crews started building the cantonment on 51,971 acres in the middle of the North Carolina-South Carolina maneuver area. By the time the crews were finished six months later, the camp contained 1,750 buildings, 65 miles of hastily paved roads (which, many months later, were still rough and either dusty or muddy), a 1,200-bed hospital, five theaters, six beer gardens, and three five-thousand-foot all-weather runways formed in the shape of a triangle. The first plane touched down on one of the new runways on 8 February 1943; the plane brought in General Chapman and the first elements of his Airborne Command staff, which had moved from Benning to Bragg only a few months before.

On that same date, 8 February 1943, the War Department published General Order Number 6, which officially changed the name of the camp from Camp Hoffman to Camp Mackall to honor Pvt. John T. "Tommy" Mackall, a young paratrooper of the 509th Parachute Infantry Battalion, originally from Wellsville, Ohio. He was one of the first paratroopers killed during World War II, during the first U.S. airborne operation of the war, a precursor of Operation Torah.

Camp Mackall was a prime example of the very difficult problem of constructing barracks, mess halls, hospitals, supply rooms, and other basic installations on a crash and money-saving basis. In going to the theater of operations type of construction, the engineers had double bunked the men in the barracks; then they planned the mess halls, latrines, dayrooms, and recreational buildings on the number of barracks, not on the number of men who would occupy them.

General Swing, of course, found this arrangement totally unacceptable. Displaying the no-nonsense, aggressive, "do-it-now" personality that the men of the division would come to admire and respect, and occasionally damn, through the long days of training and the arduous months of combat, he took immediate action. He directed Brig. Gen. Albert Pierson, who had been designated the assistant division commander, to call the chief of engineers in the Pentagon and report to him the intolerable situation at Hoffman and request, in strong terms, that the chief of engineers remedy the problem with some haste and effectiveness.

The chief of engineers reacted promptly and the problem was at least partially solved before the bulk of the fillers arrived. The problem did not go away totally, however. Throughout the division's stay at Mackall, because of a shortage of barracks and BOQs, many officers and enlisted men lived in winterized pyramidal tents.

One might debate the relative comfort of the tents versus the BOQs and barracks. The BOQs and barracks were so flimsily built and the lumber was so green that the walls split and the floors cracked, permitting scrub shrubs to grow up through the floors. In the BOQs, at least, some officers permitted the plants to remain, giving a rather homey touch to what were otherwise very drab and drafty rooms. Heat was another problem. The potbellied coal stoves in the buildings heated the men nearest them but did little to warm those five or more feet away. And getting to the outside latrines and showers in the early morning cold was designed primarily to build character and goose bumps.

In early December 1942, Generals Swing and Pierson, Brig. Gen. Wyburn D. Brown, the designated 11th Airborne Division artillery commander, and Col. Francis W. Farrell, the designated chief of staff of the division, had met in Washington with the staffs of three other divisions slated to be activated in February 1943. General McNair, who had the responsibility for activating, training, and equipping all new divisions, greeted the men in his office. Then he turned the division teams over to his general and special staff sections for four days of briefings and orientations in their particular fields of expertise.

Even though these division teams were composed of fairly high-ranking officers, nonetheless they went next to Fort Holibird for four days of orientation on the operation and maintenance of various motor vehicles. This included, preposterously, requiring the generals and colonels to drive a 6 × 6 convoy through the streets of Baltimore, Maryland. Perhaps with some misgivings, and probably glad to get rid of their high-ranking charges, the NCO ordnance examiners duly awarded the generals and colonels their operators' permits. Colonel Farrell was the only member of the Division Headquarters who opted to try to qualify on a motorcycle. Unfortunately, he skidded out of control on the track and, as a result, for many years bore ingrained on his forehead a patch of Holibird dirt. The NCO in charge of motorcycles awarded Colonel Farrell an "A" for effort and an "E" for competence; he did not award him a motorcycle operator's permit.

The 11th Airborne Headquarters group next went to Aberdeen Proving Grounds for several days of orientation on current weapons. Lost in files is whether or not they learned much about pack 75s, folding stock carbines, or spring-loaded jump knives, items with which they would become intimately familiar over the next few years and which had not been in wide use previously in the army. The artillerymen may have been familiar with the pack 75; they were not accustomed to thinking, however, that the prime mover for the pack 75 would be seven or eight men—not a group of stubborn mules.

General Swing and Colonel Farrell moved on to Fort Leavenworth, where they picked the officers who would be the original chiefs of the division's general staff sections.[1]

The 11th Airborne Division was not the first airborne division in the U.S. Army's history. But it was the first to be organized as an airborne division from the ground up. The rapid, extraordinary growth of the airborne venture, from a test platoon to division-sized units in a little more than two years, is a reminder that in time of war, with the nation and its diversified resources of manpower, intelligence, and will mobilized totally, the impossible is accomplished rather rapidly. The 11th Airborne Division was a product of this one concentrated, determined effort in a series of many other efforts to ready the U.S. Army for its varied and multifaceted role in World War II.

The airborne concept developed gradually and, at times, fitfully, just before and in the early years of the U.S. involvement in World War II. One stumbling block was that many senior officers felt that the "airborne" concept was ill-conceived and only marginally beneficial to the overall war strategy. They could not possibly imagine that paratroopers could be useful for anything more than small, daring, and suicidal raids on enemy headquarters, bridges, or communications centers. Nor could they visualize the use of gliders in combat. And the heavy drop technique, which the Germans had developed early in the war, was beyond their imagination and comprehension.

John Keegan in *Six Armies in Normandy* writes about the lethargy

---

[1] G-1, Lt. Col. James W. Smyly, Jr.; G-2, Maj. Clifford L. Dier; G-3, Maj. Robert A. Ports; G-4, Lt. Col. Glenn A. Ross. At Fort Sill, General Brown met two of his battalion commanders, Majors Douglass P. Quandt and Lukas E. Hoska. At Benning, General Pierson met the two glider regimental commanders, Colonels Robert H. Soule and Harry Hildebrand. Colonel Oren Haugen, USMA 1930, the designated commander of the 511th Parachute Infantry Regiment, was in Toccoa, Georgia, assembling his regiment.

of the Allied armies in developing parachute units. He mentions that, in 1936, British and French observers had witnessed a Soviet maneuver in which paratroopers had been dropped, however primitively and dangerously, from a giant Tupolev aircraft. The paratroopers clung "desperately to the rail along its fuselage as they breasted the chord of its monstrous wing and then, at a signal, releasing their grip in unison to be whirled away like needles from a mountain pine in the first storm of winter."[2]

In 1938 and 1939, Gen. George C. Marshall, the brilliant and decisive army chief of staff, had been receiving reports from his attachés that a number of the major powers in Europe, including the French, Italians, Russians, and Germans, were experimenting with airborne troops, delivered both by parachute and air-landing techniques. The attachés reported that the German development of parachute, glider, and air-landed troops was especially well conceived and organized under the expert leadership of Gen. Kurt Student. The attachés pointed out, for what it was worth, that the German airborne troops remained under the command of the Luftwaffe. General Marshall decided to take action with respect to the idea of delivering troops to combat via parachutes.

Consequently, in April 1939, he directed his G-3 to send a memo to General Lynch, the chief of infantry, requesting that he "make a study for the purpose of determining the desirability of organizing, training, and conducting tests of a small detachment of air infantry with a view to ascertaining whether or not our Army should contain a unit or units of this nature." The memo also said: "It is visualized that the role of this type of unit will be, after being transported in airplanes, to parachute to the ground a small detachment to seize a small vitally important area, primarily an air field, upon which additional troops will later be landed by transport airplane. The air infantry unit or units will in all probability be small and lightly equipped. Their training should include a considerable amount of athletic drill, utilization of parachutes, demolitions and exercises in security functions." And finally, the memo concluded in the peculiar, unnecessarily polite, yet demanding jargon of staff officers: "It is believed desirable that the study referred to be initiated without delay." The last rejoinder was unnecessary; the chief of infantry favored the idea and had been doing spadework on the idea for some months.

In five days, General Lynch had back on General Marshall's desk

---

[2] Keegan, *Six Armies in Normandy*, p. 69.

a lengthy study that discussed the Soviet and French use of airborne forces on maneuvers; the U.S. utilization of airplanes to carry cargo, soldiers, and field artillery units; and a 1934 Fort Benning test that proved that an entire infantry battalion and all of its equipment could be transported by aircraft over great distances during both day and night. General Lynch recommended extensive tests to determine the size, missions, and equipment of air infantry units; he even recommended that the Air Corps assign him a squadron of nine transport aircraft so that he could begin the experimentation and tests at Benning forthwith.

It was seven months before General Lynch had any positive reply from the army staff on his "air infantry" recommendations. General Marshall had passed General Lynch's recommendations to Gen. Hap Arnold, the Air Corps branch chief, who in turn had passed them to his Air Corps Board at Maxwell Field and to his plans division in Washington for comments and recommendations. One of the more startling replies (at least it seems startling in view of what has happened to both the Air Corps and airborne forces in the intervening fifty or so years) to General Arnold came from Col. Walter Weaver, commandant of the Air Corps Tactical School at Maxwell Field, speaking for the Air Corps Board.

> I recommend that we create in the Air Corps an organization similar to what the Marines are in the Navy; that this organization perform such functions as the following:
>
> 1. Man antiaircraft equipment . . . for the protection of airdromes.
> 2. Be charged with the neutralization of gassed airdromes.
> 3. Provide the guard for the protection of . . . airdromes and supply centers.
> 4. Perform such military ceremonies as have heretofore been customary at army posts, such as firing of salutes and rendering of honors for distinguished persons.
> 5. Provide the guard for prisoners.
> 6. Furnish the guard for aircraft forced down in the vicinity.
> 7. Be so organized and equipped as to perform the functions of parachute troops or landing parties from air transports.
>
> It is believed that there is a real need for such an organization within the Air Corps. It might be well to consider building up such an organization under the existing Military Police, now found at most of our large stations.

As a suggestion of a name for this organization, it might be called the "Air Grenadiers" or "The Air Corps Grenadiers"[3]

Lieutenant Colonel Carl "Tooey" Spaatz wrote the air plans division study on the question and reported to General Arnold that, in effect, the Air Corps had far more important projects to worry about than air infantry. He also pointed out that no extra transport aircraft were available to support this new undertaking. General Arnold forwarded to the chief of staff the Spaatz recommendations; General Marshall bought the Air Corps view, at least temporarily. The project then lay dormant until January 1940, when General Arnold decided that he could spare a few transport aircraft for Benning and so reported to General Marshall, who then gave the project top priority and directed his chief of infantry to assume the responsibility for commencing the training of the air infantry.

General Lynch immediately assigned Maj. William C. Lee, one of his smartest and most dedicated staff officers, to run the project for him. Major Lee was forty-three years old at the time and had been on active duty since World War I, in which he had served as a platoon and company commander in combat in France. Once he had received the assignment, Bill Lee was off and running. He first contacted the Air Corps and asked for transport aircraft, the development of a static line–activated parachute, and the loan of two riggers and two trained parachute jumpers and several equipment chutes for tests by the Infantry Board at Benning. In three weeks, the Air Corps responded to part of the request and sent the planes, men, and equipment to Lawson Field at Benning. And by May 1940, the Air Corps test center at Wright Field had developed the T-4, a backpack, static line–activated personnel chute, twenty-eight feet in diameter, and a smaller, rip cord–activated reserve. By June 1940, the Infantry Board was ready to start live jump tests.

The original test platoon was organized at Fort Benning, Georgia, shortly thereafter in the summer of 1940. Two lieutenants, both from the class of 1936 at West Point and from the 29th Infantry at Benning—Lieutenants William T. Ryder and William P. Yarborough—were among the seventeen officers who had volunteered to lead the test platoon. Lieutenant Ryder had had an interest in airborne forces long before

---

[3] Letter from Col. Walter Weaver, commandant of the Air Corps Tactical School at Maxwell Field, Alabama, to General Arnold, dated 7 September 1939.

General Lynch decided to form a test platoon. He had studied the use of airborne forces by the Russians and the Germans, he had seen some of the test equipment drops at Benning, he had read everything he could on the subject, and he had written a number of papers on the combat employment of airborne forces that he had submitted to the Infantry Board. When the day came at Benning for the Infantry Board to test the seventeen volunteers to determine who would lead the test platoon, Lieutenant Yarborough was not present; he had just received orders to report to Camp Jackson, South Carolina.

Lieutenant Ryder passed the written exam with flying colors and walked out of the test room at the Infantry Board a full hour before any of the other candidates. He won the job in short order.

The enlisted volunteers for the test platoon came from the 29th Infantry Regiment, stationed at Fort Benning. Shortly, the test platoon was detached from the 29th and moved to Lawson Field. In July, the platoon flew up to Highsmith, N.J. The two towers at Highsmith were 150 feet high, unlike the 250-foot towers that the Ledbetter Construction Company of Birmingham, Alabama, would later build at Fort Benning. At Highsmith, one of the towers was rigged for controlled jumps using vertical steel guide cables from the top of the tower's extended wings to the ground; the other tower was without the cables and permitted the paratrooper to flow with the wind once he was released at the top. On both towers, each paratrooper's chute was attached to a large metal circle on the ground, which in turn was attached to a cable that ran to the top of the tower. When ready, the paratrooper was pulled to the top of the tower by the cable. Once the paratrooper reached the top, the cable operator pulled the entire rig up against the extended arm of the tower, which caused the chute to fall clear of the metal circle to which it had been clipped.

During the training at Highsmith, General Lynch paid a surprise visit to the platoon and, even though he was in his early sixties at the time, took a ride on the controlled parachute rig. His jump proved to the applauding test platoon men that he was indeed one of the senior army generals totally in favor of the airborne concept and that he did all he could to foster its growth and development.

After the platoon finished its ten days of training on the towers at Highsmith, it returned to Benning for the final phases of its training. By the platoon's sixth week of training, it was a physically fit and enthusiastic group of well-disciplined, highly motivated soldiers. Each man in the platoon by then had learned to pack his own chute. The platoon was ready for its final test—actual parachute jumps. The first two jumps in the eighth week of training were "tap-outs," wherein the trainer in the door would tap the leg of the jumper when it was his turn to go out. The last three were mass jumps, each man following the man in front of him as fast as he could get to and out the door.

When the big day finally arrived, the platoon was ready. The C-33 carrying the first ten jumpers took off from Lawson and leveled off at an altitude of 1,500 feet, flying large circles over Lawson Field and the drop zone (DZ) in neighboring Alabama. A few minutes out from the drop zone, Warrant Officer Wilson, the Air Corps instructor, gave the required commands to stand up, hook up, check equipment, sound off for equipment check, and close in the door. He checked each man's static line and then motioned Lieutenant Ryder to take up the jump position in the door. Wilson stuck his head out into the 110-mile-per-hour slipstream and looked for the DZ. The pilot throttled back to slow down to the proper jump speed. Over the "go point," Wilson tapped Lieutenant Ryder on the leg, and Ryder made a forceful jump out the door. The next man to jump had won his honored position in a lottery the night before. The man who would jump behind Lieutenant Ryder was in an enviable position because he was to be the first enlisted man in the U.S. Army to become a paratrooper. Unfortunately, the man who would become number one froze in the door on the first pass and froze again on the second. Thus the honor fell to the number two man, Pvt. William N. "Red" King, who, when it came his turn to make his first jump, flung himself out the door, giving himself no time for second thoughts.

The word "Geronimo" is in the lexicon of every paratrooper, even to the present day. Its use by the airborne goes back to the day when the test platoon made its third jump—its first mass jump. The night before the jump, three paratroopers of the test platoon went to a movie at the Fort Benning post theater. The movie was a western in which U.S. Cavalry troops chased the renowned Apache chief Geronimo and a band of his Indian braves. After the movie and on their way back to their tents near Lawson, one of the moviegoers chided Pvt. Aubrey Eberhardt about the extent of his enthusiasm and willingness to make the mass jump the next morning. Eberhardt drew himself up to his full six-foot-eight-inch height and declared that not only was he not afraid to make a mass jump but, to prove how relaxed he was, he would yell "Geronimo" when he exited the plane.

Word spread throughout the platoon about Eberhardt's claim. The next morning, the men in Eberhardt's plane and those who had already jumped and were on the ground waited for the yell. True to his word, when it came time for Eberhardt to leap out the door, he yelled a loud "Geronimo" and followed it with an equally resonant war hoop so loud that the men on the ground could hear it. Thus, without intending to or even knowing it, Eberhardt established one of the many traditions of the U.S. paratrooper.

The test platoon's fifth and final jump was scheduled to be a mass jump of the entire platoon from three aircraft. Once on the ground, the platoon would carry out a tactical assignment in which they would attack an enemy position on the edge of the DZ using weapons, ammunition, and equipment that they would have dropped with them in separate parachute bundles. So significant was this jump that the top War Department brass decided to come to Benning to watch it. First to arrive at Lawson was General Lynch, the airborne enthusiast, accompanied by Major Lee and several other staff officers from the infantry branch chief's office. The next plane carried not only General Marshall but also, previously unannounced, Henry L. Stimson, the secretary of war.

The jump went off with only two minor flaws. One involved Pvt. Steve Voils, who had the first Mae West and pulled his reserve to slow his descent and land safely; the second involved Pvt. Leo Brown, one of the last men to jump. Before he could land, he was caught in an updraft and drifted over the heads of the VIPs on the edge of the DZ. He finally came to earth not by way of his parachute but by way of a ladder: He landed on the roof of a hangar at Lawson and needed the ladder to get down.

The men of the platoon carried out the U.S. Army's first airborne tactical mission with well-drilled precision. They double-timed through all of their actions, assembled their weapons and gear, and attacked their objective with enthusiasm. The VIPs were duly impressed with the performance. General Marshall told them later at lunch that the army would activate whole battalions of paratroopers and that they would have a large part in training the new outfits.

After the test platoon completed its eight weeks of training, it was split into two teams. One, under Lieutenant Bassett, went to Chanute Field, Illinois, for a comprehensive and exacting course in parachute maintenance and rigging. The other stayed at Fort Benning under Lieutenant Ryder and would perform two functions—form what would eventually become the parachute school, and supply the cadre for the army's first parachute battalion. When Lieutenant Bassett returned to Fort Benning about seven weeks later, he was amazed to find that the test platoon's original four tents had grown into a large tent city and that construction crews were hard at work building two-story barracks adjacent to the tent city. Scores of enlisted men swarmed about the area. Lieutenant Bassett soon discovered that these men were the volunteers for the first parachute battalion—the 501st.

In those early days of the U.S. airborne endeavor, the army staff had not yet decided under which branch's tutelage the paratroopers belonged. The chief of engineers, Maj. Gen. Eugene Schley, thought that the engineers should control them because paratroopers would require extensive training in the use of explosives; Gen. Henry H. Arnold felt that the Air Corps should have them because the parachutists were entirely dependent on aircraft to deliver them to their target. General Lynch was so livid at the other branch chiefs' attempts to gain control of the airborne troops that he requested a meeting with the army chief of staff to settle the dispute. On 6 August 1940, the three branch chiefs met with General Marshall in his office. One by one each branch chief presented his case. Finally General Lynch had his say. "Once on the ground," he said, "the parachutist becomes an infantryman and fights as an infantryman." He also added, as a clincher, that the test platoon was already in training at Fort Benning and that any increases in the parachutist effort be kept under the direction of the chief of infantry at Fort Benning.

General Marshall, as was his wont, listened quietly to the presentations of the three branch chiefs. Then he said: "Gentlemen, you've all presented convincing arguments as to why your particular branch should take charge of this vital project now under way at Benning. I want you to know that we are in fact going ahead with plans to form a parachute battalion. The first one will be activated in just a few weeks. It is my decision to place the formation and development of that battalion under the control of the Infantry at Fort Benning. Thank you for coming here today, gentlemen. Good day."

True to General Marshall's word, the army staff issued a War Department order on 16 September 1940, which stated in part: "The 1st Parachute Battalion is constituted and will be activated at the earliest practical date at Fort Benning, Georgia.'' On 26 September, the War Department issued an amendment to that order, changing the designation from the 1st Battalion to the 501st Parachute Infantry Battalion. The reason: The Marine Corps was also forming parachute battalions and was also numbering theirs starting with number one. To avoid confusion the army elected to number parachute battalions in the 500 series, giving the marines the numbers 1 to 499. On 7 October 1940, the 501st Parachute Infantry Battalion was activated at Fort Benning under the command of the recently promoted Maj. William M. Miley, West Point class of 1918. Two-and-a-half years later, Major Miley would become Major General Miley, in command of the 17th Airborne Division.

Even though the 501st was still in its formative stages, gathering recruits and officers, putting them through jump training and even watching barracks and messes being built for them, in early November 1940, the War Department issued orders to form three more parachute infantry battalions in 1941. The 501st was ordered to supply cadres for the new battalions and to supervise their training. Between 1 July and 5 October 1941, these three battalions came onto the army's rolls: the 502d, under Maj. George P. Howell, Jr. (West Point class of 1919); the 503d, under Maj. Robert F. Sink (West Point class of 1927); and the 504th, under Maj. Richard Chase (Syracuse University class of 1927).

The army staff decided not to neglect the possibility of using troops in an air-landing role, presumably to come into an airfield in transport aircraft after the field had been seized by parachutists. On 1 July 1940, the army activated the 550th Infantry Airborne Battalion under Lt. Col. Harris M. Melasky from the West Point class of 1917; later, on 10 October 1941, the 88th Airborne Infantry Battalion came into existence under the command of Lt. Col. Eldridge G. Chapman, who would later command the 13th Airborne Division in France in 1945.

Major Miley realized the difficulty of training his own battalion and having the responsibility for jump qualifying three more battalions. Consequently, he recommended to the chief of infantry that he, the chief of infantry, organize a special group to jump-train the new battalions and that, thereafter, the jump-qualified battalions be moved to their home stations for tactical training. The chief of infantry bought the recommendation and, on 10 March 1941, formed the Provisional Parachute Group under the direction of recently promoted Lt. Col. William C. Lee, the man who had done so much in the very early days of the development of the airborne concept that he is known widely as ''the Father of American

Airborne Troops.'' General Lynch also gave Colonel Lee the mission of developing suitable tables of organization and equipment and tactical doctrine for the employment of airborne troops. Colonel Lee transferred to Benning and immediately took a crash course in jumping from the men who would make up the Provisional Parachute Group.

Colonel Lee was the driving force behind the development, installation, and use of the various devices at Benning that generations of paratroopers have come to remember with respect, if not fear. There were the 250-foot towers, on which fledgling paratroopers made their first controlled jumps, some with the benefit of four vertical cables to keep the paratrooper in bounds, and some with only the winds to guide them to their landing areas. (Three of the original towers are still in use at the parachute school. The fourth was blown down by heavy winds in 1950.) There were the 34-foot jump towers, which gave the paratroopers an idea of the opening shock of the 28-foot main canopy. (For some reason, there were more washouts on the 34-foot tower during training than there were either on the 250-foot towers or from aircraft actually in flight. It may be that the towers, only 34 feet above the ground, heightened a man's sense of acrophobia.) There were the mock-ups of the passenger compartment of the C-47 to train the recruits in the proper techniques of exiting the plane. There were the landing trainers to teach men how to hit the ground and tumble without breaking more legs than necessary. And there were the suspended harness contraptions that taught a paratrooper how to guide his chute while in the air. The fledgling paratrooper learned later that it was easier and more comfortable to control the actual parachute in the air than it was to manipulate the suspended harness in the mock-up shed.

The original test platoon spawned a group of instructors who were the envy and the idols of the neophyte paratroopers. Soon after their own training ended, and as soon as they took up the mantle of leader and trainer, the test platoon veterans took on an air of competence, efficiency, self-confidence, and expertise that imbued the student paratrooper with his own feeling of self-confidence. Even young officers going through the course were completely intimidated and impressed by the parachute school instructors. At calisthenics, for example, the muscle-bulging instructor had a disconcerting habit of starting the class doing push-ups in the sawdust pits while he, on the platform, did the push-ups with one arm while counting cadence with the other over the struggling students in the pits. But no matter what the class—parachute packing, tumbling, tower jumps, mock-door training, rope climbing, long-distance running doing the "paratrooper shuffle" (the runner moving fairly slowly, not lifting his feet far off the ground, so that he could move long distances carrying mortar plates or other heavy loads on his shoulders)—the students showed total respect for the demanding, ever-watchful, well-built, erect instructors in their singular uniform of white T-shirts, fatigue trousers, spit-shined jump boots, and baseball caps. Students labored through their grueling day in one-piece coveralls and GI shoes.

Crete is a case history of a successful though costly airborne operation. It was so costly in manpower and aircraft that Hitler thereafter lost confidence in his airborne forces and did not use them again in their primary role. As a matter of fact, after October 1941, the shortage of trained German ground units forced the German High Command to use its trained airborne and parachute units as straight infantry in the Russian campaign that followed Crete. General Student admitted, in a postwar interview, that "Crete was the graveyard of the German parachutists."

But the Crete operation taught the Allies some valuable lessons in airborne tactics. Control of the air and the sea, if the operation is near the sea, is essential. The command channels must be clear and simple: The German chain of command was simple and direct; the British chain was not. In the Crete operation, for example, on 27 May, when General Freyberg was already starting to evacuate his forces, Churchill sent a message to his commander in chief, Middle East: "Victory in Crete is essential at this turning-point in the war. Keep hurling in all you can." Other valuable lessons learned by the Allies in the Crete operation were that surprise is vital; that airborne commanders must be flexible and adapt their tactics rapidly to changing situations; and that strong reserves, ready to be committed by air or sea, are fundamentally necessary.

Because for the first time in the history of warfare a nation was able to seize a large island entirely with airborne and air-landed forces, the Crete operation is historically significant. Its lessons were not lost on the Allies, who were, in 1941, still in the throes of deciding the size and composition of their own airborne units. Crete demonstrated that the Germans were far ahead of the Allied effort in developing the airborne tactic to include even the heavy drop of artillery pieces. (The Germans dropped a large antitank gun lowered by five large parachutes onto Crete.) That Crete gave added impetus to the development of airborne divisions in the United States Army is without question. Thus, the 11th Airborne Division, and the other four airborne divisions that would eventually make up the airborne contingent of the U.S. Army, probably owe their very existence to the German demonstration of airborne potential on Crete. And the U.S. Army high command must be given great credit for having the foresight to move from battalion-sized parachute units at the time of Crete to division-sized units in less than eighteen months. Perhaps without the Holland and Crete operations, there would have been no U.S. airborne divisions.

Thus, at Camp Mackall, North Carolina, in February 1943, with the birth of the 11th Airborne Division, the U.S. Army airborne concept came to full fruition.

CHAPTER 2

ACTIVATION

On 7 December 1941, the Japanese attack on Pearl Harbor, one of the most brilliant tactical feats of the war, achieved what the leadership of the United States had been unable to do previously: It solidified the country immediately behind the war effort. For the first time in its history, the United States went to war with almost total unanimity of popular support. And also for the first time in its history, the United States entered a war with a large army already mobilized and an industrial system partially geared up for wartime production. Before Pearl Harbor, the country had been supplying munitions and combat equipment to the Allies. But after Pearl Harbor, the illusion that the United States could sit in isolation and serve only as "the arsenal of democracy," furnishing the Allies with weapons but not men to use them, vanished in the smoke and fire of its eight devastated battleships along Battleship Row and scores of burning and wrecked aircraft on the parking ramps and taxiways of Wheeler Field on Hawaii. In the wake of the Japanese attacks throughout the Pacific, President Roosevelt told Secretary of War Stimson: "We must not only provide munitions for our own fighting forces but vast quantities to be used against the enemy in every appropriate theatre of war." The United States was finally totally engaged with its Allies.

On 7 December 1941, the army had, in its active ranks, 1,643,477 soldiers in training at scores of new camps around the country organized into twenty-seven infantry, five armored, and two cavalry divisions. There were as yet no airborne divisions. This was a giant leap forward from the 165,000 soldiers in the army's undermanned and inadequately and primitively equipped units in 1938. In 1942, under a newly formed "victory program," the army planned an ultimate mobilization goal of 10 million men. In that same year, the army reached a total of 3.6 million men and women under arms and added thirty-seven divisions to the thirty-four already activated. The 11th Airborne Division followed shortly thereafter.

The Army Ground Forces Command activated divisions in the early stages of the war by forming division cadres in a division already in training and then sending those cadres to new camps to form new divisions. Thus one division begat other divisions in a geometric progression. The process skimmed talent and experience from the divisions supplying the cadres; but with the ever-increasing requirements for combat divisions, the system did produce satisfactory results efficiently and rapidly.

The 11th Airborne came into being partially under this concept. Except for the regimental commanders and their executive officers and the field artillery battalion commanders and their executive officers, the officer cadres for the two glider infantry regiments and the two glider field artillery battalions came from the 76th Infantry Division at Fort George G. Meade, Maryland. Special Orders Number 149, Headquarters, 76th Infantry Division, dated 11 December 1942, ordered, in the peculiar and arcane language of adjutants general, the cadres to report to the CO of Laurinburg-Maxton Army Air Base, Laurinburg, North Carolina, on 27 December 1942 to

pursue sp course of instrn. Upon completion of this course o/a 8 Jan 1943 these O's WP from Laurinburg, NC to Ft Benning, Ga rptg to Comdt The Inf Sch on 10 Jan 1943 for further temp dy to pursue a course of instrn. Upon compl of this course o/a 5 Feb 1943 these O's WP fr Ft Benning, Ga to Hoffman, NC rptg thereat for dy not later than 8 Feb 1943.

The glider infantry regimental commanders and their executive officers and the glider field artillery battalion commanders and their executive officers joined the cadres at Laurinburg for the two-week airborne orientation course and then moved to Benning with their cadres for the month-long New Division Officers' Course. The enlisted cadre for the glider infantry and field artillery units came from the 88th Infantry Division at Camp Gruber, Oklahoma. These men had had no previous airborne training. The cadres for the engineer, ordnance, signal, medical, quarter-master, and antiaircraft companies and battalions came from their parent technical service schools and installations.

In 1940, Capt. Oren D. Haugen, West Point class of 1930, thirty-two years old at the time, was a member of Major Miley's 501st Parachute Infantry Battalion at Fort Benning. Major Miley had handpicked Haugen to be the commander of A Company of the 501st. In the same battalion were many officers who would later become famous as airborne command-ers in combat.[1]

When the 502d Parachute Infantry Battalion was activated on 1 July 1941, George Howell became its commander. Captains Haugen and Glen McGowan went with him from the 501st, Haugen as the S-3 and McGowan as A Company commander. When the 502d Parachute Infantry Regiment was activated on 2 March 1942 under Lieutenant Colonel Howell, Haugen and McGowan stayed with the regiment and were both promoted to majors. On 12 November 1942, the 511th Parachute Infantry Regiment was formed (but not activated) at Fort Benning, and Lieutenant Colonel Haugen, who had in the interim been promoted and had become the executive officer to Col. James Gavin in the 505th Parachute Infantry Regiment, was named its commander by the Airborne Command.

When Haugen moved to the 511th, he took Major McGowan with him. Airborne Command notified the 504th Parachute Infantry (PI) Battal-ion and the 502d, 503d, and 505th PI Regiments to supply the cadre to the 511th. Haugen and McGowan personally interviewed each man. McGowan remembers that it was a "conglomeration but all good men." The cadre moved into a few buildings at Benning that had been vacated by the 502d, which had moved into the permanent barracks formerly occupied by the Benning school troops, the 29th Infantry. One week before Thanksgiving 1942, the cadre of the 511th moved by train from Benning to Toccoa, Georgia, still under Airborne Command's jurisdic-tion.

---

[1] Among them were Major Miley, Maj. George Howell, Capt. Roy Lindquist, Lt. John Michaelis, Maj. Robert Sink, Capt. Bill Yarborough, Capt. James W. Coutts, and Lt. William Ryder.

When the cadre arrived at Toccoa in the damp cold of a Georgia mountain winter, it found the camp "unfinished, dank, and a sea of mud." Among the officers already with the cadre were Lt. Col. Ernie LaFlamme, in command of the 1st Battalion cadre; Lt. Col. Norman Shipley, who had the 2d Battalion; Glen McGowan, who commanded the 3d; and Frank Holcombe, later to become well-known throughout the division as "Hacksaw Holcombe," who was the S-3. Because Haugen had no executive officer, he gave the job to McGowan in addition to his job of running the 3d Battalion cadre. The cadre found Camp Toccoa a sharp contrast to the permanent barracks and military orderliness they had left at the Infantry Center.

To fill out the slots for junior officers in his regiment, Haugen sent McGowan and Holcombe back to Benning to cull through the parachute units there and recruit who they thought would be the best. Unfortunately, according to McGowan, "Sink and Dunn and Gavin were there first and as a new lieutenant colonel (18 January 1943) I had to take what was left." Given the combat record of the 511th, what was left must have been of superb quality. Major Ed Lahti was one of the officers recruited; when he arrived, he was assigned as executive officer of the 3d Battalion cadre and shortly thereafter the commander of the 3d Battalion when McGowan became the XO of the regiment. As McGowan wrote later,

> The fillers for the 511th came from parachute volunteers from among the various Infantry Training Centers. Earlier, I was placed on TDY (temporary duty) with the Airborne Command. My assignment was to visit all the Infantry training centers and the Artillery center and "sell" parachuting. I had three riggers and three volunteer jumpers. We went to each center, showed the old movie *Parachute Battalion,* had various rallies, and I gave them the sales pitch. We gave a few ground demos and a jump where there was a field large enough. The CGs at the various Centers had been instructed to permit any officer below the rank of major and any EM that wanted to volunteer would be processed and at the end of his basic training shipped to the various units before being assigned to jump training. The Centers let many that were not totally physically fit to be a trooper come to the various units. We had to send them back as we gave all a rigorous PT test. In our case in the 511th, we accepted for the most part high school graduates. The record showed that we built a fine team. . . .

Henry J. Muller was a young captain in January 1942 when he went to jump school at Benning. Next, he completed the G-2 course at

Leavenworth, after which he was assigned to the 511th cadre, still at Benning. Colonel Haugen, according to Captain Muller, "set him to work preparing very detailed plans for processing our fillers who were to join us in Toccoa. He wanted it to be a masterpiece of administrative efficiency and, under his close control, it was—small groups moving on the double to each processing station. I then became the S-1 of the 511th."

The processing and selection of the volunteers made a great impression on one of them, C. Smith Poole, from Seattle, Washington. He was almost twenty-three, a few years above the average age of the volunteers. He had been inducted into the army at Tacoma, Washington, shipped to Fort Lewis, Washington, and immediately requested assignment to the paratroopers. According to Smith Poole, while he was at Fort Lewis, four other inductees volunteered for the airborne and "five of us were shipped to Toccoa, Ga. by rail, in style, in a compartment. The five of us were from three states, Washington, Oregon, and California. Only remember one of the five, a great fellow, Morry Bryant, who wound up with me in D. Company. . . . We hit Toccoa on January 25th, 1943. Stood before Major Shipley, naked, with coat over left arm. He asked me, 'How many three cent stamps in a dozen?' 'What is the hair style in Washington?' 'Why do you want to be a paratrooper?' 'How can I be sure that you will make that first jump?' 'How many pushups can you give me?' " Poole passed Major Shipley's careful scrutiny and became one of the select fillers for the 511th.

The fillers—unbooted paratrooper volunteers—quickly filled the ranks of each of the 511th's battalions at Toccoa. The regiment immediately began a modified unit training program because, as far as Colonel Haugen knew, the regiment would remain a separate one, not part of a division, and would probably be destined for service in the European theater. And because the fillers were scheduled for jump school in the very near future, Colonel Haugen made certain that his men would not fail the rigorous physical fitness training requirements of that demanding four weeks at Benning.

Near Camp Toccoa was Currahee (Indian for "stand alone") Mountain, a high and rugged piece of terrain that the troopers of the 511th would learn to hate with some passion because Currahee fitted intimately and vigorously into their daily training program. The 511th recruits double-timed up the mountain and down it and around its base until they were sick of the mountain but more physically fit with each passing day.

Smith Poole remembers that "Toccoa was 'A' Stage. You couldn't get any more basic—tied to Flagpole, ran Currahee, issued rifles, close order drill, endless formations including PX and P—Call, hurting and hungry all the time." The weather was still cold. Frank Lewis was one of the fillers who joined the regiment at Toccoa. "I remember the mud," he wrote later, "frozen in the morning, soft at noon, and frozen again before we returned from the field. The barracks sounded like a TB sanitarium and Camp Mackall, N.C. appeared to be paradise when we first arrived."

And "Hard Rock" Haugen, practicing leadership by example, led most of the runs. He was as physically fit as any man in the regiment in spite of the fact that he smoked at least two packs of cigarettes a day. One of his officers later guessed, perhaps apocryphally, that Colonel Haugen lit only one cigarette a day—the first one—and chain-smoked from that one all day long.

The 511th was formally activated on 5 January 1943, and was thus the first unit of the 11th Airborne Division to be formed. At that time, the Airborne Command had designated the 511th Parachute Infantry Regiment (PIR) as a separate regiment and had slated it to move to the European theater of operations as part of an airborne task force when it had finished its training. But in January 1943, Gen. Albert Pierson, the designated assistant division commander of the 11th Airborne Division, paid an unexpected visit to the 511th at Toccoa. General Pierson spent the night with the 511th and, according to Colonel McGowan, "looked over our operation of examining and testing volunteers for parachute training. At that time, General Pierson told us in confidence that he understood that we were to be the Parachute Regiment in a newly formed airborne division, the 11th. This came to pass after the 11th was activated."

After a few weeks at Toccoa, the regiment moved to Camp Mackall to complete basic, start some unit training, and prepare for jump school at Benning. After Toccoa, Poole wrote, "Camp Mackall was next. Don't remember date but it was like home, in comparison. I was in formation at dedication ceremonies. Fort Benning was next and back to Mackall."

Bob LeRoy also remembers Toccoa.

Yes, we were at Toccoa in February '43. Mostly close order-drill in the red mud, etc. Moved to Mackall in mid-March, 1943. New ones [recruits] kept coming in until about April 1st. Started our basic training. . . .

Then July went to Ft. Benning for 3 weeks, it seems. Very hot . . . area called "The Frying Pan." Double-timed until men fell out from heat prostration, etc. Diet was changed somewhat. Received a boil on my left arm that week, but made all my 5 jumps on schedule daily during our 3d week there. We packed our own chutes each AM and jumped at 1:00 PM for 5 days in a row. Then building confidence in our chutes, ourselves and our God! Lots of double-time to and from our barracks etc (110 degrees in shade and little shade).

Leo Crawford wrote about the training at Toccoa, Mackall, and Benning. He remembers that a number of the recruits he met at Toccoa were "fresh off the farm" and had been in the army only a few days. They had had no

basic training or any training at all to speak of. Training at Camp Mackall was vigorous. After completion of basic training we went to Fort Benning where the new men took jump training while the officers took Jumpmaster training. Each company originally had a strength of about 180 men. The authorized strength of a parachute rifle company was, as I recall, 8 officers and 115 men. This allowed the retention of only the very best. By the fall of 1943 every man in my platoon of D Company had an AGCT test score (IQ Equivalent) over 115 which was higher than the criterion for going to OCS.

How the 511th came to be part of the 11th Airborne Division is a bit unusual. The numbers 511 and 11 are probably just coincidental. (But the 513th PIR was a part of the 13th Airborne Division, and the 517th was a part of the 17th Airborne Division.) In January 1943, before General Pierson's visit to Toccoa, General Swing had looked over the records and the training status of the 501, 502, 504, and 505 PIRs. He also talked to General Lee of the Airborne Command, who gave the 511th "high marks." On this basis, General Swing opted for the 511th to become the parachute infantry regiment of the 11th Airborne Division.

That the former members of the original test platoon were spreading their talents throughout the airborne world is evident by the fact that two members of the test platoon ended up in the 511th. Lemuel T. Pitts went to Benning's OCS shortly after the test platoon disbanded; he became a platoon leader in E Company of the 511th. His company commander was Hobart B. Wade, who had been the first sergeant of the test platoon, and who had also gone to OCS at Benning.

Parachute artillery was a few steps and many months behind the parachute infantry in its development and growth for the simple reason that there were few visionaries in the army who could imagine dropping a two-and-a-half-ton or so artillery howitzer by parachute, or any other way, from a C-47, the Air Corps' workhorse troop carrier. But by the summer of 1942, the top planners and commanders in the army were talking about airborne divisions and that, perforce, meant artillery.

In July 1942, newly promoted Brigadier General Lee went to England to discuss with the British airborne experts their airborne plans and achievements. One of the most important items he brought back with him was the recent British decision to go ahead with an airborne division. General Lee met with General McNair as soon as he returned and recommended that the U.S. Army also activate an airborne division, giving the army the capability for large-scale operations, not just raids and small units' parachute assaults. General McNair promised to consider the recommendation. True to his word, he announced in August 1942 that the army would activate not one but two airborne divisions, the 82d and the 101st. In actuality, these two divisions became "airborne" on 15 August 1942.

A division obviously was not complete without its supporting artillery—"the greatest killer on the battlefield"—a phrase that the instructors drummed into the heads of all students at Fort Sill, the artillery school, and still do. To 2d Lt. Joseph D. Harris fell the task of developing a system whereby artillery weapons and their ammunition, radio equipment, fire control instruments, and other gear could be safely dropped, reassembled, and moved on the ground to positions to support the infantry. His was a formidable assignment. (That the army in those days would assign a second lieutenant to such a task is evidence that the "old" army believed in giving a man a job and letting him do it.)

Harris became commander of the newly activated parachute test battery at Fort Bragg in the spring of 1942. His men came from volunteers from the various artillery battalions stationed at Bragg, among them the 36th, 17th, 178th, 4th, 6th, and 97th. The test battery went to Benning and went through jump school as a unit. Thereafter, the test battery and Lieutenant Harris began to try to solve the problems thrust upon them by the Airborne Command. Lieutenant Harris realized that the 105mm howitzer, the standard division artillery weapon, weighing in at 4,980 pounds and unsuited for easy breakdown and reassembly, was out of the question as a parachutable artillery piece. But he knew about pack 75s, 1,268-pound howitzers with a range of 9,475 yards, almost 3,000 yards shorter than the 105mm howitzer. Harris reasoned that the relatively short range of the pack 75 would not be particularly disadvantageous because the artillery would be dropped in with the infantry behind enemy lines and would presumably, therefore, be quite close to its targets. Harris also knew that the pack 75s were the mainstays of mountain artillery because they could be broken down into seven pieces weighing about 180 pounds each for transportation over rugged terrain on the backs of mules. He knew that a 180-pound load could be parachuted safely to the ground. With this hint of a solution, Harris and his test battery went to work.

In March 1942, the War Department had reorganized itself with a series of radical changes in its major subordinate departments, one of the most important of which was the establishment of the Army Ground Forces under General McNair and the Army Air Forces under General Arnold. Shortly thereafter, General McNair established the Airborne Command at Fort Benning under Colonel Lee. The Army Air Force, recognizing the expansion of the airborne effort, had set up the Troop Carrier Command at Stout Field near Indianapolis, Indiana, under Col. Fred C. Borum.

Harris worked with the Troop Carrier Command to develop a rigging system whereby the C-47 could drop a total of nine loads, each weighing about 200 pounds including the parachute and containers. The nine loads would include the front trail assembly, the rear trail, the bottom sleigh and recoil mechanism, the cradle and top sleigh, the tube, the breech ring, the wheels, and ammunition and an ammo cart. The Troop Carrier Command and the test battery finally developed a system whereby the C-47s were rigged with six so-called "bomb" racks under the main fuselage. Each rack had a streamlined cup in front, behind which one of the bundles was hung from the fuselage. The other three loads became "door bundles." Early on, a problem arose because, after the nine loads were dropped, they scattered over large areas on the drop zone, and it became time consuming for the cannoneers to locate all of the pieces of their own howitzers, reassemble them, and get them into firing positions.

Colonel John B. Shinberger, of the Airborne Command at Fort Bragg, came up with an ingenious solution to the problem of keeping all pieces of each howitzer close together on the ground. He evolved a system whereby the nine loads were all linked together along a "daisy chain," a long nylon strap. When the green light went on over the door of the C-47, the jump master standing in the door of the plane shouted "go." At that command, two men near the door threw out the three door bundles and followed them out the door. Simultaneously, the jump master, using a toggle switch, rapidly pushed a button to release the loads in the bomb bays under the C-47. Meanwhile, the rest of the stick was going out the door. The jump master then followed the last man out. Once the nine loads of the howitzer and its ancillary equipment were in the air, the static lines of the parachutes popped the chutes open. The guide lines of the loads were all looped to the daisy chain; thus the loads were free to move along the daisy chain and not become entangled. And because they were all linked together, the loads landed fairly close together on the drop zone.

After the parachute test battery completed its experiments and had developed a reasonably practical method for dropping artillery pieces by parachute, it evolved into the first Parachute Field Artillery Battalion, the 456th, activated at Fort Bragg on 24 September 1942. Lieutenant Lou Burris was one of the original artillery paratroopers. He wrote recently of that experience.

In the first class of artillerymen to go through jump school at Fort Benning, Ga., in 1942, in a sweating formation, in one-piece coveralls, at the double, shouting cadence was Major Douglass Quandt, Lieutenants Norman Martin, Nick Stadtherr, Lou Burris and others. We grumbled together, swearing we would kill some of those instructors if they ever came to a unit of ours. All movements were at the double and infractions were punished with pushups, starting at 50.

All artillerymen from that class, and those immediately following, went to the Test Platoon at Fort Bragg, to devise ways of packing and dropping the 75mm. Mountain Howitzer. The test platoon became a battery and then a battalion as the officers and men flowed in. The battalion was designated the 456th Parachute Field Artillery Battalion, a part of the new 82d Airborne Division.

The best of this group then formed the cadre for the 457th and moved to Camp Mackall, a freshly drained swamp 20 miles west of Fort Bragg, to form the 11th Airborne Division.

The cadre for the 457th began forming at Bragg in January 1943. Paul S. Childers had been a corporal in the 456th and had completed jump school on 5 June 1942. To be selected for a cadre often meant rapid promotions. Paul Childers's case is illustrative. When he joined the cadre of the 457th at Bragg, he was a corporal but was immediately promoted to staff sergeant to head up the detail section of B Battery. He remembers that "Sgt. Barbagallo was to be supply sergeant, Sgt. Geunch was to have a gun section. Another individual had been assigned as First Sergeant but never showed up which left me holding the bag as First Sergeant." The 457th cadre moved to Mackall in February 1943 and started a few weeks of cadre training. Major Douglass P. Quandt, West Point class of 1937, was the new commander of the 457th.

United States experimentation with and development of the glider as a means of transporting men into combat, like the paratrooper concept, lagged far behind the German effort. On 10 May 1940, the Germans launched their blitzkrieg against the West with massive assaults in a brilliant and successful campaign to outflank the so-called impregnable Maginot line. One part of that effort was the glider-borne assault against Fort Eben Emael, a concrete and steel underground fortress near the juncture of the Meuse River and the Albert Canal along the Dutch-Belgian border, about fifteen miles north of Liège. Both the Allies and the force of some 780 men guarding Fort Eben Emael thought it was invulnerable to attack; it was Belgium's most modern fort. The German High Command knew that Eben Emael had to be knocked out in the early hours of the attack to prevent its guns from being used against what would have to be their fast-moving, ground-bound assault forces.

In a maneuver allegedly conceived by Hitler himself, a small contingent of seventy-eight glider-borne German soldiers in about a dozen gliders soared silently in from their release point over German terrain and landed relatively quietly, directly on top of Fort Eben Emael in the dark, predawn hours of 10 May. The principal armaments of the glider men were fifty-six 110-pound explosive devices, each of which could blast a six-inch hole through solid steel. The power of the explosive derived from the effect of its "shaped charge," first developed by an American scientist, C. E. Monroe, and later perfected by the Germans. The German glider men quickly dropped the explosives into the guns and into the fort's exits, thereby not only neutralizing the power of the fort but also trapping its contingent in what was now a blasted, wrecked, and useless prison. Twenty-eight hours later, the helpless Fort Eben Emael garrison surrendered to the small band of German attackers.

Early in 1941, spurred on by the German success in combat with gliders, Gen. Hap Arnold directed his staff to start work on a classified project—to study and make recommendations on the possibility of using gliders in combat. After his staff came back with positive recommendations, he set up an Air Corps glider branch at Wright Field, near Dayton, Ohio. In a very short time, enthusiasm ran high for the glider both in the Air Corps and in the army. The Air Corps made plans to train as many as 36,000 glider pilots and actually set up a schedule to qualify twice that many. In the army, Colonel Lee envisioned that the glider could easily provide paratroopers with artillery howitzers, antitank guns, jeeps, miniaturized engineer bulldozers and other equipment, and large numbers of reinforcing troops who would need no special training (except perhaps a dose of psychological indoctrination to make them at ease in the dark, crude innards of the awkward and fragile-looking oversized kites). And at about this time, General McNair, commander of the Army Ground Forces, suggested that all standard infantry divisions be trained in aircraft- and glider-landing procedures before being shipped overseas.

The U.S. glider program did not achieve the rather lofty goals that had originally been programmed. The grand total of glider pilots active at any one time probably never exceeded 7,500. And General McNair concluded that training all infantry divisions in air-landing and glider techniques would put too much of a strain on the training base. He therefore limited glider training to designated glider units.

Eventually, the Air Force Materiel Command expended $500 million on the glider program and built a number of experimental and limited-production models. It was a substantial undertaking that had to develop a glider almost from scratch. The program was riddled with scandal. The cost per glider ranged from $15,000 to $1.7 million, and even the most inefficient companies were permitted to furnish parts for the gliders. The legitimate airplane manufacturers were swamped with orders, and they were not able to supervise or control the quality of the parts they were receiving from their subcontractors.

On 1 August 1943, a Waco built by a manufacturer in St. Louis was making a demonstration flight over the city. The glider carried the company's chief executive officer, the mayor, local VIPs, and some military representatives. Midway into the flight, the glider's fabric began to tear. The glider vibrated, rattled, and swayed out of control. One wing began to fold slowly backward and then collapsed. The glider, unhooked from the tow plane, cartwheeled to earth. There were no survivors.

Wright Field developed a number of prototypes and finally settled on the Waco CG 4A, a boxlike contraption with wings, whose skeleton of small-gauge steel tubing was covered with canvas. It had a wingspan of eighty-four feet, was forty-nine feet long, and could carry 3,750 pounds. That equated to two pilots and either thirteen fully combat–loaded soldiers or a jeep and six men. The passengers entered the glider through a side door in the rear. The nose of the glider and the pilots' cockpit was a compartment hinged at the top so that, when raised, jeeps or artillery pieces could be loaded underneath it from the front.

By the time the CG 4A went into full production, some forty-five companies in fourteen states had a part of the action and built a total of more than 16,000 gliders of which 13,909 were CG 4As. Not only were specialized airplane manufacturers building all or parts of the CG 4A, but so were a host of other factories, including a refrigerator company, a piano builder, a furniture factory, a coffin shop, pool table and canoe makers, and even a pickle company and a brewery. If the glider men of the 11th had been aware of the origin of the gliders they were expected to ride in with no extra pay and no right to refuse, they might have been even more trepid about their flights around and over Mackall and Maxton. And if they had been aware of the accident rate of the glider (in 1943, the Airborne Command reported the loss of three to six gliders daily in training), they might have been even more outspoken in their abhorrence of the glider. One poster at Maxton summed up their feelings: Beneath a series of photos showing glider wrecks, a glider man had written: "JOIN THE GLIDER TROOPS! No flight pay; no jump pay; BUT Never a Dull Moment!"

The honor of being the first glider unit falls to what had been the 88th Airborne Infantry Battalion, trained originally in air-landing techniques. It was stationed at Fort Bragg in the spring of 1942. In May of that year, it was enlarged to 1,000 men and redesignated the 88th Glider Infantry Regiment. In the fall of 1942, construction of a training camp at Laurinburg-Maxton was finished, and the CG 4As began to arrive in sufficient quantities to permit the start of serious glider unit training. In October 1942, the 88th hiked the fifty-five miles from Fort Bragg and took up their new location at Laurinburg-Maxton. The army's glider training program was finally underway.

At Camp Hoffman, beginning on 6 February 1943, each day's entry in the division's diary recorded the arrival of additional officers and men—members of the cadre or of previously activated units. The Division Artillery Band and the 511th Parachute Infantry Band, for example, had both initially entered the federal service with the National Guard and had both been playing for the Field Artillery Brigades at Fort Bragg before joining the 11th. The 711th Airborne Ordnance Company and the 408th Airborne Quartermaster Company were also activated prior to the division and joined the division as already-formed units.

In the early weeks of February, the cadre set about the task of making their barracks, mess halls, orderly rooms, supply rooms, and headquarters buildings as functional and as livable as possible, given the stage of construction, the presence of construction crews still at work on roads and buildings, and the absence of even the most basic office furniture, office supplies, and communications.

The completion of the cadre training coincided with the date of activation of the division. On that date, the division published General Order Number 1, which listed the following organic units of the division:

Headquarters, 11th Airborne Division
Headquarters Company, 11th Airborne Division
Military Police Platoon, 11th Airborne Division
408th Airborne Quartermaster Company
511th Airborne Signal Company
711th Airborne Ordnance Maintenance Company
221st Airborne Medical Company
127th Airborne Engineer Battalion
152d Airborne Antiaircraft Battalion
Headquarters and Headquarters Battery, 11th Airborne Division Artillery (Band)
457th Parachute Field Artillery Battalion
674th Glider Field Artillery Battalion
675th Glider Field Artillery Battalion
187th Glider Infantry Regiment
188th Glider Infantry Regiment
511th Parachute Infantry Regiment (Band)

The total division strength, officers and men, was 8,321, just slightly more than half the strength of a standard infantry division. Moreover, the airborne division's weapons, all of which had to be capable of delivery to the battlefield by parachute or glider, were necessarily light, two facts that would be lost on the senior commanders in combat when the time came to commit the 11th Airborne. The division also had a peculiar organization when compared to a standard infantry division. Whereas the division had three regiments, the glider regiments had only two battalions and the glider field artillery battalions that supported them had only two firing batteries of six guns each. The parachute regiment did have three battalions and the parachute field artillery battalion had three firing batteries of four pack 75s each.

In the airborne divisions that went to Europe, the basic organization changed. The 82d and the 101st eventually had two parachute infantry regiments and one glider infantry regiment. Occasionally, separate additional parachute and glider units were attached for specific operations. The 11th, on the other hand, retained its general basic structure almost until the end of the war.

Meanwhile, at Division Headquarters in the early days of February 1943, the G-1 formed a classification group of unit personnel officers and clerks whose duties would be to receive, classify, and assign the recruits as they arrived and to speed them swiftly and efficiently to their permanent assignments and locations.

But someone had to meet the trains at the Hoffman train depot, where the bulk of the recruits would be arriving. It fell to the lot of then Maj. Ernie Massad, a field artilleryman from Oklahoma, to form a "casual detachment" of ten officers and forty-six men whose duties would be far more demanding than the adjective in their title might suggest. The casual detachment's functions were to meet the trains in Hoffman; transport the recruits to camp; feed them and house them; and, with the assistance of the Classification Group, check their service records, assign them to divisional units, and see to it that they got there. Division Headquarters assigned to the casual detachment for their temporary use a number of barracks and a mess hall in the currently unoccupied 511th area at the west end of the camp.

The first fillers for the glider elements of the division arrived at Hoffman on 2 March 1943 at 0200 on a cold and miserable night. The few lights of the Hoffman station house blinked feebly through the soggy Carolina mist. Beyond the station, the casual detachment's line of soggy, dull green, two-and-a-half-ton trucks stood with motors idling and tailgates down. To the fillers, some still in their civilian clothes, it was not a sight to fill them with warm emotions of patriotism, duty, honor, and country, and an ardent desire to take up a rifle and charge.

The casual detachment NCOs lined up the recruits as best they could and tried to answer their questions. "Where are we?" "At Hoffman, North Carolina." "What's at Hoffman, North Carolina?" "Camp Mackall." "What's at Camp Mackall?" "The 11th Airborne Division." "The 11th wwwhat?" "Airborne." "What's airborne?" "Paratroopers and glider riders." "What's a glider?" At about that point, the cadre man called attention, gave a right face, and marched the bewildered recruits to the waiting trucks for the cold and wet ride to Mackall. Their wartime tour with the 11th Airborne Division had begun under less than auspicious circumstances.

Edward A. Hammrich remembers well his arrival at Hoffman and Mackall.

> My first realization that I was a Gliderman, [drafted] into the Airborne Army, was when I disembarked from the train at Hoffman, N.C. I emphasize the word drafted, because to this day—45 years later—I think we were given a dirty deal in not being able to volunteer nor receive the additional pay for hazardous service in the Airborne service. . . . My first impression on seeing Camp Mackall was one of surprise, thinking that these tar-paper shacks must be the temporary buildings till the regular barracks are put up. It did not take us long to find out otherwise. . . . It was nice being able to see what was going on outside of the buildings without going to a window, just look through the cracks.

The men of the division came from all sections of the country. Each Service Command supplied men for the division in the ratio of the civilian population of the Service Command to the population of the entire United States. Practically all of the fillers came directly from reception centers at Camp Wolters, Texas; Fort Sill, Oklahoma; Fort Lewis, Washington; Fort Dix, New Jersey; and Fort Meade, Maryland. Those men who had volunteered for parachute duty at their reception centers were assigned directly to one of the parachute units of the division; all others were assigned, unasked, to the glider units.

The quality of the men who came to the division as fillers was particularly high. The majority of them were eighteen to nineteen years old, although a few were older. At full strength, the division average age was slightly less than twenty years old. Sixty percent of the enlisted men had a score of 110 or higher on the army general classification test; 110 was the minimum intelligence standard for admission to Officer Candidate School (OCS). More than one recruit felt that he had an intelligence and a capability exceeding those of some of his superiors. Eventually, in combat, many superb young men were commissioned on the battlefield, proving to some of them that they were right all along. Because the division would not be called upon to cadre another division, and because very few of the division's men went to OCS, the quality troops stayed with the 11th Airborne Division, a factor that would prove vital in hard months of combat to come.

Private Edward W. Jacobs was a newspaperman by trade until he was drafted in late 1942. Right after the war, he wrote about his feelings on arrival at Hoffman.

I arrived at Hoffman, North Carolina, thoroughly confused and bewildered. Once outside the train, I saw a sign which read something about the 11th Airborne Division. As the full meaning of the word "airborne" struck me, straight from the press bars of Philadelphia and tipping the scales at a scant 230, I was convinced that Army paperwork was as loused up as Reception Center rumor had predicted. I thought seriously of making a wild dash for the safety of the retreating train but immediately realized that I was in no condition to make it. Instead, my fellow recruits and I from the big cities of the East stood around making disparaging remarks about the metropolis of Hoffman, North Carolina; they were soon cut short by sharp-voiced sergeants. They organized us into some sort of formation, marched us to waiting trucks, saw us safely loaded, and started the convoy to Camp Mackall. . . . After a short ride, we arrived at the Casual Detachment barracks, were assigned a temporary location, and then marched to the messhall for a hot meal.

After a much too short rest, and the lapse of a few seconds, or maybe hours, our names were called again. We gathered our barracks bags and other gear, formed in line and started the march from the western end to the eastern end of S-3 Street. Along the road we saw for the first time the brand new signs marking the headquarters of the various units of the Division. At the first sign, "188th Glider Infantry," we halted. A list of names was called out. Those men fell out and were turned over to the noncommissioned officers of the 188th. From this time forward, they were doughboys. Similar stops were made at the 187th Glider Infantry, the 127th Airborne Engineer Battalion, and the artillery and antiaircraft battalions. Some of us dropped off at each stop, and, finally, the remaining men knew they were assigned to the Special Troops units by a process of elimination.

For the fillers, life at Camp Mackall had begun. The military procedures that would fill the days ahead would transform the fillers from civilians to soldiers. The process was inexorable.

CHAPTER 3

FROM TRAINING TO COMBAT READINESS

With the completion of cadre training and the arrival of the fillers for its glider elements, the 11th Airborne Division began its march on a sometimes rocky, sometimes relatively smooth, but usually strenuous path to cohesiveness, combat readiness, and maturity as a division. During training, however, the troops of the division were not aware that full maturity would not come to them until their specific small unit, platoon, company, or battery was committed to combat and had had its first taste of incoming enemy fire or was making its first tense, tactical patrol into enemy territory, unaware of the enemy's positions and unable to see him in the jungle. The first burst of a Japanese machine gun digging up dirt at his feet or whistling past his ear, or a mortar explosion within a few yards, would be sufficient to mature him rapidly. He had to know instinctively what to do. Then the long hours of training, but more important, his close relationship with the men in his small unit would pay off. The greatest motivator on the battlefield would prove to be one trooper's unwillingness to let his "buddy" down. Foxhole camaraderie would be the payoff. Pride in one's unit came next.

Like all new divisions of the World War II era, the 11th Airborne went through basic, unit, and maneuver phases of training. Basic training lasted from 15 March to 21 June. As the days of basic training went by, the training settled into a routine. The shouts of marching men counting cadence bounced off the scrub oaks, pine trees, and barracks and rolled away across the Carolina sand hills. Training areas had been hacked out of the undergrowth and pines around the unit areas. The recruits, dressed in fatigues, helmet liners, and GI boots and leggings, sat around easels and portable blackboards while young lieutenants and sergeants in khakis and helmet liners tried to drive home the essential points that would convert the recruits into soldiers. Classes in map reading, weapons operation and disassembly, first aid, foxhole construction, rules of land warfare, dry firing, customs and courtesies of the service, personal hygiene, communications, use of hand grenades, patrolling, and a multitude of other subjects and skills pertinent to the specific needs of the various units crammed the scheduled hours of the duty day. The 11th Airborne was slowly acquiring the skills that in about eighteen months would be put to the ultimate test of its soldiers—combat against a wily, ruthless enemy on the uncharted, mud-blanketed mountains of Leyte.

One of the most important and hence most thoroughly covered subjects during basic training was on individual weapons. In the words of Private Jacobs:

Our first indication that the division would have some use for us came when we began to receive individual weapons instruction. Our introduction was the invariable lecture by a lieutenant standing before us, shy and tentative, holding in hand a carbine or an M-1, explaining each part. At a succeeding session, a few sample weapons were distributed among us. We spread our shelter halves on the ground, and, with a weapon to each group of five or six soldiers, together we started to field-strip them. Finally, we were considered sufficiently trustworthy to be issued a weapon of our own, and realization dawned that a problem, as well as a possession, had been issued.

When it first came to us, it was packed in Cosmoline, which had to be removed completely. When we thought we had finished cleaning our guns, there was twice as much goo on us as ever there had been on the weapon, and still the same amount on the gun as before. The new parts worked stiffly—screws resisted all efforts to loosen them and springs came to life, grew, bounced, hid, and buckled. Out to the inspection we went, exhausted but triumphant, with extra parts that wouldn't fit stuffed in our pockets. At least it was clean, we said. Those that didn't fall apart in the captain's hands when he smacked them, released clouds of dust and rust. . . . At one inspection, rifles were supposed to be dry; at the next one they were supposed to be oily. If the piece was oily, it picked up the dust of the sand hills country; if dry, it got rusty. When we took it to the field, it picked up sand which meant another cleaning. We hated to take it out, preferring to enshrine it, clean and oiled, in the rifle rack, and borrow someone else's for the trip. Little tricks of the trade, such as using Blitz Cleaning Cloth as a rifle patch, steel wool to remove pits, or pencil lead to cover rust spots, soon boomeranged, but what was a burdensome task stretching into hours finally became a chore which could be attended to in a brisk ten minutes.

Learning how to fire our weapons was a process which started with much enthusiasm, descended into monotony, and finally wound up in an unbelievable wave of interest and sense of accomplishment. Preliminary Rifle Instruction—PRI—started in the thorough and methodical manner typical of what we had come to expect of the Army, and was followed by instructions on positions—standing, kneeling, sitting, and prone. Muscles creaked and rebelled at the unfamiliar attitudes and Southern coon hunters held forth with contemptuous critiques, but the positions soon became second nature. There followed the seemingly endless dry runs in preparation for the range, and when we were thoroughly sick and tired of the whole business, we received our schedule for firing on the range.

Range days were somehow different from all others. We rose early, and there was early chow. The gang selected to work in the pits went off in trucks even earlier to have the targets ready for our arrival. We marched at ease the three odd miles out Range Road in the early dawn, gossiping and humming, and by the time the sun was rising over the horizon, we were ready to fire. On the firing line, we had our last dry run followed by five shots to zero-in our pieces. Almost before we knew it, we were ready to fire for record, and dry runs were of the past. The range officer repeated the old calls which have become ritual: "Ready on the right? Ready on the left? Ready on the firing line? Flag is waving, flag is down, targets UP!" The first startling crackle of one or two impetuous riflemen, probably firing by mistake, gave heart to the hesitant, and a fusillade broke the morning stillness. Down went the targets to be marked, and the babble of time-worn remarks rose from the firing line: "I'll bet you five dollars" and the frantic yell, "JAM! JAM!" A hush, and the targets reappeared, spotted with the white and black discs, and, now and then, the slowly waving red flag—Maggie's Drawers—signifying a miss.

As the days of the basic phase wore on, the training became more complicated and more field oriented. The cadre taught the budding soldiers how to erect various types of hasty field fortifications and a skill that would become second nature in combat, how to dig a foxhole. The sandy North Carolina soil made foxhole digging relatively simple but still arduous and unnecessary, thought the sweating troops, after the first one. They knew how to dig a foxhole; it really wasn't necessary to keep practicing that art. The cadre men did not agree.

There began also the short overnight field problems, "bivouacs" in the army parlance of the day, which put to the test a number of skills learned previously around the barracks or in a classroom setting: tactical marches, night movement, squad and section combat deployment, tent pitching, eating in the field using mess kits, field KP, and field sanitation, a euphemism for construction and use of outdoor privies. Washing and shaving in a "steel pot" became a useful art.

The artillery had a problem different from that of the infantry: The artillery troopers had to take their pack 75s with them into the field for field training. And to compound the problem, in the very early stages and during basic training, the pack 75s' wheels were the same as those used by the mule teams—thin, wooden-spoked wheels whose rims were iron. The prime movers for the pack 75s were about eight men, tugging the artillery pieces behind them. In the Carolina sand, the thin wheels of the pack 75s dug in deeply. And in very soft terrain, the wheels occasionally went up to the hubcaps. The artillerymen felt a great sense of relief when their pack 75s were fitted out with wheels with wide rubber tires.

The other units of the division—the engineers, the signalers, the ordnance men, the quartermasters, the medics, and the antiaircraft gunners—fitted their special skill requirements into their basic training as the weeks progressed.

The officers of the division participated not only in their unit marches and bivouacs but also in something divined by and reserved for them alone by General Swing. The first of these sessions occurred at 1600 on Friday, 19 March 1943. All officers in the division formed in their unit area, then marched to division headquarters. General Swing, General Pierson, and General Brown, who was then the artillery commander, fell in at the head of the column of officers. Behind the generals were the division staff officers. General Swing then led the column on what had been previously described as a short, brisk exercise walk. The pace was brisk and the walk was not short; it turned into a run, and it lasted nearly an hour. General Swing was so enthusiastic that he continued what inevitably came to be known as "Swing sessions," every Friday afternoon that the division was at Mackall, give or take a few Fridays when the division might have been in the field.

The highlight of the basic training phase for the paratrooper volunteers came in the months of May and June 1943, when they went, a battalion at a time, to Fort Benning for jump school. Ordinarily, jump school was four weeks long, with the first week devoted to getting the jump volunteers into good physical condition. In the case of the 11th's volunteers, the Airborne Command sent a team to Camp Mackall to look them over and to judge their physical condition. The team found the volunteers in such good physical shape that it waived the first week of jump school, A Stage, for the 11th's would-be paratroopers.

B Stage was a mixed schedule of learning how to tumble on landing, climbing on the plumber's nightmare, listening to lectures, exiting the mock door to a precise set of instructions (stand up, hook up, check equipment, sound off for equipment check, close in the door, go!) as if from an aircraft in flight, leaping out of the thirty-four-foot tower and sliding down a cable to a pile of sawdust some hundred feet away, swinging from the suspended harness in some discomfort, and learning how to pack a parachute. The students were also expected to climb a twenty-foot suspended rope in a matter of seconds, an exercise designed to strengthen the muscles needed to control a parachute in the air.

C Stage was devoted to using the 250-foot-high jump towers, a somewhat leveling experience that made a paratrooper more than ready to leap out of an airplane, and continuing to learn to pack a parachute with precision.

D Stage was the big week in which the trooper made his five qualifying jumps. One nervous, soon-to-be jumper described his first jump and D Stage this way:

After a sleepless, tossing night of half-hoping it would rain, and half-hoping it wouldn't rain so I could get it over with, we marched down the hill in the grey dawn to the packing sheds, drew our chutes, and moved to the bull pen to sit and await our planes and our turns. Across the way, grim and serious faces told of similar uneasiness deep inside, and we tried—but failed miserably and self-consciously—to laugh at the high, nervous pitch of the wisecracks flying back and forth. Soon my turn came, and I took my place in the waiting plane. Once aloft, I stretched my neck and looked out of the open jump door at the sight of the brownish fields below—way below. Before I knew it, I was hooked up, and in an irresistible rush, out, with eyes tightly closed and lips tightly clamped. I landed safely, tumbling as instructed, rolled up my parachute and was ready to do it again. There was nothing to it—provided I could do it again—right now. But with four more I was qualified. Later I would get to savor the thrill of jumping. I would feel no more the sickly uneasiness— only the anticipatory tingling, the pleasurable trembling that precedes arrival at the "Go Point." We all went back to Mackall with a fierce pride and the right to wear our hard-earned jump wings and jump boots. I was finally a paratrooper.

When the army began to form airborne divisions, there were only a handful of senior officers who were jump qualified. As a consequence, many of the airborne division commanders and their principal staff officers were not jumpers. General Maxwell Taylor, for example, made only one jump at Benning after watching students go through their training for a few hours. His second was a combat jump into Normandy leading the 101st Airborne Division in the invasion. And his third and final jump was during Operation Market-Garden, the mighty Allied airborne invasion of German-held Holland. General Mathew Ridgway had also made only one jump prior to jumping with and leading the 82d Airborne Division into Normandy.

In the 11th Airborne Division right after its activation, none of the principal division staff officers were jumpers. As Henry Muller, who would become the division G-2, put it, "The Division staff officers were all non-jumpers and hence looked upon like non-flyers in the Air Force. In order to correct this, General Swing made five quick jumps himself with only a few hours training. He then offered all of his staff an opportunity to qualify if they so wished. Actually, this put them under some pressure."

One of the staff officers was a heavyset man who could not possibly make the grade as a paratrooper and summarily asked for reassignment out of the division. The G-2, Lieutenant Colonel Dyer, injured his back on a jump and had to be reassigned. Henry Muller said that "as the only Leavenworth G-2 type in the division, General Swing called me to his office and told me I was to be the 'Acting G-2.' I recall that he put unnecessary stress on the word 'acting,' but I don't blame him. He was still suspicious of unrepentant paratroopers and particularly a brand new major just turned 26. It was five or six months before he very casually informed me I was the G-2."

General Swing was indeed suspicious of paratroopers even though he had become one. He realized that he was commanding an outfit made up, on the one hand, of cocky paratroopers with special jump pay, and, on the other hand, of glider troops who had had no voice in their assignment to the division and no extra pay to compensate for being forced to ride to war in a rickety, undependable glider just as hazardous as jumping out of an airplane. Unless he took some drastic actions, General Swing could foresee that the division would be split down the paratrooper-nonparatrooper crease—a fault line that might inevitably become a major problem in the division.

Some of the officers of the 511th were aware of the reputation that the "high-spirited youngsters" of the regiment were making for the 511th. Reports had filtered back to General Swing at Mackall that the 511th troopers were full of hell, rowdy, hell-raisers, and lacking in the discipline that he intended to instill in his soldiers. The reports may very well have been exaggerated; nonetheless, when the regiment joined the 11th at Mackall, General Swing was ready for them. Henry Muller remembers that union.

It was quite a shock to us. General Swing, who had heard terrible reports about the alleged rowdyism and unprofessionalism, determined to "make us over right." The first thing to go were the leather jackets [Air Corps "bomber jackets" issued to flight crews] worn [and authorized] by paratrooper officers. Next were the beloved boots for all ranks! We were in a state of shock. That dreadful morning when we all had to put on "leggings" . . . nearly broke our spirits—but not for long. The old horse artilleryman [General Swing] knew what it would take to bring a high spirited horse under control. In the long run, it was good for us too-cocky paratroopers and helped prevent unhealthy rivalry between the paratroopers and the glidermen. The glidermen were referred to as "Haimens" at this point.

Those were the negative steps that "the old man" took. On the positive side, he decided, quite radically, and apparently without authorization from higher headquarters, and this would not be the last time that he acted unfettered by the staff of his superior commanders, that the whole division should be able to enter combat either as paratroopers or as glider men. To achieve that goal, he eventually set up the division's own jump schools at Camp Polk, in New Guinea, and in the Philippines.

General Swing wanted all men out for training—officers, NCO, troops. First Sergeant Paul S. Childers, B Battery of the 457th Parachute

FA Battalion, remembers quite vividly his first contact with the division commander.

> Shortly after we began basic training, the General made an unannounced visit to the battery areas. I was in the orderly room working on the morning report, duty roster, and sick book. There were two officers in the day room working on a lecture or class they were supposed to give. Sgt. Barbagallo was in the supply room when the General came in and he really read the riot act to these two officers, then proceeded to work on Barbagallo. By that time, I began to think maybe I should raise a window and take off. Maybe by the time he got to the orderly room he had run out of gas for when he came in, I reported, and he asked me what I was doing. He seemed to accept my answer. Nevertheless, within the next day or two, the order came down that there was to be no one in the battery area after drill call.

Toward the end of basic training, the various units increased emphasis on their own particular skills. Each artillery battalion, for example, moved to the ranges at Fort Bragg to see what happened when the number one man pulled the lanyard after real live ammunition had been jammed home in the tube. Until then, they had had to take the cadre's word that the things they had been pulling through the Carolina sands had some actual useful purpose in combat.

On 22 May 1943, a truck convoy carrying the 152d Antiaircraft Battalion left Camp Mackall for Fort Fisher, North Carolina, to practice antiaircraft firing with their .50-caliber machine guns. The battalion returned to Camp Mackall on 5 June, having successfully completed yet another hurdle on the road to combat readiness as a battalion. But as Private Jacobs tells the story, the battalion really surmounted two hurdles, the first of which happened even before the battalion left Mackall.

> Just as the men were lined up in front of the trucks ready to go to Fort Fisher, General Swing inspected unexpectedly. Proudly they stood, knowing how well they looked. But not for long, and soon pride gave way to trembling. He was looking through duffle bags, of all things! Everything came out, and that means everything from civilian clothes to beer cans. Back to barracks marched the chastened 152d. Back to the motor parks went the trucks. Four hours later, another 152d, lighter by tons, drew up for inspection, passed, and moved out. Word spread like wildfire, and units moving out thereafter scrupulously packed according to the book.

On 21 June, the division finished basic training and entered a new phase—unit training program (UTP)—a period that the troopers of the division would find far more interesting than basic. The UTP welded together individuals, by now schooled in the ways of a soldier, into units of a division. During this phase, the regiments held platoon proficiency tests at Fort Bragg; all men went through the infiltration, transition, and close-combat courses.

Private Jacobs did not particularly take to the infiltration course.

There, a couple of fiendish machine gunners fired at our ground-hugging, crawling, pack-laden bodies. A demon with a switch in his hand waited until we were directly over his explosive charges and then detonated them in our faces. The urge to abandon our snake-like crawl and walk erect as we had been taught since childhood was emphatically discouraged by the sound of the bullets skimming just above our backs. We crawled through the weeded, blast studded, barbed-wire entangled mantrap and pulled our dirty exhausted bodies out of the other end with just enough energy remaining to jeer at the more obese and less agile still creeping toward the half-way mark.

During the UTP, airborne training also progressed from individual to unit technique. First there were squad jumps, followed by problems on the ground. Then came platoon, company, and battalion jumps, in daylight, at twilight, and finally by the light of the moon.

Lieutenant Leo Crawford, a platoon leader in D Company of the 511th, who had joined the 511th at Toccoa right out of jump school and OCS, remembers in some detail one of his platoon jumps that was to be followed by a tactical problem on the ground.

It was a night jump where the planes flew a triangle of 100 mile legs. As it was a long flight, I had the men unhook their leg straps so as to be more comfortable. As we were on the final leg, I thought I recognized our location from the lights of a town. I went forward and asked the pilot: "Is that Hamlet down there?" He replied: "Heck, I don't know. I'm just following that plane up there." I promptly went back and had my platoon hook up their leg straps. This was my first disillusionment with Air Corps navigation.

During July, all units went on ten-day bivouacs that were tactical only in part. The artillery battalions went to Bragg again and fired their weapons under tactical conditions, with the forward observers practicing the skills learned at Fort Sill in the basic officer course, which would stand them in such good stead once they got to combat and were firing at live targets.

The various glider units of the division started their formal glider training at Maxton Air Base and mastered the intricacies of rope tying; slide-rule manipulation; and loading and lashing of jeeps, howitzers, and other pieces of engineer, signal, and medical equipment. It was in this period that the glider riders took their first rides in the motorless contraptions and came to realize that they had been right all along— glider riding was hazardous, scary, and a "helluva way to enter combat."

To emphasize that feeling of fear and nervousness toward the glider as an accepted mode of transportation, the division suffered its first training fatalities on 16 September when, during a combined parachute and glider training exercise, a glider, coming in to land at the Mackall strip, crashed and killed six men. Four were from the 674th Glider Field Artillery Battalion and the other two were the pilot and copilot of the glider.

The paratroopers suffered a fatal accident on 29 October during a night jump. One of the C-47s carrying men of Headquarters Battery of the 457th Parachute Field Artillery Battalion attempted to land at Mackall after one engine had conked out. The plane overshot the field, and, as it rose and banked to turn and try again, its wing caught on a pine tree and spun the plane around and down. The casualties were heavy: Ten of the 457th's men were killed. Five lived; one, Corporal Sczeswick, was killed later on Luzon.

Captain Lou Burris, who commanded Dog Battery of the 457th from its activation until the end of the war, felt a great deal of emotion about that crash. He said later:

Some members of Dog Battery, including me, took that loss pretty hard because it was my plane we had been forced to turn over to Headquarters Battery. We objected vigorously because the pararacks under the plane's belly had to be re-rigged, requiring hours of hard work. During flight the plane developed engine trouble at a low altitude. The men of Headquarters Battery, under the command of Captain Joe Unger, were hooked up ready to jump and could have saved themselves and the plane by lightening the load, but the young 2d lieutenant co-pilot ordered them to un-hook, sit down and ride the plane down. The plane hit the trees with one wing and crashed in the pine forest and burned.

Leo Crawford remembers the training at Mackall.

[It was] vigorous [with] a lot of emphasis on physical conditioning. At Mackall, a fantastic esprit de corps developed. The loyalty within platoons, companies, battalions, and regiments was fantastic. The one mistake Division made was not fostering enough "division" loyalty. . . . In retrospect, it would have been very wise to make the 187th and 188th Paraglider at the very beginning. When I moved to the 188th, I was amazed at how unanimously the members accepted jump qualification and how many were already jump qualified. Having 188th and 187th personnel jump with the 511th at Mackall and having 511th personnel ride in gliders with the others would have been a good idea.

But that was in the offing. One suspects that General Swing knew he had to train the division first as basic soldiers and then as units; then later—especially in New Guinea and on Luzon—he could concentrate on the cross-training of his paratroopers and glider riders.

During July 1943, while the 11th Airborne troopers were training as units in the summer heat of North Carolina, across the Atlantic the 82d Airborne Division was making history by taking part in the first large-scale Allied airborne operation of the war. The 82d was part of Operation Husky, the Allied invasion of Sicily. The airborne phase of Husky would have a significant impact on the 11th Airborne in particular, and on airborne operations in general, and would almost cause the demise of the concept of an airborne unit as large as a division.

The tactical plan for the invasion of Sicily on 10 July was divided into two major parts: General Montgomery's British Eighth Army of four divisions to land on the southeast corner of the island and make the main thrust up the east coast; Gen. George Patton's U.S. Seventh Army with four divisions to land on Montgomery's left and protect his flank. The airborne phase of the operation would precede the amphibious landings by three hours.

The first airborne portion of Husky called for 1,600 men of the British 1st Air Landing Brigade to land in gliders just below the city of Syracuse at 2230 on 9 July and then to seize the road network and a keystone bridge in the area to facilitate Montgomery's advance into Syracuse. The second airborne operation was scheduled for 2330 on 9 July. In this attack, Col. James M. Gavin would lead his 505th Regimental Combat Team into an area near Gela on Sicily's southern coast. His missions were to block the roads leading to the coast near Gela and to hold the drop zone for the drop of Col. Reuben H. Tucker's 504th Regimental Combat Team on the night of 11 July.

The planned flight of the 52d Troop Carrier Wing, which would carry the 82d to Sicily, was 415 miles long, circuitous, and dangerous, given that the flight would be at night under blacked-out conditions and at 200 feet above the Mediterranean. It was so circuitous because the planes had to fly a dogleg around the flank of the 3,000 Allied ships carrying the amphibious forces and had to avoid the Axis shore batteries on Sicily.

The weather on 9 and 10 July was also a factor; it deteriorated to the point that General Eisenhower considered postponing the assault for twenty-four hours. After consulting his weather experts, however, he decided to go ahead as planned.

The planes carrying the airborne troops ran into such high winds shortly after taking off from North Africa that their vee formations were broken up and many of the planes flew off course. The inadequately trained American aircrews scattered the 3,400 paratroopers of the 505th over a wide area of southern Sicily. The British glider men fared worse: Of the 144 gliders that left North Africa, nearly 70 were released prematurely and fell into the sea; 50 crash-landed on shore. Only a dozen reached the planned landing zone.

The first phase of the 504th's drop, led by Colonel Tucker, on the night of 11 July started off on schedule and on course, but there the precision ended. In the second and succeeding serials, some of the planes were far off course. An Allied antiaircraft gunner thought that the errant planes were German. He opened fire on the transports and started a chain reaction throughout the fleet anchored offshore. Of the 144 planes that left Africa carrying the 504th, 23 never returned, 37 had major damage, and half of the planes required major repairs before they could fly again. Eighty-two paratroopers were dead, 131 were wounded, and 16 were missing. In the next twenty-four hours, Colonel Tucker could account for only a quarter of the 2,000 men who had left North Africa.

But because the paratroopers and glider men had been so widely dispersed, the Axis intelligence had no idea of how many men had dropped. After the war, Field Marshall Albert Kesselring, the German commander of all the German troops in the Mediterranean, wrote: "The paratroopers effected an extraordinary delay in the movement of our own troops and caused large losses." General Karl Student, the father of the German airborne effort, said: "It is my opinion that if it had not been for the Allied airborne forces blocking the Hermann Goering Armored Division from reaching the beachhead, that division would have driven the initial seaborne forces back into the sea."

But those Axis conclusions were far from those formed by General Eisenhower, concerned about the future of airborne and irate at the commanders who had not foreseen the difficulties that resulted in the Sicily debacle. He sent an after-action report to General Marshall in which he stated:

I do not believe in the airborne division. I believe that airborne troops should be reorganized into self-contained units, comprising infantry, artillery, and special services, all of about the strength of a regimental combat team. Even if one had all the air transport he could possibly use, the fact is at any given time and in any given spot only a reasonable number of air transports can be operated because of technical difficulties. To employ at any time and place a whole division would require a dropping over such an extended area that I seriously doubt that a division commander could regain control and operate the scattered forces as one unit. In any event, if these troops were organized into smaller, self-contained units, a senior commander, with a small staff and radio communications, could always be dropped in the area to insure necessary coordination.

General Eisenhower's after-action report to General Marshall caused the army's high command grave doubts about the wisdom of pursuing the airborne division concept and very nearly prompted the Army chief of staff to abandon the idea and to disband the five airborne divisions (the 82d, 101st, 11th, 13th, and 17th) already in existence. Even some of the army's original small cadre of airborne enthusiasts were split among themselves. One confident and optimistic group was planning for an airborne corps (which, of course, eventually came to pass in the European theater of operations) while another group, far less committed to large airborne formations, felt that battalions, for quick in-and-out raids, made more sense. Even Lt. Gen. Leslie J. McNair, the tough and demanding commander of the Army Ground Forces, who was originally very much in favor of airborne troops and large airborne units, was disillusioned by the bungling and misfortunes of the Sicilian airborne campaign. General Ridgway, then in command of the 82d, was also disillusioned about the value of airborne divisions after the Sicilian campaign but changed his mind later. Before General Marshall would take final action on the matter, however, he directed the convening of a special board to study the problem and to determine the War Department policy on the mission and scope of the U.S. airborne program and operations.

The first board was headed by General Pierson, then the assistant division commander of the 11th. "I was ordered into the Pentagon to study the matter," he wrote recently. "I saw Mr. Stimson, the Secretary of War, and then reported to General Thomas T. Handy, Operations Division, to head a board of officers with Air Corps and Marine Corps members. We concluded that division organization for airborne troops could be supported in combat and recommended that the division be retained." His board also concluded that "an airborne division could be sustained by air for 3–5 days" but, General Pierson added, "some of my supporting documents were rather sketchy. . . . However, not much came from this report but the Swing Board which followed became the all-important doctrine."

The War Department selected General Swing to preside over a second board of officers to investigate the same matter. General Swing was an obvious choice for the job because he had been present in Sicily as General Eisenhower's airborne advisor, had watched the 82d's miscarried operation, and was currently an airborne division commander. General Pierson wrote recently:

> Why Eisenhower required an "airborne advisor" stumped me. I talked at some length about the operation after he [General Swing] came back. Weather affecting the flight of the troop carriers had a lot to do with the faulty drop of the 505th. The flight had to change direction so as to avoid flying over the Navy convoy to keep from being shot down by our own Navy. He deplored the action of the troops on the ground shooting down our planes the following morning.

In September 1943, the War Department's second airborne board of officers, shortly and thereafter to be known as the "Swing Board," met at Mackall. The board members included experienced paratrooper and glider officers, artillerymen, and Air Corps troop carrier and glider unit commanders and staff officers. For a couple of weeks, the board reviewed both the Axis and Allied airborne operations to date, studied the organization of the airborne division, and analyzed the problems encountered by the Air Corps troop carrier units in the North Africa and Sicily operations. They reviewed navigational problems, interservice communications, and command and control of airborne forces before and after commitment. By the end of September, the board had finished its deliberations and recommended that the War Department publish a training circular that would define the relationship between the Airborne and the Troop Carrier Commands, their several responsibilities, and the details of airborne operations from takeoff to drop and assembly. In short order, the War Department published Training Circular 113, which became the "bible" for subsequent airborne operations.

Training Circular 113 did not, however, satisfy Generals Marshall and McNair that airborne divisions were here to stay in spite of the fact that the 82d, less the 504th still fighting in Italy, and the 101st, under the command of "the father of airborne," General Lee, had already been deployed to England and were in the throes of getting ready for an invasion of the Continent. Generals Marshall and McNair wanted proven beyond the shadow of a doubt that an airborne division could function as conceived. General McNair ordered the 11th Airborne Division to plan a division maneuver for December 1943; on its success or failure would depend the future of the airborne division.

Major Muller remembers the "flap" over the ultimate optimum size of the airborne unit.

General McNair was responsible for force structure and logically it was he who would monitor our operations and make the judgment. However, the woods were filled with those who opposed large airborne forces. The Air Corps feared that the troop carrier requirements would cut into their "all important" strategic mission. The ground force people, particularly the armored officers, believed that airborne units would be too light to handle the heavy German divisions. . . . Aside from the recognized problems of finding the DZ's at night (later proved in the Normandy jump) we had the problems of locating ourselves on the ground, assembling with others in our unit, and finding our equipment.

General Swing had me do a lot of research on this while at Mackall working with the G-2 of the 17th Airborne Division, our neighbor. We suspected that the dispersion would be so great that we even tried celestial navigation. Handling the sextant and bulky tables at night proved infeasible. The best solution was to mark the azimuths of all roads on the maps. A lost unit would move to the nearest road and take azimuth then move to the nearest junction or intersection and take another azimuth reading. We believed it would be unlikely that two such azimuths could be duplicated in the same area assuming the Air Corps dropped us within several miles of the DZ. I don't know that this system was ever used, but we had planned to do so had we gone to Europe, where there were sufficient roads to use the system.

For assembly we tried lights, sounds and even hydrogen balloons to hold lights aloft but this had obvious shortcomings. The Army finally did adopt whistles, powered by nitrogen gas, which could be set at various pitches and frequency intervals. These were to be attached to equipment bundles and were activated either when the parachute opened or when the bundle struck the ground. I don't recall that they were ever used at least in our division.

For at least all of these reasons, the future of larger airborne units was in doubt and did, in part, depend on the success or failure of our Knollwood operation. . . .

I suppose after Sicily and Normandy some of the opponents may have had the opportunity to say "I told you so." In our case, as things turned out, we would have been better off with a full strength infantry division with 105 mm. and 155 mm. support.

The real advantage of airborne may have been the wonderful esprit of the volunteer units as well as the potential threat which forced the enemy (in Europe at least) to disperse his defense forces.

The Secretary of War was also concerned about the airborne concept and its place in the tactics and strategy of winning World War II. He decided to see for himself. He came to Mackall on 23 and 24 November. On 23 November, the division staged an infantry-artillery, parachute-glider maneuver, which was a success. But it was not the entire division, and it was not staged under the trying circumstances of long flights over water. The December performance would have to examine that total picture.

General Pierson remembers Mr. Stimson's visit.

Mr. Stimson, our Secretary of War, was concerned about our airborne losses in the Sicily operation. He undoubtedly knew about the British glider losses too. At any rate, I recall a vivid night glider exercise at Mackall where a number of very senior individuals came down to observe night glider landings. I was present at a glider landing field with a group consisting of General Arnold and I believe Mr. Stimson, observing gliders come in for perfect landings on this particular field. I am sure that General Swing was there too. After several gliders came down, we heard music coming from the sky. It was some time afterward a glider came down for a landing and approached the tree-line where the observers were standing. It rolled up abreast of us, the nose of the CG-4A opened and out came an Air Force orchestra complete with their instruments. It convinced the observers of the effectiveness of night glider operations.

WAR DEPARTMENT
WASHINGTON

November 27, 1943

My dear General Swing:

I wish to thank you for the many courtesies and kindnesses extended to me during my stay at Camp Mackall. I believe I got more of value from this particular inspection trip than from any trip I have made. I was particularly impressed by the drive and enthusiasm displayed by the troops under your command and by the painstaking care and detailed planning which their training bespoke.

The Airborne Infantry Division will play a great part in our future successes, and I know that the 11th Airborne Division will render outstanding service to our country on some not too far distant D Day.

I wish to congratulate you personally and through you all ranks under your command on the outstanding condition of your division as to physical toughness and high degree of training.

With every good wish for your continued success, I am

Very sincerely yours,

HENRY L. STIMSON
Secretary of War.

Major General Joseph M. Swing
11th Airborne Division
Camp Mackall, N. C.

The objective of the December operation was the capture of the Knollwood Airport in North Carolina; thereafter, in airborne history, this action would be known as the Knollwood maneuvers. Army Ground Forces directed that the maneuver be conducted according to the recently published Training Circular 113, and they designed the maneuver to provide practical and straightforward answers to the following questions. Could an airborne division fly a three- to four-hour instrument course, at night, across a large body of water and arrive on schedule at precisely selected drop and landing zones? Could such a force land by parachute and glider without sustaining excessive landing casualties? Could the division then wage extended ground combat? Could the division so landed be resupplied totally by air and air landings? General Swing, his staff, and principal commanders thought that it could; now they had to prove it.

Through the months of the fall of 1943, the 11th Airborne Division was honing its collective skills in the various arts of war. Small-unit training gave way to company-, battalion-, and regimental-sized maneuvers. The artillerymen learned to mass their fires based solely on the observations and calls for fire from a single forward observer with an infantry company; the 127th Airborne Engineer Battalion became adept at small bridge building, road cutting, demolitions, and bulldozing in general. The 221st Airborne Medical Company practiced their skills on the drop zones and prepared for the inevitable casualties that combat would eventually bring. (Little did they realize that in a short time they would be performing surgery under tents in the most primitive of conditions on the muddy hills of Leyte.) The 511th Signal Company communicated over longer and longer distances with greater and greater speed; the 152d Airborne Antiaircraft Battalion tracked planes through their sights and imagined that they were Zeros; the 711th Airborne Ordnance Maintenance Company put together weapons smashed on drops and kept the division's jeeps and two-and-a-half-ton trucks operational; and the 408th Airborne Quartermaster Company packed chutes, rigged equipment bundles, invented new ways of dropping equipment, and practiced resupply of all kinds of supplies both by ground and by air transport. The units of the division learned and trained, driven by the certain knowledge that they would fight the enemy somewhere, sometime soon. They developed new ways of doing what other units might take for granted because this was an "airborne" outfit, basically different in organization, tactics, esprit, and means of entering combat. The units of the division had few books to follow; in fact, they wrote their own books.

Dog Battery of the 457th was a special case. Originally its ninety-eight men and seven officers were organized into two platoons: One was a jumping antiaircraft platoon armed with .50-caliber machine guns on ground mount tripods; the other was a glider-riding antitank platoon armed with antique 37mm antitank guns. (Later, in New Guinea, the battery would get pack 75s like the rest of the battalion, but that was some months off.) The battery had no motors section, no mess section, no personnel section. According to its commander, Capt. Lou Burris, from the spring of 1943 through the end of combat,

> Dog Battery was a bastard outfit, organized so that it couldn't possibly do anything of significance alone and was cut off from the parent battalion by lack of appropriate armament. The training was put together as an after-thought while that of the other batteries was carefully planned. We became a dumping ground for those men and officers who were less than productive or too rebellious for the firing batteries, and later as punishment.
>
> Our morale plummetted. The anger, frustration, and belligerence felt by the members of the battery had to be channeled into training. Men had volunteered for parachute duty at age 17 at Toccoa, Georgia, where our own battalion introduced them to the Army. There was no Reception or Replacement Center or basic training by anyone else. It was a new concept for officers and men. The knowledge that these were the men and officers we would take into combat created an entirely different attitude.
>
> In North Carolina, Dog Battery trained in infantry small unit tactics along with every other skill we could dream up that we may use, not knowing just what our combat mission would be.
>
> Training and tests were designed for artillery batteries, not anti-tank, anti-aircraft units like Dog Battery. We were allowed to set up most of our training schedules and exercises, but we were also used for work details to preserve the integrity of the firing batteries. The battalion was graded on combat readiness of its firing batteries and we were treated as second-class members of the battalion. It irritated us and we trained harder, ran farther and imposed on ourselves a more stern discipline. When we took the part of "Enemy Forces" against our own battalion, we did it with enthusiasm, stealing everything we could from gun sights to jeep parts. Unfortunately, this attitude carried over into off-duty time and Military Police reports poured in.
>
> We all developed that arms length relationship which is necessary among soldiers to prevent an emotional breakdown when one is killed.

By December 1943, the 11th Airborne was a functioning, well-trained, combat-ready, highly disciplined division able to enter combat by parachute and glider or amphibiously if the occasion demanded. Starting on 4 December, the Knollwood maneuvers would test the combat and airborne readiness of the 11th Airborne.

On 4 December, after intensive planning and preparation, the units of the division moved out of Camp Mackall in a series of truck convoys.

The soldiers were loaded down with their individual packs and weapons. The paratroopers wore their jumpsuits and brown jump boots; the glider riders wore fatigues and canvas leggings. The ride was dusty but, for a change, not hot. December in North Carolina can be cold, and the troops would remember this particular operation for a lot of things—one of which was the freezing-cold weather. The truck convoys moved to five airfields in North and South Carolina: Pope Field at Fort Bragg, North Carolina; Mackall; the air base at Florence, South Carolina; and the army air bases at Lumberton and Laurinburg-Maxton in North Carolina. Most of the officers and noncommissioned officers of the division were aware that the results of the Knollwood maneuvers would determine the future of the airborne division as a unit; that knowledge added a tension to their preparations, above and beyond their normal predrop anxiety.

Army Ground Forces designed the Knollwood maneuvers to test the feasibility of loading up an airborne division in its jump transports and gliders, flying a four-hour triangular course—for the most part over water—hitting the drop and landing zones at night under blacked-out conditions, assembling the units into combat formations speedily, and then attacking the defending forces aggressively. The test results would answer two questions: Is the 11th Airborne Division combat ready? Is the airborne division a valid and practicable idea?

On 5 December, the Army Ground Forces test team had deployed a composite combat team from the 17th Airborne Division plus a battalion from Col. Duke McEntee's 541st Parachute Infantry Regiment around the objective, the Knollwood Airport and several other critical points.

The 11th Airborne Division, with the 501st Parachute Infantry Regiment attached, was originally scheduled to take off on the night of 5 December, but adverse weather conditions forced postponement for twenty-four hours. Under Secretary of War Robert Patterson and General McNair were on hand for the scheduled 5 December takeoff, but, with the postponement, they flew back to Washington. The importance of the maneuver to the Army was so critical that they came back again to watch the takeoffs and landings on the night of 6 December. Other VIP observers included General Ridgway, temporarily back from command of the 82d Airborne Division in England, and Brig. Gen. Leo Donovan, the new commander of the Airborne Command. Additionally, there were several teams of high-ranking inspectors from the War Department, the Army Ground Forces, and the Army Air Forces.

At the five departure airfields, the paratroopers and the glider men made ready for the takeoff. The paratroopers trucked up to their planes, with each truck carrying the load for a specific plane. Once at planeside, the paratroopers struggled into their main chutes; adjusted their loads of field gear, weapons, and ammunition; and then clipped on their reserves across their chests. The jump master of each plane checked each of his men for proper adjustment of parachutes and field packs. Fully rigged for jumping, the paratrooper was bent over from the tightness of the parachute harness and the weight of his personal gear. Then the paratroopers lined up in reverse order of jumping, waddled to the planeside, and climbed laboriously up the three steps into each C-47. They sat down on the canvas benches along the bulkheads of the planes and tried to get as comfortable as the harness would allow. They did not relish the long ride and would have far preferred to take off and jump as soon as they reached jump altitude. But that was not to be this time.

The glider men dismounted from their two-and-a-half-ton trucks near their assigned gliders and unloaded. The artillerymen shoved their pack 75s into the gliders through the front of the CG 4A, whose nose, containing the pilots' compartment, was swung upward. Other glider men loaded jeeps, small bulldozers, communications equipment, medical paraphernalia, trailers, and the whole range of supplies, weapons, and equipment needed by the division in the field for a sustained operation. Then the glider men, without parachutes but loaded down with their own personal gear, filed into the gliders, sat down on flimsy canvas seats along the sides of the gliders, and tensely awaited the hookup to their tug aircraft and ultimately their takeoff.

The takeoffs from the five airports were timed so that each serial would join the column in its proper place in line as the entire division became airborne. The planes were in a vee of vees, nine ships wide, as the formation grew longer and longer. The column headed east, across the North Carolina shoreline, out over the Atlantic, then turned north and finally headed back west toward the designated drop and landing zones, which were located in the area to the west of the Fort Bragg reservation. Golf courses around Pinehurst and Southern Pines, open fields outside the towns, and areas adjacent to the Knollwood Airport were the drop and landing zones. At 2300 on the moonlit night of 6 December, the first paratroopers in the lead ships jumped into the dark onto drop zones marked by pathfinders who had jumped earlier. As each successive vee of vees droned over its assigned area at about 1,200 feet of altitude, the sky was filled with paratroopers floating silently to the ground and with CG 4As, suddenly cut off from their tug ships, dropping rather rapidly on a sharp glide path to the moonlit landing zones (LZs). The drop and landing zones were soon covered with grounded chutes, opened equipment bundles, and empty gliders, in a scrambled and helter-skelter pattern, the noses of the gliders swung up to permit unloading of the cargo.

One of the more spectacular jumps that night was the drop of the 457th Parachute Field Artillery Battalion. In the black of the night, the fifty-two C-47s carrying the 457th came over the proper drop zone in a perfect vee of vees. The red and green wing lights of the planes and the bluish exhaust flames added a technicolor beauty to the formation, silhouetted against the starry sky. But as the jumpers leapt out of the planes and the jump masters toggled off the loads from the racks on the bottom of the planes, the sky became filled with free-falling colored lights, as if a giant, multicolored hailstorm had suddenly engulfed the area. The cause of the shower of illumination was the battery-operated lights on the artillery bundles, which were properly turned on by the opening shocks of the equipment parachutes but which were improperly attached to the bundles, causing them to break off and free-fall to the ground. The artillerymen had cleverly rigged the lights to the various bundles in a formula of colors to identify each battery's loads on the DZ but had, not so cleverly, used the wrong strength cord to attach them to the loads.

Almost all of the jumpers and gliders hit the proper DZs and LZs. The division chief of staff and his glider load, however, landed on a road on the Fort Bragg artillery range.

As soon as they landed and got out of their parachutes, the infantry paratroopers located their bundles, dug out crew-served weapons, assembled on the DZs, and then formed into their tactical echelons for the attack on their assigned objectives. The artillery paratroopers searched out their loads for the pack 75s, assembled them, and then moved out to their firing positions, tugging their weapons behind them. The rest of the units went about their tasks as rapidly as the night and the locations of their bundles would permit. The glider elements unloaded their gliders and joined their units for movement to assigned areas and missions. In a few hours, the division was reasonably well assembled as a unit and was in pursuit of its primary mission—the capture of Knollwood Airport. By dawn, the airport was in the hands of the 11th Airborne Division.

On the following day, a steady succession of troop carrier aircraft, this time loaded with all classes of supply, commenced landing at the airport, where the division had established an airhead. For the next five days, the division waged simulated combat against the defenders over the sand hills and dunes of North Carolina. By evening of the sixth day, Army Ground Forces declared the Knollwood maneuvers over. General Swing ordered his units back to Mackall. That night, in a cold, driving rain from which the jumpsuits and fatigues offered little protection, the units mounted up in two-and-a-half-ton trucks for the freezing ride back to the tar-paper shacks they called home at Camp Mackall.

Once back at Mackall, the division staff reviewed the operation from start to finish and, with input from all of the subordinate commanders, prepared a postoperational report for General Swing. In turn, on 16 December, he submitted his Division Commander's Report to General McNair. In reply, General McNair wrote:

> I congratulate you on the splendid performance of your division in the Knollwood maneuver. After the airborne operations in Africa and Sicily, my staff and I had become convinced of the impractibility of handling large airborne units. I was prepared to recommend to the War Department that airborne divisions be abandoned in our scheme of organization and that the airborne effort be restricted to parachute units of battalion size or smaller. The successful performance of your division has convinced me that we were wrong, and I shall now recommend that we continue our present schedule of activating, training, and committing airborne divisions.

That ended the debate. The airborne division concept had been tried and tested, and found credible, workable, and functional. The five U.S. airborne divisions were safe from further cuts, doubts, and controversies.

One problem did remain, however, and it would be the 11th that would feel the strain and difficulties. That problem was the fact that an airborne division had only about 60 percent of the manpower strength and only a fraction of the firepower of the standard World War II infantry division. When an airborne division was used in an airborne role, higher headquarters both understood and expected what role the division would play and what it could reasonably do with its limited resources. But when the airborne division was used in a ground role, as was the 11th through all of its combat, higher headquarters equated the airborne division with a standard division and expected from both the same results. And of the five airborne divisions, it was the 11th Airborne Division that was used most extensively in a straight ground role. Someone said that when an airborne division was committed to combat for the first time, it had already taken enormous casualty losses because of its reduced strength.

In the minds of the airborne troopers, particularly those in the 11th, the airborne division was equal to a straight infantry division because it made up for its smaller size and understrength firepower with willpower, discipline, drive, enthusiasm, and esprit. They felt that airborne troopers were several cuts above the "legs," and they stood straight, raised their chests, strutted in their highly polished jump boots, and boasted of their prowess. They knew that jumping out of airplanes or riding gliders into combat set them apart from the ordinary GI, and, at least overtly, they longed for the excitement and challenge of battle. The airborne soldiers never for a moment doubted their skills, their endurance, and their combat readiness. They had confidence in themselves and their units. And in a few short months, they would have the opportunity to prove themselves on the field of battle.

CHAPTER 4

CAMP POLK

January 1944 Headlines

1 January: Soviet offensive west of Kiev moves to within twenty-seven miles of Polish border

6 January: U.S. Army discloses the development of a propellerless fighter plane capable of flying at speeds of 500–600 miles per hour powered by jet propulsion

8 January: Selective Service announces that no further occupational deferments will be granted to men in the eighteen-to-twenty-one age group with few exceptions

18 January: Allied forces open a new offensive in northern Burma in the Kyankshaw area

21 January: Australian troops advance to the watershed of the Faria River in Ramu Valley of New Guinea

22 January: In a surprise landing, Lt. Gen. Mark Clark's Fifth Army establishes beachhead at Anzio, Italy

23 January: Allies announce Gen. Dwight D. Eisenhower will command U.S. forces in the European theater as well as being the supreme Allied commander

29 January: American troops fight their way to a point one mile north of Cassino

30 January: U.S. landing forces are put ashore in the Marshall Islands at Roi and Kwajalein, first territory held by Japanese before Pearl Harbor to be invaded, and meet strong opposition

To the men of the 11th Airborne Division, January 1944 was a month that marked another abrupt change in their relatively short lives as soldiers; this change, however, was more radical than any of the previous ones. In the future, of course, there would be greater changes and upheavals in the order of their lives as they drew closer and closer to that momentous day when they would fire their first shots at the enemy. In the January 1944 move, the division would be transported en masse from one post to another, and, whether or not the men were aware of it, they would be a party to the quickening of the growth and the maturing of the division. In a few short weeks after their arrival at their new post, they would see a change in their day-to-day status as well, as the Army Ground Forces' umpires tested them in the field under conditions as close to combat as they could make them. Pure training, sometimes monotonous, sometimes exhilarating, would give way to testing, sometimes reasonable, sometimes exasperating. But the result of the examination would be, if the division passed, an imaginary diploma certifying that the 11th Airborne Division had in fact graduated and was combat ready.

For the Division Headquarters' officers and men, 1 January 1944 would be a day they would long remember—and not only because the previous evening had been New Year's Eve. On 1 January 1944, the Division Headquarters at Camp Mackall burned to the ground, causing, as the division diary so tersely and unemotionally put it, "minor losses of equipment and records." As the division historian recorded,

On the next day, 2 January, the first units of the Division started for Camp Polk, Louisiana. In twenty-two trains, we made the trip, and it was neither a "sentimental journey" nor a luxury cruise. We went in troop trains—some fortunate ones in Pullmans, and some in the railroad's adaptation of the "plumber's nightmare," the troop Pullman, a car with canvas bunks swung on rattling frames. As we pulled in on the Polk siding, a corps headquarters was moving out to war, and we gaily waved them on their way. Some Angels claim that this interlude on a railroad siding represented the best relations the Division ever had with a corps headquarters. Adaptable as ever, we soon took up the customs and habits of the natives in our new home, deeply hidden in the South.

By 10 January, the Division had closed at Polk and we had explored the possibilities of life within and outside the camp. We found ourselves not too welcome. Our intense pride as airborne troops immediately clashed with the pride of that other proudest and most arrogant branch of the

Army: the Armored Force. Camp Polk was the home of the armored troops, and we felt like outsiders. There is no doubt that the armored troops regarded us as interlopers. They wore facsimile jump boots and we didn't like that, though later we were to see jump boots on everything from a New Guinea native to a USO show girl. Throughout our short stay at Polk, we felt and acted like hostile dogs in the same room, ordered to lie down by our masters.

After living in the cantonments at Mackall, the post at Polk seemed luxurious. Barracks were spacious and well heated, and had showers and latrines inside, doing away with those cold, Chic Sale runs. Battalion messes were unheard of at Polk, and each one or two companies had a messhall and kitchen of its own. The system improved the general food condition, and unit commanders went wild fixing cozy, family-style meals. Post Exchanges were well stocked and had a large variety of supplies, including 3.2 beer and other soft drinks. Service clubs were well located and had better facilities than we had seen before.

The hard life at Mackall, the intensity of the training, and the rigidity of the discipline of the previous year had produced a combat-ready division. "When we left the sand of North Carolina for the mud of Louisiana for final maneuvers," Leo Crawford remembers, "I don't think the United States Army ever had a more physically fit unit with better morale. The only thing lacking was for the officers and NCOs to have combat experience. I'm sure all of us look back at times when we might have made a little better decision that might have kept one or more of our men alive if we had known then what we knew a couple of wars later."

C. Smith Poole, who was a private first class in Company D of the 511th, was somewhat perplexed by the move from Mackall to Camp Polk. "Camp Polk was next but I don't know why," he wrote. "It was kind of like we had to be somewhere and were waiting for something." Smith Poole was right—the division was waiting for something—final exams, overseas deployment, and combat. The stateside days were dwindling down to but a few.

The division completed its move to Camp Polk in the first week of January 1944. The division historian wrote,

We came to Louisiana to be tested, and the tests were not long in arriving. On 10 January, we started a week of intensive training for individual training tests which were given to us by Third Army. On 18 January, the Division was assigned to XXI Corps. In a telephone conversation on the afternoon of 20 January, Corps outlined our schedule for the next few weeks. We were to close in the maneuver area on 3 February, maneuver, and return to Camp Polk on the 19th to continue our preparation for movement overseas. We were assigned an A-2 priority for equipment, and we were tentatively alerted for movement to the port of embarkation on 15 March.

General Pierson remembers many of the details of the Polk testing period in a way with which the young troops in the field were familiar. General Pierson in a recent letter wrote:

The XXI Corps, commanded by Major General William H. Morris, ran our maneuvers—a two weeks or so series of controlled exercises. They were the usual—the march, the attack, the withdrawal and the defense. Tests were conducted by officers from the Third Army at Fort Sam Houston. We then had several weeks to get ready for the DA Inspector General's team to see if the division was ready for overseas movement. Personnel and equipment were carefully scrutinized—it was essential that everybody and everything be in first class combat condition. Individual equipment, inoculations, teeth, records, organizational equipment as laid down in T/O's—or what have you. I was told that organizations had been turned back at the port by IG Teams. You know Uncle Joe would never stand for that. We removed all evidence that we were the 11th Airborne Division and became Shipment #1855.

But not quite yet. The division historian wrote about the Polk maneuvers, tests, and inspections from a lower level on the pyramid of the division's chain of command.

We moved into the field—by foot, of course—on the morning of 5 February, and bivouacked that night near Hawthorne, Louisiana. When the sun went down that evening we confidently expected to see it again, but we saw it only briefly once or twice, and then it came out in a sneering, temporary way to shine fitfully on us as we stood rain-soaked, shivering, and mud-caked. Maneuvers was a series of four flag exercises (the enemy was a group of flags), and each exercise lasted about three days. Each three-day period was styled "tactical" which, translated, meant that we could have no fires, could use no lights, and had to dig all of our installations into the ground. Breaks between exercises lasted about twenty-four hours, and they were styled "non-tactical." During these breaks we caught up on sleeping, eating, and warmth. The exercises took us rapidly through the various stages of a campaign. During the first, we made an approach march. In the second phase, we attacked, and in the third, we defended. During the fourth and final phase, the ruthless flags broke through our lines and we were forced to withdraw through the swampy Calcasieu mud fields during the night.

The salient feature of the maneuvers was the rain. The 127th Engineer Battalion spent the entire time building corduroy roads over two feet of sticky clay, or hauling mud-bound vehicles to some sort of dry ground— usually an island in the vast sea of Louisiana gumbo. The artillerymen were forced at times to take apart their pack howitzers, hub deep in the mud, displace piece by piece to a new position, and reassemble them on planks to prevent their sinking into the viscous, brown earth. The dough-boys, as usual, lived with the soil—cold, wet, and muddy.

Edward A. Hammrich, who had been in Headquarters Company of the 1st Battalion of the 188th, remembers the Polk tests and maneuvers. He wrote:

In January of 1944, we moved to Camp Polk, Louisiana. This was for advanced training and ground maneuvers. In the few weeks we were out in the field, we had everything as far as weather conditions, snow, sleet, rain, and hail. The mud was up to our—well, let's say it buried a jeep. Need I say more? I do remember some of the men hunting wild pigs, using their rifles with bayonets as javelins; some of the men, that is the farm boys, had roast pig that night.

The division historian continued:

After two weeks which seemed like two months, we emerged from the Calcasieu Swamp, muddy and tired, and by 20 February we were settled once again in Camp Polk, intensifying our preparations for movement overseas. We took additional tests. Division Artillery took and passed the Army Ground Forces Artillery tests—examinations covering all possible conditions under which division artillery, by battery, battalion, or all battalions together, might be required to shoot. The infantry engaged in squad, platoon, company, battalion, and regimental problems involving the attack of a fortified position, marches to the attack, withdrawals, and construction of defensive positions.

While tactical tests were being conducted, G-4 was making showdown inspections. Each unit was checked for serviceability of equipment and correctness of supply as compared with the unit tables of equipment. Short but sweet combat intelligence tests were conducted. Finally the War Department inspector descended upon us and gave us a harrowing period. Johnny's shots and dental fillings were checked, and woe betide the company commander who neglected to initial a service record erasure. We stood in awe and nervous apprehension of Colonel Barrett and his staff of IGs, for we knew that, no matter how well we had performed to date, he was the man who could, by a mere scratch of the pencil, keep us from going overseas to fight. We had heard of how divisions had been turned back from the port because they had been found wanting at this inspection. We shined, clicked heels, boot-licked, anything to pass and push for overseas.

General Swing was the consummate commander. He would have been successful commanding an infantry division, an armored force, or, for that matter, a rear-echelon Service Command—although neither he nor the Service Command troops would have been very happy if that unlikely scenario had come to pass.

To train the 11th's glider riders as paratroopers, General Swing had applied to Army Ground Forces, and had received permission, shortly after the division arrived at Polk, to establish a jump school. General Swing initially selected Colonel Haugen to operate the jump school because he was the most experienced paratrooper in the division in a senior command position. But shortly after Colonel Haugen and his team had drawn up the plans for the school (which was actually located at DeRitter Army Air Base), General Swing and Colonel Haugen differed seriously and vociferously on the basic curriculum for the course. Colonel Haugen proposed to follow the standard Fort Benning jump school procedures, which required four weeks of training, considerable emphasis on physical conditioning, and the routine hazing made famous by the instructors at Benning.

Major Burgess, then in the 187th Glider Infantry and not qualified as a paratrooper, was at Col. George Pearson's quarters at Polk for dinner one evening a few weeks after the division had closed at Polk. Also present that evening, among others, were General Swing and Colonel Haugen. According to Major Burgess,

Swing was in a hurry [to establish the jump school] as time was short before we were to go overseas. Swing thought Haugen was spending too much time on physical conditioning, which was really unnecessary at that point, and too little on the jumping phase. As they both had several drinks, their faces became red and their voices rose. . . . Swing turned to me and said, "Burgess, what kind of shape are you in?" I thought he was referring to whether I was drunk or sober. I responded that I was "in Goddamn good shape," and left the room.

The next morning at 0530 Colonel Hildebrand [CO of the 187th] came to my quarters and told me that I was to report to General Swing at 0600, and wanted to know what I had done to incur his wrath. Hildebrand knew nothing of the events of the previous evening and concluded that I must have committed some breach of duty or behavior. I had the same thought.

When I arrived at Division Headquarters at five minutes to six, Swing's office doors were closed but I could hear both him and Haugen screaming at each other. Haugen finally came out the door, beet red, gave me a dirty look, and went on by. I went in and reported to General Swing, who opened the conversation by the observation that the night before I had told him that I was in Goddamn good physical shape. He went on to explain that he didn't like the way the parachute school was being run, told me to run it, and said that I could have any parachute qualified instructors and other assistance I needed. He also wanted the school in operation in a week, with ground training for a week and then jump qualification in the second week.

At that point, the best qualified and most experienced parachutist was Haugen, so, being a naive young Major, I went down to ask him for help. Haugen was disgusted at being relieved of the assignment. He informed me that he had nothing against me personally, but he wasn't going to help me with a parachute school, as he didn't approve of Swing's methodology. He would not accept any responsibility for the program, nor would he allow his men or officers to participate in the jump training. So much for my second contact with Haugen.

Thereafter, I went to see Lt. Col. Doug Quandt, who commanded the 457th Parachute Field Artillery Battalion, and Lt. Col. Davis, who commanded the 127th Airborne Engineer Battalion, and obtained instructors from them.

A parachute jump school was established using training stations. One was a mock fuselage where one learned to hook up, shuffle down the plane and jump out the door. Several other platforms of varying heights were employed to "leg up" the muscles for jumping and learn the landing position of the legs and feet. When we were ready to start training troops, Swing told me he would give me two days to get it running, and then he'd come down and inspect it. On the morning of the third day Swing appeared, accompanied by Colonel Farrell, the Chief of Staff, and Doug Quandt. I reported to General Swing. He watched for about two hours. He never made a single comment and left. The next day he was back. Again he watched, spending several hours, and again left. On the third day Swing repeated the procedure. As he left, Doug Quandt remained, and made the remark, "Well, you just made it with General Swing." Thereafter Swing's visits were at decreasing intervals.

And thus was the first division jump school started. General Swing's vision of a division, totally "airborne" and qualified to enter combat either by parachute or glider or both, depending upon the situation and availability of aircraft and gliders, began to come closer to fruition.

A description of the jump school through the eyes of a student is a bit different than one through the eyes of the jump school commander or the division commander himself. A captain in the 188th, R. E. (Jack) Kennington, remembers:

In early March, I took two weeks' leave to visit my recently widowed mother in Indiana and spent a week in Louisiana with Jeanne, my wife. I flew back to Shreveport and was waiting for Jeanne to arrive by train on Saturday, 11 March, when I received a call from the adjutant to the effect that a jump school would start on Monday morning—would I be there? (I had requested a transfer to the 511th while at Mackall which was disapproved by Colonel Soule.) I asked if there wouldn't be another one, but was told that it was then or never, so the "honeymoon ended" at Polk Monday morning.

I think the jump class consisted entirely of 188th company grade officers and NCO's, about 3 plane loads of 69 scared people. We had checked into the guest house at North Camp, so Jeanne had the pleasure of driving me each a.m. Monday, we jogged and tumbled off the mockup. There was no 30 foot tower. On Tuesday, we jogged and tumbled and hung in the harness. We were told not to worry about water jumps, as we wouldn't make any over-water jumps in Louisiana. Wednesday was jump day and we entrucked at dawn for DeRitter Army Air Base. I told Jeanne she wasn't allowed at the drop zone near Lake Charles, because I wanted to be macho, and didn't want it to look like I needed her to hold my hand. However, she was invited by Colonel O'Kane and Padre Moore, already a jumper, to follow their jeep, so when my chute opened, the first thing I saw was my Chevrolet below. Jeanne had picked up a couple of cases of coke and pickled pigs feet en route, so all the officers flocked to my car on landing. Jeanne said she had brought a stack of blotters along for evidence to support a life insurance claim if my chute didn't open. But I fooled her. One of the captains suffered a broken leg.

We completed the required five jumps, including a night jump, during the rest of the week, with the usual Air Corps foul-ups, such as late arrivals, shortage of planes, and one jump aborted in flight due to wind, plus one that should have been aborted, but wasn't. Every night, we all gathered at the O Club to drink and discuss the various aspects of becoming expert descendants.

The first two days of the following week, some of us underwent jumpmaster training. This led Colonel Soule to ask me: "What are you doing for the 188th Glider Infantry these days?" I don't recall any more jump activity until New Guinea. . . . The Camp Polk jumpers received no jump pay until New Guinea, but I believe we got our back pay, tho we couldn't use it.

My jump certificate is dated 13 March 1944 and is signed by Robert E. Conine, "War Lord."

There was relatively little time for the men of the division to engage in extracurricular activities off post, given the constant and time-consuming schedule of testing and inspecting by Army Ground Forces and the continuous training by the commanders of the units of the 11th. But there was some outside activity. The division historian, very proudly and arrogantly and perhaps even taking a bit of liberty with the facts of the matter, reported the situation this way:

The cities and towns around Camp Polk felt the weight of the presence of the Angels as did the units stationed at Polk—notably the jump-boot wearing armored divisions. Leesville, whose main streets were typical of those in all boom towns near Army posts, knew the 11th Airborne had arrived. Where once tankers had reigned supreme, came paratroopers, ready to unboot any boot-clad non-jumper. Many tankmen went home in stocking feet to find their boots neatly piled in their orderly rooms.

Shreveport, DeRitter, Lake Charles and even cities as far away as New Orleans played host to the strutting soldiers with shiny boots, sharply pressed uniforms, cockily worn overseas hats, and the red, white and blue airborne patch.

Some people complained that the soldiers of the 11th thought they were tough. The people were absolutely right, for the Angels knew they were tough and took occasion to prove it. People complained that we were cocky; again they were correct, for we knew there was no other outfit like our Division and we were spoiling for combat to prove it to all doubting Thomases. We figured that there were not enough Japs to stop us if we could only get through with tests and inspections, and get on our way.

By March 1944, as the division's stay at Polk lengthened, the men of the division began to feel apprehensive about their ultimate combat role. Rumors were rampant. Some of the men reasoned that the invasion of Europe was imminent and that another airborne division—in addition to the 82d and the 101st already in Europe—would be required for the inevitable and costly assault on fortress Europe. Others reasoned that because there was no airborne division in the Pacific (the 503d Airborne Regimental Combat Team was, however, already in that theater), the Pacific was the next likely target for the 11th. In all probability, the War Department reasoned that Europe already had two airborne divisions and that General MacArthur in the Pacific needed a full airborne division in addition to the 503d. General Pierson remembers, "We presumed that Polk was selected for the 11th and that we were slated for the Pacific. But when we arrived at Polk, we found another division that was shipped later to Europe."

General Swing was probably not privy to the War Department's discussion of the division's combat theater. General Pierson wrote recently, however, that "General Swing was positively pleased when he learned that we were slated for MacArthur's command. I gathered from conversations with General Swing that if he were asked for a choice of theatres, he would have selected the Pacific. We know that MacArthur considered the 11th as his 'secret weapon.' "

By whatever route the War Department decided that the 11th Airborne should go to the Pacific—logic, logistics, staff studies, guesswork, happenstance (after all, the Allied High Command had made the strategic decision early in the war that the greatest effort should be directed toward the Germans and Europe)—no matter the reasoning—the War Department ordered the 11th Airborne to move to the Pacific.

The division historian wrote shortly after the war,

We had been alerted to move out of Polk on 15 March, but we were delayed over a month. By 15 April we were restricted to the post. Patches were removed from all uniforms, jump boots were packed away; we were inoculated for all and sundry diseases, and an intensified recreation program was inaugurated to keep us from missing the little world outside of Camp Polk. We were under wraps. Censorship lectures and posters drummed into our heads the absolute need for not divulging or discussing any facts, no matter how small, that we might have known; we weren't told where, how, or when we were going but the clamps put on us served to notify us that we were going. The POE was not far away now. We were no longer the 11th Airborne—we were merely a number—1855. Physical inspections for each of us were over, the inspector had gone over our records with a fine-toothed comb, G-4 and ordnance had made certain that we had all the equipment our T/E said we should and that it was in excellent shape. Testing teams representing all branches had examined us and our abilities minutely; we had passed; graduation day was upon us. Our study and training were over, at least as far as the Zone of the Interior was concerned. We had our diplomas: tickets to the POE, and passages on a west bound ship.

On 20 April we started boarding trains for our trip to the POE, our last train trip for many long months. We all felt a little differently this time, more settled perhaps, or at least more thoughtful. Good-byes had been said which would have to last for a seemingly endless number of months. By 28 April, the Division had closed at Camp Stoneman, California, there to complete its final preparation for overseas movement.

Camp Stoneman, about thirty miles east of San Francisco, was located in one of the most beautiful parts of California. It was flanked by scenic hills and lay in a fertile, green valley. It was designed specifically for the purpose for which it was used. Camp Stoneman received units destined for movement overseas; supplied them with odd items of equipment that they might have been unable to obtain beforehand; gave final inoculations to the west-bound units; fed the units extremely well; and entertained the soldiers with many and various movies, stage shows, and concerts. By the time the 11th Airborne Division processed through Camp Stoneman, the men and women who made up Stoneman's permanent party were professionals at their business. The division historian noted, somewhat pessimistically,

Stoneman fattened us for the kill. Each of our units spent an average of about six days at Stoneman getting processed. We had a day to learn about what to do on a ship, where the life rafts were, how they operated, what was in the life-raft kit and how to use it. We practiced climbing up and down a rope net; we learned how to jump into the water from a sinking ship; and we found out how to wear, adjust, and operate individual life belts. There could be no doubt in anyone's mind, now, but that we were going to make a long water trip over the Pacific Ocean—destination unknown.

Censorship of letters began at Stoneman. After the initial reluctance to write letters which we knew would be read by someone in our own unit, we settled down and wrote what we wanted, within security limitations, of course, seemingly forgetting that they would be opened before reaching their final destination.

Some soldiers, but particularly highly trained and proud paratroopers, have a penchant for getting into trouble regardless of the circumstances or the locale. The members of the 11th were no exception. Leo Crawford remembers:

> The division moved to Stoneman from Polk for embarkation. Someone overoptimistically tried to smuggle 8,000 intensely proud and highly charged young men through Stoneman. Taking off patches and jump boots was ineffective. Routing them through Stoneman at the same time as an Engineer outfit wearing boots while they were forbidden theirs was a disaster. The Division accumulated a record number of AW 104's during that period, including one myself. After an altercation at the Officers' Club, I had to report to General Swing after a preliminary chewing by Colonel Haugen. Facing those two in the same day is surpassed only by something on the order of the Bataan Death March. I reported to General Swing bearing a black eye, which I had tried ineffectually to conceal with borrowed sunglasses. His opening remark was "Are you an officer?" I replied, "Yes, Sir." He said, "You look like a damned hoodlum to me." After those niceties, he bore down. He concluded: "You are under arrest to quarters until I relieve you." Some eight or nine months later, I got a combat promotion to captain. Since he had never released me from arrest, I may be the only one who was ever promoted to captain while under arrest to quarters. My big fear at the time was that I would not get to go overseas with the division. My punishment was a $125 fine and a transfer to the 188th. I was very unhappy about leaving my platoon in D Company, 511th. One other officer involved was transferred to the 187th.

On 2 May 1944, the first units of the division marched out of Camp Stoneman, moved to nearby Pittsburg, California, and then boarded inland boats for the trip to San Francisco, the division's port of embarkation (POE). The trip from Pittsburg to San Francisco was down Suisun Bay through the Carquinez Strait, through San Pablo and San Francisco Bays, and then under the Oakland Bridge. The ships tied up at the Oakland Mole, near the oceangoing ships on which the division was to sail, and the troops debarked. They marched into a large, wharf-side shed where smiling young Red Cross women cheerfully dispensed coffee and doughnuts. "The condemned man" syndrome was becoming more and more obvious to any of the troops who took time to think such philosophical thoughts.

Spilling coffee and doughnut crumbs, the troops marched to the dock near their assigned ships. After a very short delay, the order to board the ships passed along the columns of troops. The historian recorded,

> If anyone had gangplank fever, it wasn't obvious. The only questions under discussion seemed to be the comfort of the ship, where we were going, how long it would take to get there, and how much farther we had to carry our duffel bags and full field equipment.
>
> If anyone had expected a luxury cruise, or even for that matter a comfortable one, he was due for a jolt. We went overseas in the days when a lot of other men were going overseas and we were crowded. Once aboard ship, we were directed to our holds, told to take a bunk, get on it, and await further orders before we moved from it. Each of the ships carried at least three battalions so it was necessarily a lengthy process to get all men aboard and to their proper areas. We weren't too happy about the accommodations. The holds had been refitted to carry troops and a seemingly endless number of bunks had been jammed into each section. The bunks were merely canvas strips stretched between pipe frames and drawn tightly by an interlaced rope around the edges. The outlook for our voyage of at least twenty-seven days was not bright. Back under the Oakland Bay Bridge we went, through San Francisco Bay, and then under the majestic Golden Gate Bridge out into the Pacific. We were finally on our way.

CHAPTER 5

CROSSING THE PACIFIC

Just two days out of San Francisco, the already dismal conditions aboard the various ships transporting the Angels across the Pacific in a south-westerly direction took a turn for the worse. The cool San Francisco type of weather gave way to the stifling heat and high humidity of the tropics. The troops were ordered to put away their woolen uniforms and don khakis. The next time the men of the 11th would see their woolens would be in Japan, some eighteen months hence. The fresh milk and vegetables ran out about the same time as the pleasant weather, and Spam sandwiches became the lunch of record—but not the lunch of choice—for the next twenty-five or so days of the trip. Many years later, veterans of that trip across the Pacific report that never again were they able to eat Spam, in any form. At other meals, the troops learned that dehydrated potatoes, cooked to the con-sistency of pebbles; powdered eggs, unrecognizable except for the color; and hot dogs of no discernible pedigree were constants on the menu.

Shortly after the trip began, the ships' crews enforced the security rules, which forbade lights above deck after sunset, which required that all portholes—for those fortunate enough to have them—be covered, and that double blackout curtains be hung over all hatches. In May 1944, the waters through which the ships traveled so leisurely—or so

it seemed to the bored troopers—were not teeming with Japanese subma-
rines, but the high command running the operation was taking no chances
with the remote possibility that one errant hunter might be lurking in
these waters. The blackout measures on an unair-conditioned ship raised
the temperature in the crowded holds to an almost intolerable level.
The troops had two choices each evening: Go on deck, where it was
relatively cool, or stay below. The historian recorded:

> Above decks there was nothing but talking to be done, but below, in
> the holds, the heat was unbearable. Lying around in shorts, a man sweated
> freely and though one could read by dim lights, write a letter to be
> mailed at some future unknown date, or play cards, only fitful sleep
> was possible.
>   During the day there were lifeboat drills. Each man had a definite
> spot to report to during the alert and a specified raft or boat to get near.
> We had calisthenics in the mornings and afternoons to keep us in some
> kind of physical shape. Some men washed their fatigues by tying them
> to a rope and throwing them over the side, but after a few times of
> dragging in a rope with an oily rag on the end of it or no clothes at all,
> or forgetting to tie the rope to the boat, this time-saving, labor-free method
> was abandoned. The entertainers of each unit came to the fore, and skits,
> songfests, and accordion solos helped pass the time. Boxing bouts broke
> up some of the monotony of the lengthy trip, and the lazy could just
> plain sunbathe and play cards on deck.

Ed Hammrich was a member of the 188th. He recalls that his trip
across the Pacific was not so pleasant.

> I sailed out of Oakland, California on the U.S.A.T. *Cape Cleare*—Captain
> Edgar I. Freeman, commanding—on 17 May 1944. The troops were treated
> very badly by the merchant marine crew, and there was no love lost
> between them and the troops. After an unbelievable twenty-seven days
> and nights sailing "zigzag" along the equator, we arrived in New Guinea
> 12 June 1944 at Oro Bay. The hot days and nights were not very pleasant
> aboard ship but I did get my Certificate of Merit, stating I no longer
> was a Pollywog but now a Shellback for crossing the Equator on 25
> May 1944. . . . I also have my Troop Mess Ticket, two meals a day
> and no going back for seconds.

Miles W. Gale was in H Company of the 511th. He remembers in
considerable detail his trip across the Pacific.

If anyone had told me that at the age of 32, I and some 2,100 other men would be traveling from northeast to southwest on the bounding main for a month on a ship—impossible, no way—especially on a ship that had been assembled in a month or two, labeled "Liberty Ship." But in May 1944, our 511th Parachute Infantry Regiment was aboard the Liberty Ship SS *Sea Pike* somewhere in the Pacific with destination unknown. The voyage ended at Oro Bay, New Guinea, about 28 days later.

When we staggered up the gangplank of the *Sea Pike* . . . , loaded down with all our gear and field equipment, the American Red Cross gave each of us a ditty bag. It was like the extra straw. The ditty bag contained toothpaste, toothbrush, cigarettes and gum. Also, as an added bonus for those musically bent, we all received either a harmonica or an ocarina. The two thousand non-musical paratroopers with sweet potatoes and mouth organs all practicing at one time was sheer torture. Mercifully, after one day, the ship's captain placed a one hour limit on the music practice. After the third day, any loose or unattached instruments were tossed overboard. Bergland's Regimental Band provided popular music for the rest of the voyage. Below decks it was hot, humid, and crowded with lots of soldier company bunking around, only separated by a few feet. Bunks were 12 tiers high from floor to ceiling and each tier was so tight for space that the guy in the bunk above was about ten inches over your nose. Our days were filled with activities, so all sleeping was done at night and some of the best musical snoring I ever heard took place.

Shipboard food was so bad that nobody asked for seconds. The two meals a day were just enough to keep one's skin and bones separated, but barely. Most of us subsisted on the chocolate bars we brought along just in case we met some nubile girls along the way. We envied the Merchant Marine crew and Navy gunners, who ate regular meals and big snacks of meat sandwiches between meals. Submarine alerts were too frequent to be true as the *Sea Pike* zigzagged and worsened sea sickness cases. Onion soup! While on board we were given tasks to do, namely, cleaning up the ship, hosing down decks, dumping garbage off the fantail at night, K.P., life-boat drills, etc. A few classes were conducted on seamanship and many on navigation. Celestial patterns were explained and the North Star was important in our night viewing. Much better than looking for moss on tree trunks to determine North. Recreation took place with boxing matches, band music, and a few movies. Old movies. The movie screen was suspended amid-ship and we viewed on both sides of the screen. The lucky guys who had the projector at their backs saw the images and printing as normal. The backside of the screen had things reversed. The ship lights were blacked out at night and the crew worked under dim red lights. Day by day, time dragged slowly. New fatigue uniforms were dragged from the stern on long lines to launder and also soften for the torrid tropics ahead.

The best sleeping spots were on deck with a musette bag for a pillow. At the first light of dawn, on the command, "Clean Sweep—Fore and Aft," the decks were watered down with fire hoses and sleeping paratroopers would wake up in a river of salt water. A lot of vulgar language was directed at the hose crew, who seemed delighted in their job. Lying on deck at night afforded us lots of time to reminisce about the past. With no landmarks in sight, we were lost. The familiar Dipper and North Star were in view, but they gradually changed position and faded from sight. So, like the ancient mariners and now to infantry soldiers, the most important set of stars was the Southern Cross, or Cruz. Actually, the Southern Cross is a constellation of four bright stars shaped like a cross with the staff pointing South.

Nights were very pleasant. We encountered no storms, rain or heavy seas. The breeze was soft and warm. A few dolphins, white and steely blue, joined us at San Francisco and played around the ship's bow to our final destination. We landlubbers spent hours at night marveling at the changing colors of the ocean, especially the bioluminescence. Its source is the many forms of marine life having luminescent qualities. These forms, which function close to the surface, become part of the bow-wake and at night the luminescence is visible from the ship. To me the lighting effects seemed to be large banks of light under the surface that were switched on and off. When a dolphin or flying fish hit the water surface, a tiny spark of light would flash. In the moonlight, the ship's wake would shimmer like a river of liquid silver.

On crossing the Equator, the ship's crew, a scruffy lot of fat, out-of-shape sailors, acted as King Neptune and his Court. Pollywogs is the label meted out to anyone who never crossed the Equator. At the Equator all Pollywogs are initiated into the Neptune Society by Neptune and other Shellbacks. Since we had a large complement on board, a random group of officers and noncommissioned officers went through the ceremony for everyone. Non-participants watched the proceedings from the decks, rigging and bridge. To King Neptune, Pollywogs are the lowest form of sea life, and we were the Pollywogs. The unfortunate novitiates were blindfolded and branded with mustard, catsup, doused with fuel oil and had eggs crushed on their heads. The Royal Barber tried to cut hair, but we were crew cut already, so haircutting didn't work. The Royal Executioner had a canoe paddle which was applied to rears when action was slow. As the ceremony ended after a few hours, the ship's crew broke out fire hoses and tried to water down the audience. In seconds we captured the hoses and doused the ship's crew, putting them to rout with boos, hisses and laughter. The 511th ruled at the end, and now we are all Shellbacks, entitled to all rights and privileges of Neptune's Domain.

The ship's course was plotted carefully, so we never saw any land or ships in that 28-day cruise except: One fine morning we woke up and a sleek little destroyer was next to us. The ships never stopped but, when we were about 100 feet apart, hose lines were exchanged and the *Sea Pike* refueled the destroyer. We lined the rails watching the proceedings and the sailors looked us over and we looked the sailors over. Lots of chit-chat was exchanged with laughter. The refueling took a couple of hours and as this was going on, one of our troopers on the *Sea Pike* spotted his sailor brother on the destroyer. They hadn't seen each other for several years. It was a happy reunion. A line was passed between the two ships, and the brothers passed their latest letters from home to each other. T-shirts and candy bars came over from the destroyer crew. Finally, refueling was finished. The lines and hose were withdrawn. The destroyer took off like a scared rabbit, and was out of sight in an hour. Our meeting lasted only a few hours, and then we were back to seeing nothing but sky and water again. The most beautiful and stirring thing that I remember about that "chance meeting" was the red, white, and blue flag fluttering at the mast of that destroyer. It made me very proud.

Captain Jack Kennington of the 188th had, as he put it, "the honor" of serving as the police and prison officer aboard the SS *Cape Cleare,* which carried the 188th Glider Infantry Regiment and the 511th Signal Company to New Guinea. Life aboard ship did not suppress his sense of humor. He recalls,

The hardest part of my duty was to accompany the regimental commander, Colonel Soule, on his daily inspection. He gave me hell every day because there were no stoppers in the latrine wash bowls. I had the ship's carpenter working full time, making wooden stoppers, and, every day, before inspection, I assured myself that the stoppers were in place. Yet, everytime the inspection was made the stoppers were missing. We made more stoppers than there were people aboard ship—so where did they go? Did the Japs get them?

Those inspections were pretty formal affairs, with the regimental exec and staff participating, so that when myself and the Provost Sergeant were added to the group, we had a good-sized party.

One day I was right behind Colonel Soule as we came up a ladder (ship talk for stairway) from one deck to the next. He picked a towel off a stair railing and handed it to me, saying, "Towel on the railing!" Then he continued on into the next compartment. I turned to the officer behind me, gave him the towel, and said: "Towel on the railing." I then stepped aside to see what would happen. Each person, in turn, handed the towel to the fellow behind him and repeated the remark. In this way, the line moved forward, but the towel stayed in approximately the same position. The last person in the parade was the assistant adjutant, who accepted the towel, looked at me and said: "What the hell am I supposed to do with it?"

I said, "Why don't you hang it on the railing?"

He did so, and we then fell in at the tail of the column, with the glorious feeling that we were making a substantial contribution to the winning of the war.

With the passage of the days, the talk among the troops increasingly centered on the division's destination. Word began to make the rounds that it was, in fact, New Guinea. The troops met this announcement with some perplexity. No one seemed to know just where New Guinea was or the combat situation there. Most of the troops guessed, however, that New Guinea was not a paradise populated with beautiful and passionate females. Some of the more realistic and well-read had learned something about the New Guinea natives and, in typically derogatory GI parlance, had dubbed them "fuzzy-wuzzies."

The more optimistic and less combat-hungry troops had hoped at least for a sojourn in Australia; the more contentious and bellicose were ready to get to combat, no matter where—Burma, western New Guinea, or on some of the remote and previously unheard-of Pacific islands about which they had been reading. Neither faction got its wish; the division's destination was in an area of New Guinea previously fought over in terrible battles that raged through the jungles in almost unbearable heat and humidity and took an inordinate toll of Japanese, Americans, and Australians. The area where the division was to locate itself for the New Guinea chapter of its history was now completely clear of the enemy and was as safe as Camp Mackall but more secure than the towns outside Camp Polk, like Leesville (with its unique wooden sidewalks), Shreveport, DeRitter, and Lake Charles.

The division historian recorded,

Finally, some three or four weeks later, depending upon the speed of the particular craft in which we had crossed the Pacific, we sighted land—green, thickly vegetated, beautiful mountainous terrain. As we sailed slowly up the winding, lush-bordered channel of Milne Bay, we got our first glimpse of the tropic, luxuriant jungle we were to know so well.

Milne Bay was a water stop only. We pulled alongside the water dock and were regaled with advice from the shore-bound veterans who had arrived a month or so before. Sure, the Japs were right in those woods, they told us. Every day they had to shoot four or five. Gullible recruits that we were, we paid little notice to the feverish service activities on the makeshift docks or to the myriad lights gleaming openly after dark. Soon we sailed again, and this time, after skirting the New Guinea coast, pulled in Oro Bay, another harbor abuzz with many ships of various types all in one stage or another of unloading supplies and personnel. The tide of battle was moving rapidly up along the coast. This was one of the larger bases, but already the fighting troops had deserted it and it was now a staging area.

By the time the ship had dropped anchor we were ready to debark. Equipment had been gathered and donned. Holds, of course, had been scrupulously policed, and we had detailed instructions for leaving the ship. Finally a fleet of beach taxis, DUKWs, pulled in along the ship and we started to unload over the side via rope-net ladders. The DUKWs plowed through the water, up and over the beach and started the trip to our new areas. We drove by huge sprawling warehouses filled with rations, past fields covered with mountains of crates, through ordnance dumps with ammunition and bombs of all kinds mathematically arranged according to size and distance between piles, and past row upon row of vehicles from jeeps to ten-ton wreckers.

After a few miles of dusty roads we came to our new camp site centered around a pierced-steel planked airfield. The war had gone on and the Air Corps had moved farther up the New Guinea coast, leaving the fields around the Buna-Dobodura area deserted. We were fortunate to get the location, for much back-breaking clearing had already been accomplished. As soon as the DUKWs stopped, we unloaded and put our feet on land for the first time in over three weeks. It was then we felt the heat of New Guinea descend on us like a cloud of hot steam—sweltering and humid. Perspiration broke out and soaked us to the skin. So this was it—this was the land of jungles and mountains, Fuzzy-Wuzzies and thatched houses, kunai grass and mosquito breeding swamps. We sat down wearily on our packs and took stock of the situation. We could see the airfield and its various adjacent taxiways along which we were to live. We could see the hills in the distance and the tough, tall kunai grass bordering the roads and the airfield.

We formed into company units and marched to our areas, which had already been laid out by a detail which had preceded us. Again we took off our equipment and this time we went to work.

The 11th Airborne Division had found a new home.

CHAPTER 6

NEW GUINEA

To call the Dobodura area the new home of the 11th Airborne Division is somewhat of a misnomer. When the 11th arrived at the site, there was not one building or structure of any sort to mark the area as a "home." There was a main airfield made of pierced-steel planks, lots of taxiways through cleared areas, and gravel side roads cut through the thick jungle. It was in this setting, inherited from the 5th Air Force, that the troops of the 11th proceeded to build a home.

The first order of business was to put up some sort of shelters. The 408th Quartermaster Company led a convoy of trucks to the Dobodura quartermaster (QM) area warehouses, where the men of the company and details from the division's various units loaded hundreds of pyramidal tents onto their two-and-a-half-ton trucks. Then the 408th drove through the division area and dropped off the tents from the backs of their trucks in the various battalion sites. It fell to the lot of each company and battery-sized unit to lay out its camp in its assigned area. The division troopers had not seen many pyramidal tents in the past, but, for the next sixteen or so months, they would become unpleasantly familiar with them. To this day, anyone who had spent some time under a pyramidal tent in New Guinea and the Philippines remembers the smell of the canvas and the heat of the interior as the tents baked in the tropical sun. He may also remember that in the monsoon rains and strong winds, the pyramidal tent qualified only marginally as a shelter.

The first day in New Guinea was hectic, according to the historian.

Kitchens had not been unloaded and meals were prepared in Australian chuck wagons and served over the sides. A clearing in the kunai grass served as a messhall. At that first meal we were introduced to a type of ration which was to sustain us for the length of our New Guinea stay. Fresh foods were things of the already dim past. The only utensils a cook needed to serve meals were a can opener and a knife for hacking open boxes of dehydrated potatoes.

Australian bully beef, tinned fruit, canned vegetables, and dehydrated potatoes, which even when cooked had the consistency of gravel, became the menu for the main meals. Breakfast was a constant succession of dehydrated eggs and soggy pancakes flavored with sugar and water and a butter specially designed for the tropics, which was not supposed to melt in the heat. The troops soon found that their stomachs were not warm enough to melt the so-called butter either. They termed the concoction variously as axle grease, GI lubricant, or other expressions of raucous and bawdy origin.

The division spent the first month—June 1944—in New Guinea getting acclimatized to the heat and humidity and building up the living areas. The 127th Engineers developed a prototype frame for the pyramidal tent, which greatly increased its size and comfort. The center pole sat on a vertical log about three feet high, and the sides of the tent were framed to tighten the canvas and raise the whole tent off the ground. With the frames, the tents lost their sagging, loose, unmilitary look and took on a semblance of orderliness and trimness. Each tent had a rack in front where the troopers could hang their mess kits and canteen cups. Each small-unit commander sent a man to the 127th area to measure the sample pyramidal frame and then appointed a team of pseudoengineers to supervise the construction of the frames in his area. Each properly framed tent could house at least four men, with room for their folding canvas cots, each properly festooned with a mosquito net over the length of it, duffel bags, foot lockers, and such other furniture as the occupants could build and get past the routine NCO inspections.

While the division had been making its slow and tedious way across the Pacific from California to New Guinea, General Swing took another route and another mode of transport. Prior to the division's move from the States, the War Department had allocated the division four spaces for its representatives to fly to New Guinea by way of Australia. The War Department had also directed that General Swing report personally to General MacArthur in Australia. The four air spaces thus went to General Swing; his aide, Maj. George Oliver; Lt. Col. Douglass Quandt, CO of the 457th; and Staff Sergeant DeBaca, General Swing's driver at Mackall. (DeBaca would continue to drive for General Swing in combat and through the occupation.)

The day before General Swing was to leave by air, he was in the hospital with malaria, which he had apparently contracted during his tour as General Eisenhower's airborne advisor in North Africa and Sicily. General Pierson suggested that he delay his departure until General Swing was out of the hospital. But General Swing insisted that it would work out correctly. It did: General Swing left the next day by air, and General Pierson sailed the same day on the army transport *Shanks*.

Swing island hopped by air from California to Brisbane, Australia, where General MacArthur's general headquarters (GHQ) was then located. General MacArthur's staff briefed General Swing on the general situation in the Southwest Pacific area; MacArthur personally informed Swing that without a doubt, in the near future, he would commit the 11th Airborne Division to combat in a "large operation," preferably by airborne assault, after the division had spent some more time in training and in getting acclimatized to the weather and conditions of the area.

General Swing then flew to New Guinea and was on hand to greet the division when it arrived in Dobodura. General Pierson reports that General Swing "looked hale and hearty. He gave Colonel Farrell a copy of orders which had promoted him to brigadier general some weeks previously. General Swing told General Farrell and me of his warm reception by General MacArthur. They had known each other before and MacArthur said he had heard some fine things about the division. We were to be his 'secret weapon.' "

During the first few days after the division landed in Dobodura, General Swing called each major unit together and told it of his conference with General MacArthur. He added that the division would train in New Guinea for a few more weeks but that "there was no question about the division's being committed to combat within a short time." The men of the division began to feel that combat in the near future was now a positive factor in their lives and one to be reckoned with as they started a new phase of training.

The new training centered on combat in the jungle with emphasis on live firing exercises. In addition, General Swing, anxious to qualify as many men as possible as paratroopers, ordered Maj. Henry Burgess, who had started the division jump school at Camp Polk, to detach himself from the 187th and to set up the New Guinea branch of the division jump school. A week after he started, Major Burgess qualified as a paratrooper. The first men through the new jump school were the men who had started at Camp Polk but who had not finished their training. Then came volunteers from all the division units. At one point, the division's percentage of qualified paratroopers was very high; 75 percent of the enlisted men and 82 percent of the officers were jumpers.

The Division Headquarters established other schools and sent men to courses operated by Sixth Army at various locations in New Guinea. During August and September 1944, the division operated a glider school in conjunction with the 54th Troop Carrier Wing at Nadzab to qualify selected paratroopers and replacements who had joined the division after Camp Polk. General Swing wanted paratroopers trained as gliderists because he envisioned the day when he might have to transport parachute unit equipment in gliders.

From July to September, the division and the 54th Troop Carrier Wing conducted a combined airborne–troop carrier program, with a different troop carrier squadron training each week. This program provided valuable training, in formation flying and dropping paratroopers, for troop carrier pilots whose main mission to date had been hauling cargo. The wing and the division established a joint standing operating procedure for airborne–troop carrier operations that would prove its value in the days ahead.

In August and September, the division practiced amphibious operations at Oro Bay. The training was somewhat limited. It consisted of selected units loading and unloading men and equipment in mock-ups near the division's base camp at Dobodura and then going to Oro Bay, where the 4th Engineer Brigade provided the landing craft for actual landings. According to the historian, "It became an invariable and fiendish custom of higher headquarters to give the 11th Airborne amphibious training whenever possible."

Sixth Army conducted various schools for units under its command. One school from which the division's Provisional Recon Platoon reaped a great deal of benefit was the Alamo Scout School at Humboldt Bay. The Alamo Scouts unit was an organization conceived by General Krueger, the Sixth Army commander, to provide him with intelligence that the Scouts obtained from deep and independent incursions into and behind the Japanese lines. In the 11th Airborne Division, General Swing had created a similar organization, the Provisional Division Recon Platoon.

The first leader of the recon platoon was Lt. Jim Polka, who had graduated from Fort Benning's OCS in February 1943 and immediately volunteered for parachute training. After jump school, he was assigned to the 11th Airborne Division as the platoon leader of the Headquarters Company's I and R Platoon. In the fall of 1943, Maj. Henry Muller, the division G-2, asked for a volunteer to form a provisional recon platoon. Jim Polka volunteered and Major Muller selected him. Polka in turn asked for volunteers from throughout the division. He received about three hundred applications from which he selected the original group of thirty-five men. He recalls,

> I had very definite ideas about training and instruction and tried very hard to maintain a high level of interest. Our subjects related to the type of mission of a recon unit, stressing communications, survival, etc. My enthusiasm was never dampened by Major Muller or Captain Patrick Cotter, Assistant G-2. We had one non-com, Sgt. Frank Flowers, who had been a college professor at Louisiana State University before the war. "Doc" was a tremendous asset to our unit. At some later date he was sent to OCS and eventually reached the rank of major.

Terry R. Santos was a member of the original platoon. He knew that Lieutenant Polka made his selections for the recon platoon with certain capabilities in mind.

> [Polka] made certain that, inasmuch as we were basically an infantry platoon, there were artillerymen, engineers, signalmen, and medics among us. In the final analysis, every man was as close to being an all around Utility Trooper as time and training would permit. Hand to hand combat techniques were practiced on a daily basis (one of my specialties).
>
> We "bivouacked" within the confines of the assigned Division area, usually near Division Headquarters, but in our "own sector." This had positive and negative aspects. The positives: No one interfered with us or our training; not many knew of our existence; we did not become

involved in the mundane aspects of garrison life; the platoon leader always had access to the G-2 and had the ear of the CG. The negatives: It was usually "beg, borrow, or steal"; we were always "attached" for mess and brought up the rear in the "chow line." In total, most of us thought the positives outweighed the negatives.

"Doc" Flowers, the leading non-com, left for OCS in Australia. There were three remaining NCOs: Ira C. "Pop" Davis (S/Sgt), Vinson B. Call (T/5), and I was a corporal. As long as we remained a Provisional Unit, there were no promotions. Many of us were called "Sergeant" but were not officially paid as such. . . . I was the Lead Scout, knew the native language (Tagalog), and volunteered for all missions and patrols.

I would like to explain the reason we were designated a Provisional Unit. Provisional, by definition, denotes temporary or conditional. In the lexicon of the Army, this meant that we did not officially exist. In short, the Recon Platoon was not an authorized unit of the 11th Airborne Division. It would be similar to being born and existing, without a birth certificate to prove it. Therefore, members of the Platoon, for administrative purposes, were, on paper, assigned to various units within the division, e.g., 511th, 187th, 188th, Div Hqs, etc. We became the ghosts, the men who weren't there. The platoon was the brainchild of General Swing. The General wanted a small, well-trained, all volunteer unit at his disposal—to use as he deemed necessary without the necessity for explanations.

The men selected by Lieutenant Polka to form the platoon were an elite group—cocky, self-confident, resourceful, and well trained. The platoon took on an aura of elitism and attracted a select group of energetic, courageous, and adventurous soldiers. Martin Squires exemplified the character of the platoon. He joined the 511th while the division was still at Mackall and volunteered for the Recon Platoon as soon as he heard about it through a college friend who had volunteered for and was accepted by Lieutenant Polka. Squires was not accepted for the platoon at Mackall, but he kept volunteering and finally became a member in New Guinea in June 1944. He said:

We were primarily under Colonel Muller. . . . We were a small group— mostly college men—crazy as Hell, and intensely devoted to our leaders, Lt. Polka and Colonel Muller. We had superior training, I believe—most of us were outdoorsmen to begin with and grew up with a familiarity to hunting, hiking, and camping. Our additional indoctrination to Alamo

Scout training while in New Guinea was also very valuable. I came out of a heavy weapons basic at Camp Wolters near Mineral Wells, Texas, so it was natural after joining the 511th and then the division recon that I was considered somewhat of an "infantry weapons" expert for our patrols.

In New Guinea, selected members of the Recon Platoon went to the Alamo Scouts School for additional training, and Del Motteler, Cliff Town, and Terry Santos made it through the tough and exacting course and received certificates of completion from the training center. Leon W. Sapp did not complete the course because he became ill with dengue fever, but he did rejoin the platoon in time for combat on Leyte and Luzon. Two other members of the original Recon Platoon were lost to the platoon in New Guinea: Gil Cox remained with the Alamo Scouts and Dave Head was transferred to the I and R Platoon of the 188th.

Prior to New Guinea, according to Terry Santos,

training was more "conventionally" oriented, i.e., European or traditional. With the Australian New Guinea Administration Unit (ANGAU) conducting jungle training, in concert with the Australian trained Papuan Infantry Battalion (PIB) and the return of three of us who graduated from the Sixth Army's Alamo Scout Training Center in Dutch New Guinea, the Platoon's training took on a concerted, no-nonsense jungle atmosphere. Traditional fire and movement tactics were not forgotten, although stealth, patience, camouflage and survival (living off the land) became primary. We devised and used our own "Brevity Signals." New Guinea was where we became a cohesive Platoon.

Since no one became a Platoon member after New Guinea, we, the members of the Provisional Reconnaissance Platoon, consider all who were in the "Provisional Platoon" as original members, inasmuch as many who were initial choices "volunteered out." In that vein, several members "volunteered out" after the Leyte campaign and also after the Los Banos Raid. No questions were asked. If anyone wanted "out," he was reassigned immediately.

Another school that members of the 11th attended was a jungle training course conducted by ANGAU near Higatura. The officers and men who attended that course came back to the division "full of the lore of the jungle," according to the historian. "They knew everything from how to eat hearty meals of jungle vegetation to how to move swiftly and noiselessly through the dense vegetation in the manner of

Jungle Jim and Kolu. The jungle-wise men then conducted schools in their respective units.''

A few weeks after Maj. Henry Burgess had started the division jump school in New Guinea, he recalls,

I was detached and assigned to the Planning Committee of the G-3 Section of Sixth Army Headquarters situated several hundred miles up the New Guinea coast. My contribution at the G-3 Section was to advise on the feasibility of employing paratroopers in some future operations. While nothing came of this assignment at that time, I did learn a great deal about staff work and planning.

About six weeks later I was assigned to the S-3 Section of a Task Force Headquarters and participated in the invasion of Noemfoor, which involved the 503d Parachute Infantry drop on D-Day plus 1 to reinforce the amphibious landing which would be made by the 158th Regimental Combat Team. The drop was a disaster. The plan had been to fly at about 600 to 700 feet over the strip for the drop. However, clouds had obscured the island at an elevation of 450 to 500 feet. The planes came in just under the clouds, and when a paratrooper dropped, his chute opened, oscillated once and the trooper hit the ground. Many fractures occurred, both from the low altitude and from the fact that the equipment working on the runway 24 hours a day was not given time to get off the runway, which resulted in many men crashing into the equipment and breaking bones.

On several occasions I went on patrols which resulted in firefights. It was interesting to observe that many of the men never really aimed their shots but fired rapidly with no significant number of hits. They seemed unaware of the distances to the target. Many of the shots were impossible to make and a waste of ammunition.

Upon return to the Division, I related these observations to Colonel Haugen. He seized upon the report to persuade Division Headquarters to put all battalions through firing exercises employing the artillery and using ball ammunition and mortars, machine guns and artillery fire. This resulted during the training exercises in two men being killed in the firing and several wounded, but the Division units gained great experience and an opportunity to coordinate all of the units, infantry, artillery, and engineers, into an attack with live ammunition.

The exercises that General Swing ordered as a result of Major Burgess's and Colonel Haugen's intercession were based on a combat team comprised of an infantry battalion, an artillery battery, and an engineer platoon supplemented with such additional support elements as were necessary to form an independent team. The training site was an abandoned airstrip at Soputa. Each unit went through the training. The 187th historian, wrote,

By the time the last outfit had pulled out of the area, the strip was a complete shambles of leafless trees and burned up grass. "Fire and movement" was a phrase we were beginning to like.

Our New Guinea interlude was to put the finishing polish to our pre-battle training. . . . By now every man knew how to sustain himself in the jungle. Each was proficient at snap-shooting at unexpected targets, and in throwing grenades in dense Hunai grass, growing to eight feet in height. Squads and platoons had been taught to crowd in close behind mortar and artillery barrages, thus taking advantage of the enemy's momentary shock to administer the coup-de-grace with grenade and bayonet. All knew the efficiency of demolition and flame-thrower technique in reducing enemy pill-boxes and similar installations. The regiment (the 187th) had been well-grounded in amphibious operations, and 90 percent of its personnel had been qualified as paratroops.

Perhaps as important a factor in our pre-preparation as either the technical or physical training we had undergone was the psychological benefit of our airborne instructions. Men who had slept through night-long tactical glider flights and pulled twisted tubing from the tangled bodies of pals, killed in crashes, had learned poise; and men who had jumped into hundreds of feet of space after seeing other pals trailed by streaming, unopened chutes, plunge to violent death, had learned nerve control the hard way.

Nor was our ground training free from casualty. Captain Farrell was killed during a demonstration of Japanese hand grenades; six men from "B" Company were mutilated by a rifle-grenade's premature explosion; a man from "G" Company was killed while manipulating a jungle target at which his squad-mates were shooting. Scrub typhus claimed the lives of two men bitten by the deadly typhus mite while they were in an overnight bivouac, located deep in the jungle. Considering the intensity of our ground-training, and the hazards of our airborne specialties, however, our pre-battle casualty rate was extremely low. The regiment, thanks to the nagging care of our medical officers and General Swing, was remarkably free from malaria, dengue, scrub typhus and many other tropical diseases.

The 11th Airborne Division did not spend the sweltering months in New Guinea totally committed to such necessary but difficult training as struggling through almost impenetrable jungle thickets with machete-wielding stalwarts leading the way; mass jumps into kunai grass–covered drop zones; firing exercises wherein the artillery and mortar rounds whistled overhead, machine guns rattled the air with staccato bursts, and the frontline infantrymen laid down as much fire as their M-1s and machine guns could generate or their grenades could blast. In addition to the days and nights spent in the field, there were evening and weekend off-duty events and army regulation–violating escapades that helped pass the months at Dobodura.

General Swing inaugurated a division-wide recreation program shortly after the division arrived in New Guinea and the 127th Engineers had completed the division bowl, an amphitheater ridged with rows of backless benches and a stage complete with lights and sound equipment. The bowl could seat almost the entire 8,000-plus men of the division.

The historian reports,

> While in New Guinea we had USO shows—two of which were outstanding. The first was the Jack Benny Show on 1 August 1944. Five hours before the show was to start the Bowl was already half-filled with an eager, candy-eating audience. By show time, the crowd had overflowed the seats and had climbed the bordering trees. Armed with field glasses and being elevated, the tree-sitters probably had better points of vantage than the early comers on the seats below. The show went full well for fully five minutes. Then came catastrophe. All the lights and the sound equipment went out. The engineers pulled out their bag of tricks; someone brought in more generators from other units; the band played on by touch and memory; in the breaks between numbers Lanny Ross, appearing with the show, got a song-fest started; Jack Benny ad-libbed at the top of his lungs, got hoarse, and retired to await the repair of the loudspeakers and lights. Finally, with everyone's patience exhausted, the system went back in shape and the show went on.

In July 1944, Lt. Col. Douglass P. Quandt, who had activated and trained the 457th from its infancy, moved to the division staff to become General Swing's G-3, replacing Lieutenant Colonel Ports. Major Kuelkhe, who had been the 457th Battalion executive officer, assumed command of the battalion. Captain Nick Stadtherr, a small (five feet four), dynamic, levelheaded, well-muscled man from Cole Camp, Missouri, was the executive officer. He claimed that he was one of the two toughest men from Cole Camp and that the other had been electrocuted. After some questioning, Nick revealed that the other "tough" from Cole Camp had been electrocuted accidentally while working for an electric utility company. Nick, before his induction, had gotten a master's degree in engineering from Columbia and had worked for DuPont in Leominster, Massachusetts.

Captain Norman Martin, a forester who graduated from Cornell, had worked for the Firestone Tire and Rubber Company on their Liberian plantations. Norm Martin was a consummate artilleryman and was the battalion S-3. He would put his considerable artillery skills to good use in the months ahead.

Captain John Conable, formerly the commander of B Battery, was the S-4. Captain Conable was an OCS graduate who had spent the years from 1934 to 1940 at Cornell, first as a liberal arts major and then in law school. While he was at the Field Artillery Training Center, shortly after he had been inducted, the reality of social life in and around army posts struck home.

> I occasionally went to Church Sunday mornings. The chaplain would get an invitation to bring three or four truckloads of soldiers to some function at a church in the area. I went to a dance at one of these churches. My eyes fell upon a good-looking young lady and I cut in on her. When I inquired about her name and where she lived she responded with, "I don't go out with Privates." The stark realities of the military caste system were driven home to the young Ivy League lawyer.
>
> Another time, at a similar function, I was attracted to another good-looking woman only to discover that she had one irremediable fault—a husband. These experiences made me realize that the Army was a poor place for romance. Since my wife-to-be was 13 in 1941, this was a very wise decision on my part.

Major Kuelkhe's command tour as CO of the 457th lasted only a few weeks. One of the 457th officers, Lt. Mel Levin, was an instructor in the New Guinea jump school. According to John Conable,

> [Lieutenant Levin] and Major Kuelkhe got into a war of some sort up at the school. This was reported to General Swing. After the General was through investigating, Mel was the Graves Registration Officer at the 408th Quartermaster Company and Major Kuelkhe was the Division Parachute Maintenance Officer. The General and Q [Quandt] came down to the battalion and asked for Nick Stadtherr. I was close enough to hear

the conversation. The General asked Nick what he thought should be done. Nick told him that in Nick's opinion, he should bring in an officer who had had no connection with the Division. The General said: "If I give you the battalion, will you accept it?" Nick said: "Yes, Sir, and I will do my best." The General then indicated that Nick was the new Battalion Commander.

Again, combat was to prove that the general's decision in this case, as in many others involving the selection of regimental and battalion commanders, was shrewd and correct.

By the time Nick Stadtherr became the commander of the 457th in August 1944, and Major Dorius had been transferred in from the 711th Ordnance Company to become the executive officer, the troops of the battalion had been working their bootlegging operation for some time. As John Conable recalls:

> Boys will be boys and almost immediately (after the Division's arrival in Dobodura) the New Guinea Distilling Company began operating. I suspect it was started by Pace, McKenna, Howard, Hurchalla and company. They apparently saw a demand for potable alcohol and made a good profit.
>
> While I am not sure of what happened, I believe that Captain __ tried to cut himself in for a substantial cut out of the profits. I think that Pace went to Q and told him about it. __ was immediately transferred out and Lt. Flanagan became the Battery Commander of B Battery.

But that did not put an end to the bootlegging operators in the 457th. One evening about a month after Nick Stadtherr had become the CO of the 457th, he derided John Conable, the S-4, because there was no sugar in the mess for his coffee. John, "Honest John" he was dubbed for his unfailing sense of integrity in all matters, assured the battalion CO that he had personally delivered 200 pounds of sugar to the mess hall that morning and that something was certainly amiss in the sugar department. Nick then told him: "In that case, I think the two of us should inspect the guard tonight. Meet me at Battalion Headquarters at 2100."

John Conable recalls,

> I reported at the appointed time. It was a warm still tropical night with only a very light wind. As we walked around the area, we could

smell the stills working. By using the short sniff method of triangulation, we located at least four operating stills. The next night Nick called the Battalion together and told them that the rations were to be used for food, not to be converted into alcohol and that it was partly his fault because he didn't think it necessary to lock up the food.

In the meantime, he had sent me out with a detail of five officers with instructions to destroy the stills. We got four complete stills and C Battery's mash, boiler and bottle supply. I couldn't find C Battery's coil which escaped destruction. We also found a barrel of apricot mash which was apparently destined to become apricot brandy. I was sure that there had to be a thief somewhere in the battalion because two of the mash barrels were full of fresh potatoes, and I had been issued no fresh potatoes since leaving Camp Polk. I was not so naive as to think that the bootlegging was finished. But the scale of the operations was substantially reduced, and Nick had plenty of sugar for his coffee. I was, of course, known as Carrie Nation Conable.

General Swing epitomized the leader who took care of the troops. He took care of them in one way that the troops would not really appreciate until they got into combat: He trained them hard and well and demanded the discipline that they would need to survive in battle. In another way, he took care of them by insisting that his staff and commanders consider and bolster the welfare and morale of their men where possible. When the division left the States, for example, General Swing insisted that the company, battery, and battalion funds be turned over to the division special services officer. (In the States, these funds were normally used to buy beer for company and battery parties.) A lot of the unit commanders balked at the requirement. But General Swing, with some wisdom, reasoned that in the tropics, the young enlisted men, whose average age was nineteen, would rather have ice cream than extra 3.2 percent beer. He directed the special services officer to buy ice cream machines and ice cream mix for later use. As it turned out, General Swing was right and a lot of commanders who lost their funds were wrong: The 11th Airborne Division was the only outfit whose units had ice cream regularly—every tenth day. And that was a very popular day.

General Swing was also an avid sports fan and set up interregimental and intraunit sports competition wherever possible. In New Guinea, the division had volleyball, softball, and even tackle football (for which a farsighted special services officer, no doubt prodded by General Swing, had remembered to bring uniforms and equipment) at various levels of competition. The senior football league had teams from the 511th, 187th, 188th, and Division Artillery. The coaches of the regimental-level teams were not rank amateurs. The 511th, for example, was coached by Capt. Tom Mesereau, C Company commander, who was a first-string lineman at West Point, class of January 1943. The DivArty team was coached by Gus Dorius, who had been an outstanding "scat back" at Cornell, and John Conable, who had been a third-string center and lineman, also at Cornell. With that kind of coaching and with many ex-college players filling the ranks, the competition was outstanding.

By early September, the division had become acclimatized to the heat, the jungle, the humidity, the boring food, the pyramidal tents, the dusty roads, the outside latrines, the jumps into the razor-sharp kunai grass, the still-busting officer "revenooers," the onerous work of unloading ships on the docks, and the Atabrine tablets that suppressed the malaria and turned one's skin yellow but did not turn away the mosquitoes. The jump school had converted almost all of the division's glider riders into paratroopers. And the War Department authorized all paratroopers in the division, regardless of unit assignment, to collect jump pay—$100 for officers and $50 for enlisted men.

In an apparent effort to see if his division could still march as a unit, General Swing ordered a division review on the steel-planked runway at Dobodura in September. The troops turned out in khakis, steel helmets, web belts, and jump boots. General Swing's comments as he watched his men pass in review were somehow not recorded for posterity. Photos indicate, however, that the troops looked smart, sharp, thin, and disciplined. And not one mustache graced the upper lip of an 11th Airborne trooper; General Swing despised them, and thus they were verboten—period.

Most of the men in the division were unaware of it at the time, but the division was authorized "battle honors for participation in the New Guinea Campaign." John Conable remembers that "we received a battle star for New Guinea because we were the reserve unit for the Hollandia Operation. We were not committed. As far as I know, no one in the Division fired a shot at any of the enemy. Our status did require plane loading plans and a combat alert."

The official authorization for the battle star for the New Guinea campaign is General Orders Number 26, Headquarters United States Army Forces in the Far East (USAFFE), dated 11 February 1945. The pertinent paragraph reads as follows:

> Pursuant to paragraph 21b (2), Army Regulations 260–10, 25 October 1944, the following units are entitled to battle honors for participation in the New Guinea Campaign during the period 24 January 1943 to present date: 11th Airborne Division.

> By command of General MacArthur:

> RICHARD J. MARSHALL
> Major General, General Staff Corps
> Chief of Staff

October brought a plethora of rumors that increased in quantity and quality until some of the rumors turned to fact: The division was going to move out. Shortly, the rumors caught up with another fact: The division was headed for Leyte.

On 12 October 1944, General Swing received an order from Southwest Pacific Command to move his division "administratively" (not combat loaded) to Leyte to prepare for an operation on Luzon. At the time of the order to move to Leyte, apparently USAFFE had no intention of using the undersized 11th Airborne as a "ground outfit" in the Leyte campaign. Eventually, the enemy situation on Leyte would demand the commitment of all available army units.

General Pierson wrote recently about the move of the division from New Guinea and his trip to Leyte ahead of the division.

> The 11th Airborne Division and the 503d Parachute Regimental Combat Team were originally slated to go into Leyte as follow-up on available "turn-around shipping." I presume that GHQ had no appropriate mission for airborne troops in mind at that time.
>
> I recall that we were alerted early in October for movement to Leyte. The landing took place on October 20th by the Sixth Army. The impedimenta of an airborne division with its parachutes and allied equipment exceeds ordinary tonnage and we were assigned a number of ships which would leave us one short. General Swing was not about to leave any of our equipment in New Guinea, and when our G4 personnel found a cargo ship in Oro Bay without an assigned mission, General Swing sent me up to GHQ in Hollandia to obtain the release of that ship. I saw Colonel Rehm [later BG] in Operations and he steered me to a Navy Lt. Commander.

He made one telephone call and we had that AKA added to our shipping.

General Swing sent me to Leyte ahead of the division to make arrangements for the arrival of the division. My advance party consisted of Lt. Colonel Glenn McGowan, G1; Major William Crawford, G4; Major John Atwood, Signal Officer; and my driver, Corporal John Archbold. We flew to Biak in a C-47 taking my jeep along. Maj. General Warren Carter, our Troop Carrier friend, had the 5th Air Force unload a C-47 of its lumber cargo and we were on our way to Leyte.

We stopped overnight in Angaur, an island in the Palau group. I flew to Peleliu in a borrowed L-4 to see Maj. General Paul Mueller, Commanding General of the 81st Division who was engaged with tenacious Japanese forces—"mopping-up" after the Marines. Our advance party slept under the wings of the C-47 that night.

We arrived off Leyte shortly before noon the following day in the midst of a Japanese air raid on the airfield at Tacloban. We were shooed away but fortunately the C-47 veteran pilot had made the Tacloban trip before. He found an out-lying air strip of grass that the Japanese had hacked out of a palm tree grove with what looked like an impossible, short runway for the C-47. The pilot made the landing without a foot to spare and we thanked him, deplaned my jeep and left the C-47 when the pilot said he would get out all right.

We went to Sixth Army Headquarters at Tacloban. I saw General Decker, the Chief of Staff, and General Eddleman, G-3. There was nothing that they could tell me at that time for any possible missions. Brig. General Sturgis, Sixth Army Engineer, showed me on a map two possible camp sites for the division and promised to take me the following day to inspect them.

I met with General Krueger that first night. He welcomed me. We discussed the combat capabilities of an airborne division vis-a-vis a full infantry division. The facts that the airborne division had only seven infantry battalions as against nine and that there was no armor or heavy artillery in the airborne division were brought up.

Both camp sites that General Sturgis showed us were far from ideal. One was on Bito Beach and the other was inland. My selection of Bito Beach proved to be the better choice.

By 11 November, the division had loaded its nine ships, the men had trooped aboard and loaded their personal gear in the crowded holds, and the navy indicated that it was ready to sail. The convoy of nine APAs and AKAs pulled out of Oro Bay escorted by nine U.S. Navy destroyers. The long and sometimes tedious months of training, moving, and speculating were about over. The division's "test by fire" was almost at hand. According to the historian,

Fortunately, the trip was made in Navy-manned ships. It was fortunate because the food we had was the best we had eaten since we left Camp Stoneman. . . . As far as we were able to determine, the trip was uneventful—no Jap planes or ships showed up to harass us—with one exception. One sub did venture within detecting range; we were immediately alerted and sent to our emergency positions. But a DE took off after the Jap craft and the alert was called off.

Aboard ship, the troops spent their time talking endlessly about the immediate and post-war future. Some gambled the days away. . . . Underneath the surface of gaiety aboard the ships we were tense. We had thought for a long time about this combat; we could look around us and know that within a very short time some of the faces we saw would be gone. This was a time for thought and mental preparation for what lay ahead. Our physical needs, the knowledge of what to do and how to do it, had been taken care of by long months of hard training. Now we had time to ponder and we found ourselves ready for combat. We didn't know then—no one knew—how soon we were to be committed, but it came sooner than any of us anticipated. The Angels were about to make fighting history.

CHAPTER 7

SITUATION IN THE PACIFIC

"It is with the deepest regret that I must inform you that conditions over which I have no control have necessitated the surrender of troops under my command." On 20 May 1942, with these disheartening words, Lt. Col. Theodore M. Cornell informed Bernardo Torres, the governor of Leyte, that the United States was giving up control of the island in the Philippines that it had governed since 1898. It would be almost two-and-a-half years before the Filipinos of Leyte would see the Americans return to liberate their island and begin the first phase of the recapture of the entire Philippine archipelago.

By 7 June 1942, the battle of Midway was over, but it would still be twenty-eight months before MacArthur would be able to land American forces on the island of Leyte. In those twenty-eight months, there would be many battles on land, on sea, in the air, and in conference rooms at the highest levels of the Allied governments.

The prewar strategic plan for the defeat of Japan was based on the premises that the U.S. would have only Japan to fight and that the U.S. Pacific Fleet would be intact. But the destruction of the Pacific Fleet at Pearl Harbor and the entrance of Germany and Italy into the war negated the basic assumptions of the strategic plan. In 1942, after the loss of the Philippines and the unchecked advance of the Japanese Southeast Asia Co-Prosperity Sphere, the Joint Chiefs of Staff (JCS)

97

decided that the first priority was to limit the advance of the Japanese and to keep open the lines to Australia. The JCS divided the area into two commands: On the southern flank was the Southwest Pacific Area Command headed by General MacArthur; on the northern flank was the Pacific Ocean Area Command headed by Adm. Chester W. Nimitz.

In 1942 and 1943, the Allied forces had halted the Japanese drive at Guadalcanal and at Papua in New Guinea, thus saving Port Moresby and, by extension, Australia. After those battles, the Japanese were on the defensive and the Allies were on the attack. The JCS developed a strategy for defeating Japan that called for the eventual invasion of the home islands and the unconditional surrender of Japan. To accomplish this objective, the Allies needed to secure a large base from which they could invade Japan. Initially, the plan located this strategic base in China; later, the Mariana Islands were substituted for China. Later still, as the war developed, the JCS had to decide between the Philippines and Formosa as a stepping-stone to Japan. But that was yet to come. What had to come first was the Allied advance across the Pacific to the west.

The JCS plan for operations in 1943 and 1944 called for the main effort through the waters of the Pacific Ocean to acquire successive island bases to be used as stepping-stones, projecting the Allies closer and closer to an ultimate showdown on the Japanese home islands. This plan would shorten the sea routes and deny the Japanese bases from which they could attack the Allied sea lines of communications. The JCS directed Nimitz to proceed west through the mandated islands while MacArthur fought northwest along the New Guinea coast.

After the defeat of the Japanese at Papua in October 1942, MacArthur implemented the JCS plan by a series of attacks up the northern coast of New Guinea to eliminate some of the Japanese bases, to set up his own logistical support areas, and to bypass Japanese strongholds that would "wither on the vine" from lack of resupply and reinforcements. MacArthur and his Southwest Pacific Command (of which he was the supreme commander but preferred the title commander in chief) moved forward from Milne Bay to Buna, Lae-Salamaua, the Huon Peninsula, Hollandia, Aitape, Biak, Noemfoor, and Sansapor. The final New Guinea attacks and landings near the northern tip of the island secured airfields that would be used to support attacks in the Philippines and the Marianas. By July 1944, an entire Japanese army had been cut off and isolated in

New Guinea. Admiral Nimitz and his Pacific Ocean Area Command, during the same period, had been island-hopping through the Solomons, the Gilberts, the Marshalls, and the Marianas.

By the spring of 1944, the operations in the Pacific were exceeding the most optimistic expectations of any of the JCS planners. As early as 12 March, the JCS ordered General MacArthur to plan to invade Mindanao, with a target date of 15 November 1944. On 15 June, MacArthur issued his plan: He would land on southern Mindanao on 25 October, and then invade Leyte, which he knew occupied a commanding position in the Philippines, on 15 November with forces mounted from New Guinea.

By September 1944, on schedule, the two elements of the Pacific Area Commands were approaching the southernmost island of the Philippines, Mindanao. MacArthur's advanced elements had reached Morotai Island, 300 miles south of Mindanao; Nimitz's forces were in the Palau Islands, 500 miles east of Mindanao.

At this point in the war, Nimitz and MacArthur, two highly competitive commanders, each jealous of his turf—or ocean—agreed that they should take Mindanao next, in accordance with the JCS plan. But after Mindanao, they were in disagreement on their final strategy for the invasion of Japan. MacArthur not only had a strong emotional tie to the Philippines and felt that the United States was honor-bound to liberate it as soon as possible, but he also felt that it would be "unsound" to bypass the Philippines and attack Formosa directly, without land-based air support any closer than Hawaii, which was 5,100 miles away. He had presented his case in an emotion-filled message to General Marshall on 18 June.

Nimitz, on the other hand, was interested in the Philippines only as a way station on the route to Formosa from which he believed he could sever Japan's sea-lanes, thereby blocking her supply of raw materials from the south. From Formosa, Nimitz felt that he could jump to the China coast, where he could build air bases for the final attack on Japan and support the amphibious invasion of Japan, which all experts agreed at this point was necessary.

General Marshall invited MacArthur and Nimitz to Hawaii to hear their individual plans for the future of the Pacific war. MacArthur arrived on 26 July, and to his surprise, President Roosevelt was present. Roosevelt invited the two commanders to dinner, and afterward drew out a map of the Pacific and reportedly said: "Well, Douglas, where do we go from here?'' MacArthur, allegedly not aware that strategy was on the agenda for the postdinner discussions, nonetheless, with his usual eloquence, launched into a long and fact-filled talk, giving the philosophical and military reasons for the necessity of taking Luzon before moving on to Formosa. Luzon, MacArthur said, could be taken more easily because of the vast network of Filipino guerrillas already in place and because of the friendly, cooperative population, eagerly awaiting liberation. No doubt he also mentioned the necessity of freeing the POWs and Allied civilian internees. He added that the prestige of the U.S. was at stake and that the U.S. should free its own territory first. According to reports, Nimitz did not enter the conversation that evening.

The next day, Admiral Nimitz presented the navy strategy: Bypass the Philippines and enter the Western Pacific to attack Formosa. General MacArthur commented on the navy plan: "For this purpose [the attack on Formosa], all of my American forces, except a token group of two divisions and a few air squadrons, were to be transferred to the command of Admiral Nimitz, who was to continue to drive across the Central Pacific. By the summer of 1945, he would be ready to invade Formosa. Just how to neutralize and contain the 300,000 Japanese troops left in his rear in the Philippines was never clearly explained to me. . . . I was in total disagreement with the proposed plan, not only on strategic but psychological grounds.''

A number of observers and planners at the conference felt that General MacArthur had made the stronger case, but President Roosevelt did not make an immediate decision on the overall strategy for the Pacific. In fact, he probably never did make one.

One result of the conference was an agreement for MacArthur to invade Leyte after landing on Mindanao. Still in abeyance, however, was the strategy that would follow Leyte—Luzon or Formosa?

On 8 September, the JCS issued missions to MacArthur and Nimitz generally as follows: "General MacArthur, after conducting the necessary preliminary operations, will take the Leyte-Surigao area on 20 December, with Admiral Nimitz furnishing fleet support and additional assault shipping. Both commanders to arrange for coordination of plans and mutual support of operations.''

On 31 August, however, MacArthur had jumped the gun and had issued his own directive. The Southwest Pacific forces were to "seize objectives in the Mindanao, Leyte and Samar areas in order to cover subsequent operations to complete the reoccupation of the Philippines.''

The Leyte operation was known as King II. The assigned target dates were Mindanao, 15 November 1944; Leyte Gulf–Suriago Strait area, 20 December.

The Luzon versus Formosa debate within the Joint Chiefs of Staff went on for some time after the July conference in Hawaii. By the end of September, however, most members of the JCS were wavering on the necessity of invading Formosa at all. All of the military criteria seemed to point toward a strategy of securing Luzon, steering clear of Formosa and the China coast, and heading straight for Okinawa. The only holdout on the JCS for the Formosa strategy was Admiral King, the navy representative. King argued that MacArthur's invasion of Luzon would tie up all of the Pacific Fleet's fast carriers for at least six weeks and that therefore the plan was unsound.

During September, MacArthur's deputy chief of staff, Maj. Gen. R. J. Marshall, was in Washington on official business. When he became aware of King's last-ditch stand on Formosa, he alerted MacArthur by cable. MacArthur quickly countered King's position by a cable to the JCS in which he stated that he needed the carriers for only a few days during the initial assault on Luzon to provide close air support for the ground forces and that, thereafter, his engineers would carve out airfields behind the invading troops for land-based close air support. (MacArthur's faith in his airfield-building engineers was valid: On one occasion, his engineers built a 2,500-foot runway of pierced-steel planks in two days.) He also pointed out quite logically that his requirement for the fast carriers would be for a far shorter time than would be needed for an invasion of Formosa, particularly if Luzon were still in enemy hands.

Based on these considerations, Admiral Nimitz recommended to the JCS that the invasion of Luzon be scheduled for 20 December and that his own forces attack Iwo Jima in late January 1945 and then Okinawa on 1 March 1945. Admiral King finally accepted the Luzon scheme of maneuver after Nimitz had backed down. With King's belated acquiescence, on 3 October the JCS directed MacArthur to invade Luzon on or about 20 December and ordered Nimitz to attack Iwo Jima and Okinawa according to his timetable.

The JCS 3 October directive finally settled the strategic debate that had been occupying the JCS for months. The directive also endorsed MacArthur's overall plan for his command—one that he had developed and pursued almost since the day he left Corregidor in 1942. His plan was called "Reno." General MacArthur wrote in his *Reminiscences*,

"Reno" was based on the premise that the Philippine Archipelago, lying directly in the main sea routes from Japan to the source of her vital raw materials and oil in the Netherlands, Indies, Malaya, and Indo-China, was the most important strategic objective in the Southwest Pacific Area. Whoever controlled the air and naval bases in the Philippine Islands logically controlled the main artery of supply to Japan's factories. If this artery were severed, Japan's resources would soon disappear, and her ability to maintain her war potential against the advancing Allies would deteriorate to the point where her main bases would become vulnerable to capture. Mindanao was selected as the tactical objective in the Philippines. . . .

MacArthur, Nimitz, and the JCS were all in agreement that Mindanao would be the initial objective for an attack on the Philippines and the base from which the rest of the islands could be assaulted. Admiral Halsey and his Third Fleet, however, changed that plan and even moved up the schedule for the landings on Leyte. On 9 and 10 September, Halsey's Third Fleet carrier-launched aircraft began attacks on Mindanao in preparation for landings there. Halsey's pilots found a surprisingly weak reaction to their attacks. They met few Japanese aircraft in the air and ineffective air defenses on the ground. General MacArthur, not missing a chance to take a little credit for his own forces, wrote, "Further probing disclosed that Southwest Pacific land-based bombers, operating out of New Guinea fields, had caused severe damage to enemy air installations."

On 12 and 13 September, Halsey's aircraft attacked the Japanese in the Visayans. Again they found weak defenses and heavily damaged Japanese air bases and aircraft on the ground. General MacArthur concluded: "It became more and more apparent that the bulk of the once mighty Japanese air forces had been destroyed in the costly war of attrition incidental to the New Guinea operations."

Vice Admiral Marc Mitscher commanded Third Fleet's Task Force 38. His planes had attacked Mindanao and the Visayans. After the raids, his pilots reported that they had destroyed 478 Japanese planes, most of them on the ground, and had sunk 59 ships against little opposition.

Admiral Halsey's reaction when he read the report was that it was "unbelievable and fantastic" and that the Japanese strength in the Philippines was a "hollow shell with weak defenses and skimpy facilities." Accordingly, he wired Nimitz with the recommendations that the invasion of Mindanao be cancelled and that the timetable for the attack on Leyte be moved up.

"Such a recommendation," Halsey wrote later, "in addition to being none of my business, would upset a great many applecarts, possibly all the way up to Mr. Roosevelt and Mr. Churchill. On the other hand, it looked sound, it ought to save thousands of lives, and it might cut months off the war. . . . I sent for my aides and told them, 'I'm going to stick my neck out.' "

Nimitz agreed with Halsey's point of view and passed on his recommendations to Washington and incidentally to Quebec, where the Joint Chiefs of Staff were about to meet with Roosevelt and Churchill. MacArthur wrote later,

> At the time he [Halsey] radioed the suggestion, virtually the whole strategic apparatus of the United States government had moved to Quebec in attendance at the conference then being held between Mr. Roosevelt and Mr. Churchill. My views were requested on the proposed change of the invasion date for Leyte, and I cabled my assent to Halsey's proposal. Thus, within ninety minutes after Quebec had been queried as to the change in plans, we had permission to advance the date of our invasion of Leyte by two months.

That same evening, 15 September, as General Marshall was on his way to his quarters after a formal dinner given by Canadian officers in Quebec, he received a cable from MacArthur: "Subject to completion of arrangements with Nimitz, we shall execute Leyte operation on 20 October. . . . MacArthur."

On 3 October, the JCS ordered MacArthur to invade Luzon on 20 December, the date originally set for the occupation of Leyte. The die was now cast; the strategic decisions had been made. General MacArthur and his U.S. forces would return to the Philippines just as he had predicted two-and-a-half years previously.

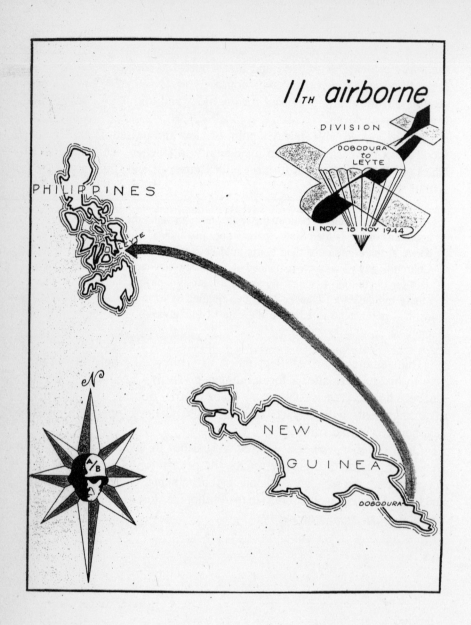

CHAPTER 8

THE 11TH AIRBORNE DIVISION ON LEYTE

The 11th Airborne Division periodic report for 18 November 1944 reported in terse military terms that, on that date, the division "joined the King II operation [the code name for the battle of Leyte] by landing unopposed on Bito Beach." The brevity and sterility of the report belied the division's difficulties in unloading the ships, landing on the beach, and setting up some sort of accommodations for its 8,000 or so men. It was not to be the sort of beach life to which the men of the division would like to become accustomed.

The *Calvert*, for example, arrived in Leyte Gulf early in the morning of the 18th. According to Eli Bernheim,

> The tail of the convoy, miles back, was welcomed by an attack from three Zeros, one of which was shot down by ack-ack and the others pursued to the westward by our P-38's. The Navy made no bones about wishing to be rid of us, and our loads, and in a hurry. This unseemly haste was engendered by the frequent attacks by Japanese suicide planes on the hundreds of ships now jamming the Gulf.
>
> Troops and their duffle bags, rations and ammunition, were taxied to the beach by naval landing craft where they were unceremoniously dumped. Heavier equipment was jammed ashore by LCT's and two-hundred

man work details around the clock, sometimes shoulder deep in water, as they carried the materiel ashore. Rough tent camps sprung up, and, during the frequent air alerts, some felt uneasy because Bito Beach was one big ammunition dump, and no one was working more than a few yards from huge piles of 155 mm. projectiles, 81 mm. mortar shells and other explosives.

Because of the constant threat from the by-now depleted but still dangerous Japanese Air Corps, many of whose pilots were, in desperation, transferring ceremoniously and religiously to the ranks of the kamikazes, Sixth Army ordered the division to unload its nine APAs—personnel transports—on the day of arrival and the two AKAs—cargo ships—as soon as possible thereafter.

General Al Pierson and his advanced detachment that had flown up from New Guinea had, before the arrival of the division's ships, marked off Bito Beach into unit areas. Bito Beach is a long, narrow spit of land about a hundred yards wide, bounded on the north and the south by swift, unfordable rivers, on the east by Leyte Gulf, and on the west by a coconut grove about 150 yards deep. Behind the grove was a bottomless swamp. In effect, Bito Beach was an island. No vehicles could move off the beach until the engineers had built bridges across the rivers and the swamp.

When he landed at Bito, General Swing was aware only that the division would be there for some time and would, perhaps, not face combat until the invasion of Luzon. But the increased Japanese buildup of their ground forces on Leyte was soon to change that supposition.

By 1800 of the 18th, the division had unloaded all of its APAs, and they sailed away into the night. By 23 November, the unloading of the AKAs would be complete. That task might have been accomplished earlier had it not been for the air alerts.

On 19 November, the men working on the beach saw a lone Japanese plane fly down the beach from the north. Another outfit, unloading near the 11th, saw the plane and raced for cover. But the men of the 11th, veterans of one day on Leyte, held their ground because they knew that the plane was a kamikaze and was more interested in the ships unloading in the gulf than it was in individual soldiers. And as the troopers of the 11th suspected, when the plane was almost overhead, it turned 90 degrees to the left and began its final dive at a transport about 1,500 yards offshore. The ack-ack on the ship took the plane

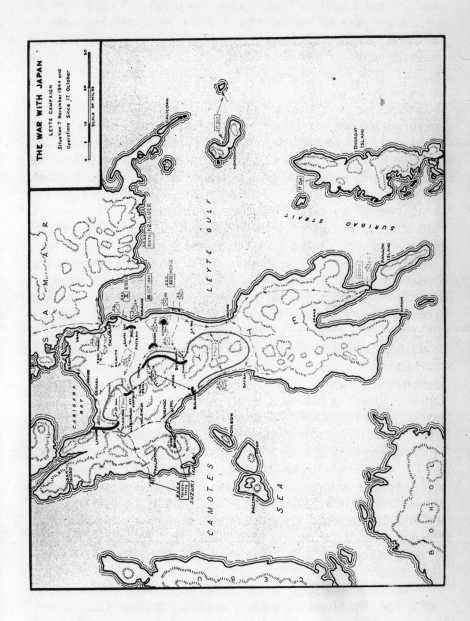

THE WAR WITH JAPAN

LEYTE CAMPAIGN

Situation 7 November 1944 and
Operations Since 17 October

SCALE OF MILES

under fire and actually bounced a couple of rounds off its bottom. But the Japanese pilot did not swerve in his dive. He clung desperately to his course and hit the transport directly below her bridge. The ship eventually sank in the shallow water and remained there as one more reminder of the Japanese penchant for suicidal exploits and devotion to the emperor.

Eventually, the hull of the ship above water became a base point for artillerymen of the 11th. A few days after the 11th landed, the Allied High Command became concerned about possible enemy landings near Bito Beach. Sixth Army directed the 11th and other artillery units still in the area to lay their guns to sea to take under fire any enemy landing craft. The 11th Division Artillery surveyors carefully triangulated the position of the sunken transport and reported its location to the firing batteries. Thereafter, the forward observers of the 11th Division Artillery had very accurate firing data for the targets that never arrived.

Dogfighting between the Zeros and the P-38s was a diversion that distracted the troops from the work at hand. There were only a few per day, but the troops applauded when one of the planes went down in flames, knowing full well that it was the P-38 that had emerged victorious.

During the nights, the troopers worked under floodlights to speed up the organization of the division bivouac area. But, fairly routinely, one Japanese bomber would appear over the area. The troops would douse their lights and continue to work by flashlight. The bomber became known as "washing machine Charlie" from the erratic sound of its old engine. The only damage "Charlie" did in the division area was to drop a bomb on a causeway that the 127th Engineer Battalion of the 11th had been so laboriously building.

The 127th Engineers had taken on the difficult and vitally essential task of building bridges and causeways off the Bito Beach "island." The construction of a road through the swamp was particularly frustrating and arduous. The battalion decided to build a causeway on piles through the swamp, but it lost many a pile in the depths of the swamp before it began to find some footing. "Charlie's" one bomb set back the project a number of days.

After about four days on the beach, the division was reasonably well settled. The bivouac areas were nestled under the coconut groves, and the piles of supplies were fairly well segregated, camouflaged, and piled neatly back from the water's edge under the trees.

As the troopers of the division settled into the routine of setting up camp, they also looked about them at the local landscape and, in particular, those Filipinos who trod it with bare feet and scanty clothes. The 187th historian recorded:

> Our first bivouacs were near the villages of Abuyog and Balay Baban and, at once, each soldier provided himself with a servant—or rather a personal helper. Unarmed, but anxious to help, the local Filipinos attached themselves to the various individuals and did yeoman service, cleaning rifles, building nipa huts and foraging for fruit. Basic wages were paid in cigarettes, and a ragged undershirt settled a whole week's account.
>
> Dreams we'd once had of beautiful scantily clad South Sea Island Belles—but that was before we landed in New Guinea where the jet-black fuzzy-wuzzies abruptly shattered that. Now our illusions were almost revived as the brown-skinned Filipino women, half-naked, wandered through camp almost at will, soliciting laundry and other work. And, as competition developed, they made no distinction between a dressed or undressed trooper.
>
> To the acute distress of the more impressionable, these Filipino country maidens proved extremely virtuous. Assisting Lt. Col. Pearson, Commanding the 1st Battalion, 187th, in the protection of his men's morals was the mayor of Abuyog who made profuse apologies when he found that an enterprising lady, of ill-repute, had attempted to set up business conveniently near the bivouac. But the mayor saved the virtue of the 1st Battalion by promptly throwing her into the local calabozo.

By this time, the Allied High Command and Sixth Army realized that the Japanese were progressing in their buildup and that, concomitantly, more Allied ground troops would be needed to win the battle of Leyte. And the rains, unceasing almost from the day the division landed, still came down.

By 14 November, General Krueger had four divisions, less two regiments, along a fifty-mile front from Pinamopoan on Carigara Bay in the north to Abuyog, just south of Bito Beach, in the south. (One regiment of the 1st Cavalry was on Samar and the 32d Regiment of the 7th Division—less one battalion—was on the west coast at Baybay.) The line ran generally in a southeast direction just west of Burauen and almost to the Leyte Gulf coast at Abuyog. On 12 November, General Krueger had ordered Colonel Kangleon and his guerrillas of Leyte and Samar to relieve the 6th Ranger Battalion on Dinagat Island. The 6th also evacuated Homonhon and Suluan Islands on which they had landed on 17 October. General Krueger placed the 6th Rangers in army reserve at Tanauan.

The steady buildup of the Japanese greatly concerned General Krueger. On 8 November, when General MacArthur had visited him at his command post at San Jose, near the south end of the Tacloban airstrip, General Krueger had briefed him on his situation. He told General MacArthur the details of the Japanese buildup, the inability, to date, of the navy and the air elements to stop the landings near Ormoc, and, most significant, that his army was short some 12,000 officers and men, a deficit particularly acute in the rifle companies. Seventy-nine percent of his casualties occurred in the infantry units. He expected that his losses would, of course, increase as the offensive progressed. (By 22 December, Sixth Army would be short more than 22,000 men.) He requested, therefore, that General MacArthur make available to him such replacements as were on hand. In actuality, General MacArthur did not have to order up any additional troops because there were a number of units already on hand or en route to Leyte.

The Headquarters of XI Corps, the 32d Infantry Division, and the 112th Cavalry Regimental Combat Team had reached Leyte on 14 November; besides the 11th Airborne, the 503d Parachute Regimental Combat Team also arrived on 18 November. Southwest Pacific Area Command (SWPA) assigned these units to Sixth Army on arrival. All of these units, except the 32d Division, which was the Sixth Army reserve, had been brought to Leyte for use in later operations. But because of the seriousness of the current situation, they were all directed to prepare for immediate combat. General Krueger assigned the 11th Airborne Division to General Hodge's XXIV Corps, the 32d Infantry Division to General Sibert's X Corps, and the 112th Cavalry Regiment to the 1st Cavalry Division.

The 77th Division arrived on Leyte under rather peculiar circumstances. In early October, the 77th was on Guam, and SWPA Headquarters had designated it as a reserve division for Sixth Army. General Krueger fully expected that it would join Sixth Army on Leyte. But on 29 October, SWPA Headquarters had released Maj. Gen. A. D. Bruce and his 77th from attachment to Sixth Army and had failed to notify General Krueger's headquarters. In early November, the 77th was on its way to New Caledonia for rest and rehabilitation. As soon as General Krueger found out about the situation, and in view of the Japanese buildup, he immediately brought the situation to General MacArthur's attention. General MacArthur reacted promptly and ordered his staff to divert the division, which was already nearing Bougainville, to Leyte. It arrived on 23 November.

For a time, the division was actually a burden to Sixth Army. In somewhat restrained prose, General Krueger wrote: "As the division [the 77th] had left much of its equipment on Guam and brought with it only a limited supply of rations and ammunition, it reached Leyte short of many things. In consequence, the arrival of this fine division, welcome as it was, augmented our already critical supply situation and made its preparation for combat quite a difficult problem, solved only by withdrawing equipment and supplies from other units."

General Krueger's plan for the final victory on Leyte directed a double envelopment of the island, reinforced by the amphibious landing of a division in the vicinity of Ormoc and by the westward attack of the 11th Airborne across the mountainous waist of the island. The double envelopment involved the attack of the now-committed 32d Division down Highway 2 from Limon just south of Carigara Bay and the attack north of the 7th Division from Baybay, about twenty miles south of Ormoc. In addition, on 7 December, the 77th Division would land amphibiously at Deposito, some four miles south of Ormoc. And meanwhile, the 11th Airborne would fight its way across the treacherous, rain-swept, muddy trails through Burauen to the west coast. The plan squeezed the enemy on the west coast while at the same time blocking him from bulging out to the east by the attack of the 11th through the middle. But before that plan would be consummated in success, there would be weeks of hard fighting ahead.

On 22 November, four days after the landing of the 11th Airborne Division on Bito Beach, General Hodge's XXIV Headquarters issued Field Order Number 28, which included this mission for the 11th Airborne Division: "The 11th Airborne Division will relieve the 7th Infantry Division along the line Burauen-La Paz-Bugho and destroy all Japs in that sector."

By the middle of November, the 24th Division in the north had seized and occupied the high ground held by the Japanese north of the town of Limon. At that point, Maj. Gen. William H. Gill led his 32d Division onto the line and passed through the ranks of the 24th and continued the attack to the south. The 24th Division, weary after prolonged fighting since A-Day, moved over to the Cavite-Jaro area and assumed a narrow sector on the left flank of X Corps. The 24th left the 34th Regiment and three of its artillery battalions temporarily with the 32d.

Major General Roscoe B. Woodruff took over command of the 24th after the relief of Maj. Gen. Frederick Irving, ostensibly for failing to take Breakneck Ridge on schedule. General Irving took over the rather innocuous job of commanding the Leyte Garrison Force, the unit that would hold Leyte after completion of the operation.

The 1st Cavalry Division, with the 112th Cavalry Regimental Combat Team (RCT) attached, was attacking southwest toward Cananga. General Krueger said: "Although serious hostile opposition on the front of the division was largely confined to the center and left, heavy downpours, extremely rugged and densely forested mountain terrain, and supply difficulties all greatly hampered the operations all along the line. But on the 22d, the 12th Cavalry Regiment seized heights from which observation of Cananga could be obtained."

On the XXIV Corps front, a battalion combat team of the 32d Infantry Regiment of the 7th Division had pushed forward from Baybay to Damulaan on the west coast, about twelve miles south of Ormoc. The rest of the 7th Division was attacking a strongly held series of enemy positions in the rugged, monsoon-swept hills west of Burauen. General Krueger reported:

> After several days of hard fighting, [the 7th] had reduced them and by 18 November had driven the surviving defenders into the mountains. On 20 November the 11th Airborne Division began to relieve the 184th Infantry Regiment (7th Division) in the Burauen area so it could concentrate on the Baybay area on the west coast, where it closed on the 25th. The 11th Airborne Division was assigned a zone of action which included the Burauen area and extended through the Cordillera (a very rugged, heavily forested mountain range which extends from Carigara Bay in the north to Cabalian and Sogod Bays in the south) in the west and almost to Abuyog in the south, its mission being to seize and secure the eastern and western exits from the Cordillera within its zone of action, in order to assist the advance of the 7th Division toward Ormoc.

The 96th Division, to the right of the 11th after the 11th relieved the 7th Division, patrolled the area from Mount Laao southeast to Mount Lobi.

General Suzuki had four divisions deployed along the line. The 1st opposed the 32d in the north; the 102d held that portion of the central mountain ridge against which the 1st Cavalry and the 24th were attacking; the 16th was dug in and defending the mountains in front of the 96th

Division and the 11th Airborne; the 26th stretched from Ormoc to Albuera and into the hills in front the 11th Airborne's route of attack.

Time magazine for 20 November 1944 summed up the military situation succinctly: "The U.S. drive on land slowed down to a walk after it had overrun about 50% of the northern half of Leyte. Ormoc, the key western port where the Japs landed and deployed in a 10 mile semi-circle, could be approached only from the north or south unless the U.S. troops attempted to come over the mountains between Dagami and Jaro, a long, difficult pass."

The 511th Parachute Infantry Regiment of the 11th Airborne was the first unit of the division committed to combat and would lead those U.S. troops attempting "to come over the mountains" through "a long, difficult pass." That pass was across the mountain range just to the south of Mount Majunag and Mount Lobi and wound its circuitous way along cliffs, up rocky slopes, around 180-degree corners, and through thick jungle vegetation and narrow slits in the rocks through which carabao could not and would not pass. On a map, the route seemed to run rather directly from Burauen in the east to Albuera on the west coast south of Ormoc. In reality, the route was uncharted, unphotographed from the air, and in places nonexistent. And everywhere, it was thick with slippery, slimy mud and rocks and overhung with dripping tree branches and wet, intertwined vines.

At 0700 on the morning of 21 November, Col. "Hardrock" Haugen led the 1st Battalion of his regiment, the 511th, commanded by Lt. Col. Ernie LaFlamme from its bivouac area on Bito Beach north to Dulag, "by guess, by God and by LCT," according to one of the participants. At Dulag, the regimental S-4 borrowed trucks and used them to shuttle the 1st Battalion west to Burauen. The 3d Battalion, under Lt. Col. Ed Lahti, followed the same route on 23 November; the 2d Battalion, under Lt. Col. Norman M. Shipley, moved north on 26 November. By the twenty-sixth, Colonel Haugen had assembled his regiment on the mud flats next to the Daguitan River not far from Burauen. One of the paratroopers claimed that his company "occupied carabao wallows just as soon as a company of the 7th Division slithered its way out of them." By 28 November, the last elements of the 7th Division had been relieved by the 511th, and Colonel Haugen had started "feeler" patrols moving to the west from Burauen to locate trails, barrios, and the Japanese.

General Hodge, CG XXIV Corps, met with General Swing at XXIV

Corps Headquarters a few days after the 11th landed on Leyte and after Corps Headquarters had issued Field Order Number 28. In his discussion of the 11th's mission, General Hodge told General Swing that not only was he to relieve the 7th in place but he was also to attack to the west through the pass and to protect and secure all corps and air force installations within the division zone.

The road from Dulag to Burauen was clogged on both sides with headquarters of both air and ground units, rear-echelon troops, and supplies that back up the combat units to the front. The corps quartermaster had tried to locate his supplies on dry ground, but the incessant rains shortly turned his supply dumps into quagmires. (In the month of November, 23.5 inches of rain fell on an already-soggy Leyte.) The 44th General Hospital, 5th Air Force Headquarters, 155mm firing batteries, truck battalions, field hospitals, ordnance depots, motor pools, ammunition dumps, signal centers, and headquarters of various other units were jammed into clearings in the palm trees or in areas hacked out of the growth along the road. But with the increased traffic and the incessant, heavy rains on the Dulag-to-Burauen road, that route soon became impassable for about two miles on each side of Burauen. The engineers rebuilt that part of the road by dumping a three-foot-deep layer of gravel over it. The remainder of the road was kept open most of the time by allowing only one-way traffic. The other roads were just as bad. Some were often under two feet of water.

In *Leyte, The Return to the Philippines*, M. Hamlin Cannon reported:

> Upkeep of the roads in general required a "profligate expenditure of engineer troops." It was found that a battalion could accomplish no more in a month than a platoon could have carried out in a week under good weather conditions. The roads required a rock or gravel foundation one to three feet thick, whereas a road-metal surface of three to four inches on an earth base was normally adequate. Since priority was given to work on the principal roads and airfields, the construction of access roads, as well as hardstands for hospitals, depots, and other needed installations, was greatly delayed.

John Conable, who had been the S-4 of the 457th, was by this time the assistant division quartermaster, an assignment that he fought unsuccessfully to avoid. He described the problems engendered by the mud:

It was the rainy season on Leyte and by December 10th the road to Dulag of 10 miles was nothing but mud up to the bottom of a 2½ ton truck's radiator. This mud had an enormous appetite for brake lines. Fortunately, even a loaded ammunition truck didn't roll very far when the brakes failed in the mud. The other Divisions on the Island were having similar troubles and the supply base ordnance types got used to hearing all of us beg.

The mud was omnivorous. It would eat an infantryman's combat boots in seven days. The tree roots in the rain forest probably served as teeth. Uniforms rotted rapidly. While we were in the tropics some of the rains were cold. It was tough to keep the wounded warm until they could be evacuated.

These were the major problems facing supply. There were also minor problems. General Swing wanted a 300 watt light bulb for his maps. Leyte was not a sophisticated island and the best we could do was 100 watts. All scavengers were alerted to our need. Finally our G-4 (Bill Crawford) himself obtained one. He got it from a battleship operating room (medical) in exchange for his 1946 Army-Navy football game tickets.

Within a three-mile radius of Burauen were three airfields in various stages of repair—Buri, Bayug, and San Pablo. The engineers had worked constantly on these three strips, but in spite of their efforts, they remained generally unstable. On 25 November, the Army Support Command dropped all work on them. However, 5th Air Force, the air unit backing Sixth Army, felt that it was necessary to continue work on the Bayug strip, and one aviation battalion remained to try to make that strip usable.

For an attack across a mountain along passes so narrow that men had to proceed in single file, the 511th Airborne Infantry Regiment was well suited. Not only were the paratroopers in superb physical condition, thanks to the leadership and discipline of "Rock" Haugen, but also the regiment was organized for movement by foot or, in some limited circumstances, by such pack animals, usually carabao, as were available. Each battalion in the regiment had only three relatively small rifle companies—no heavy weapons companies as in standard infantry battalions. The battalion headquarters company had a communications section, a light machine gun platoon, and an 81mm mortar section. By any standard of measurement, the airborne infantry battalions, both parachute and glider, were small and lightly armed. The condition made movement easy, but the airborne infantry, just like the standard infantry outfits, needed heavy firepower support when it hit the enemy bastions.

By 24 November, the 11th Airborne Division Headquarters had moved to San Pablo, a small barrio outside of Burauen, and occupied the command post area vacated by the 7th Division. General Swing had assigned Col. "Shorty" Soule and his 188th Glider Infantry Regiment (composed of only two very light battalions) the missions of securing the southern sector from La Paz south to Bugho, of protecting the left flank of the 511th as it advanced to the west, and of patrolling its area to determine the location and size of the enemy forces in its sector. The 1st Battalion, 188th, just north of Bugho, had the additional mission of patrolling as far as the west coast of Leyte. The 2d Battalion, 188th, at La Paz, was to patrol to the northwest and contact the 511th. The boundary between the regiments passed through Patog.

Edward A. Hammrich was the message center chief of Lt. Col. Mortimer J. O'Kane's 1st Battalion of the 188th. He remembers the movement of the 1st Battalion to an area near Bugho.

We fought our way into an area between a place called Bugho and La Paz. Up on a small plateau in this mountain area, the 1st Battalion 188th set up its CP.

I'll never forget the stench of dead bodies that greeted us as we took up positions on this location, relieving the 7th Infantry Division. The position on top of this plateau was so isolated and dangerous to get in and out of, that all food, medical, and other supplies had to be air dropped to us.

Initially, General Swing assigned Colonel Hildebrand and his 187th Glider Infantry Regiment (also with just two light infantry battalions) the mission of protecting the division rear area at Bito Beach. But as the battle progressed, first one of the 187th battalions would move forward into the mountains and then the other.

Lieutenant Colonel Jim Farren moved his 152d Airborne Antiaircraft Antitank (AA) Battalion to San Pablo airstrip to provide AA protection to the strip and the division and corps installations around Burauen. In a short time, however, the men of the 152d would prove their worth as ground fighters.

Lieutenant Colonel Davis had his 127th Airborne Engineer Battalion "scattered at every mudhole in the Division sector, sometimes bridging them, sometimes scraping them, and sometimes in the more hopeless holes, just plumbing for depth and sunken trucks," according to one of the men of the battalion. "The bulk of the battalion was at San Pablo repairing the Burauen Road and the San Pablo Airstrip."

Recounted the division historian,

> The Division Bands were trained as DUKW drivers, and back at Bito Beach loaded supplies and DUKWed them to us. All of the Special Troops, except the rear echelon at Bito Beach, were assigned defensive missions around the CP at San Pablo. There, just behind the Operations tent, the Division Artillery Headquarters set up, and from their jerry-built tents conducted big-picture battle with two acting infantry battalions (Lt. Colonel Lukas E. Hoska Jr and his 674th Glider Field Artillery Battalion and Lt. Colonel Mike Massad and his 675th Glider FA Battalion—both battalions without their pack 75 mm. howitzers), a battalion of 75's, and Marine and Corps Big Toms. This was the setup as we shifted our weight and started into the hills. All liaison planes of the artillery were based at San Pablo Airstrip, a quarter mile below the Division Command Post.

On 27 November, Colonel Haugen ordered his regiment into the hills to the west of Burauen. The regiment's first objective was a small guerrilla camp named Lubi, which stood astride the junction of two trails going west into the mountains from Burauen. Ernie LaFlamme moved out first, leading his battalion, less C Company, along the north trail. In the flat area just to the west of Burauen and before the trail rose into the hills, the men of the 1st waded knee deep through sucking mud that made their progress slow and difficult. Once into the hills, the trail was muddy but not deep. The battalion moved slowly along the north trail through a deserted guerrilla camp, and then through the empty barrios of Catabagan, Anonang, and Lubi. The battalion, in single file for most of the march, wound through Lubi, up a streambed to a tabletop rising about 150 feet above the riverbed, surrounded on three sides by sheer, jungle-covered cliffs and on the fourth by a more gentle slope. Across the river, which made a rectangular island out of this small, wooded plateau, jungle-covered mountains rose high and forbidding—the central mountain range of Leyte. The small tabletop of land, approximately 200 yards long by 70 yards wide—about two football fields laid end to end—on which the men of the 1st Battalion, 511th, now stood, was fringed with coconut trees. The Filipinos called the mesa "Manarawat." It was destined to become the hub of all of the 11th Airborne's operations in the central Leyte mountain range. The 1st Battalion, 511th, had not seen or heard any Japanese en route.

Colonel "Rock" (over the months, the men of the 511th had dropped the "Hard" from Hard Rock's semiaffectionate nickname) Haugen, the men of his headquarters, and Capt. Tom Mesereau's C Company, 511th, followed Ernie LaFlamme by about three hours up the north trail. A guerrilla guide led them. In the vicinity of Anonang, where the river splits in two, the guide advised Rock Haugen to abandon the path followed by Ernie LaFlamme and move up the right fork of the riverbed on what he assured him was a shortcut to Lubi. Haugen was forced to trust the guide because the maps of the area were completely untrustworthy. Many sections of the maps simply stated: "uncharted." The column moved up the riverbed in single file, with scouts out.

One of the men on the march reported: "It was eerie. It was raining, and we, who had not yet seen a Japanese, suspected that there was a Japanese behind every rock and tree. Slowly and silently we moved, burdened with heavy mortars and machine guns, and slipping exasperatingly in the infuriating, root-tangled mud."

Not far up the riverbed, one of the lead scouts signaled ENEMY IN SIGHT, and the men in the rear of the column heard two shots. The scouts had spied two enemy soldiers washing in the stream and had killed them both. The jubilation of the lead scouts was short lived. At some signal, perhaps the two shots, Japanese on both sides of the streambed opened fire on the column. C Company of the 511th and the headquarters element of the 511th had been sucked into a classic ambush. Tom Mesereau sent his 1st Platoon to attack the enemy on the right bank. The platoon lost eight men and killed twenty of the enemy, but it became cut off from the rest of the company and was forced to withdraw toward Lubi.

The main portion of the company tried to dislodge the enemy from the left bank of the stream but was unsuccessful. Finally, C Company plus the headquarters element crossed the streambed and assaulted the right side, which the 1st Platoon had been unable to overcome. By a combination of hand-to-hand fighting, grenades, and close-in rifle fire, C Company managed to expel the enemy from the high ground and set up a defensive position. But they were immediately beseiged by the Japanese.

In the fight that followed, the regimental S-3 and about twenty men became separated from the rest of the company and fell down a sharp cliff. By nightfall, this group had retraced its steps back along the trail to Burauen and the division CP. The S-3 talked to the division G-3, but his report was exaggerated and confused. Other men of the group held that most of the company and the regimental headquarters had been wiped out in the ambush. In addition, they were unable to locate the ambush site on a map. The division G-3, Lt. Col. Douglass Quandt, ordered the artillery liaison planes into the air to search for the rest of C Company.

Lieutenant Colonel Norman E. Tipton was the 511th regimental executive officer and was bivouacked with the rear elements of the 511th in the Burauen area near the Division Headquarters. Tipton ordered Lieutenant Colonel LaFlamme and the 1st Battalion, 511th, to move out from Manarawat in an attempt to locate C Company and relieve them. LaFlamme sent a platoon-sized patrol under Lieutenant Varna to lead the march. After a couple of hours, Varna and his patrol found a portion of the Japanese force that was surrounding C Company. The enemy force was dug in on the defensive and was large—too large for Varna's platoon. The Japanese killed Lieutenant Varna at the head of the patrol that returned to Manarawat without having located C Company.

General Swing ordered Lt. Col. Harry Wilson and his 2d Battalion of the 187th to move up from Bito Beach to replace Lt. Col. Norman Shipley and his 2d Battalion of the 511th in defensive positions on the heights just west of Burauen. Swing ordered Shipley's battalion to prepare to move out along the north trail to assist the 1st Battalion, 511th, in finding and relieving C Company.

The trip of the 2d Battalion, 187th, from Bito Beach to the low mountains just to the west of Burauen was an eye-opener for the men of the battalion. Wrote CWO William G. Nelson, personnel officer of the 2d Battalion, 187th:

> The Second was literally ferried to its new position in those strange vehicles called amphtacks. Enroute, we stared like yokels at a starlet, as we crossed the coastal plain between Dulag and Burauen, for up to this time, we had no idea of the magnitude of the American effort on Leyte.
>
> We passed ammunition dumps by the dozen; 155 batteries; truck battalions; field hospitals and many special-unit headquarters. Finally, as we neared Burauen, we clanked past airstrips jammed with P-38's. All these installations were literally bogged down in the mud. In fact, the typhoons of October and the continuing deluge had all but washed out Sixth Army's Service troops and the 5th Air Force back across the beach.
>
> Arriving at Burauen, the battalion found the dry areas—the relatively dry areas of the town already occupied by an Air Force MP platoon, an

Ordnance Battalion, and the 44th General Hospital. The battalion of the 511th we were to relieve was preparing to move out. Air Force files cheerfully informed us that the Nips bombed away at the strips almost every night, although lately his nightly application had become a bit feeble.

Down near one of the airstrips was located the headquarters of our division. This half-flooded landing field had been allotted to the Eleventh and from it aerial resupply missions were being launched in support of the 511th, which had already penetrated so deeply into the mountains that this method of replacement supply was the only one feasible. Up on the hill, at the edge of town, was Fifth Air Force Headquarters, where it overlooked the three airstrips of its fighter squadrons.

At any rate, the job of the 2d Battalion was to protect this whole gigantic, and confused, melange, and, accordingly, it occupied positions about eight hundred yards west of the town on a low hill dominating the surrounding flat-land.

C Company and the 511th Command Group, meantime, were having a rough time in the middle of the Japanese force that surrounded them. Their ammunition, fired more recklessly in the first heat of combat than was economical, was running low. Their food supply was even lower. But the men on the ridge were beginning to learn to conserve both. They used fire discipline and fired only when it was absolutely necessary to hold their positions against the enemy probes. They also conserved their own grenades by throwing back at the enemy their unexploded ones.

On the second day of the ambush, 28 November, a group of Japanese approached C Company's perimeter with demands that they surrender. The Japanese were led by the Filipino guide who had steered the company into the ambush. He was promptly killed while Rock Haugen got rid of the Japanese summarily.

That night, Haugen took eight men and stole out of the ambush site. He sent six of the men to Manarawat to lead the 1st Battalion to C Company, and, with the two other men, made his way back to Burauen and Division CP on 30 November, the fourth day after the start of the ambush.

On the day before Haugen arrived at Burauen, Lt. Donald E. Neff, a liaison pilot from the 675th Glider Field Artillery Battalion, was circling over the mountain searching for C Company. He spotted a flash of a mirror, a can, or a piece of glass. He returned over the area and heard some small-arms fire. He could see nothing through the thick foliage,

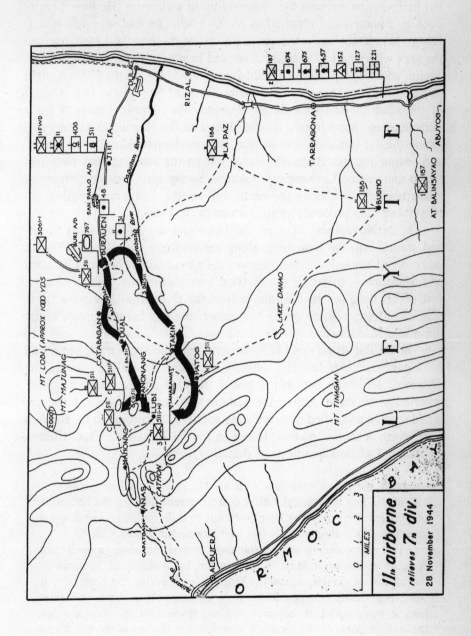

11ᵗʰ airborne
relieves 7ᵗʰ div.
28 November 1944

but he fixed the position by a bare stump in a clearing. He flew directly back to Burauen and reported to the G-3 what he had seen and heard. Doug Quandt got out some aerial photos of the area and Neff selected the spot where he had seen the flash and heard the firing. Quandt called Tipton and Shipley, CO of the 2d Battalion, 511th, to the CP that night and pointed out what Neff had found. General Swing was fully abreast of the situation and took decisive action. He ordered Tipton to get a parachute and jump from a liaison plane into the clearing at Manarawat, where the 1st Battalion was located, assume command of the regiment, and, using the 1st Battalion, move out to the clearing that Neff had found and rescue C Company. General Swing also ordered Shipley to move his battalion along the north trail on the following morning, 30 November, and proceed, by forced march, to Lubi.

On 28 November, Lt. Col. Ed Lahti and his 3d Battalion, 511th, had started into the mountains along the southern trail. General Swing had ordered him to leave one company at Patog, midway between Burauen and Manarawat, to secure the division's southern flank, and to take the rest of his battalion to Mawala, across the river from Manarawat. He was due to arrive there on 29 November, the day before Tipton would jump into Manarawat.

The 3d Battalion, early in its march along the south trail, had found no Japanese. Lahti left H Company at Patog not only to secure the division's left flank but also to patrol the area and to locate Japanese reported to be there. Before the battalion arrived at Mawala, however, it had spotted and killed its first enemy soldiers. According to Lt. Richard V. Barnes, a mortar platoon leader in the 3d Battalion, Capt. Clinton A. Ashford of Headquarters, 3d Battalion,

surprised and killed three Japs with his M1 rifle. After being searched, one of the Japs was found with a detailed terrain map of the area west of Burauen. This map was later flown out by a liaison plane and dropped back in to the battalion three days later, translated into English.

The next morning the 3d Battalion moved out along a creek bed from its perimeter at Mawala, to join the 1st Battalion at Manarawat. As the last of the Headquarters Company was leaving the perimeter, it was brought under intense rifle fire from the gorge below. Upon investigation, it was found that the creek bed had made a hairpin turn and that the lead elements of the battalion were firing at the top of the hill where they had just left. Luckily, all shots were wild and no one was hurt. The rest of the trip to Manarawat was upstream and very slow; but by late afternoon, the battalion, less H Company, joined the 1st Battalion and became part of the perimeter defense.

Upon arriving there, the battalion found that Manarawat was being cleared for a liaison plane strip. The next few days were spent clearing the strip and in receiving a small amount of supplies dropped by liaison plane.

The 81 mm. mortar platoon of Headquarters Company left Burauen without any of its mortars. The probability of its employment in our advance to the west made it necessary for the platoon to be able to provide at least a small amount of support to the battalion. As a result, two mortars and approximately 60 rounds of H.E. light ammunition were dropped by liaison planes. The tube, bi-pod, and ammunition were dropped by parachute; but the base plate was merely thrown out of the plane. It was here that the 3d Battalion received the first of several casualties by aerial drops. Pfc. Jack Jones, of the mortar platoon, was hit on the back of the head by a free falling base plate and died the same night.

The division G-4, Lt. Col. Bill Crawford, also started using liaison planes to drop food and ammunition to the clearing that Neff had spotted in the hopes that C Company could get to them. Most of the supplies landed in the middle of the clearing, but later it was obvious that the area had been swept by enemy fire, and C Company had been unable to retrieve any of the much-needed resupplies.

On the morning of 30 November, Lieutenant Colonel Tipton made what was probably the first combat jump ever from a Cub plane when he parachuted into Manarawat. It would prove to be only the first of many combat jumps from Cub planes that the 11th would use to put troops in the right, tight spots when necessary. Before the Leyte campaign would be over, moreover, the 11th would find many innovative uses for the eleven liaison planes of the Division Artillery Air Fleet, uses far more exciting and valuable than their originally conceived employment, that of simply flying artillery air observers over an enemy position to direct artillery fire thereupon.

Doug Quandt was in another liaison plane circling over Manarawat when Tipton jumped in. Once Tipton was on the ground, he radioed Quandt overhead that he had assumed command of the 511th and was prepared to move out on the mission assigned by General Swing.

On the morning of 30 November, after Haugen had arrived at the division CP, he checked the photo on which Neff had identified the probable location of C Company and said that he was reasonably certain that that was where Mesereau and his troops were located. One of the two men who accompanied Haugen out of the hills was a young trooper named Berg, a member of his S-2 Section. Haugen and Quandt discussed the situation, and they concluded that the most rapid way to reach and relieve C Company was to lead the 2d Battalion, Shipley's, now on the north trail, to the C Company position.

Berg volunteered to make the combat jump to the 2d Battalion from a Cub plane. His drop zone would be the narrow, muddy trail in front of the 2d Battalion. Berg had only one problem: His jump boots were worn out from the few days he had used them in the mountains. He checked Doug Quandt's boots and suggested that they would be acceptable. And so the deal was made—new boots for a combat jump from a Cub plane. That afternoon, Berg climbed into the backseat of the Cub—the pilot occupied the only other seat, in the front—and with Berg's legs hanging out the door, the plane took off. They flew up the trail, and then Berg jumped out when he saw the point of the 2d Battalion. He landed directly in front of the point men of the battalion.

Colonel Tipton left Manarawat the next morning with Company G of the 511th, according to Lieutenant Barnes, "to relieve C Company. Their attack combined with the attack of the 2d Battalion, moving up from Burauen, finally effected their relief." The 2d Battalion remained in contact with the Japanese in the area; G Company, C Company, the 1st Battalion of the 511th, and the regimental command element moved back to Anonang. Colonel Lahti and his 3d Battalion had, meanwhile, replaced LaFlamme's battalion at Manarawat.

The question of which man in the 11th Airborne killed the first of the enemy is a debatable one. On 28 November, while the 1st Battalion of the 511th was moving into the hills west of Burauen, Lt. George Skau, from the G-2 Section of Division Headquarters, was traveling by jeep from the Division Headquarters to the CP of the 188th. Patrols operating in that area had found relatively little evidence of the enemy. Some distance down the road from the division CP, a Japanese soldier stepped out in front of Skau's jeep. Skau was quicker on the draw and killed the enemy soldier. Skau searched the body and discovered the soldier's paybook. He was Superior Private Takanaka. Presumably, to George Skau goes the distinction of being the first 11th Airborne trooper to kill one of the enemy.

At 0245 on 27 November, the Japanese began the first phase of their plan to regain the initiative. Three enemy air transports, U.S. code-named "Topsy," looking much like the U.S. Air Corps' C-47s, flew over Leyte Gulf at an altitude of fifty feet with their lights on. They were flying north up the shoreline. Ten minutes later, one of them crash-landed about twenty-five yards offshore in the area of the 728th Amphibian Tractor Battalion some three miles north of Tarragona. A battalion guard, thinking that the plane was in fact a C-47, climbed on the wing and offered his assistance. The Japanese swarmed out of the plane, and one of them threw a grenade at the friendly guard. The men of the battalion were alerted, and a number of them fired at the Japanese. Two enemy soldiers were killed with small-arms fire, but three managed to escape into a swamp west of the landing point.

A second Japanese transport crash-landed on the Buri strip and all the occupants were killed.

The third plane landed on Bito Beach near the river that formed the northern boundary of the 11th Airborne Division's rear area. An antiaircraft machine gun crew was on the alert near the downed plane. One of the American soldiers shouted across the river: "Need any help?" "No, everything OK," came the reply. And, according to the division historian, "the machine gun crew went back to watching the skies for enemy aircraft." With the exception of one enemy soldier who was killed by a patrol shortly after dawn, all of the Japanese in this plane escaped to the west. The Topsy, with a bright red sun gleaming on its tail, was a constant reminder to the 11th Airborne men at the Bito Beach base camp that the Japanese had a unique way of bringing in their pathfinders.

The men of the 728th Amphibian Tractor Battalion searched the plane near their area and found many demolition charges. In view of this discovery and the fact that the Japanese made no attempt to follow up the crash landings by a parachute attack, the intelligence officers at XXIV Corps concluded that the Japanese who crash-landed had been on a suicide mission whose aim was to destroy the airfields in the Burauen and Dulag areas. There had been little damage from the mission, but Radio Tokyo claimed that it had been "most successful." Some intelligence officers concluded from that remark that there might be a follow-up airborne attack, either by raiding parties or by a larger contingent of Japanese paratroopers. The latter would prove to be the case.

As the units of the division moved into the mountains, the division communicators found it difficult to maintain a telephone net from division to the regiments and the other units. Too many men were required to guard the wire over the long routes through the mountains. And too many men were required to repair the wire lines, which the Japanese cut in many places during the night. The regiments and smaller units could and did lay wire and maintain telephone nets, but it was apparent that the division could not communicate by wire west of the Burauen area. The division adopted two expedients to solve the communications problem. One was the "Mosley milk run" and the other was the "Godfrey relay."

The Mosley milk run was named after Capt. Art Mosley, a member of the division G-3 Section. He teamed up with a liaison pilot named Lt. Jack Keil of the 674th Glider FA Battalion. Each day of the Leyte campaign, at 0730 and again at 1630, these two officers would climb into Keil's Cub plane, set the radio, and fly off into the mountains, dodging the hills as they flew through the low-hanging clouds. They would circle over each unit on the ground, no matter how small, contact it on the radio, drop messages and orders, talk to the commanders and staff officers, receive reports and orders for supplies, listen to gripes, and plot the unit position on the "milk run" map. Then they would return to the division strip, and Mosley would go to the G-3 operations map, plot the new locations of the units, and relay messages to the G-3 and the G-4.

Many days, fog closed in on the milk run, and the trip would be hazardous. On one occasion, Keil was flying low because of bad visibility. The plane ran into a Japanese telephone wire. The plane snapped the wire, but the only other damage was an ugly cut across Mosley's right cheek.

Each morning, Mosley picked up copies of the division newspaper, the *Static Line,* and dropped them to the units as the plane flew over. This was almost the only news the mountain-bound soldiers had of the outside world. One morning, Doug Quandt picked up one of the rolls of newspapers and noticed that it was addressed not to one of the 11th's units, but as follows: "To the girls, with the compliments of Art Mosley and Jack Keil. Phone Glider 3." After some discussion, Mosley reported that on the way out of the mountains, Keil flew over the WAC camp and Mosley dropped the greetings from the 11th Airborne. Quandt felt that such a procedure had merit.

The "Godfrey relay" was the result of a mission that General Swing assigned to Lt. Col. Jim Farren, the CO of the 152d Airborne AA-AT Battalion. Colonel Farren's mission was to gather as many SCR-609 radios as he could find and, with security men from his battalion, follow the infantry into the mountains and establish radio relays wherever he thought necessary to link the units in the mountains with the division CP at San Pablo. West of Burauen, there were a number of abandoned farms and barrios, all with a name but without a Filipino in residence. At a number of these clearings, the 152d set up relay stations. Godfrey 12 was at Manarawat, and Godfrey 8 was at Anonang. There were other stations at Catabagan, Takin, and Patog. "Godfrey" became the password of the Leyte mountains. Gossip, news, orders, rumors—all were available at a nearby Godfrey station. Infantrymen on patrol came to know the relay station operators by name, and some passing patrols brought the outpost guardians small gifts—chewing gum or an extra K ration.

The Japanese recognized the purpose and value of the Godfrey linkup. At Catabagan, the Japanese attacked the small outpost, but the lieutenant in charge called for artillery fire over the Godfrey net. The artillery from positions west of Burauen responded and dumped a large concentration on the Japanese. Thirty-two of the enemy died in their aborted attack.

Technical Sergeant Alexander Ruzycki of the 152d and three of his men manned the relay station outside Burauen. Early one morning, Sergeant Ruzycki saw two Japanese about fifty feet away crawling toward his lean-to shelter. He calmly picked up his M-1 carbine and killed them both and then called battalion headquarters and reported two dead enemy in his position. Ten minutes later, Sergeant Ruzycki saw three more of the enemy outside his position. In the ensuing firefight, he lost a finger. He also received a grazing wound on his thigh, but he hobbled back to his radio, reported his situation to battalion headquarters, and suggested that the battalion send a patrol to his area because he was certain that there were more of the enemy nearby. When the patrol reached the vicinity of Ruzycki's lean-to, the approaching soldiers heard the sounds of a small firefight. They crept on cautiously and found that Ruzycki and his three men were surrounded by the enemy but were holding their own in the firefight. The patrol attacked and, in forty minutes, killed twenty-two Japanese. The patrol and Ruzycki's team had only one casualty. Later, Sergeant Ruzycki received the Silver Star.

From Manarawat to the west, the three trails across the mountains again diverged, and the nebulous maps seemed to indicate that they converged again at Anas, a deserted barrio on the west slope of the central mountain range. The 511th promptly dubbed the trails North, South, and Middle. General Swing ordered Colonel Haugen, who had rejoined his regiment, to "proceed to Mahonag, secure the Jap supply trail in that vicinity, with the secondary mission of attacking west on 7 December in a coordinated attack with the other elements of the 6th Army operating on Leyte." (From the Journal of the 511th Parachute Infantry—Leyte Campaign.)

On 2 December, Colonel Lahti gave I Company the mission of locating the route to Mahonag and finding the Japanese supply trail. To Lieutenant Fenske fell the reconnaissance task. He left in the morning, and by 1700 he and his patrol had returned to the 3d Battalion perimeter at Manarawat with the information that they had found a trail to Mahonag but had been unable to find the Japanese supply route. The trail he found was from Manarawat to Mount Catmon and over Mount Catmon to Mahonag, a distance of about seven miles, up and down the muddy, vine-entangled, dripping landscape. After Lieutenant Fenske had returned and reported his findings to Colonel Lahti, Colonel Lahti called his company commanders to a meeting at his CP—a couple of foxholes and a radio under the tree line—and told them to be prepared to move out the next morning.

At 0800 on 3 December, the 3d Battalion left the perimeter at Manarawat, tracking along the same route that Fenske had found the previous day. Initially, the battalion used a few carabao to carry the mortars and ammunition and other supplies, but the carabao soon became useless. The condition of the trails, because of the incessant rain and steep inclines, made the carabao too slow for the march. And the carabao were too fat to squeeze through some of the tight spots on the trail. Lieutenant Richard V. Barnes, the 81mm mortar platoon commander, had his platoon unload and hand carry the mortars and ammunition the rest of the way. By late afternoon, the battalion had closed on Mahonag, without discovering any of the enemy along the South Trail.

Mahonag was a stump-studded clearing, about 400 by 500 yards, on top of a commanding hill. It had been used by the Filipinos, and then the Japanese, apparently as a *cammote* (sweet potato) patch. The troopers of the 3d Battalion found that the hill was covered with defensive positions dug by the Japanese and also showed evidence of use as a bivouac area. But the enemy was no longer there. They had apparently fallen back into the surrounding jungle and hills. As soon as the battalion arrived on the hill, it immediately set up a perimeter defense. Once more, Lieutenant Fenske set out to look for the missing Japanese supply trail. By 1700, he was back with the word that the trail was about 1,000 yards to the south of the position and that there were Japanese in the area. He and his patrol had killed ten of the enemy without getting into a full-scale firefight and had also located a Japanese telephone line. He had tapped the line but had heard no conversations.

Late on 3 December, the regimental headquarters and most of the 1st Battalion arrived in the perimeter. They had used the Middle Trail. After Colonel Lahti briefed Colonel Haugen (who had also jumped into Manarawat by Cub plane) on the situation, Colonel Haugen ordered a company to set up an ambush on the supply trail and to take along a wire tapper and an interpreter.

The 2d Battalion of the 511th was still fighting a large force in the area of C Company's ambush. Based on the Japanese defenses and their ability to withstand the 2d Battalion's attack, Colonel Shipley, the 2d Battalion CO, had determined that the enemy was deeply dug in and apparently guarding what appeared to be the command post of a large installation. The battalion had twice tried to reduce the position, but, to date, had been unsuccessful.

On 2 December, back on the hills west of Burauen, General Swing had ordered Lt. Col. Harry Wilson to follow the 511th into the hills. According to Chief Warrant Officer Nelson, "We moved off light, each man carrying his own weapon, with ammo and two day's K rations. In our wake moved Lt. Bernheim's supply train; its rolling stock a herd of sluggish, patient carabao loaded with heavy weapons, spare ammo and the heavier signal equipment. Such was life in the 'modernized war.'"

Eli Bernheim had more than his share of trouble with the carabao and resupplying the 2d Battalion, 187th.

I had the problem of getting an adequate ammo resupply to the battalion area through the incredible mud. Colonel Wilson had issued me a substantial amount of pesos. I bought a number of carabao and a couple of young Filipino herders. We built some heavy bamboo sleds and dragged the ammo to the Battalion area. . . . I became somewhat notorious as the chief of the carabao pack train. There were some humorous incidents. We didn't know that males and females had to be separated. Unfortunately, we had one female who went into heat, and the males started fighting and goring, resulting in some severe wounds. The Filipinos kept yelling "creosote, creosote" which we didn't understand until it became apparent that this was the prescribed treatment for gore wounds. We had no creosote, but there was the usual supply of the World War II delight—Dubbin, and for once it was useful.

I won't go into the details on the horrors of the march through the mountains; I can recall more than one night spent in a hole with water up to my chin or places where you couldn't dig a hole and tried to sleep on the mud covered by a poncho. Eventually, we could take the carabao no further. We lost two heavy machine gun cradles when a carabao fell off a ridge. We finally turned the carabao loose, and the herders tried to backtrack. I don't know whatever happened to them, but if we had known what was ahead, we might have considered a slaughter and butcher operation.

On 2 December, the 1st Battalion of the 187th had moved up from Bito Beach, where, along with elements of the 503d Parachute Infantry Regiment, it had been patrolling deep into the area behind the beach, more intensely after the crash landing of the Japanese transports. The battalion had succeeded in eliminating a number of the Japanese who had survived the crash landings. The battalion moved by amtracs, and occupied positions on the east end of San Pablo airstrip, across the road and about a mile east of the 11th Airborne Division Headquarters.

Lieutenant Charles "Pop" Olsen was the commander of C Company of the 187th. In New Guinea, Olsen had succeeded to the command of C Company when the previous company commander was killed during a demonstration of a Japanese grenade. The morning after the 1st Battalion moved into San Pablo, Lieutenant Olsen made a trip to the division CP with Colonel Pearson, the 1st Battalion CO. General Swing directed Colonel Pearson to send C Company into the hills behind the 2d of the 187th, which had already departed. But he also told them that he wanted one platoon of C Company to jump into Manarawat.

Olsen returned to his company position and alerted the company to get ready to move out. When he finished briefing his platoon leaders, he told Lt. Chester J. Kozlowski, who had transferred to the division from the 503d Parachute Infantry Regiment after that regiment's operation on Noemfoor Island, that he and his platoon would remain behind and that he was to report to General Swing at the division CP.

Chet Kozlowski wrote recently,

Not privileged to be in on the "Know," I can not say why the 187th was selected for the jump on Manarawat. The only thing I can think of was that the 511th was committed in the jungle and we were there at the time we were needed.

As soon as the company left, I went over to where General Swing and his staff were to report in as directed. General Swing told me that he had heard of me and he wanted me to take my platoon and jump into combat. He then asked me if we needed any supplies and equipment. After being in the boonies for so long, all of our socks and underwear plus fatigues were worn out so I requested same. The General himself made two trips to the QM Supply Point and returned with arm loads of socks. During this time he asked me if there were any other items I needed. I told him that we needed machine guns since the platoon itself was not authorized any. He turned to his Ordnance Officer and told him to break some out of cosmoline, clean them up and bring them to me ready to fire.

The colonel tried to protest his having to clean them himself but the General told him to DO IT. I also requested an A-5 container. While waiting for the container, I sent word back to my platoon sergeant to send a few men to pick up the supplies and help pack the container. General Swing watched as we packed the container, stating that he never saw one being packed.

As soon as the platoon was ready, General Swing had the aircraft (a Cub L-4) taxi to us so that we can be briefed on how to get into the plane, sit with our feet out the door, and our static line hooked up into a D ring. Then, when we received the word to go, it will be more of a hand signal and we were to roll out the door.

I was the first to get aboard the aircraft and take off. We had about six light aircraft (L-4's and L-5's) at the strip. I and my runner took the first two planes. After about fifteen minutes we were over the DZ at 400 feet altitude when the arm went up to GO. The opening shock was not there. Actually it was a nice smooth opening and upon landing, we gathered our chutes and set out to establish a perimeter and fields of fire.

The strength of my platoon was 24 men and it took several trips for the planes to drop them all. About the third day following our drop, the rest of C Company arrived and expanded the perimeter.

The farther the infantry battalions of the 11th moved into the hills to the west, the less was the artillery support available to reinforce them. By 3 December, the 511th was beyond the supporting range of the smaller caliber artillery and even of most of the 155mm guns that had been attached to the division from XXIV Corps Artillery. And even though the Corps Artillery had forward observers with the 511th, and air observers overhead, the 155mm guns, even in the areas they could reach, could not give the 511th the close-in fires it needed in the mountain fighting. To the division staff and particularly to the G-3, Colonel Quandt, it was obvious that even the light pack 75s of the Division Artillery could not be towed into the hills, the carabao could not carry them, and the paratrooper artillerymen, capable and physically fit as they were, could neither drag nor carry them up the slippery, muddy trails. And though the "pack" artillery had been traditionally packed by mules, there were no mules available and, even if there had been, they could not have moved the artillery up into the mountains.

On 3 December, the 457th was still in the bivouac area at Bito Beach. The battalion had set up its guns along the coconut tree line behind the beach to be prepared to fire to the east in the event the Japanese tried to make an amphibious landing in the area. On the night of 3 December, Doug Quandt, at Division Headquarters, called Lt. Col. Nick Stadtherr, the CO of the 457th, and told him to parachute one of his firing batteries into an area near Manarawat, from which he could fire in support of the 511th in its attacks to the north and the west. Quandt also alerted Stadtherr to the possibility of dropping in the rest of his battalion. Nick Stadtherr, an imaginative and determined officer, accepted the mission as fairly routine, even though he had no idea of how he was going to perform it. He selected A Battery, which he formerly commanded, to make the jump, no doubt believing that it was the best battery. Stadtherr asked John Conable to jumpmaster the drop.

Conable ordered Lt. Milton R. Holloway (known to some as "Bobo" and to others as "Jelly Belly" because of his obvious size) to move his battery to San Pablo strip, one of the three strips along the road from Dulag to Burauen. Conable went on ahead to try to find out what aircraft he had and how he was going to get everything he needed— particularly equipment and personnel chutes—in a hurry.

When Conable arrived at San Pablo, he found problems. There was only one C-47, an air-sea rescue ship that had never been used for jumping paratroopers. He also found out that all other C-47s in the area were urgently needed for aerial resupply missions, that the clouds usually hung low over the mountains, and that there were no jump fields like the ones at Mackall or in New Guinea. The pilot of the air-sea rescue plane found out about Conable's problem and offered his assistance. He said that when the plane was not in use for his rescue work, he and his crew would be glad to drop Conable up in the mountains. That was all the encouragement Conable needed.

Fortuitously, the division supply men in the 408th Quartermaster Company had had sense enough to bring along parachutes and other equipment for dropping elements of the division when required. Conable ordered pararacks for the C-47, equipment containers, and equipment and personnel chutes brought up from Bito Beach. The equipment arrived late in the morning. By that time, Holloway and the battery had unloaded themselves and their howitzers and other gear from the DUKWs that had ferried them from Bito Beach. They began immediately to attach the pararacks to the bottom of the air-sea rescue ship. Colonel Stadtherr was also present, helping to organize the effort. While the battery was in the middle of getting ready for their jump, a jeep arrived from Division Headquarters. The driver told Captain Conable to report immediately to Headquarters. "After some speculation as to what was up," he remembered later, "I piled in the jeep and went to Division Headquarters which was close to the San Pablo airstrip at Burauen. Upon arrival I received orders relieving me from assignment to the 457th FA and appointing me Assistant Division Quartermaster. I sent the jeep back to report what was happening to me to Nick."

Colonel Stadtherr took over the job of getting A Battery ready to jump into Manarawat. Ordinarily, a parachute artillery firing battery requires twelve C-47s for a drop. Stadtherr had to make do with one. He had the aircrew strip the door off the C-47 and tape the sharp spots around the door. He had the pararacks fastened to the underside of the plane. Then he loaded one-thirteenth of A Battery and one-fiftieth of his battalion headquarters into the plane and took off. It was the afternoon of 4 December and the 11th Airborne Division was about to make its first unit combat jump from the airborne workhorse—the reliable and battle-worthy C-47.

The division staff had selected for a drop zone an area about two rough and mountainous miles from Manarawat. The DZ was fairly wide and even free of trees and presumably safer than trying to drop into the confines of the Manarawat clearing. But after the first drop, Colonel Stadtherr decided that he could hit the Manarawat clearing and save the battery the backbreaking trek overland with its howitzers in pieces. The new DZ at Manarawat measured about 500 feet long by 150 feet wide. Cliffs dropped off the DZ on all four sides and tall mountains rose to enclose it on three sides. The mountains around the gorge in which Manarawat sat like an island forced the C-47 to approach the drop zone by following a deep, moon-shaped canyon, hit the field immediately after a blind curve to the right, and then zoom sharply up and to the left when it passed the end of the short drop zone.

Wrote the division historian,

> Beautiful flying by the pilot of Rescue and tremendously proficient jump-mastering by Colonel Stadtherr, who personally jumped each planeload, landed all equipment and men in thirteen plane trips, directly in the center of the field. Because nine loads of equipment had to be dropped each trip (six from the belly and three from the door), personnel sticks were restricted to five men in order not to drop off the far end of the jump field. No injuries were sustained—except to ''Jelly-Belly'' Holloway's pride which had to suffer the march from the original drop zone to the battery position—even though the men jumped from three hundred feet. From that day on, A Battery provided 360 degree support to all the infantry fighting in the mountains.

With the movement of the infantry battalions of the division farther and farther to the west, and the increasing difficulty of directing their operations and of communicating with their commanders from the division CP at Burauen, General Swing decided to establish a forward CP at Manarawat. ''Swing blew a fuse,'' reported one of his staff officers, ''when he read a message from Manarawat that the Signal outfit had closed down for the night because they 'drew fire from the Japanese.' ''

On the afternoon of 4 December, Col. Doug Quandt jumped from a Cub plane into Manarawat to begin that phase of the campaign. Captain Wells Albade from the G-3 Section, Capt. Joseph ''Bo'' Seay from the 127th Engineers, Capt. Jack Atwood, and a detachment of the 511th Signal Company with an SCR-694 radio also jumped in from the one jumper-troop carrier transport—the L-4.

It was also readily apparent to General Swing and his division surgeon, Lt. Col. Frank Regnier, that they needed an expeditious and reliable means of treating the increasing number of wounded men close to the action in the hills and of bringing out the wounded when they could be moved. The manpower and security needed to move the wounded men down the trails would be an almost impossible drain on the slender soldier resources of the division. The division commander had solved part of his problem of the almost impassable trails by parachuting men and equipment forward; he determined that he would reverse the procedure and fly out his wounded. There was one major problem: There was no airstrip in the mountains. General Swing directed his division engineer, Lt. Col. Douglas C. Davis, to build one.

On the afternoons of 4 and 5 December, a platoon of 127th Engineer Battalion, led by Lieutenants Clift and Brugh, parachuted into Manarawat using the same Cub planes that had dropped Lieutenant Kozlowski and his platoon. The planes also dropped in bundles of shovels, saws, axes, and picks for clearing trees off the plateau and making a strip long enough to accommodate the Cubs. But before the strip was ready, the Cub planes also dropped in medical personnel to establish a forward hospital at Manarawat.

The medical unit organic to the division was the 221st Airborne Medical Company. Attached to it for the Leyte operation were two portable surgical hospitals. In this case, the term "portable" took on new meaning. Three surgeons and ten medical technicians dropped into Manarawat and established a nipa-thatched, silk parachute–lined "hospital" capable of providing medical and surgical care for the wounded of the division. The units brought their wounded into the clearing at Manarawat for treatment. As soon as the walking wounded were able to make the trip, they caught the first patrol going back to Burauen or, if their condition warranted it, back to their units for more fighting. Seriously wounded stayed in the "hospital" until they could be evacuated by Cub plane.

As soon as the engineers had cleared the strip, the L-4s (but not the slightly bigger and more powerful L-5s) began to land. The medics fitted up each L-4 with a piece of plywood over the backseat, long enough to accommodate a wounded man on a mattress and long enough to bump the pilot in front on the nape of his neck.

Captain Tom Brady, the commander of A Company of the 511th, was wounded seriously in the head and was litter-borne into Manarawat. In the rough clinic there, Captain Nestor performed a skillful brain operation that kept Captain Brady alive. For three days, Brady lingered between life and death. Then he was flown out in Lt. Sid Lanier's "ambulance" plane to the Dulag General Hospital. From there he was flown back to the States.

About 6 December, Brig. Gen. Al Pierson arrived at Manarawat to take over command of the division CP forward. He recalls, "I flew to

Manarawat airstrip by L-4 Cub piloted by Lt. Lanier, considered by all of us as the most experienced pilot able to take off successfully from the short Manarawat airstrip. We outfitted his plane with a board so that it could carry litter patients and I was flat on my back for that short flight from San Pablo. . . . I had my driver, Corporal John Archbold, with me. He parachuted in from an L-4, missed the strip, and landed in a tree. However, no injuries.''

The problem of supplying the troops in the mountains became more and more acute the farther the units attacked to the west. For all of Sixth Army, there were only between two and six C-47s available for resupply missions at any given time. They were rarely available to the division, and Colonel Crawford, the division G-4, could not rely on them for resupplying the units in the hills. The planes had to be ordered forty-eight hours in advance, with the supply loads specified; scheduled flights were cancelled in the event of an emergency in another area; the C-47s would not fly without fighter cover, which was not always available; the constant and prevailing bad weather prevented flights by the C-47s into the mountains for days at a time; and the restricted and small drop zones made the trips hazardous for the pilots and for the recovery of the supplies that were dropped.

On 2 December, one C-47 on a ration supply run to the 1st of the 511th failed to pull up soon enough from its run into the drop zone and crashed into the side of Mount Catmon, about 500 yards into enemy territory. Colonel LaFlamme immediately sent a rescue party to the downed plane. The party reached the area in about an hour. The rescue group pulled the dead and wounded out of the plane, recovered a small portion of the supplies, and headed back to A Company's perimeter. Then A Company sent out a carrying party to recover the rest of the supplies. By the time the group climbed back to the wrecked C-47, the Japanese had taken out most of the supplies and booby-trapped the plane. The carrying party grabbed up what was left of the rations, rebooby-trapped the plane, and left.

To solve the supply problem, the division G-4 and the quartermaster developed a system of aerial resupply that was more dependable than the C-47s. The division used its own men and planes plus some L-5s and pilots borrowed from a very cooperative nearby outfit, the ''New Guinea Short Lines.'' All together, the division assembled sixteen planes at the San Pablo airstrip Number Two, also called Bayug, just a short distance across the road from the division CP. There the Quartermaster Company established a stockpile of all types of supplies, packaged for Cub plane delivery. Captain Davy Carnahan, from the division staff, was the boss of the enterprise, more formally known as "the chief of the aerial delivery section of the 11th Airborne Division," and set himself up in a pyramidal tent in the trees on the other side of the runway from the Dulag-Burauen road on San Pablo Number Two. He had a varied crew to manage. The pilots of the planes were under Maj. Edwin L. Harloff, the Division Artillery air officer. Carnahan's other group was a collection of mechanics and small, lightweight division soldiers who pushed the cargo out of the planes over the DZ. Once the operation was going at full speed, the aircraft parking area was on the west end of the runway; scattered in the trees along some high ground to the north of the strip were the officers' tents, a mess tent, a radio shack where Clifford P. Johnson of Division Artillery headquarters battery held forth, aerial resupply tents, and a supply fuel dump.

The San Pablo strip was busy. Wrote one of the men who had been a party to the operation:

Planes were constantly landing and taking off to deliver supplies far into the mountains to the west, and, daily, personages of high station landed or took off from the dirt strip. Systematic supply runs were planned and executed at this nerve center of the Division supply. At peak operation the 16 planes of the center delivered an average of 21 tons of supplies a day to the front line troops in the mountains. (The air distances were actually quite short. The distance from San Pablo to Manarawat, for example, was only about ten miles.) It was not sporadic delivery, but continuous, high-speed delivery, day after day, throughout the month of December and the first part of January. Without it, the Division would not have passed the first foothills west of Burauen.

On many days, thick, grey fog closed to the ground in the mountains, and the pilots had to circle looking for breaks into which they could dive and deliver. Often as not, once through, the break in the clouds would close on the pilot and a nightmarish, circling climb back to sunlight and safety ensued. On one such day our only pilot loss occurred: gallant Lt. John A. Ricks, from the air section of the 457th. He crashed somewhere in the fog-covered hills attempting to deliver food and medical supplies to the ground soldiers.

Pilots flew from daylight to dark, ten and twelve hours a day, in fair weather and foul. Their only recreation was bombing the Japs on the way to and from the target runs. Each time they took off, they placed a few hand grenades or bazooka rounds in their laps, and on the way dived and hurled the lethal weapons at any unfortunate Nip who dared to show himself on the ground. Whether they ever hit one, no one knows, but the pleasure and satisfaction of watching scurrying Nips partly repaid the "biscuit bombers" for the splendid, fatiguing work they performed.

Michael J. Kalamas was a member of Headquarters Battery of the 457th. Shortly after the division landed on Bito Beach, Kalamas saw a notice on a makeshift bulletin board in front of the battery orderly tent. It said: "Men, under 135 pounds, needed for aerial resupply detail at Division Headquarters. Apply at the orderly tent immediately."

The next morning, 24 November, he showed up at the battalion headquarters, against "the better judgment of my close companions," and went by jeep to the rear division CP at Bito Beach. "There, along with ten other undernourished looking young men, we climbed aboard two DUKWs that were waiting for us. We headed up the rough road to Dulag, where we saw some P-38s parked along the runway of Dulag Airfield. Then we continued on up the Dulag-Burauen road."

By midafternoon, Kalamas and the other volunteers, among them Patrick Bowen and Mac Martino from the 152d AA Battalion and Robert Brooks from the 408th QM Company, were dropped off at a "wide spot in the road." The driver of the DUKW said that the division CP was in some trees on the side of a hill. Then he said that their destination was an airstrip about a quarter of a mile across a field. Kalamas recollects,

The place sure didn't look like much. In fact, it looked so peaceful, you would never know that there was a war going on around us. It was very quiet, and except for two mechanics, working near four or five observation (Cub) aircraft, you would never know that there was anyone here at all.

The long dirt runway sort of ran East and West. It ended in some more scrub brush and trees, and beyond that, we discovered later that another airstrip (Buri) was located, but not occupied.

Not far from where we were standing, a tarp covered what looked like supplies and on the other side were some gasoline drums, standing on end. Over on the north side, some distance away, was some sort of a bamboo shack with a coconut leaf roof that was barely visible among the brush.

I turned to my left, and beyond the small trees were rolling hills, and in the distance were the mountains, green and misty. This was a beautiful valley, and except for the war, I'm sure the people liked living here.

I walked over to the mechanics and told them who we were, and asked who we should report to. They said to talk to Capt. Carnahan. "You will find him in a tent, over in that bunch of trees." I couldn't see the tents from here, but I went over and finally located him.

I told him that there were ten guys sitting on the strip, and we wanted to know what we were supposed to do. He said we would have to rough it until some tents and the supplies came up from the beach. There were ten-and-one rations under the tarp we could use. There were no cooks up here, so everyone made his own meals.

Except for air raids and Washing Machine Charlie visiting every night to see what the Americans were doing, it was fairly quiet. We used to watch when the antiaircraft guns over Dulag and Tacloban filled the sky with fire and smoke that disturbed our rest period.

When the supplies and equipment began arriving from Bito, we quickly found where we fit into the scheme of things. From dawn to dusk, rain or shine, the planes started taking out the stuff as fast as we could load it. I can't recall any bunch of men who were more eager to fill an assignment, under somewhat unorthodox conditions.

The pilots of course were outstanding. They never complained. They flew in the rain, when the mountains were fogged in, and at the end of the day, they nearly fell out of the aircraft with weariness.

. . . . Before the strip was completed at Manarawat, most of us flew every day, and I must admit it did get tiring after a time. We would sit in the back, piled high with boxes, blankets or whatever, and go sailing off into the hazy mountainous areas. Skimming over the tree tops, it was a dark green jungle, as far as the eye could see. When we found the drop area, the pilot just dropped the plane as far down as possible, and we unloaded as rapidly as possible.

Then on the 29th of November, one of the truck drivers told us that a Jap plane full of paratroops had crashed at Buri. He said that another had cracked up on the beach, and most of the men had escaped. We were just a little concerned because Buri airstrip was just a couple of miles away from us.

. . . . We had gathered a large amount of blankets, boots and other supplies together and someone told us that it should be dropped by C-47. So, on December 2d, trucks were ordered and we loaded them and went up to Tacloban. At operations we found where the planes were, and with help from the Air Force people there, we loaded two C-47's.

We wanted to go along on the drop because it would have been our first time but they told us that they had enough men to handle it. So we went back to operations. We filled our canteens at a lister bag, and sat down to rest up before heading back to San Pablo.

While we relaxed, we could see both ends of the field and we watched the activity going on. Just overhead, we spied some Corsairs coming in to make a landing. One came in and as soon as it touched down, it spun out of control, and before our eyes, just broke into pieces. Another veered to the right, and plowed into a bomber parked along the runway, and burst into flames. The pilot pulled himself out and collapsed on the ground. Some men ran over and pulled him away from the burning plane to safety.

Several minutes later, one of the Air Force men came out and told us that one of the C-47 aircraft we had loaded had crashed into a mountain. We thought about that for a few minutes, and decided to go home, where it was more peaceful.

On our way to Dulag, a Jap fighter came down out of the blue and began strafing us. We could see the slugs tearing up the dirt on the road in front of us, and as he went by, I could look into the cockpit and see the cloth flying helmet he was wearing. This just didn't seem to be our day.

When we arrived back at the airstrip, a cook had prepared a meal and we had our first hot dinner in a long time. That was the first time I had seen most of the people that were around there, and I guess that there may have been about 35 or 40 altogether.

I believe it was the 3d of December that Lt. Ricks made a flight into the mountains. We waited until dark, and when he didn't return, we knew something may have happened. We found out the next day. Another pilot told us he had somehow stalled the plane about a hundred feet off the ground and it had fallen straight down, and the plane was completely destroyed. We all felt pretty bad about it, even though we knew it could happen to anyone at any time.

With the exception of the ambush of a part of the 511th Regimental Command team and Tom Mesereau's C Company, the period until 5 December was characterized by patrol action rather than sharp firefights or prolonged battles. There were casualties and there were paratroopers killed in action, but, in general, it was a period in which the infantry battalions maneuvered, patrolled, reconnoitered, and felt out the Japanese defenses, in preparation for the final push through the mountains to Ormoc. The support elements of the division located themselves so that they could provide artillery fire, signal communications, resupply, a medical base, transportation, and engineer effort to the infantrymen in the hills. The major battles of the 11th Airborne on Leyte were yet to come.

CHAPTER 9

THE BATTLE OF THE AIRSTRIPS

By the end of November 1944, the U.S. land-based air strength on Leyte had begun to expand. The Japanese Imperial General Headquarters recognized that such a buildup would jeopardize the line of communications between the homeland and the South Pacific area, particularly if the Americans were able to transfer their air strength from New Guinea to Leyte. In the latter part of November, Gen. Tomoyuki Yamashita, who commanded the 14th Area Army, sent a liaison officer from his headquarters in Manila to the command post of Lt. Gen. Sosaku Suzuki, commander of the 35th Army on Leyte, at Ormoc. General Yamashita's order to Suzuki, paraphrasing the feelings of his seniors, said: "If the construction of air bases on Leyte is permitted to continue, the communications between the Southern areas and the homeland will be cut and this would be a serious situation. Therefore, we must occupy Burauen airfield as soon as possible and at the same time neutralize Tacloban and Dulag airfields. Moreover, we must annihilate the enemy's air power."

Given the advances already made by the U.S. ground forces on the east and north coasts of Leyte and the continuing U.S. buildup of supplies and fighting forces on the island, the Japanese tactics to carry out the edict of the Imperial General Headquarters were desperate and hazardous. The plan developed by Yamashita's and Suzuki's staffs involved both the Japanese army and air forces. From 23 to 27 November, the air force mission was to eliminate the U.S. air elements on Leyte. On the night of 26 November, aircraft loaded with demolitions and specially trained demolitions experts would crash-land on Dulag and Tacloban airstrips and blast them out of commission. On the night of 5 December, the 3d and 4th Airborne Raiding Elements of the Katori Shimpei Force would take off from Luzon and jump on the Burauen airfields.

The ground scheme of maneuver required the 16th Division and the 68th Independent Mixed Brigade to attack from positions in the mountains west of Dagami, near Mount Lobi, south toward Buri, the northernmost of the three airstrips around Burauen. Units of the 26th Division, at the time fighting the U.S. 7th Division on the western shores of Ormoc Bay, were ordered to break contact with the 7th, cross the mountains to the east, and attack the Bayug and San Pablo strips. The 26th Division would move generally through the Mahonag-Anas Pass, across which the 511th Parachute Infantry Regiment was deployed. General Suzuki was optimistic enough to order the 26th Division commander to continue his attack east, after he had captured the Burauen airstrips, and seize the Dulag airfield. The ground units were directed to be in their attack positions, just west of Burauen, early on the morning of 6 December to assist the paratroopers who would have landed the night before.

The Japanese generals ran into difficulty coordinating the plan. General Suzuki on Leyte requested a postponement of forty-eight hours because he felt that he had not made sufficient preparations. General Yamashita denied the request but at the same time did postpone the airborne attack twenty-four hours, until the night of 6 December, because of a forecast of bad weather. General Suzuki's staff succeeded in getting the change of dates to the commanding general of the 26th Division but, because of radio difficulties, he was not able to inform General Makino, CG of the 16th Division. General Makino's 16th Division had been decimated since the U.S. landings on Leyte. He was able to assemble only one battalion of effective troops, about 500 men, from his entire division, some 8,800 men at the beginning of the Leyte campaign.

General Suzuki considered the battle for the airfields so important that he personally took command of the Burauen operation, and, on 1 December, he and part of his staff moved from the west coast, near Ormoc, to a position in the mountains near Burauen. He left Maj. Gen. Yoshiharu Tomochika, his chief of staff, in command of the operation around Ormoc. "Unwittingly," according to M. Hamlin Cannon, "the Japanese were flogging a dead horse. General Krueger had stopped all work on these airfields [the ones around Burauen] on 25 November." The heavy and unceasing rains had made such mires of the roads, airstrips, parking ramps, and taxiways that the engineers were unable to make them usable. The P-38s up to their wheel tops in the mud simply could not taxi.

On or about 2 December, General Makino and the remnants of the 16th Division, about 500 men, assembled in the foothills southwest of Dagami. The men rested, ate what rations they had, and moved out toward the Buri airfield. En route, U.S. artillery and tank fire killed approximately two hundred of the enemy. The rest of the force moved into a deep gorge about 6,500 yards southwest of Dagami and prepared to move out on 5 December to join with the paratroopers in a combined assault against the Buri airstrip. "The Americans later learned from interrogated prisoners that the morale of the men of the 16th Division was very low at that time," wrote M. Hamlin Cannon. "They were living on coconuts and bananas, since the officers had taken the few remaining rations. Wounded men in the force had to be abandoned."

This force from the 16th Division was still unaware that the paratrooper drop had been postponed for twenty-four hours. Therefore, on the night of 5 to 6 December, General Makino led this bedraggled group quietly toward the Buri strip. Stationed at the Buri strip were about 47 men from the 287th Field Artillery Observation Battalion and 157 men from various service units attached to the U.S. 5th Bomber Command. In addition, some small elements of engineer troops and a signal company were at the foot of a bluff, near the northern edge of the Buri strip.

By 5 December, the XXIV Corps G-2 felt that the area around the three Burauen airfields was secure. The 2d Battalion of the 511th and the 1st Battalion of the 187th had moved west into the mountains. The 3d Battalion of the 306th Infantry, which had been northwest of the airfields, had reverted to the 77th Division for the amphibious landings near Ormoc. The XXIV Corps G-2 periodic report for 2000 on 5 December on the situation in the Burauen-Dagami-Mount Alto area read: "An examination of reports of action in this area since 1 Nov may well warrant the assumption that organized resistance had about ceased." Next morning, what was left of the Japanese 16th Division came out of the hills.

At 0600 on 6 December, men from the 287th saw the Japanese

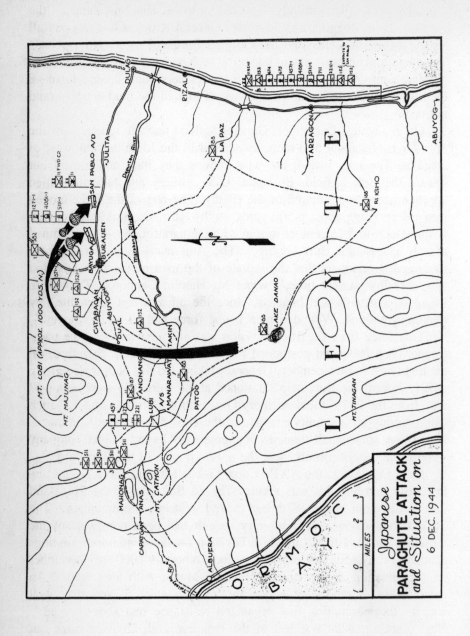

Japanese
PARACHUTE ATTACK
and *Situation on*
6 DEC. 1944

cross the main road south of the battalion's position and head east toward the Buri field. The 287th immediately radioed this information to XXIV Corps Headquarters. After the 16th had crossed the main road, the Japanese moved into a swamp near the airfield. One fifteen-man unit set up a machine gun in a Filipino shack about 300 yards west of the highway. At 0630, the enemy force launched its surprise attack on the Buri strip. It was lead by a traitorous Filipino who was later captured and turned over to the Filipino guerrillas for swift justice.

The Japanese broke into the service units' bivouac area around Buri while most of the men were still asleep. The enemy bayoneted some of the American soldiers in their bunks or before they could grab their weapons. Some who could get to their weapons held off the Japanese until they could run out of the area, many clad only in underwear and without shoes. These men ran up to the road or up the bluff to the Headquarters of the 5th Bomber Command. After the 11th Airborne Division Headquarters found out about the attack, it radioed XXIV Corps that the service troops "were firing at everything that moves and . . . probably inflicting casualties among our troops." What was left of the attacking forces of the Japanese 16th Division entrenched themselves in the woods north of the Buri airstrip.

General Hodge, meantime, had ordered the CG of the 96th Division to turn over the 1st Battalion of the 382d Infantry to the operational control of General Swing and to send the battalion south along the Dagami-Burauen road. A reinforced company of the 382d was already in the area north of Buri.

On 5 December, Lt. Col. Robert MacCleave with part of the regimental headquarters of the 187th plus Lt. Col. George Pearson's 1st Battalion of the 187th, less C Company, which had parachuted and marched into the hills the day before, had moved up from Bito Beach to San Pablo airstrip. Colonel Hildebrand, CO of the 187th, had gone separately to Division Headquarters for orders. Wrote Chief Warrant Officer Nelson, 1st Battalion, 187th,

As had the troops of the 2d Battalion, we of the 1st goggled at the wide variety of service units, glumly settled into the mud of countless bivouacs along the Dulag-Burauen Road. Long since we have learned that there were more than a hundred such camps . . . and they were all immobilized, scarcely able to meet their own supply needs.

Moreover, the fighter squadrons of the 5th Air Force were moribund, trapped in the ooze of their operations fields. The only planes still functioning in the San Pablo area seemed to be our little resupply "Cubs" which puttered in and out on their vital supply missions. Protection of this entire service area fell to the responsibility of the 11th Airborne Division, and the First of the 187th was the single infantry battalion immediately available to the Division commander for the task. Weakened by detachments, we numbered at the time exactly fourteen officers and two hundred and ten men.

The 11th Airborne staff had been alerted to the possibility of a Japanese airborne attack somewhere on Leyte. Hank Burgess wrote recently,

On the evening of December 4th or 5th 1944, at this point I can't recall the exact date, I was the Duty officer in the evening when a coded message entitled "Alamo Report" was received by the Communications Section advising a force of Japanese paratroopers had left Formosa the day before for airfields in Luzon, which were then in Japanese possession. It was believed that they would jump in Leyte to recapture the airfields at Burauen. Not knowing what "Alamo Report" was but sensing that it must be important, I took it to Swing, who immediately came into the operations tent and spent a great deal of time looking at the maps of the area and determining what might be done if the Japanese did attack our areas of responsibility. He was excited and related that an "Alamo Report" was top secret and reliable.

The only combat infantry unit quickly available to the Division at either Bito Beach or Burauen was the 1st Battalion of the 187th . . . which was the Division reserve. A 155 mm. artillery battalion of Marines and a battalion of tanks that had been stuck in the mud were within several miles of Division Headquarters and close to 5th Air Force Headquarters. All of the troops in the area were under the command of Colonel Hildebrand. . . .

Early on the morning of 6 December, after General Swing had become aware of the situation around Buri, he briefed Colonel Pearson and then directed him to take a platoon and fly it to Buri in the division liaison planes. He also directed him to have the rest of his battalion follow on foot. Colonel Pearson went back to San Pablo, selected the platoon, and, with Maj. Hank Burgess, who was the acting G-3 because Doug Quandt was at Manarawat with General Pierson, flew up to Buri. The liaison planes had to make three rounds-trips each to ferry the platoon,

Pearson, and Burgess. On the strip, they were met by a group of very excited service troops and Air Corps men.

After Colonel Pearson calmed them down enough to get some idea of what had happened in the early morning hours at Buri, he left Capt. Sterling R. Nesbitt and one squad on the strip to give it some security. Then he divided the rest of the platoon into three patrols to comb the area west to the Dagami-Burauen road. He told the patrol leaders to reassemble in the Service Battalion bivouac area after they had completed their missions. Wrote Chief Warrant Officer Nelson,

> Up until the time Colonel Pearson was guided to a neighboring signal service battalion bivouac, he had believed that the Jap assault was made by a small combat patrol. Now he was to see mute and sickening evidence that the Japs had attacked in considerable force. The signal camp was deserted—deserted except for several tents full of soldiers who lay on their bunks, still sacked up in their mosquito netting—dead and horribly so. Forty bodies were counted there, and all had been clubbed or bayoneted to death while they slept.

Occasionally, Colonel Pearson could hear firing from the direction in which he had sent the patrols. In about half an hour, the patrols reported to him in the Engineer Battalion bivouac area. Lieutenant Paul G. Bashore reported that his patrol had killed eighteen of the enemy and that another patrol had accounted for eight more. Colonel Pearson was now convinced that there must be many more of the enemy in the area of Buri.

At about 0900, the rest of the battalion arrived at Buri after a muddy march from San Pablo. Colonel Pearson now had just 180 men present for duty against the remnants of the 16th Division. He prepared to attack. Wrote the 187th historian,

> None of us will ever forget the denseness of the jungle growth to the north and east of our rendezvous. Tall, thick bamboo; sago palms; dense rain forest—in fact all the lush, treacherous vegetation of the tropics covered the area and the Japs could have concealed a very large force indeed within its depths.
>
> The battalion formed in lines of skirmishers, two-yard intervals between men, and advanced to the northeast. Not five minutes after we entered the jungle, we flushed our quarry and a series of gun-fights ensued at point-blank range. Occasionally we'd break through the underbrush into

the open of flooded rice paddies, where we'd see Nips floating face down-
ward in the water, apparently dead. Prodded with bayonets, most of them
would prove plenty lively until we ran them through and they became
real corpses.

For two hours, the battalion continued to grope and fight its way
through the steaming jungle to the north of the strip, attacking the Japanese
soldiers in their defenses, often in hand-to-hand combat and at close
range where grenades and bayonets were the weapons of choice. Finally,
Colonel Pearson called a halt to check his men and their situation. The
company commanders reported a total kill of eighty-five of the enemy
while suffering only two wounded themselves. One, Sergeant McKenna,
had his backside creased. This was the first combat mission for the 1st
of the 187th.

General Swing landed in a Cub plane at Buri during the 1st of the
187th's fight to the north. Captain Nesbitt reported to him and gave
him a rundown on what was happening. General Swing told Nesbitt to
join the battalion and to tell Colonel Pearson to "take up positions
along the Dagami-Burauen road and keep it open and to look to his
west from which we soon expect plenty of trouble."

In line with these orders, Colonel Pearson deployed his small battalion
along the road, with A and B Companies on line and the battalion
command post, covered by a section of heavy machine guns, on a small
mound nearby in the engineer bivouac area. Colonel Pearson had arrived
at Buri under the impression that his mission was to be one of reconnaissance and would last only a few hours. Since he had been impressed
with the need for speed, he had ordered the battalion to leave heavy
equipment, packs, and mess equipment at San Pablo. Lieutenant Carlson,
the mortar platoon commander, had no mortars; he took his section
down the road to an ordnance depot and borrowed two mortars and
ammunition. It turned out to have been an auspicious move.

At 1500, Colonel Pearson sent Lieutenant Hanna and a patrol to
gain contact with the 1st Battalion of the 382d Infantry of the 96th
Division to the north of Buri. "An hour later," according to Chief
Warrant Officer Nelson, "a great deal of activity was noted in the hill
to our West. Observers from the companies (along the road) estimated
that there were several hundred men in that area and believed them to
be Japs. Later it was found that the force numbered between ten and
twelve hundred men. When a patrol from B Company determined defi-

nitely that the observed force was Japanese, the battalion commander called for and got artillery fire placed on the Nips.'' Unfortunately, the fire soon lifted because, said Division Headquarters, ''it was landing smack on the boundary between divisions and there was a probability that the target area was occupied by troops of the 96th Division.''

All afternoon, the battalion was harassed by sniper fire, but by 1800 the 1st of the 187th had driven the enemy back from Buri airstrip, although a few pockets of Japanese still remained around the edges of the strip. Recalled Chief Warrant Officer Nelson,

Soon it was twilight, and except for the raucous chorus of night birds and insects, inevitable in the tropics, all was quiet. No packs and no rations and we didn't know when we'd get them up. Grimly we eyed those hills toward the west and dug our slit trenches deeper. Troopers on the rims of the perimeters squinted down their final protective lines and diligently cut away brush and kunai to lengthen their fire lanes. The lads inside the perimeters sharpened their knives and checked their grenades. Squad leaders circulated around and were free with their advice. Don't get trigger happy—don't advertise your positions with tracer bullets—you men on the perimeter, use your grenades—you men inside, don't use grenades—if the Japs come inside the perimeter, use your knives and bayonets.

The 1st Battalion of the 187th settled in for the night. Its false tranquility was soon to be shattered.

On the evening of 6 December, Michael J. Kalamas, a member of the aerial resupply team, and a friend of his were washing their mess kits after supper. The mess tent was on the north side of the Bayug strip, about halfway between the ends of the runway. Kalamas recalls,

The next moment, the peaceful, warm evening erupted in complete bedlam. Incendiary bombs were exploding all around us. The noise was deafening, and pieces of white hot magnesium were flying through the air and covering the ground like so many hailstones.

We stood in our tracks not knowing what to do, and, as I looked skyward, I could see several bombers overhead. I expected them to return and make another run, possibly with something harder this time. I yelled to my friend, and I took off running to my tent to get my carbine and steel helmet. Trying not to step on any of the burning fragments, we discovered that the roof of the tent was filled with holes from the hot magnesium and was all over the dirt floor.

I couldn't locate my web belt, so I grabbed my carbine and helmet and I went out the back way, with my friend on my heels. I was heading for the safety of the trees, but before we got there, we heard the loud whine of an aircraft engine. Out of the corner of my eye, I saw a fighter plane diving in our direction, with guns belching fire. I dove into a nearby ditch, and my friend landed on top of me. The barrel of my carbine dug into the ground, so I tried to find a stick to unplug it. Seconds later, the Jap fighter zoomed back into the sky from where it had come, and by then I was able to clear the barrel.

We stood up to see what else was happening. Two men were near our tent, looking at the trees at the far end of the airstrip and they were yelling that they had seen a lot of parachutes coming down in that area. I asked who they were, and he said he thinks they may have been Japanese. And with that, they took off across the runway running as fast as they could.

Kalamas and his friend ran into an officer on the north side of the strip. They got into a jeep and tried to make it across the runway. Just as they broke into a clearing near the strip, they could see men coming down the strip in their direction. Recalls Kalamas,

They were singing and shouting and carrying on, and we knew all at once that they were not our guys. The officer driving the jeep put it into reverse and headed back to the brush north of the strip. Then the jeep bogged down in a marsh.

The officer jumped out and said, "Let's go." With that, he headed out towards the runway. Stumbling through the brush, we emerged into the clearing, very close to where most of the aircraft were sitting. The three of us stood still in silence, watching as we tried to catch our breath.

Everything was on fire. The drums of gasoline were burning. Also the two supply tents, on the other side of the runway. The planes farther away from us were also on fire, and a couple of Japanese soldiers were tossing hand grenades into the cockpits, as they were heading in our direction.

Kalamas and two friends headed west and ran into a guard from a U.S. unit who took them in for the night. The next morning, they made their way to the 11th Airborne CP. They reported to the operations tent, thinking that they were bringing surprising news. In fact, the Japanese paratroopers had been more visible to the men around the division CP than they had been to the men around the Bayug strip.

Private First Class Mort Ammerman was in B Company of the 188th Glider Infantry Regiment and, on 6 December, he was in a four-man team on an outpost guarding a bridge in the Burauen area. Their outpost was some miles distant from their company perimeter. Sergeant Harrell was in charge. The other two men were Holloway and Hooper. About dusk on the 6th, Mort Ammerman remembers that he and his outpost crew

. . . saw many aircraft flying overhead—at their altitude and in the subdued light conditions—we assumed that they were C-47's and recall that we thought some unit of the 11th AB was making a night jump. . . .

We set up arrangements for guard duty and sleep, and thought no more of the aircraft that had flown almost directly above us. It was raining, and I was sleeping under my blanket on one end of the bridge—estimate between midnight and one A.M. Holloway was also on sleep assignment—Hooper and Sgt. Harrell were presumably awake on guard duty.

I suddenly awoke, resultant of hearing a burst of automatic weapon fire, and almost simultaneously felt sharp pain in my lower legs—and figured that I had been hit (correctly). I rolled off the edge of the bridge onto the creekbed below—just a short drop. It was pitch black out—and raining hard—and like a damned fool, unable to locate my M-1 rifle which had been next to me while sleeping. I crawled under the bridge and pulled out my trench knife—at that moment I figured that it was the end of the end, as I heard Sgt. Harrell groaning—he was dying, and there was no word from either Hooper or Holloway.

I believed at that moment that of the four of us, I was the only one left alive and anticipated further assault by the enemy. I recall the blackness of the night around me—could see absolutely nothing.

Several minutes passed and I heard no further firing or movement. Sgt. Harrell—somewhere close by was still alive—I could hear him groaning and knew he had to have been hit badly—then I heard somebody whispering above me on the bridge: "Anybody alive?" It sounded like Holloway and it was.

I could not stand due to my leg wounds—whispered to Holloway to extend his rifle barrel down to me and haul me up on the bridge. He did so. I groped around in the darkness—located my rifle and ammo. Told Holloway to move to the far end of the bridge with his weapon and cover from there while I crawled to the closed end of the bridge to cover from that end. . . . I heard no more signs of life from Sgt. Harrell, but located Hooper lying on the bridge nearby. He was quiet and still and did not respond to my whispered queries—I assumed correctly that he was no longer alive. Evidently, Sgt. Harrell was dead also.

At daybreak, Holloway ran back to the perimeter, and in about half an hour, trucks carrying Captain Mayberry and men from B Company of the 188th arrived at the bridge site. They dismounted and sprayed the foliage on both sides of the road with rifle and automatic weapons fire. An ambulance with the company hauled Ammerman to a hospital; later he was evacuated to Guadalcanal but rejoined the 188th on Luzon.

At dusk on 6 December, some of the division staff were just sitting down to supper in the mess tent when they heard the drone of aircraft overhead. They all ran outside to see a number of transport planes— C-47s, they thought—flying low almost directly overhead. The cabin lights in the planes were on, and each plane had a man standing in the door. Henry Burgess turned to the officer next to him and said, "You count the planes and I'll count the jumpers." Burgess guessed that about 250 paratroopers had jumped on the San Pablo strip.

What the men of the 11th Airborne Division had been witnessing from various scattered points around the Burauen area was the airborne phase of General Yamashita's plan to recapture the airfields in the Burauen-Dulag area. The schedule called for the transports to begin dropping paratroopers at 1840 on 6 December with an escort of fighters whose mission was to neutralize the airstrips. Just before the jump, medium bombers were slated to strafe the Buri, San Pablo, and Bayug strips. At the same time, light bombers were to hit AA positions between Dulag and Burauen. The Japanese assigned a total of fifty-one aircraft to the operation.

Just before dark, as planned, thirty-nine enemy transports with fighter and bomber escorts roared over the Burauen area. The bombers dropped several incendiary bombs on the San Pablo strip, setting a gasoline dump on fire and burning a liaison plane. Fighters raced up and down the strips, strafing as they went. Eighteen of the planes were shot down by U.S. antiaircraft guns. The commander of the 3d Parachute Regiment jumped with about 60 of his men on the Buri strip; between 250 and 300 Japanese paratroopers landed near San Pablo. The Japanese transports destined to drop paratroopers at Tacloban were shot down by antiaircraft fire; the transports assigned to Dulag crash-landed and killed all the paratroopers.

At the San Pablo strip, the Japanese paratroopers landed and unsnapped their parachute harnesses. The Japanese version of the parachute had a harness with a quick release, apparently not totally trustworthy. Some men of the 11th reported seeing paratroopers falling to their deaths when the quick releases sprang open on opening shock. Later, in another peculiarity, the 11th troopers found, on the bodies of the Japanese paratroopers, bottles of liquor whose labels indicated that they were for use only in flight.

For assembling on the ground after the drop, the Japanese used a system of bells, whistles, horns, and even distinctive songs for the smaller units. At the San Pablo strip, the Japanese paratroopers talked in loud voices and allegedly yelled slogans, to include: "Everything is resistless. Surrender, Surrender. The great Japanese Army is descending. Everything is resistless." And, "Hello. Where are your machine guns?"

The paratroopers who landed to the west of the San Pablo strip were midway between that strip and Bayug. After landing, they spread out. Some of them moved down both sides of the San Pablo strip and others moved off to the west to Bayug.

At the Bayug strip, the enemy paratroopers set fire to a number of the liaison planes that the 11th needed so desperately to keep the troops in the hills supplied. They moved into the bivouac area of the men who manned the resupply site and destroyed the camp. On the strip at the time of the attack were some seventy-five American officers and men. Most of them dug in and defended the south side of the strip until morning. Captain Felix H. Coune, from Headquarters of the 11th Airborne Division Artillery, was killed when he tried to move to the south side of the strip. Another patient but thoroughly frightened pilot spent fourteen hours lying in a drainage ditch while the enemy walked around and about him. For Capt. David Carnahan, the commander of the aerial resupply operation on Bayug airstrip, his greatest loss was his prized air mattress.

At the San Pablo strip, the Japanese ran up the north and south sides of the runway and assembled on the north side. They burned three or four more liaison planes, a jeep, several tents, and a gasoline dump, on which, for some effect or other, they threw ammunition. The only U.S. troops in the area were elements of the 127th Engineers, a portion of the 511th Signal Company, Headquarters Battery of Division Artillery, and parts of the 408th QM Company, the 711th Ordnance Company, and some Air Corps service troops. According to Capt. Charles Bellows, who made a report of the paratrooper landings to the G-3 of XXIV Corps, "There was uncontrolled and disorganized firing and much difficulty arose in establishing a co-ordinated command."

Notwithstanding that comment, during the night of 6 to 7 December,

Lt. Paul J. Pergamo and a platoon from the 127th, armed with three machine guns, succeeded in scattering a group of the enemy and then dug in on the southwest corner of the strip on some slightly higher ground. The Japanese charged the position three times during the night; Pergamo and his engineers repulsed all three of the attacks with "heavy loss to the attackers." One of the attacks came within fifteen feet of the position before the Japanese withdrew. At dawn, most of the paratroopers who had jumped on San Pablo assembled and moved north and west to the northern edge of the Buri strip and joined parts of the Japanese 16th Division.

At Buri, Sgt. Jack S. Blessing and an assistant were just getting out of L-4s when the paratroopers landed. They were bringing much needed radio equipment to the 1st of the 187th west of the strip. Sergeant Blessing was killed, but his assistant managed to make it to the perimeter. At daybreak, Pfc Joe E. Rangel, B Company, 187th, was found dead under two of the enemy, one of whom he had knifed. The other had apparently held a grenade to Rangel's back.

During daylight of 7 December, the Japanese sniper fire increased on elements of the 1st of the 187th, who killed three of the enemy in a supply tent near the battalion CP. In the medical aid station, Capt. Hans Cohn, the battalion surgeon, was working on a wounded man. A sniper shot a plasma bottle out of his hand. He calmly lowered his patient into a slit trench and continued his work.

Early in the morning of 7 December, Lt. Col. Douglas C. Davis, CO of the 127th Airborne Engineer Battalion, gathered together the miscellaneous service troops of the division, including some units from his own battalion, into a composite force to protect the San Pablo strip.

Michael Kalamas and his friend had arrived at the 11th Airborne CP at daybreak on 7 December. One of the staff officers told Kalamas that the airstrip would have to be retaken as soon as possible. Kalamas recalled,

> We would move out immediately and pick up anyone along the way. The new arrivals headed for the strip in single file and we followed them.
>
> As the last of us were crossing the road, I heard the sound of an airplane and there in the distance came a Jap fighter. As soon as I heard the gun fire, I dove beneath a truck parked along the road and watched as the machine gun bullets tore up the dirt in front of me. He was quickly gone and I got up to see if he would be back.

The fighter made a turn to make another run, and then from another direction, a P-38 came to the rescue. He headed straight for the Jap Zero, which then turned tail, and tried to get away. Tracers from the P-38 seemed to follow him, and suddenly the Zero seemed to stop. It turned over, very slowly like a dead bird, and fell toward the ground with a trail of smoke lingering in the sky. The P-38 headed back in our direction, did a couple of barrel rolls and was gone.

Sometime late on the night of 6 December, it became clear to General Swing that the enemy airborne attack was more than a simple suicide demolition mission or a reconnaissance. Accordingly, he ordered Lt. Col. Lukas E. Hoska, Jr., CO of the 674th Glider Field Artillery Battalion, to leave his pack 75s on Bito Beach and to move to San Pablo as soon as possible. General Swing charged Lt. Col. James Farren and what men he had left from the 152d Airborne AA Battalion with the defense of the division CP. No Japanese, however, approached the CP's perimeter.

At daylight on 7 December, Colonel Davis and his multibranched force started to move out to attack across the San Pablo strip to clear it of the enemy and to relieve the troops, some of whom were from his own A Company, who had been caught in and around the strip. Just as he was about to launch his attack, Colonel Hoska and his glider artillerymen, turned infantry overnight, arrived in DUKWs. They dismounted hastily, and, armed only with their carbines, moved on line to the right of Davis's troops. General Swing, meantime, had arrived on the scene. Wrote the division historian,

To anyone who had read of the Civil War battles, the similarity of this morning's fight will immediately become apparent. On the left were the engineers, drawn up along the southern edge of the strip. On the right was the artillery, similarly drawn up in battle formation. . . . In the center, between the two outfits was General Swing, shouting as he directed the two commanders in the attack. They in turn bellowed at their units, and the attack moved off. The Japs were holed up all around the strip, but initially the strongest resistance was met in front of the engineers. However, by maneuvering his companies, Colonel Davis succeeded in pushing across the strip and three hundred yards north of the airstrip. . . . Behind them, dead Japanese were removed from the strip, and the few L-4 planes remaining after the Japanese attack immediately took off, harassed by sniper fire, to deliver much needed supplies to the mountain troops.

After advancing across the runway, the engineers ran out of ammunition. The 674th moved forward to a coconut grove to the north of the strip. Colonel Davis closed the gap between the two units with a strong patrol, and that evening the two ersatz infantry outfits went into a tight perimeter. They remained in that area in defense of San Pablo for the next few days.

Lieutenant Leo Crawford was a platoon leader in C Company of the 188th. Prior to the Japanese parachute assault, the 188th had been patrolling an area from Bugho to La Paz. Crawford remembers,

When the Jap paratroopers dropped we were in a quiet area. One plane load of Japs missed their drop zone and had brought the rear areas (around Bito Beach) almost to a stop. No traffic, etc. We never saw a live Jap. A couple of shots were fired at us from some trees and, in true Ft. Benning style, I had some men establish a firebase while others went around the flank. When we reached the place we thought the shots came from, whoever fired was gone. Later that day we met a Filipino carrying a Japanese paratrooper's head with the cloth helmet still on it. . . . The Filipino spoke little English but we finally determined that the Jap had been wounded (by us?) and had come to the Filipino's hut wanting tubik (water). When the Jap was off guard he took his head off with a bolo. It was a nice neat job. We were unable to locate any more Japs and returned to the battalion. Evidently all of them were trying to rejoin the main group and had left the area. It was amazing how much those few paratroopers had brought things to a standstill in the rear areas.

Near Buri, the 1st of the 187th had moved west along the Dagami-Burauen road on 6 December. By the middle of the morning of the next day, the Japanese who had jumped near Buri had completely occupied the undefended strip. They took advantage of arms and ammunition abandoned by the Air Corps and other service troops who had left the area abruptly. Second Lieutenant Rudolph Mamula of the 767th Tank Battalion had been charged with recovering the abandoned weapons and ammunition but had not been able to do so.

When General Krueger had learned of the Japanese airborne attacks, he requested that General MacArthur release to him elements of the 38th Division that had just landed and were to stage on Leyte for "future operations." General Headquarters (GHQ) assigned the 149th Infantry to Sixth Army; on 6 December, General Krueger in turn assigned two battalions of the 149th to General Hodge; he, in turn, put the two battalions under the operational control of General Swing for use against the Japanese paratroopers in the Burauen area. At 0200 on 7 December, General Swing ordered the two battalions of the 149th to the San Pablo strip. They arrived in the early afternoon of the seventh.

General Swing met the advanced elements of the 1st Battalion of the 149th and said, according to Maj. Martin C. Grigg of the 1st Battalion, 149th Infantry, "Glad to see you. I am General Swing of the 11th Airborne Division. We've been having a hell of a time here. Last night approximately seventy-five Jap paratroopers dropped on us of which we have accounted for about fifty. Fifteen hundred yards from here on an azimuth of 273 degrees is another airstrip just like this one. Between here and there are about twenty-five Jap troopers. It is now 1400. I want that strip by nightfall."

The men of the 1st of the 149th moved out at 1430 and covered the first few hundred yards with no difficulty. Then they came to a swamp through which they had to wade, shoulder deep in some places. The companies lost contact with one another in the swamp. A Company arrived at Buri at about 1630, but C Company, which had had a brief firefight, did not get to the south side of the strip until 1800. Because it was so late and because they had run into more Japanese than General Swing had allegedly told them about, they dug in for the night.

After the Japanese parachute attack on the Buri strip, General Swing ordered the 1st of the 187th to clear the strip as soon as possible. During the morning of 7 December, the battalion, still northwest of the Bayug strip, had taken machine gun fire from a platoon west of the Dagami-Burauen road. The battalion held this force in check while Colonel Pearson organized an attack on the strip to the east. The 1st of the 382d had arrived in the area at 0930; at 0945, the two battalions attacked toward the Buri airfield. Lieutenant Carter and his A Company, 187th, led the attack. Twice, Lieutenant Pickle's platoon of A Company fought its way to a precarious foothold on the northwest corner of the strip; twice they were blasted off by heavy enemy fire. Companies A and B of the 382d also advanced aggressively but faltered when the company commander of A Company was wounded. Colonel Pearson decided to withdraw both battalions to the north to consider another avenue of approach.

He made a personal reconnaissance around the west end of the Buri strip and crawled to within fifty yards of the enemy positions. He decided that he could move up a ravine on the west and then move south to a clearing on the south side of the strip. Here he could get supporting fire from Lt. Clayton B. Farnsworth's heavy machine guns and Lieutenant Carlson's mortars.

The attack moved off at 1400, but the ravine had already been booby-trapped by the Japanese. Then the attack moved south. Farnsworth and his eleven men set up their machine guns a few feet from the edge of the landing strip. He remembers:

> The Japs were thicker than flies around what planes they had taken from our Air Corps men. They did not expect our presence from that point, and most of them seemed to be busy stripping guns and ammunition from our planes. Several Japs were carrying them [the guns] across the open airstrip to the point where we had been trying to make a break onto the strip all morning.
>
> There are two things which I think made it possible for me to get those two machine gun crews so close to the edge of the air strip when there were so many Japs in plain sight.
>
> The biggest help was from the fact that when we ran over the top of the hill about a hundred feet from the edge of the strip . . . Colonel George Pearson was with us. This put a good heart in the men and they figured that if a Lt. Col. could be up there, then they could also.

When Farnsworth's men had the machine guns only partially set up, three Japanese jumped up from the grass about thirty feet to their front. Fortunately, they did not have their weapons ready to fire. Farnsworth told the men to keep setting up the machine guns and that he would take care of "the three Japs." With his first shot, three more of the enemy popped up out of the grass. None of them had a weapon ready, and Farnsworth, a superb shot, took them under fire. He recalls,

> These six shots were the fastest six that I have ever fired at anything. In the matter of less than a minute, the crews had the guns operating. As to how effective their fire was, I cannot say. They may have only scored on a couple dozen or so or it could easily have been several times that many. I did catch the first burst out of the corner of my eye and it was directly in line with a bunch of Japs hurrying across the strip. The tracer bullets showed the fire a little low but the bullets ricocheting from that hard air strip floor should have been more deadly than if it had been directly into the enemy.

Farnsworth left the machine gun firing up to his crews and crawled over to an old foxhole nearby. It was deep enough for him to stand

and to rest his arms on the top, making a perfect platform from which he could shoot well-aimed fire. In the next three minutes, he got off five shots. From his position, he could spot the enemy soldiers through the scope of his rifle as soon as they raised their heads. But his luck did not hold. He took a Japanese rifle shot through the stock of his rifle, which not only shattered his rifle stock but also a bone in his right arm. He used his belt as a tourniquet to stop the flow of blood.

After the machine guns had been firing for about fifteen minutes, the crews ran out of ammunition. Two men crawled to the rear to get more. They came back with the word that Farnsworth was to withdraw his machine guns. "After having a clear look across the strip this seemed like a heartbreaking thing to do," Farnsworth said later, "but we lifted the guns from their cradles and started to drag them back. That is, the men did it, I had all I could do to drag myself."

On the way to the rear, the crews began to take fire from behind them. Private Miller, crawling along with a tripod on his back, came to a palm log that formed a barrier across his path. Instead of crawling around it, he tried to make a dash across it. A burst of fire picked him off. The bullets continued to kick up dirt around him after he had fallen.

Farnsworth's crews suffered the loss of Private Miller and, they thought, of Sergeant MacKenna, and the wounding of four others on their return to the rear. Sergeant MacKenna's helmet was perforated with .50-caliber bullets, and he fell in the mud, apparently dead. He was left where he lay. As Farnsworth and his men tried to move back to the area with the rest of the battalion, the enemy closed in around them. Farnsworth directed his men to strip the guns and "destroy their vital parts to keep them from falling into the hands of the Japs." Then Farnsworth signaled his men to withdraw. They dragged their dead and wounded with them.

To the west of Buri, the battalions regrouped, and Colonel Pearson ordered A and B Companies of the 187th to attack abreast to the northeast, and Company A, 382d, to attack due east. The units advanced against heavy fire but, by 1600, were holding a footing at the southwest corner of the strip. By this time, ammunition was low, the troops were out of water, and they were dog-tired. About that time, a liaison plane flew over. The pilot revved back his motor, leaned out, and shouted: "Japs— over there." This was not a particularly surprising revelation to the soldiers on the ground.

That afternoon, a very tall Japanese soldier, hands in the air, walked into the battalion CP. About fifteen feet from where the command group was standing, he leaped for a ditch. Lieutenant Ace Parker shot him between the eyes. The Japanese soldier had three hand grenades attached to his belt.

At 1630, the 1st of the 187th made contact with the 1st of the 149th at the western end of the Buri strip. By dusk, the remainder of the 1st Battalion of the 382d, 96th Division, had arrived and taken up a position near the 1st of the 149th. At 2000, the sector was reportedly quiet.

During the night, the Japanese brought up two machine guns and emplaced them directly in front of A Company of the 382d. At dawn, the guns opened up and their grazing fire pinned down the company. Private First Class Warren G. Perkins, with bullets flying past him, found the guns and called for mortar fire within fifty yards of his position. The mortars silenced the machine guns. Private Ova A. Kelly, in the middle of the confusion, charged the machine gun position with his M-1 and a carbine. He killed eight of the enemy before he was killed. Later, he was awarded the Medal of Honor posthumously. The rest of the company charged after Kelly and secured the edge of the runway where it went into a perimeter defense.

After the 1st Battalion of the 149th arrived in Colonel Pearson's area, he was under the impression that, with the added strength, he could now attack and secure Buri. But that was not to be the case.

The 5th Air Force Headquarters was located on the Burauen-Dulag road a few miles from the 11th Airborne Division CP. It was a "critical area," according to Henry Burgess, "as it was from this location that all of the orders were prepared for the daily bombing and fighter flights over all the Philippines. The office worked twenty-four hours a day with lights on all night inside the buildings and with floodlights shining on the outside of the buildings. . . . Since the 5th Air Force Headquarters was lit up at night and the visibility was so good, it was obvious to the Japanese descending from the mountains that it was an important place and should be attacked."

Late in the afternoon of 7 December, the 11th Division Headquarters sent an order to Colonel Pearson directing him to move his battalion from the Buri area and to defend the 5th Air Force Headquarters. Colonel Pearson thought that there must be some mistake; he radioed the division, which replied that the order was indeed valid and correct. As the battalion was preparing to move south to the vicinity of 5th Air Force Headquarters, Sergeant MacKenna walked into the area under his own power.

At midnight, the 1st of the 187th (still less C Company, which was at Manarawat) arrived in the vicinity of the 5th Air Force Headquarters. The infantrymen found the pilots and staff of the headquarters posting interior guards, "cadet style," with flashlights blinking on and off all around the buildings. Nelson reported that "the flyboys were right happy to see us. They fed us coffee and Spam." The battalion moved into positions, previously occupied by the 2d Battalion of the 187th, about eight hundred yards west of Burauen, on a rise in the foothills of the mountains. They could see a great portion of the Leyte Valley and watch the 149th in its attempt to retake Buri from the very stubborn Japanese.

On 8 December, General Swing ordered Colonel Hildebrand, CO of the 187th, to take charge of all the counterattacking forces in the area of Burauen's three airstrips. On that same day, the 2d Battalion of the 149th joined the 1st near Buri.

At 1045 on 9 December, the 1st Battalion, 149th Infantry, attacked north toward the Buri strip with its three infantry companies on line. They got across the runway but then came under heavy enemy fires from positions that the enemy had dug in on a slope to the north of the strip. The 1st Battalion withdrew to the south of the strip after killing fifty of an enemy force estimated at about two hundred men. The 2d Battalion, 149th, remained in position throughout the day.

The 1st Battalion, 382d Infantry, was still in a position near Buri. At twilight on the ninth, the battalion commander had sent his rifle companies out in a circle around the battalion to locate enemy patrols that were said to be converging on the airfield. Guarding the perimeter in the immediate area were only a few mortar men and headquarters troops. At midnight, approximately 150 Japanese launched an attack on the perimeter. The service troops and headquarters types, armed only with rifles and mortars, stopped the charge. They killed fifty enemy while suffering only seven casualties.

On 10 December, the 1st of the 149th made the final push to seize control of Buri. After a half-hour artillery concentration, the 149th moved out with A and C Companies abreast and B Company in the rear. They crossed the runway, and, 300 yards north of it, A and C moved to the northwest and B went to the northeast. Together, the three companies cleared the airfield of individual Japanese and wiped out some small pockets of resistance. At 1700, the 1st went into a perimeter; Buri airstrip was clear.

But the Japanese were still not finished with the Burauen airfield attacks. On the evening of 10 December, a battalion of the 26th Division came down out of the hills to the west of Burauen. The 26th could muster only that force out of its entire strength and was four days late in arriving at its line of departure for the airfield attacks. One major reason for the delay was that the 26th was coming east on some of the trails over which the 511th Parachute Infantry Regiment was moving to the west.

At 1930, the 26th troops began firing at the buildings of the 5th Air Force; some of the bullets went through the walls of the plywood hut occupied by the 5th Air Force commanding general, Maj. Gen. Ennis C. Whitehead. "The General ducked a bullet, ordered someone to find out who the blankety-blank was responsible and that he'd blankety-blank better stop or think up a blankety-blank good reason," according to Maj. Herbert O. Johansen.

A 5th Air Force staff officer called Lt. Col. Paul V. Kaessner of the 8th Aviation Signal Battalion on the phone. According to Major Johansen, this was the conversation:

> "Colonel, you've got to stop that promiscuous firing down there immediately!"
> "Like to, Sir," answered the colonel, "but the Japs . . ."
> "Japs," shouted the staff officer, "that can't be Japs. The fire is coming from our fifties."
> "That's right . . . and the Japs are doing the shooting!"
> "Where in the hell did the Japs get our machine guns?"
> "How in hell should I know, sir?"
> "The bullets are coming right through the general's quarters."
> "Tell the general to get down on the floor. Incidentally, that yelling you hear is a Banzai raid on our mess hall."

XXIV Corps Headquarters called the 11th Airborne Division Headquarters and notified its staff of the attack on the 5th Air Force Headquarters. XXIV Corps indicated that the 44th Station Hospital was also under attack. "Rumors were rampant," according to one of the 11th Airborne Division staffers. "We heard that the Japs had gotten into the hospitals, were going down the aisles of the wards butchering the patients with sabres, and ruthlessly killing the doctors."

The rumors were highly exaggerated. Lieutenant John G. Hurster, the mess officer of the 1st Battalion, 187th, had set up his kitchen near the 44th, from which he could carry hot meals to the troops in the foothills. The CO of the 44th, rightly concerned about the security of his hospital, had asked Lieutenant Hurster to set up a perimeter around the hospital. Lieutenant Hurster had complied, using his cooks, supply men, and drivers from Headquarters Company of the 187th. On the night of the Japanese attack on 5th Air Force Headquarters and the 44th, Lieutenant Hurster and his assorted, converted infantrymen, armed with their rifles, held their position. The next morning there were nineteen dead enemy around the perimeter. The next morning, Colonel Pearson sent out patrols, which killed another seventeen Japanese in the rice paddies in front of the 44th.

This action by the disorganized remnants of the 26th Division was the last major effort to regain control of the Burauen airstrips.

On 7 December, the 77th Division had landed amphibiously just below Ormoc on Leyte's west coast. On about 10 December, General Suzuki, the Japanese commander of forces on Leyte, learned of the landings. He had moved to an area near Burauen to command the airfield operation. When he heard of the Ormoc landings, he recognized the importance of holding Ormoc at all costs. He therefore cancelled all operations against the Burauen strips and ordered all troops who had been involved with the failed attack to move to Ormoc Valley. The return through the mountains was difficult. The Japanese had lost all command unity; those who got through the 511th in the hills and through the muddy trails did so individually.

"The Japanese had failed to achieve any major objective," according to M. Hamlin Cannon. "The air transports allotted to Tacloban were destroyed by antiaircraft fire, while those destined for Dulag, crash-landed, killing all their occupants. Though they had destroyed minor fuel and supply dumps and a few American aircraft, delayed airfield construction, and isolated 5th Air Force Headquarters for five days, they had not appreciably delayed the Leyte operation."

General Swing recognized that the division's final effort on Leyte would be the push to the west and the linkup with the 7th and 77th Divisions on the west coast. On 9 December, he told General Pierson and Doug Quandt to return to the CP at Burauen, ostensibly so that he could move to the Manarawat location. "Quandt and I and a small patrol made the return trek along awesome trails to the division CP," according to General Pierson. "We returned to the division CP about three days after the Japanese attack. . . . Gen. Swing flew up to Manarawat shortly after our return . . . and just before Haugen made his final push at Anas."

The 11th Airborne and the 149th Regiment had had their baptism of fire. Neither unit had landed on Leyte expecting to be committed to immediate combat. Under the circumstances of the operation, the weather, and the surprise Japanese paratrooper attack on relatively thinly defended areas, the troops acquitted themselves superbly. Further tests were in the immediate offing.

CHAPTER 10

CLEARING THE MOUNTAINS

The 11th Airborne Division diary for most of December starts off each day with much the same entry: "Frequent showers during the day, with the weather mostly cloudy. Periods of good visibility were limited."

The constant rains and the low clouds frequently grounded the division's "biscuit bomber" fleet of L-4s and L-5s, with the result that the troops in the mountains were without sufficient food, ammunition, medical supplies, new boots, and field uniforms. For many days, three men made do with one K ration per day. Platoon leaders rationed ammunition, which the riflemen counted by the bullet rather than the clip. In the incessant mud, fatigues became soaked and rotten, and mud sloshed over the tops of boots whose soles rotted after a few days of forced marches. The night air was penetratingly cold, especially to the troops who slept in their muddy foxholes in their wet clothes and boots. Men wrapped up in ponchos at night and steam-dried while they tried to sleep. Some men went for days without taking off their fatigues or their boots. Dry socks were a luxury; a clean shave and hot bath were what dreams were made of.

When B Company of the 511th arrived back at Manarawat, General Pierson was still there with the division forward CP. Bert Marshall remembers meeting General Pierson near the general's "old shack."

The whole place was so muddy, and our boots were all muddy and wet, including our socks. One guy took off his boots, he took off his socks, and drained all the water out of his boots. Then he said, "Boy, I would give anything for a dry pair of socks." We looked up, and who was standing behind us but General Pierson, and he took off and went up to his little shack, and we all kept talking about how everything was all wet and how our feet were soaked and everything. A little while later, here came General Pierson standing behind us, and he threw a kid a pair of socks, and said, "Here is a dry pair of socks for you." That really impressed me about General Pierson and I thought, Boy, he is really a big man.

While the Japanese attacks and the U.S. counterattacks near the Burauen airstrips were in progress, elements of the 511th Parachute Infantry were slogging their difficult and hazardous way through a pass southeast of Mahonag.[1] Lieutenant Colonel Harry Wilson's 2d Battalion of the 187th had hiked up a trail from the Burauen heights to relieve Lt. Col. Norman M. Shipley's 2d Battalion, 511th, north of Anonang. Haugen ordered Shipley to follow the North Trail to Anas. The 11th Airborne G-2, Lt. Col. Henry "Butch" Muller, thought that this trail might lead to the long-sought Japanese supply trail. The main mission of the 11th Airborne Division was now to fight its way to the west coast through the mountains and link up with the other elements of Sixth Army fighting along the west coast, north of Albuera and generally along the Talisayan River.

The 2d Battalion of the 187th, like the battalions of the 511th that had preceded it, had extremely difficult terrain to overcome in its march up into the hills from the Burauen area. Chief Warrant Officer Nelson reported,

There was just one trail, so the battalion was strung out in single file. Every inch of the trail was slippery and the going was hot and tough as we crossed the flooded rice fields west of Burauen. This part of the move was pleasant strolling compared to the mountain trails we were about to encounter.

Once in them, it was a nightmare of climbing straight up the sides of sheer cliffs, cutting foot-holds as we went, pulling ourselves up by the vines along the trail. Foot by foot we scaled the greasy heights and

---

[1] Sometimes spelled Majunag.

a slip would have plunged one to his death on the rocks below. Reaching the crests, we'd catch our breath, then slip and slide down the other face of the height only to be met with the necessity of crossing a raging mountain river in the canyon below. Sometimes the trails would wind a few hundred yards along the beds, then veer sharply upward across another slippery ridge; then there'd be another rampaging river to cross. Somebody said that he counted thirty such stream-crossings between Burauen and Anonang. We don't know if that's true, but we do remember that the water was sometimes neck-deep, that we had to clutch the belt of the file in front of us to keep from being washed away and dashed to a grisly end on the rocks downstream. We do remember holding our weapons aloft with our free arms to keep them dry and clean in the streams.

Late in the afternoon of 3 December, the 2d of the 187th reached Anonang, a *cammote* and green corn patch with one rickety shack in the middle of the clearing. Colonel Wilson ordered Capt. George Ori and his F Company to occupy an old 511th outpost, two thousand yards to the northwest of the battalion perimeter at Anonang. The position commanded a view of a strong Japanese position on a plateau below. It took F Company three hours to climb up to the 511th's old outpost. When Ori reached the top of this hill, he found a phone line from the position to Anonang still workable, and Ori could call for mortar fire when he needed it. On the night of 3 December, the Japanese hit Ori's perimeter, and the phone line was a great help in bringing fire onto the attacking Japanese. F Company suffered no casualties.

On 4 December, Captain Ori decided to feel out the Japanese position. Lieutenant Kneebone's platoon led the probe and shortly broke out of the main forest into an opening stretching to the north. As soon as the platoon was in the clear, the enemy blasted it with machine gun fire sited along taped-out lanes. Kneebone and two of his men, including Sergeant Newsome, who would die that night, were hit. The enemy tried to counterattack, and Ori ordered the platoon to withdraw. F Company had run up against a very strong Japanese force on a hill that, sometime later, would become known as "Purple Heart Hill."

Butch Muller had fairly well determined the locations of the main Japanese forces still remaining within the division sector. One force was just north of Anonang, which the 2d Battalion of the 187th had also just found. The other was west of Mahonag, size unknown. And there were more Japanese retreating to the west after their failure to seize the Burauen, Tacloban, and Dulag airfields.

But even after the debacle of the airfields, the stubborn Yamashita was still not convinced that Leyte was lost. On 7 December, he sent a convoy of fourteen ships to San Isidro in northwest Leyte. Planes of the 5th Air Force sank all of the ships and shot down sixty-four Japanese planes. In spite of those losses, some two to three thousand enemy troops managed to land. On 11 December, planes of the 5th Air Force intercepted a Japanese convoy off Palompon and sank five of the transports, damaged the remaining six, and shot down thirteen enemy planes. The Japanese air effort was rapidly dwindling.

Colonel Lahti's 3d Battalion of the 511th had been at Mahonag since the afternoon of 3 December. On the night of the fifth, a small group of the enemy, using American BARs, tried to infiltrate the perimeter, but Lahti's paratroopers beat off the enemy with small arms and machine gun fire. According to Lieutenant Barnes, the mortar officer of the 3d Battalion,

> In the meantime, regimental headquarters, with most of the 1st Battalion, arrived in the perimeter. . . . The next morning (the sixth), a message was sent from Mahonag to division headquarters that all troops were out of rations; and, if rations, oil, ammunition, and signal supplies were not sent to the positions, we would not be able to continue the attack. By 1700, one C-47 and two liaison planes dropped some ammunition and K rations in a small clearing. During this ration drop, the 81 mortars of the 3d Battalion did their first firing. While the liaison planes would circle the drop zone, they would be fired on from the surrounding jungle by a Jap machine gun. A hurried shift would be made and a few rounds fired in the general direction. This went on for about five minutes. Whether or not any rounds hit or even came close to them is not known, but they soon stopped firing.
>
> On 6 December, the 3d Battalion S-2 section was sent out to reconnoiter a route from Mahonag to Anas to prepare for the advance the following day. This patrol returned with the information that they had discovered a well-developed Jap supply trail that seemed to continue on through the mountains to the west coast.

Colonel Lahti's S-2 had indeed found the long-sought Japanese supply road. In the Mahonag area, the trail was just north of Mahonag and across a river at the base of Mount Mahonag. It was a foot trail that had been widened to jeep width and padded with three- or four-inch logs to form a corrugated road in the muck. The rains had been so heavy, however, that, in some sections of the road, the logs were a foot below the surface of the mud. The trail ended just north of Lubi; its origin on the west coast was just above the Talisayan River. The trail also went north up a ridge line along the west coast of Leyte.

On 7 December, the 511th, less the 2d Battalion, moved out of Mahonag on a drive to the west toward Anas along a trail to the south of the Japanese supply trail. Colonel Shipley's 2d Battalion, 511th, moved out toward Anas following the Japanese supply trail. The interim regimental objective was to cut the supply trail at Anas where it entered the mountains from the west.

Colonel Shipley had left behind Capt. Hobert B. Wade and his E Company to serve as the battalion rear guard with orders to move out the next day. Private First Class Elmer Fryar was in the platoon, led by Lt. Norvin L. Davis, West Point class of January 1943, which would cover E Company's rear. At dawn on 8 December, as the company was preparing to move out, the Japanese hit E Company's perimeter— "a normal Jap morning Banzai attack," according to one of the by-now hardened veterans of the company. "There was no call for anyone to do anything but sit in his foxhole and shoot along the previously planned lanes of fire." But Fryar reacted differently. He crawled out of his foxhole and scrambled to an elevated position behind a log in front of the machine guns of his platoon. From there, he directed accurate fire from the machine guns and mortars and with his own M-1, even though he was being shot at repeatedly by the attacking enemy troops. Shortly, the Japanese attack was broken and thrown back.

During this fight on the perimeter, one of the sergeants in E Company had had his head creased by a Japanese bullet. He rose from his hole and stumbled dazedly away from the company toward the Japanese lines. Enemy snipers opened fire. Fryar got up from his relatively safe position behind the log, ran to the stumbling, wounded sergeant, and hauled him back to safety. Then he dressed the sergeant's wound. E Company continued to withdraw from the position. The Japanese attacked again. Once again, from an exposed position, Fryar fired his M-1 at the attacking enemy and directed the fire of the machine guns and the mortars. And once again the Japanese attack faltered and withdrew. Aid men relieved Fryar of the wounded sergeant, and Fryar rejoined his platoon for the march out. Midway in the platoon column marched Fryar and his platoon leader, Lieutenant Davis. About midmorning, a Japanese sniper arose from a hidden position and took aim at Lieutenant Davis. Without hesitation, Fryar threw himself in front of Davis and took a burst of automatic fire in his chest. He did not die immediately. "As his last act on this earth," one of his friends reported, "he pulled the pin from his belt-carried hand grenade and threw it at the Jap sniper, carefully hidden in the jungle foliage. It was a direct hit. It was, at the same time, the twenty-seventh Jap Elmer had killed that day." Fryar, at age thirty-two, was the oldest paratrooper to win the Medal of Honor during World War II.

When the two battalions of the 511th left Mahonag along the South Trail to Anas, with the 3d Battalion in the lead and the 1st Battalion some days' march behind it, they were very lightly equipped. Wrote Lieutenant Barnes,

> The ration supply had been limited since leaving Manarawat, and when the 3d Battalion started out each man had two days ration, consisting of four boxes of K's per man. All the small arms that a man could reasonably carry were issued and, in addition, each man had two or three hand grenades. The 81 mortar platoon of Headquarters Company carried two complete mortars, and each man who was not carrying part of a mortar carried two rounds of H.E. light ammunition. No ammunition bags were available and the men were left to carry the bulky rounds as best they could. The platoon carried around 30 rounds.

The 511th's route to Anas was along yet another undefined and uncharted trail through barrios that might appear, on the vague maps, in the 511th's area but that in reality might be ten miles to the north— or south. According to Lieutenant Barnes, "The trail was even more difficult than the one from Manarawat to Mahonag. The heavy rains had made it ankle deep in mud in some places and dangerously slippery in others. At some places it was necessary to pass the parts of the mortars up to a man on a ledge above, and then, the men had to help one another over the ledge. Frequent breaks were necessary and the movement of the column was very slow."

After the 2d Battalion of the 511th had moved a few thousand yards down the Japanese supply road, it passed through a deep canyon. A swift, wandering stream commanded the center of the gorge, and, on the right side, the supply trail wandered its corduroyed way. Deep in the canyon, the battalion found a Japanese campsite, at least regimental in size. When the 2d Battalion discovered the camp, the Japanese appeared to be in the process of deserting it—whether because of the 2d's advance or perhaps in the enemy's general retreat to the west is uncertain. The

2d Battalion took the camp under attack from two directions and in the ensuing "short and nasty" fight, killed hundreds of the enemy. When the troopers of the 2d Battalion finally overran the campsite, they were appalled at what they found. "Japanese flags were strewn about," one of the troops remembered, "maps, diaries, code books, and cooking utensils lay on the mossy ground of the village among the dead Japanese. Awe-inspiring above all was the sight of the Japanese wounded, deserted in caves and lean-tos on the side of the canyon. Gagged and bound and left to die, these pitiable creatures would have inspired the revolted pity of the fiercest soldier."

But it was in this canyon, between Mahonag and Anas, after the fight was over that the 2d Battalion took a number of casualties from an unexpected and still unidentified source. Corporal James T. Wentink was in the S-2 Section of Headquarters Company of the 2d of the 511th. He remembers that the battalion was on the trail the next morning when he noted that "an artillery spotter plane, L-4 or L-5, was cruising right overhead. I don't think the Japs had small artillery spotter planes in this area. Anyway, a couple of rounds hit ahead, a couple of rounds hit behind, and a couple of rounds came right in the 'pocket.' Captain Jenkins was killed, Peter Kut was killed, Elmer Burgett lost a leg, and Shipley lost a leg. I don't know how many were wounded including men on both sides of myself."

Dean Marks was a machine gunner in the 2d of the 511th. He remembers the shelling of the battalion this way:

> We got about five or ten minutes down the trail when three huge explosions hit our point. Shit, we were being shelled. The first salvo which we didn't hear coming, they were all tree bursts. Casualties were high and very selective, it seemed. Shippo (Colonel Norman Shipley's code name) had a leg ripped half off. Platt (a medic) cut it off on the spot. Captain Jenkins was hit in the upper chest. He lived about a minute. We then heard a distant muffled "boom boom boom." This was salvo number two. We hit the deck. I hid in an undercut in a stream bed right next to a half rotten carabao. The three rounds came in, but up the trail a hundred yards. It was SHZZ-BLAM, almost like a snarl then explosion. That was all we took, six rounds total. Sherlock was hit in the leg. Burgett severely in the leg. Platt or Chambers (the 2d Battalion surgeon) cut it off. A kid from E or F lost an arm and a leg. His name was Hard . . . Hard died. I can't remember all of the wounded. We had to abandon our attack toward Rock Hill. We had at least a dozen dead and close to

forty wounded, some very badly wounded. Platt and Chambers saved a lot of them. Some they couldn't. We finished making litters with ponchos and tree limbs and started back to Mahonag. Other parts of the Sixth Army had landed at Ormoc and chased a good portion of a division back toward us. When we got back to Mahonag, we found that there were Japs in the perimeter we had vacated. D and E pushed them out in a short firefight with help of 2d's 81 mm. mortars. We flopped back into our holes and dragged the dead Japs out into the jungle away from the perimeter so they wouldn't stink up the area. The next few days we found we didn't drag 'em far enough.

Who fired the artillery that devastated the 2d Battalion is difficult to assess. It would be more comforting to the survivors if they knew that it had been enemy artillery. But as James Wentink wrote recently: "Relative to the time we were plastered, very accurately, by our artillery in Leyte, I have given this much thought over the years. I think you may agree that those on the ground, the receiving end, may be able to make better judgments than anyone speculating forty plus years later."

Dean Marks seems to think that it was Japanese artillery. He recalls: "The day the artillery nailed the 2d Battalion of the 511th. Whose? The Japanese had a couple of 105's and 75's in the area. It happened when their 26th Division was to make a last ditch drive towards Burauen. Was it them or was it the 155's back on the beach at the Ormoc area? My opinion is that it was the Japs that saw our fire the night before, scouted us, figured out what we were up to and laid six rounds in on the point of our route march."

Colonel Lahti and his 3d Battalion of the 511th had proceeded along their trail to the west. Wrote Lieutenant Barnes, "Around 1300, after the lead elements of I Company had advanced up a steep, jungle covered mountain ridge . . . they surprised a platoon of Japs on top of the mountain. After a sharp firefight, the mountain was taken and most of the Japs were killed. One officer, Lt. Maloney, of I Company, was killed in this action." The mountain was promptly named Mount Maloney.

After I Company, commanded by Capt. James T. Toth, killed off the rest of the enemy atop Mount Maloney, a patrol discovered that the main Japanese supply trail came across it. Colonel Lahti then ordered H Company to organize and defend Mount Maloney and directed the rest of the battalion to pass through H Company and continue to move west along the Japanese supply trail. The battalion, less H Company, moved out on the morning of 8 December.

After moving about 500 yards against relatively light resistance, I Company came to the lower levels of another mountaintop, which was even higher than Mount Maloney. The only accessible approach to this hill was from the east, up a narrow, thickly wooded, razor-back ridge 1,200 feet long and only 35 feet wide. The slopes of the ridges were very steep, averaging about 60 degrees, and the terrain surrounding the hill was rugged, mountainous country composed of sharp ridges, covered with rain forest, thick undergrowth, and vegetation. Near the top of the ridge, it was honeycombed with Japanese foxholes and caves. Colonel Lahti ordered his battalion to proceed with the attack.

I Company was in the lead. The ridge was so narrow and confining that the company had to move in a column of squads, with the company spread back along the ridge. Assisted by artillery fire from A Battery of the 457th at Manarawat, I Company seized the hill after a bloody, exhausting attack. By this time, it was late afternoon, and Colonel Lahti ordered the battalion to halt and dig in for the night. The mountain that the 3d Battalion had just captured was a narrow, thickly wooded ridge about 400 yards long and 35 yards wide at an elevation of about 3,000 feet. The slopes on the northwest side toward Ormoc were very steep, averaging about 60 degrees. Around the hill skirted the Japanese supply trail. The hill was named "Rock Hill" after the 511th regimental commander.

At one point on Rock Hill, the tired, hungry, and rain-soaked troopers of the 511th could see Ormoc Bay in the distance—about six miles away. Lieutenant Barnes wrote that "this was indeed a welcome sight and the words 'I'm dreaming of an Ormoc Christmas' were being sung by everyone." But even though Ormoc and the west coast were within view, the regiment—and the division—had ahead of them some of the toughest fighting yet encountered before they could go back to the now-imagined luxury of Bito Beach, dry clothes, a bath, and a clean bunk.

During the day and most of the night of 8 December, H Company of the 511th, dug in on Maloney Hill, repulsed a series of Japanese banzai attacks.

On Rock Hill, Colonel Lahti was still under orders to move west. Consequently, at 0700 on the morning of the ninth, G Company, under Capt. Pat Wheeler, West Point class of January 1943, moved out along the Japanese supply trail to continue the advance. After moving only a short distance, G Company was stopped by heavy machine gun fire from a ridge to the west. In the attack, three men were wounded and one officer and an enlisted man were missing. Colonel Lahti had been monitoring the progress of the company and, at 0830, when he realized their difficulty, he ordered the company to return to the battalion perimeter on Rock Hill.

The enemy was very active in the 3d Battalion's area. On 9 December, the Japanese launched a series of attacks on Rock Hill with mortars and machine guns supporting the riflemen. One observer said that "the battalion held these two locations—Rock and Maloney Hills—astride the main Japanese supply route under a continual attack from exasperated and fanatical Japanese." According to Lieutenant Barnes,

> All attacks were repulsed. During these attacks the poor quality of the Japanese mortar ammunition was noted. Many rounds landed close to troops but the powdery fragments seemed to have little effect. A few men from H Company tried to rejoin their company on Maloney Hill but were unable to do so because of the heavy sniping between the two hills. The next day (the tenth), the battalion started clearing the top of Rock Hill so it could be located by liaison planes, for the dropping of needed rations and supplies. A trail was made on top of the hill so that the Jap trail running along the side could be used in setting up ambushes.
>
> Company H, back on Maloney Hill, had counted 244 dead Japs up to date and were continuing to repulse all attacks. Captain Van Epps, from the battalion aid station on Rock Hill, fought his way, despite the Jap snipers, to the H Company position to take care of three badly wounded men.

On the morning of 10 December, the 511th Regimental Headquarters and the 1st Battalion left Mahonag, and, by late that afternoon, they had linked up with the 3d Battalion on Rock Hill.

About 200 yards southwest of Rock Hill, a patrol had located a strong enemy position. Colonel Lahti ordered I Company to take it. Captain Toth sent one of his platoons on the mission. Lieutenant Barnes set up one of his mortars on the trail on top of Rock Hill "facing down the route of the Jap supply trail." He sent an observer and two wiremen with a roll of assault wire behind Toth's leading rifle platoon. The platoon had moved only about a hundred yards when it was taken under fire by a machine gun from high ground to the platoon's front. The platoon leader sent one squad around to the left through the jungle and the two other squads down the trail, but they were all soon pinned down by fire. The mortar observer crawled up to the lead rifleman and had him point out the approximate location of the machine gun. He telephoned the location to Barnes who fired one 81mm mortar round at a range well beyond the pinned down platoon. Then he walked the rounds carefully back to the enemy position. When he had the target range and deflection, he fired three rounds rapidly. The platoon thereafter walked in and overran the position.

At 1500 that afternoon, H Company moved off Maloney Hill and was replaced by a company from the 1st Battalion; H Company moved up and occupied the hill that had just been taken by I Company's platoon.

The next morning, 11 December, Colonel Lahti ordered H Company to advance west along the supply road toward Anas; H Company, however, ran into another strong Japanese defensive position on a ridge, sometimes called West Ridge, about 500 yards to the west of Rock Hill. Colonel Lahti then ordered Captain Wheeler to try once more to advance to the west by moving around the blocked H Company. He gave Captain Wheeler two missions: Keep moving toward Ormoc Bay and contact the lead elements of the 7th Division who had landed amphibiously south of Ormoc and were moving toward the north and the east; and reconnoiter a route by which the regiment could attack the ridge that was holding up H Company. Unfortunately, after G Company had moved out and had gone a few thousand yards, it lost contact with H Company and was not able to carry out the second part of its mission. Captain Wheeler, however, did continue to lead his company west to try to make contact with the 7th.

On the evening of 11 December, Colonel Haugen met with his battalion commanders and staff. He told Colonel Lahti that he wanted the 3d Battalion to halt its drive to the west and to hold the Mahonag-Anas pass and destroy all the enemy in the vicinity of Rock Hill and Mahonag. Colonel Lahti objected. He felt that the primary mission was to keep moving, and he wanted to follow G Company. Haugen was adamant and told him emphatically that he would stay where he was.

For a number of days, the rains had prevented any supply drops from getting to the 3d Battalion. "The battalion aid station had eighteen serious casualties on hand and the medical supplies that were desperately needed were not available," Lieutenant Barnes wrote. "The men had not had rations for four days and the supply of ammunition was low, especially in hand grenades." Colonel Lahti, in some desperation, ordered his Headquarters Company commander to carry the litter patients over the Japanese supply trail back to the so-called, makeshift "advanced hospital" at Mahonag. The men fashioned litters out of tree limbs and ponchos and loaded up the patients. One squad of the mortar platoon with a machine gun attached was formed to lead the litter bearers down the trail. After the advanced squad had gone about twenty-five yards from the perimeter, the lead scouts suddenly hit the ground. Barnes checked the squad leader and found that he had heard

> a lot of activity and the clicking of bolts immediately to our front. The machine gun was set up in the middle of the trail and started firing rapid fire on both sides while the litters were withdrawing into the perimeter. This fire was returned by machine guns and rifles. No casualties occurred.
>
> These Japs had come from Maloney Hill between our position and Mahonag; a position formerly held by H Company and elements of the 1st Battalion, before they were left unoccupied on 11 December. . . .
>
> Back on Rock Hill, the 3d Battalion was making a series of attacks on Maloney Hill but all were repulsed. The men were tired and weak from lack of food. Even walking down the muddy trail a few yards would exhaust them. Everyone had been wet from the time they left Mahonag and the continuous rain and dampness had kept them wet. Most of the ponchos and shelter halves had been utilized in making litters and in protection of the many wounded at the aid station.
>
> On 13 December, the skies cleared for the first time in many days and the liaison planes dropped rations and medical supplies for over an hour. After the first drop, each three men were issued one box of K rations. During the course of the ration drops, in the next few days, two men were killed by falling boxes and there were many "near misses."

Unfortunately, there was still no way to evacuate the litter cases from atop Rock Hill.

Colonel Haugen, determined to clear the enemy from his positions midway across the mountains between Burauen and Ormoc, ordered a coordinated attack to retake Maloney Hill. The plan called for H Company to attack to the east from Rock Hill and two companies from the 2d Battalion, now commanded by Maj. Frank S. Holcombe—Colonel Shipley's replacement—to attack to the west from Mahonag. The lead elements of H Company had just started to leave the perimeter on Rock Hill when they were fired on by a large number of Japanese who had crawled up to within a few yards of the outer foxholes on the 3d Battalion's perimeter. A sharp firefight reportedly took place, which lasted most of the morning. The two companies from the 2d Battalion were equally unsuccessful in getting back on top of Maloney Hill. Colonel Haugen ordered these two companies to join the 3d Battalion on Rock Hill.

On 17 December, "word was finally received about G Company," Lieutenant Barnes wrote. "Elements of the 32d Infantry, pushing up toward our position, had finally contacted them. These men [G Company 511th] had been without rations for ten days and most of them were suffering from malnutrition."

Lieutenant Barnes's cryptic remark does not spell out the difficulties that G Company had in finally getting to the west coast. William M. "Buzz" Miley, Jr., was the platoon leader of the 2d Platoon of G Company during its march from Rock Hill. In a recent letter, he wrote of the trials of G Company's trek west.

On the 11th (I think), Wheeler briefed the platoon leaders that later that day we would leave Rock Hill on the north side, approximately parallel the trail going west, intersect the trail behind the Japs and wait for orders from 3d Bn. to either hold on the trail or attack east to meet the battalion. (This sounds logical since H and I attacked down the trail to Hacksaw Ridge later.) Captain Wheeler made a point that he had told Bn that Co. G had no rations and no replacement radio batteries and those we had were almost dead and was told (and told Co. G) that we'd be hungry for a couple of days and we should trail wire on the way out. Which incidentally went dead two hours out so we figured the Japs cut it.

I personally led off out of the perimeter with the scouts of the 2d Plt and as I recall it, it was on an azimuth of about 10 degrees west of north, but from there on we followed a stream bed—but very slow since the hunger was catching up with us.

For approximately three days we tried to parallel the trail; then the 3d plt tried to fight back south and uphill to cut the trail. We could hear Japs talking above us. Our (plt) lead scouts made contact (going straight uphill) and Pfc Matt Pike was shot through the shoulder, came tumbling down the hill. . . . Since we were all very weak, Wheeler pulled us back and we went looking for a clearing of some sort to put out our recognition panels in hopes of getting a ration resupply since Wheeler figured both the 511th and division would be looking for us with rations and batteries. "Starvation Hill" was a small cleared area on a slope with a clear view south. We could see where the trail was on top of the ridges and saw at least two airdrops by C-47's to the 3d Bn. (−). The only food we had at this time was rice taken off Japs killed blundering into our perimeter and plenty of cammotes . . . which we dug up and cooked.

We displayed two panels, one company identification and the other a "rations required" one from the SOI. This was done because an L4 or L5 flew over or near us (up high) every day but obviously (at first) thought we were Japs since we were hit by white phos. the 2d day. We thought they were marking rounds (and dug deeper) but no artillery followed. We did have two casualties from burns. By this time we were all very weak and were cooking everything we could dig up to include the insides of palm and banana trees which made a pretty good mush or soup. There was never any problem with water since a fast rushing stream was at the bottom of the hill. I think we spent a total of ten days on the hill. About halfway thru Capt. Wheeler asked for volunteers for a daylight patrol to move west to contact the 7th Div, give them our position and get us out. There were at least 50 volunteers; a five-man group was selected and left that day. They hid and moved so well that they went all the way to the ocean but took so much time due to physical condition that we were out before they could help us. The next day, 1st Sgt Pile asked Capt Wheeler to let him take a night patrol of volunteers and they left that night. This patrol made contact with the 7th, informed them of our position and condition and was the reason they came in and got us out. 1st Sgt. Pile fell over a cliff and drowned (body never recovered). . . .

Back on Starvation Hill we received an airdrop by L5 of two cases of C rations (free drop). This was the result of the second patrol action. The rations hit, split, broke, burst and scattered chow all over the terrain, and we ended up scraping food off bushes and the ground, but not enough to do anyone any good.

On the 10th day, an American GI scout was challenged coming up the hill on the north side of our hill. (He damn near got shot.) A small patrol followed him in and said that if we could follow them out to an adjacent hill, a unit was there to carry us to the coast if necessary. We moved out and contacted the parent unit (Company K, 32d Infantry, 7th Division). We moved into their perimeter, each of us was issued one heavy can of C ration which was too much for our bellies and we got sick real quick! The next day we were escorted by this unit to the beach and told to take it easy until the 511th came out of the mountains.

During most of the 511th's trek through the mountains, a forward observer from a marine 155mm gun battery along the Burauen-Dulag road had accompanied the regimental staff. Colonel Haugen had not used the battery because he felt that the flat trajectory of its guns would make it hazardous, if not impossible, to bring fire in close to his own troops—where it was needed most. And he worried about the difficulty of adjusting the artillery in the confines of the jungle. But in order to lessen his own casualties in getting back on Maloney Hill, he did, on this occasion, ask his marine observer to put a concentration on top of it. On the morning of 18 December, after an adjustment of observed fires, the 155s plastered the hill with a number of volleys. A short time later, B Company attacked the hill and walked to the top of it with no opposition. The artillery fire had been devastatingly effective. B Company found scores of dead enemy scattered over the hill in their bombed and battered emplacements. Using the great foresight that made him a superb regimental commander, Colonel Haugen had previously ordered an ambush set up on the supply road leading off Maloney Hill to the west. When the artillery fire began raining on Maloney Hill, the ambush killed more than 100 of the enemy as they sought to get off the hill and escape the artillery fire.

During this period, the 2d Battalion of the 187th had been in a number of firefights around Anonang. On 11 December, Gen. Albert Pierson and Col. Doug Quandt arrived at Anonang. After reviewing the situation with Col. Harry Wilson, General Pierson ordered him to attack the main Jap position below Ori Hill, the hill from which Captain Ori and F Company had been repulsed on 6 December.

On 12 December, F and G Companies of the 187th launched an attack that would take G Company up the riverbeds to strike the position from the north while F Company moved through its old perimeter to attack from the southwest. The artillery forward observers, from A Battery of the 457th at Manarawat, had a very difficult time adjusting their fires because of the thick jungle overhang and the inability to see through the jungle for more than a few yards. Most of their adjustments were made by sound, a system not totally accurate.

By 1300, F Company had cleared Ori Hill and had worked down the slope toward the enemy position. Reported Chief Warrant Officer Nelson,

> Presently, it was stymied by our own artillery whose shells were bursting in the trees, above and behind it. High angle fire was infeasible when sensings were so inaccurate. Lead scouts reported that when an "over" did land in the Jap positions, it had absolutely no effect on their coconut tree revetments.
>
> Meanwhile, Captain Walters had worked G Company around to his assembly area, but found himself facing the problem of attacking without supporting fires, up a single jungle trail into a strongly fortified position. He radioed the battalion commander and explained the situation and requested permission to hold up his attack until artillery fire could be brought

in for his support. Colonel Wilson agreed and ordered the two companies to return to the battalion perimeter. G Company held up its return and organized a search for two scouts who had gone up a blind trail and were missing. They never returned. F Company, withdrawing at dusk from Ori Hill, did not reach Anonang until midnight.

The only light along the trail was a strange macabre phosphorescent glow from the jungle debris lining the stream bed. Holding onto each others' belts, we slipped and fell, tumbled into holes, bumped our heads on our lead files' weapons, tripped over logs as we felt our way through the pitch black. At hourly halts, the surgeon administered blood plasma to the wounded. Pfc Cleo Harrell, who had been wounded in the abdomen, and had walked back up to Ori Hill, holding his intestines in with his hands, died enroute and his last words were to his company commander: "Sir, did we do what you wanted?"

Early on 13 December, a detachment of the 152d working a radio relay station at Catabagan sent a message that it was surrounded by a large enemy force and needed help. Colonel Wilson sent E Company to take care of the problem. Near the 152d, E Company ran into about ten Japanese who were promptly "liquidated." The main force had apparently pulled back to the northeast. On the way back to the battalion perimeter, one of the lead scouts, Private Shadden, shot two more of the enemy. Another Japanese jumped him and grappled with him for his rifle. Shadden knifed him. His company commander made him a private first class on the spot.

On the same day, Lt. Harrison I. Merritt, of G Company, led his platoon out from the perimeter on a routine scouting patrol. The platoon ran head-on into a large enemy force about 1,500 yards northeast of Anonang. The enemy force proved to be very stubborn, and Merritt radioed his situation to Captain Walters, who rushed to his assistance with the rest of G Company. During the ensuing fight, Captain Walters was killed and several other men were wounded. Merritt took charge of the battle, called in heavy mortar fire from Anonang, and "dispersed the force." Night closed in before they could attack further. The company returned to Anonang carrying its wounded and the dead company commander.

Late in the afternoon of 13 December, Col. George Pearson and his 1st Battalion of the 187th arrived at Anonang with orders to relieve the 2d Battalion of its mission around Anonang. On 14 December, Col. Harry Wilson received orders to move west to Mahonag "to protect the drop zone at Mahonag and to block the Japanese supply trail between Mahonag and Anas.''

"It was time we moved," wrote Chief Warrant Officer Nelson. "We were completely out of rations and the cammote and green-corn patches had been picked clean. Moreover, the wild pigs had become wary of the area. By now, we were subsisting on the nourishing but tough buffalo steaks. It was slim picking we turned over to our brother battalion."

The trail that Colonel Wilson and his battalion followed to the west first led south along the streambeds, past Lubi. Then it turned west over a series of towering ridges. Chief Warrant Officer Nelson remembers:

> The going was the toughest yet and we had to hand carry our heavy equipment because caribao not already slaughtered were simply spent. They and their drivers were abandoned to make their way home as best they could.
>
> We were continually harassed along the trail by Jap delaying forces, with mortars and machine guns, who retired from ridge to ridge as we advanced. Four of our lead scouts, whose lives were downright poor insurance risks on that route, were wounded. We formed no perimeter that night but simply lay on the sides of the trail and trusted ourselves to God.

At 1500 on 15 December, Lieutenant Siegel was leading the march with his platoon. At one point on the trail, he received fire from a Japanese ambush site along the trail. Siegel moved his platoon off the trail and tried to outflank the ambush by moving through the bush. Again he was fired upon, and he returned the fire. Fortunately, no one was wounded or killed. Shortly, he heard some unmistakable American profanity from a position farther up the trail. The Americans were from the 511th and had been attacking the ambush site from one side while Siegel had been hitting it from the other. In the interim, the enemy had pulled out.

When the battalion pulled into Mahonag, it found a rather strange and desolate sight. Wrote the 187th historian,

> Mahonag was a field on a hillside, about three hundred yards long by two hundred wide, studded with stumps and fallen trees, packed with hundreds of slit trenches, littered with boxes and cans and debris of spent ration packs. Permeating the atmosphere was the horrible sickening odor

of unburied, decomposing bodies. At once we were assaulted by the largest, most prosperous swarm of flies we'd ever seen.

Nevertheless, like an old hag wearing too much makeup, this forlorn bit of real estate wore an incongruously racist face. It blossomed with green and yellow and white cargo parachutes, which the men had set up tentwise for shelter. Color and cloth for a circus. . . . Those chutes had brought in ammo and rations and the men squatted around camp fires, boiling the coffee and cooking stew in helmets, of the excellent ten-in-one rations. Many of us have since paid bucks for meals that couldn't match the taste of that hot chow, the first we'd eaten in days.

The rations and ammunition drops were not without their cost. Throughout the division, some fourteen men were killed by errant drops from the C-47s and liaison planes. In the 2d Battalion of the 187th, 1st Sgt. Teddy Sowards was injured during a drop, and Private Bircheler was killed.

On one corner of the clearing at Mahonag, the medics had set up a parachute-covered field hospital, which did yeoman service in caring for the many wounded men of both the 511th and the 187th who could not be evacuated farther. One of the ration drops narrowly missed one of the surgeons in the tent; another hit and broke the arm of one of the patients who was being operated on for a leg wound. When the patient awoke from the anesthetic, he found his arm in a splint and his leg in bandages.

"Hey, Doc," he is alleged to have said, "I thought I was hit in the leg." "You were," answered a medic, "but you were in no condition to duck a ration box. So now you also have a broken arm." "This darned war is full of nasty little surprises," said the wounded soldier.

For the next few days, the 2d of the 187th dug in its perimeter at Mahonag, sent out patrols around the area, and set up and baited ambushes along the trails. "Ambush duty was interesting and fruitful," wrote the 187th historian. "A squad, or half-squad would take up positions along the Jap trails, like hunters on a deer run, and wait until the Nips walked into the line of fire. As the kills diminished at one 'blind,' new positions would be set up and the hunt would go on. Of course, the Japs had their own blinds and we lost men to them, too."

The men not on these duties found time to clean themselves, their clothes, and their weapons. The health of the men in the battalion, like the rest of the men who had spent days in the rains in the mountains, was deteriorating. Men were sick with various jungle fevers, and some men had the beginnings of "jungle rot" on their feet and around their ankles. Many had "immersion feet." When they took off their socks, the outer layers of skin went with them. The men almost universally suffered from dysentery. So did the Japanese. Some of those who were found had cut out the entire seat of their pants to facilitate the solution to the problem.

At this stage of the Leyte campaign, it was becoming clear to General Swing that the southern part of his sector, in which the 188th Airborne Infantry Regiment had been operating, was relatively clear of any large concentrations of the enemy. Therefore, he ordered Colonel Soule to move his regiment north and to concentrate it in the vicinity of Manarawat.

Lieutenant Colonel Mortimer J. O'Kane and his 1st Battalion of the 188th moved by truck and DUKW from Bugho to Burauen and thence up the muddy trails already traversed by the 511th and the 2d of the 187th to Patog. Colonel Soule, his regimental headquarters, and Lt. Col. Tommy Mann's 2d of the 188th moved by foot from La Paz to Burauen to Manarawat, dragging their reluctant, lumbering carabao with them. Colonel Hildebrand and a skeleton forward echelon of the 187th Regimental Headquarters had moved to Anonang by way of Manarawat and had taken command of the middle section of the mountains from Anonang to Mahonag.

General Swing anticipated that when the infantrymen came out of the hills, they would need help with their wounded and would certainly need to be resupplied with equipment, rations, and uniforms. He sent the 127th Engineers by road across the waist of Leyte from Abuyog to Baybay on the west coast with instructions to find the Japanese supply trail as it entered the mountains from the west and to widen it as far as prudently possible into the hills, prepared to meet the 511th and the 187th with trucks and ambulances. He directed the 408th Quartermaster Company to set up supply points on the Ormoc coast in preparation for the infantrymen's arrival.

The 127th located the Japanese trail where it entered the mountains and sent its exact location to General Swing and Colonel Haugen. "A quick change was made in the route of advance of the 511th," the historian reported, "when it was determined that the previously obtained report of a small recon patrol was inaccurate by two ridges."

On 15 December 1944, General Swing wrote to Gen. Peyton C. March, who had been the army chief of staff from 19 May 1918 until 30 June 1921 and who was also General Swing's father-in-law.

Dear General:

Hardly know what I may write without violating censorship regulations. It appears that we are a "secret weapon" although we have been in the line since 20 November. You notice that no mention has been made of our activities in the daily communique. Nevertheless, we've killed over 2,000 Japs and have moved through the mountains to the west coast midway between the Abuyog and Baybay road, which the 7th Division took, and the troops of the X Corps on our right which have been held up for so long by so-called "impassable terrain." Two of my regiments equipped with light packs, no pup tents, no ponchos, no extra clothing or footgear, have been fighting through mountain trails for 25 days. We ran smack into the Jap 26th Division, a fresh division landed south of Ormoc. This division had the mission of advancing east on the identical trails. We have knocked them back 12 miles as the crow flies and about twice as far by mountain trail. We have them now pinched in between ourselves and the 7th Division.

From now on it's a process of extermination and they fight like cornered rats. Casualties on our side are not light because when disorganized, the individual Jap hides in a hole, up a tree, in debris around deserted barrios. There is always the danger of a lucky shot and I mean lucky or, if you will, unlucky getting one. On the whole they are lousy shots and must be within 10 or 15 paces to hit the bull's eye. Had one sniping at me the other morning from a coconut tree, couldn't locate him until some of the men shouted he was in a tree not 10 yards from me, so I ran over and stood at the base of the tree while the men riddled the so and so over my head. Fortunately many of our wounds are from 25. caliber and incapacitate for 10 days or two weeks only. Most damage is from hand grenades. Many Japs have thrown away all arms but knives or bayonets and hand grenades, then garbed in Filipino clothes or oddments from our own uniforms, they endeavor to infiltrate at night close enough to toss a couple of grenades at an outpost and if caught do not hesitate to use the grenades on their own persons.

Fortunately, I was able to drop one battery of mountain guns on a little plateau giving us range to the western slopes in the vicinity of Aubera and covering all the approaches from the mountains of Mt. Mahonag and Lobi to the northwest, north and northeast. This one battery has fired practically through a field of fire of 270 degrees. All the Jap has to combat it with is his little 50 mm. knee mortar. I have established radio relay stations every mile or so and that means an hour and a half to 2 hours apart along the line of communications. Can only afford 30 to 40 men at each station, all dismounted artillery or anti-aircraft artillery armed with carbines, light machine guns, and grenades. These posts each have an artillery liaison officer. When attacked, they are strong enough to hold until artillery fire arrives. To date, the answer always has been Japs withdrawing, carrying wounded, found 6 or 9 Japs dead, no casualties.

The supply for the whole operation has been accomplished by "jeep" artillery, liaison planes, even to reinforcements to some isolated post. Have parachuted 188 officers and men including two surgical teams without a single injury. The two teams have established two small hospitals and performed miracles, operated for belly wounds and head wounds. The men are receiving the same care they would receive in a general hospital, have even found time to drop them ice cream (we purchased an ice cream machine in Australia and persuaded the troop carrier to fly it into our base camp on the beach.) Am afraid some of the wounded will have to remain several months in the hills until they have recuperated sufficiently to be littered out by manpower.

It's a queer war, but I get a kick out of beating the Japs at their own game—the so-called tactics of ambush infiltrations to the rear, surrounding small units, etc. Hope we have this cleaned up by Christmas, but it looks kind of doubtful now.
Sincerely, Joe

The 511th was now ready to resume its attack toward the west. On 19 December, Colonel Lahti sent H Company on a reconnaissance in force to a ridge about 800 yards to the west of Rock Hill. A battery of the 457th fired a series of concentrations in support of the attack but, by 1600, H Company had made no progress against a large enemy force. Colonel Lahti ordered H Company to return to the Rock Hill perimeter.

The next day, Colonel Lahti launched an all-out attack with his entire battalion, less G Company, which was still making its way to the coast. Colonel Lahti ordered the attack with I Company, led by Capt. James J. Toth, on the right and H Company on the left. Captain Bobo Holloway and his A Battery of the 457th, firing at the extreme limits of the range of the pack 75s, laid down a heavy concentration of fire in front of the infantry. Lieutenant Barnes had sent his forward mortar observers with the lead platoons of each of the companies. Company I made good progress and by noon had reached the top of the ridge where the supply trail made a sharp turn to the right. When Captain

Toth got to the top of the ridge, he found that the enemy had abandoned the position and had infiltrated down the slope between I and H Companies. Toth sent a strong patrol down the trail to get behind the Japanese and clear the trail toward H Company.

Barnes's mortar observer with the lead patrol attempted to place mortar fire around the patrol where it would do the most good. Unfortunately, he could not see the rounds land and had to adjust the fire of the one mortar by sound. The lead patrol received heavy machine gun fire from its front. Staff Sergeant Mille, the mortar observer, was slightly wounded but continued to adjust the fire. His radio was out so he used wire that he had trailed behind him. Shortly, that too was cut and he finally used Japanese wire, which he had found along the trail, for communicating back to the mortar. Sergeant Mille brought three rounds closer and closer to the enemy machine gun. One of them hit a tree above the enemy gunner and killed him. By late afternoon of 20 December, the 3d Battalion, in what was described as a "brilliantly executed attack," had seized the northern portion of the West Ridge.

On 20 December, the infantry units in the area received new assignments. Colonel Haugen ordered the 2d Battalion of the 511th to pass through the 3d Battalion and continue the attack along the southern part of West Ridge. F Company of the 188th had arrived at Mahonag and relieved the 2d Battalion of the 187th of its security mission there. General Swing ordered the 2d of the 187th to move west to Rock Hill, with the mission of passing through the 2d of the 511th, and to continue the march to the west.

Before dawn on 22 December, however, Col. Hacksaw Holcomb led his 2d of the 511th in the predawn darkness against the enemy on the southern part of the ridge, "spurred on," said one of the observers of the action, "by a reluctance to allow the 187th to pass through and snatch the glory of the last breakthrough attack. The Japanese had never been banzaied before. The 2d Battalion found them in their bunks, such as they were, and slaughtered over two hundred of them before they could organize their defense. The attack became a rout with only sniper fire from there on." In their assault, the 2d of the 511th used all of their close-in weapons—flamethrowers, grenades, and bayonets. From then on, in the annals of the 11th Airborne Division, West Ridge became Hacksaw Ridge.

On 21 December, General Swing and Doug Quandt flew into Manarawat in liaison planes. General Swing was headed for Mahonag. At Manarawat, he picked up a four-man patrol to escort him along the route. The four men had been wounded in previous action and were on their way back to their regiment, the 511th, after having been "patched up" at the "hospital" at Manarawat. One of the men of the patrol was Pfc Clifford Servias, from G Company of the 511th. He suggested to General Swing that he remove his stars, since there were known to be enemy troops along the trail up to Mahonag. General Swing, in a predictable reply, said: "Nothing doing." A few moments later, he had second thoughts about it and put his stars on the underside of his collar, a custom followed by all of the officers in the hills. Rank insignia made officers first targets for Japanese snipers, and a tall, white-haired man wearing two stars was a prime candidate. Besides, no one in the 11th needed to see General Swing's two stars to know who he was.

General Swing arrived at Mahonag in the afternoon. He was "as muddy as any dog-faced private," one of the 187th troopers recalled. "He was accorded the honor of sleeping in the position's only nipa hut, a one day privilege as it was demolished the next day by a salvo of mis-directed ration boxes."

The 2d of the 187th at Mahonag was being resupplied occasionally by paradrops from C-47s. Many of the bundles, however, got hung up in trees or drifted over to enemy territory. General Swing decided to do something about it. Lieutenant Eli Bernheim remembered that "we erected a platform and fashioned some crude semaphore flags. My platoon sergeant, Ernie Stringham, would signal the planes as they swooped low over the area and give them a wave at the precise moment as directed by General Swing. He took a vigorous part in this operation, and there was no doubt as to who was running the show." General Swing no doubt wanted to correct the aim of the pilot who demolished the nipa hut.

At 0400 on the morning of 23 December, the 2d of the 187th moved out of Mahonag for the two-hour march to Rock Hill. Colonel Wilson had orders to "make contact with the 511th Infantry on Rock Hill and to be prepared to aid in the breakthrough attack to the coast." The 2d of the 187th moved out with General Swing near the head of the column "as we shot a few groups of Japs who insisted on dying," Chief Warrant Officer Nelson reported. "Once we passed through a canyon reeking with the smell of decomposing bodies. It was the end of the trail for the ambitious Jap 26th Division which once had planned to overrun Burauen."

In the march to Rock Hill, Colonel Wilson had G Company in the lead. "The trails were treacherous, muddy and slippery," wrote Lt. Joseph Giordano,[2] the platoon leader of the 2d Platoon of G Company. "However, the battalion made its way along the long difficult route without incident and at approximately 0600, the approaches along the slopes of Rock Hill were reached." The 2d of the 187th passed through the 2d of the 511th along Hacksaw Ridge, now "lined with enemy dead."

Continued Giordano, "The battalion went forward to overtake the lead elements of the 511th who were pushing forward at breakneck speed along the Japanese Supply Trail which ran along the razor back ridge in the direction of Ormoc. It was difficult to understand how a unit engaged in bitter fighting could keep up the terrific rate of march forward. The trails everywhere were littered with enemy dead, as were the slopes of the ridge."

At 1200, the 2d of the 187th took over the lead from the 2d of the 511th. Lieutenant Giordano and his 2d Platoon led the march thereafter.

Colonel Haugen stopped Giordano and told him: "You must keep going as fast as possible. Run if you have to, but don't give the Nips a chance to set up their weapons. We've got them with their pants down. You can't even stop to kill them all. Just push through. We are behind you and will take care of them as we come to them. Just keep going fast. Any questions?"

Giordano and his platoon had gone less than 100 yards down the trail when they were fired on by a machine gun about 20 yards to their front, where the trail turned abruptly to the left. A BAR man took the machine gun under fire, and one of the lead scouts tossed a white phosphorous grenade in the direction of the machine gun. Giordano sent his lead squad to the left in the jungle and sent a four-man team to assault the gun from the right. In a matter of minutes, the four-man team was back with the report that "the machine gun and the three men manning it are out of action."

Another 150 yards ahead, the trail disappeared into a deep gorge. At the lip of the gorge, the scouts opened fire on a number of the enemy on the trail. The Japanese returned the fire, but ineffectively. Giordano happened to look to the bottom of the gorge, where a small

---

[2] Major Joseph B. Giordano, Monograph, "Opn of G Co 187th EIR-ORMOC," The Infantry School, 1948.

stream passed through it. He saw two Japanese alongside the stream just as they blew their heads off with hand grenades.

Giordano checked the gorge carefully and decided that it was an excellent place for the Japanese, from the sides of the gorge above his position, to make a defense. He established a base of fire with one squad, and sent one squad to the right and another to the left. When he had the platoon ready, he gave the signal to advance. The enemy put up only "feeble resistance." At about that time, Colonel Wilson arrived on the scene. "What's holding up the parade?" he wanted to know. Giordano showed him thirteen dead Japanese. Two of the dead were part of the enemy security force on the right bank who had jumped off a 150-foot cliff when the second squad assaulted the position.

The platoon headed up the far side of the gorge without further incident, thanks to the third squad, which had eliminated two snipers who would have been firing down the column. The platoon reached a point high on the western slope of a steep mountain, from where the men could see the west coast plainly. Here Giordano stopped the platoon and fired a violet smoke grenade, "which was the signal for friendly forces intended to attract elements of the 7th Infantry Division that might be in the vicinity," he said. On a ridge four or five hundred yards to the west, Giordano saw answering violet smoke. He had at last made visual contact with the U.S. forces on the west coast.

"The column pushed on, down the winding trail until it reached the draw at the bottom of this same mountain," Giordano wrote later. "At this point, the company ran into another group of Japanese, who put up only feeble resistance, and were easily eliminated by grenade and BAR fire." Giordano continued to follow the supply trail and shortly reached the approaches to "an extremely dangerous looking position to the front." Here he stopped the column, put out security, and sent a patrol to reconnoiter the position. The halt once again brought forward the chain of command, this time General Swing, who had been marching near the head of the column. The recon patrol returned shortly with a report that the position to the front was honeycombed with caves and deeply dug-in foxholes, that it appeared to have been heavily shelled judging by the condition of some of the camouflage, and that enemy dead littered the area.

Giordano led the column up the steep side of the hill to the top of the peak. They found that the position was "well laid out, camouflaged and dug in almost solid rock. The battered trees and number of enemy

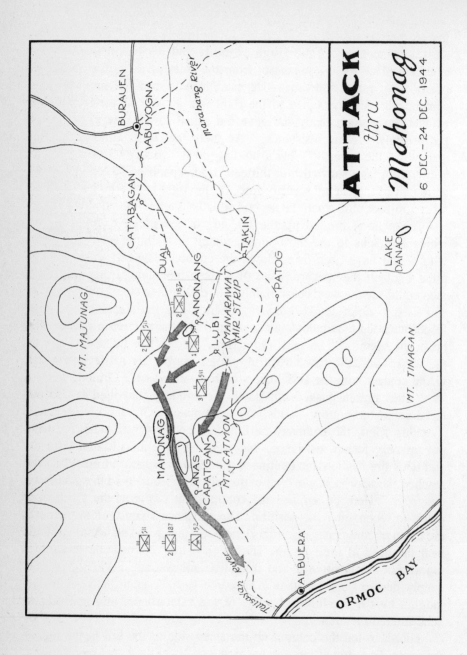

ATTACK
thru
Mahonag
6 DEC. - 24 DEC. 1944

BURAUEN
ABUYOGNA
Marabang River
CAT-ABAGAN
DUAL
ANONANG
TAKIN
PATOG
LAKE DANAO
MT. MAJUNAG
2 187
2 511
1 511
3 511
LUBI
MANARAWAT AIR STRIP
MT. TINAGAN
MAHONAG
ANAS
CAPATGAN
MT. CATMON
1 511
2 187
152
Talisayan River
ALBUERA
ORMOC BAY

dead found on top of this position, which was long and narrow in shape, served as mute evidence of heavy gunfire. Among the dead were two American soldiers that appeared to have been dead less than twenty-four hours.''

When he reached the west end of the ridge, Giordano could see Ormoc and the seacoast. And to his front, about 200 yards away, he saw the dug-in emplacements. That position, he wrote, was

> soon alive with members of the 2d Battalion, 32d Infantry. They were amazed to see fellow Americans on the same strong enemy position that had given them so much trouble. "Oh, yes," said one of the members of the 32d, "we expected you. Saw the violet smoke. But we didn't think that you were coming over that hill. Why, only last night it was solid with Nips. We lost two of our boys on it." Thus physical contact was made with the Ormoc Corridor, and the trail between this point and Rock Hill was covered with approximately 750 enemy dead. The road was finally opened between Burauen and Anas, and the area west of Mahonag was cleared.

That night the battalion spread out on clean grass beside a stream near Albuera.

After the 11th had completed its push across the Leyte mountains, General Bruce, commanding the 77th Division near Ormoc, radioed General Hodge, the XXIV Corps commander: "Have rolled two sevens in Ormoc. Come seven, come eleven."

General Swing ordered the 511th, after the 2d of the 187th passed through near Hacksaw Ridge, to secure the route from Mahonag to the coast and to collect all the litter patients and the wounded from Mahonag and Rock Hill. By 25 December, the regiment had cleared the mountains and had completed its mission. General Swing ordered the 511th back to its base camp at Bito Beach and turned the security of the western end of the Japanese supply trail over to the 2d of the 187th from its base at the head of the Talisayan River. But the fighting in the mountains was still not over for the 11th Airborne Division.

The Japanese pocket about 1,400 yards northwest of Anonang had still not been destroyed. The 1st and 2d Battalions of the 511th and the 2d and 1st Battalions of the 187th had, in turn, butted their heads against this large enemy force. Each battalion had sent probes and recon patrols to feel out the position, and each probe had been hit hard with Japanese sniper and machine gun fire and was forced to turn back. Early on, General Swing and his staff realized that the Anonang position was formidable and that it would take a well-coordinated, multibattalion force to liquidate it. General Swing decided not to attack it with strength while the major portion of his infantry was slogging and fighting across the mountains to the west. His major mission was to get to the coast; a large attack at Anonang would delay that part of his Sixth Army's dictated mission. But now that he had achieved a juncture with the 7th Division, he felt that the time was propitious to eliminate the final, stubborn cluster of the enemy in his area of responsibility.

The Japanese defenses near Anonang were on two parallel ridges. On the first ridge, the Japanese had dug sixty-four "spider holes," each eight to ten feet deep, for individual riflemen. They had also dug in machine guns, both light and heavy, on both ridges, with overhead cover and interlocking fields of fire. All faces of the slopes were studded with caves, which controlled the narrow trails. The Japanese had rolled grenades out of these caves at some of the probing U.S. patrols. In the rear of the position was a bivouac area, cached with ammunition, rations, and other supplies, large enough to accommodate a regiment. Apparently the area was a rallying point for all the enemy units in the area, and the G-2 estimated that there were at least a thousand Japanese dug in and concentrated along the ridges and gorges.

The enemy had camouflaged the entire area with the ingenuity and "devilish" artistry so typical of Japanese groundworks. They had cut the centers out of bamboo thickets, inserted a machine gun and a couple of men in each one, and then restored the thicket with such painstaking care that an American soldier could walk within two feet of the nest and not know it—until it started firing, and that was too late. In another gambit of camouflage, the Japanese would tie bushes around themselves, climb into trees, stay there motionless for hours, and blend so well with the foliage that a man directly under the tree did not know there was a sniper above—until he was shot. The rear ridge, where the Japanese had concentrated their defenses and the bulk of their force, became known among the 11th Airborne troopers, for obvious reasons, as Purple Heart Hill.

Lieutenant "Pop" Olsen had had his C Company of the 187th at Manarawat from the time that it had jumped and walked into that area. On about 14 December, a Japanese force of about company size had tried to infiltrate the Manarawat strip, presumably to knock out the pack

75s of A Battery of the 457th. Just before dawn, the enemy burst into the northeast corner of the perimeter yelling "banzai, banzai, banzai." Their coordinated and accompanying mortar fire exploded within the perimeter, and their machine guns grazed the area. The attack was well planned and achieved surprise. But the men of C Company, dug in along the perimeter, returned the fire. "Several of the Nip gunners were hit," Chief Warrant Officer Nelson reported, "but in a twinkling they were replaced by their determined buddies. Fire streaked through the Nipa hospital but the surgeons had rolled their patients into the slit trenches beneath. Lt. Olsen and another man crawled under the fire to the vicinity of the hospital and opened up on the attackers with Browning automatic rifles. The action lasted two hours until some twenty-one Japs were annihilated at a cost to us of two wounded." On 18 December, C Company rejoined the 1st of the 187th in the Anonang area.

In that area, Col. Tommy Mann and his 2d Battalion of the 188th had been probing the ridges for three days, searching for some undefended or weakly defended avenue of approach into the position. The answer was always the same: There was none. In the meantime, Colonel Pearson had pulled his 1st Battalion of the 187th back from Anonang and, circling the position on a wide arc, moved to the north, above the Japanese defenses. To the west of the 1st of the 187th was the Division Reconnaissance Platoon commanded by Lieutenant Polka. Captain Bud Ewing, from the division staff, was with them. The Recon Platoon had traveled along the slopes of Mount Lobi in an effort to determine how far to the north the Japanese position extended. The Recon Platoon found that the position extended to the west rather than to the north. The platoon dug in on the northwest corner of the Japanese defensive network. Colonel Soule ordered his F Company, now located at Mahonag, to move down the trail to the east and to set up an ambush along the trail to trap any of the enemy moving off the ridges after he launched his attack.

The units to assault the twin ridges were now in place, and Colonel Soule ordered the attack for the morning of 26 December. As planned, that morning, Colonel Mann, with his battalion on a hill southwest and across a gorge from Purple Heart Hill, pulled out of his position and headed away from the Japanese, leading them to believe that, like the four other battalions before him, he was moving out of the area. The 2d of the 188th moved into a narrow, steep-sided river bottom, which hid it from the Japanese. The battalion then doubled back and moved up along the wooded side of a ridge and climbed east up a rocky gully

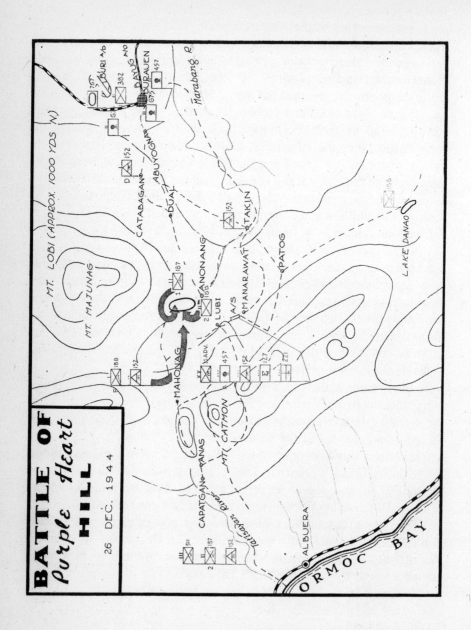

BATTLE OF
Purple Heart
HILL
26 DEC. 1944

onto the southern slope of Purple Heart Hill. Then the battalion turned left and moved up to the enemy position. The south slope of the hill was so steep that the men had to pull themselves up hand over hand on vines and bushes. As soon as they were within range and vision of the Japanese on the ridge, the lead troops were met with heavy fire from the deeply entrenched enemy.

Private First Class John Chiesa was in E Company of the 188th. He and Privates First Class Davis and Duncan were on the point going up the hill. Chiesa wrote recently,

We just got to the top of this hill when all hell broke loose. The Japs opened up with their wood peckers and rifles. Duncan got hit in the rump and he went tumbling down the hill. I hit the ground and prayed. Finally, Davis and I jumped up and went diving over the ridge. We could not see the Japs because they hide pretty good in the jungle. They were firing and we were trying to fire back, but we could not see them to know where to shoot at. Finally, our platoon leader, Sgt. Kelly, got up on one knee and started to point to show us where to shoot. About that time, the Japs got him and he was dead. He was one hell of a soldier, believe me. (During maneuvers in Louisiana, Colonel Soule told him not to point to where the enemy might be or they would know he was a leader and they would try to get him, which they did.)

Me, Pvt. Hodges and three other guys in our company went up to the side of the hill, and we laid there, waiting for someone to tell us what our next move was.

While we waited, I got hungry so I turned around facing down the hill and got out one of my K rations. I was opening up the can when twenty feet from me this Jap jumped out of the bushes. He looked at me and I looked at him. I think he was as surprised as I was. I had an M1 rifle laying across my lap. Everything was done automatically. (Our training came in handy.) I grabbed the rifle, turned and pulled the trigger. He was doing the same thing but I was luckier. I hit him smack in his Adam's apple. I can still see the surprised look on his face. . . . The thing that will always be on my mind is that if I didn't stop to eat, those Japs would of killed all five of us. I was the only one looking down the hill.

When we were back down the hill, Colonel Soule came to me and asked me what I would do to get those Japs and take the hill. I thought he was joking. Here is a colonel, and a darned good one, asking this pfc how to take a hill.

I told him, "Just bomb the hell out of them, blow the hill up." We went up the next morning, and after a good bombardment, we took the hill.

The "good bombardment" came in part from A Battery of the 457th at Manarawat. Captain Bobo Holloway, the battery commander of A of the 457th, and his forward observer team were with the leading platoon of the 2d of the 188th moving up the ridge. Captain Holloway moved to within twenty-five yards of the Japanese position and brought in a number of artillery concentrations all over the ridge. He was also able to direct the fires of some 105mm howitzer and 155mm guns from positions near Burauen. During the night of 26 December, the artillery from Manarawat and Burauen and the mortars and machine guns of Colonel Mann's battalion pounded the enemy defenses. On 27 December, the 2d Battalion stormed Purple Heart Hill and, after much bitter hand-to-hand fighting, destroyed the enemy and stayed on top of the ridge. The battalion closed in at dusk and had no time to dig in. The men simply moved into the old holes and revetments from which the Japanese had so recently been evicted.

The Japanese who had not been killed by the artillery, mortars, machine guns, and rugged, close-in fighting by the assault troops scattered to the north and the west. Those trying to escape to the north ran into Colonel Pearson's 1st of the 187th, which was attacking southward along the gorge and up the other ridge. "Three minutes before 1400 (H-Hour for the 1st of the 187th)," reported one of the men who had been in the attack, "we felt the mighty shock of the 'Long Toms' landing on the crest of the ridge and at 1400, with a cheer we clambered up to the plateau in assault, and it was like shooting ducks in a rain barrel. The concussion of the tremendous projectiles had shocked the defenders into impotence, and all we had to do was give them a dose of assault fire. Hundreds, we never knew how many, had been buried in their subterranean galleries." Those fleeing to the west ran into the ambush that F Company, returning from Mahonag after the evacuation of the Mahonag wounded, had set up along the Japanese supply trail.

The bloody battle for Purple Heart Hill was over after almost five weeks of containment followed by the final assault. The troops searched the area and found 238 dead Japanese and many fragments of bodies mangled by the artillery fire. They also found that the Japanese supply trail, which wound over the hills and through the gorges from Ormoc Bay, ended at Anonang. Butch Muller reasoned that, because of the extensive defenses, the fact that the supply trail terminated there, and because earlier patrols had seen Japanese sentries walking about with fixed bayonets on their rifles, Anonang was probably the command post of the Japanese 26th Division.

Part of the 675th Glider Field Artillery Battalion, under the command of Lt. Col. Mike Massad of Oklahoma football fame, and bereft of its pack 75s, was in the hills near Abuyogna, about a mile to the west of Burauen, acting like infantrymen. On Christmas Eve at about 2330, the Japanese attacked the perimeter of the 675th. Lieutenant Hubert W. Welton, of B Battery of the 457th, was the forward observer with the 675th. He had previously boxed in the 675th's perimeter with artillery concentrations. When the Japanese attacked, Lieutenant Welton called for the concentrations by numbers. B and C Batteries of the 457th, in firing positions just to the west of Burauen, responded with artillery fire all around the perimeter. The Japanese attack stopped shortly thereafter.

During December, the morale and the physical condition of the Japanese forces on Leyte sank to an incredible low. The Japanese 35th Army had begun to disintegrate. Desertions were common. The wounded refused to return to their basic units. Because the Japanese had scant medical facilities for treating their wounded, the problem of what to do with them became acute. The Japanese resorted to drastic measures. General Tomochika, chief of staff of the 35th Army, later said: "Commanders employing persuasive language frequently requested seriously wounded soldiers at the front to commit suicide; this was particularly common among personnel of the 1st Division and it was pitiful. However, the majority died willingly. Only Japanese could have done a thing like this and yet I could not bear to see the sight."

After 1 December, the Japanese on Leyte "were on a starvation diet and had to live off the land," according to Col. Junkichi Okabayashi, chief of staff of the Japanese 1st Infantry Division. "The men were forced to eat coconuts, various grasses, bamboo shoots, the heart fibers of coconut tree trunks, and whatever native fruits and vegetables they could forage. They were literally in a starved condition."

As they retreated, the Japanese abandoned equipment, weapons, and ammunition along the roads and trails. General Tomochika said that when the Americans captured his headquarters site, he left without any clothing. However, he picked up "a new uniform and sufficient food while on the road."

The troops of the 11th Airborne Division in the mountains and in the base camp at Bito Beach observed Christmas in a variety of ways. The division quartermaster drew 10,000 fresh turkey rations for Christmas dinner. The men in the hills got their turkey in cans and the real thing when they got back to the beach. General Swing made a special effort for the troops in the hills. He had the liaison airplane fleet drop Red Cross packages containing books, candy, and cigarettes and as much mail and as many packages from home as was possible. Some chaplains jumped and some hiked in to conduct religious services. Even the division band, under the command of Warrant Officer Berglund, trudged up the mountain trails to Manarawat and Mahonag to play for the wounded in the hospitals.

After the success at Purple Heart Hill and the juncture of the 511th and the 2d of the 187th with other American forces on the west coast, the main battles of the 11th Airborne Division on Leyte were finished. Most of the division units withdrew to the Bito Beach base camp. The 674th and 675th Glider Field Artillery Battalions, however, stayed in the hills outside Burauen, scouting and patrolling the eastern approaches to the Leyte hills. The 457th Parachute Field Artillery Battalion remained in position outside Burauen to support the other howitzerless artillerymen still in the mountains. The 152d AA Battalion maintained its chain of relay stations across the mountain chain until about 9 January. But by 15 January, all of the 11th Airborne had returned to Bito Beach.

Lt. Fred A. Renaud, XO E Company 511th PIR, briefing his men before a training jump in New Guinea, Summer 1944.

Troopers of the 511th PIR chute up on Mindoro for the combat drop on Tagaytay ridge, Luzon.

511th RCT drop on Tagaytay Ridge, Luzon, 3 February 1945.

11th Airborne Division Command Post, Paranaque, Luzon, February 1945.

Two members of C Company, 511th PIR, Cpl. Henry Kusmierczyk on left and S/Sgt Charles Egbert, chat with three rescued Los Banos internees: Hal Bowie, holding his baby, Lea, and his wife Paquita, from Barcelona, Spain.

BG Albert Pierson (right) and Frank Smith, war correspondent for the Chicago Sun Times, *examine bullet holes in the side of one of four Japanese gliders parked along Dewey Blvd., Manila PI, February 1945.*

Frank Smith (left) and LTC Glenn J. McGowan, G1, 11th Airborne Division, examine a Japanese flag captured during the Los Banos raid.

Squad of G Company, 187th Glider Infantry Regiment, on patrol near Sulac, Luzon, 9 April 1945.

General Walter Krueger, CG of Sixth Army, talks to men of C Battery, 457th PFA Battalion, at Lipa airstrip, on 22 June 1945, before their jump at Aparri, Luzon the next day. LTC Nick Stadtherr, CO of the 457th, is on the left.

Men of the 511th Gypsy Task Force assemble after their jump and glider landings at Aparri on 23 June 1945. This was the first and only occasion in which U.S. gliders were used in combat in the Pacific.

Colonel Charles Tench, Army Air Corps, a member of General MacArthur's staff, greets Major General Joseph M. Swing on his arrival at Atsugi, Japan, on 30 August 1945.

Linkup of Gypsy Task Force and 37th Infantry Division south of Aparri on 28 June 1945.

General MacArthur shakes hands with M/Sgt. John F. Krausa, 11th Airborne Division band leader, at Atsugi, 30 August 1945. General MacArthur said to Sgt. Krausa: "I want you to tell the band that that's about the sweetest music I've ever heard."

First U.S. jeep in Tokyo—11th Airborne's 511th Signal Company's, not 1st Cavalry's—is center of Japanese attention.

MG Swing greets LTG Robert L. Eichelberger, CG of Eighth Army and LTG Oscar W. Griswold, CG of XIV Corps, at Sendai Railroad Station, October 1945.

Secretary of War Robert Patterson reviews troops of the 11th Airborne Division at Sendai on 7 January 1946.

11th Airborne troopers jumping over Hokkaido in October 1947.

Camp Crawford, home of the 11th Airborne Division Headquarters and the 187th Glider Infantry Regiment, Hokkaido, Japan. In the distance is Sapporo, Hokkaido's capital city.

MG (later LTG) Joseph M. Swing, Commander of the 11th Airborne Division from January 1943 until February 1948.

CHAPTER 11

BITO BEACH AND THE INVASION OF LUZON

On 24 December, General Swing wrote another letter to General March in which he summed up the operations of the division on Leyte.

Dear General,
Am just back from a few days in the mountains, as a matter of fact I've walked clean across this d—— island and it wasn't the most pleasant jaunt I ever took. Wish you could see these young men of mine fight. It would do your heart good to see the calm joyful manner in which they kill the rats. I really believe this is the first time the Japs have run against American troops that never stop coming. It has been the custom in this so called jungle warfare for troops to start "holing up" an hour or more before sundown and form their so-called perimeter from which they never venture forth until after cooking individual breakfast at daylight—taking an hour to do so. As a result, the Japs bivouac at their ease, have scouts watch the formation of the perimeter and then heckle our troops all night. We changed that—made my troops keep going until dark, then dig in so the Japs don't know where we are located and finally got them to the point where they would start out just before the crack of dawn without breakfast. As a result, we've killed about twice as many Japs in proportion to our own casualties as had any other division. The last day,

the 22d, when we busted out of the hills to where the 7th Division was sitting on the beach—the dawn attack caught 300 Japs sleeping outside their foxholes and we slaughtered them there with bayonet, knife, and hand grenades. From then on it was a field day—had four battalions in column. As fast as one showed the least sign of tiring, sent the next one thru and by noon, we had done 4,000 yards—took a break for breakfast, and at 1430, we were on the beach and the 7th Division bivouac. Counted approximately 750 dead Japs and didn't go down the cliffs where many of them rolled off—captured two mountain howitzers, 1000 rounds of ammunition, 16 light machine guns, seven heavies, and the Japs left engineer, signal and medical supplies and many split-toed shoes along the trail. Have told the Corps commander if he wants to walk from Burauen air fields to Ormoc beach all he has to do is put a clothes pin on his nose and let a man with a strong stomach guide him.

Our identification shows that we cleaned out the 16th and 26th Division completely. The two had consolidated in the Mt. Mahonag region and initiated the attack on the airfields in conjunction with the paratrooper attack of Dec 6th. Have killed the Chief of Staff of the 16th Division and most of the staff of both divisions but unable to locate the two commanding generals. Prisoners of war say they were replaced by new commanders but believe they were evacuated by air. Of course the devils bury their officers and booby trap their bodies so we'll never know.

Am taking a week to evacuate to the beach and reequip for an airborne operation, but as I told you some time ago the staff is a pain in the neck to me so far as having a little imagination. Afraid they can't supply us once we're in and we have practically supplied ourselves with cub planes for over a month in the mountains. Come under Eichelberger's command on the 26th. He has already sent word he wants to see me about an airborne operation, so maybe we'll have a chance to do our stuff. You probably surmised the orthodox manner in which they will attack Luzon. Have a spot picked out south of Manila that would give the so and so's fits if I can convince the powers to land me there. Xmas greetings.

Sincerely, Joe

From 20 January on, the remnants of the Japanese forces hid out in the Villaba sector on the west coast of Leyte, north of Palompon. General Suzuki and his staff waited almost two months for a ship to arrive to evacuate them, during which time they reportedly had plunged into the depths of despair. Finally, on the night of 17 March, two Japanese vessels appeared off the coast. At 0300 on the morning of the eighteenth, General Suzuki and part of his staff boarded the boats and left the island.

For days they sailed from island to island in the Visayas only to find that the islands were already occupied by the Americans. On 16 April, off the coast of Negros Island, American aircraft spotted the boat in which General Suzuki was riding. The U.S. bomber attacked the vessel; General Suzuki was killed. With that death, the Leyte campaign was ritualistically finished.

The campaign had involved large numbers of troops. During January 1945, when the American forces were at their greatest strength, 257,766 U.S. Army and Air Force troops occupied the island. The total U.S. Army casualties for the operation were more than 15,500, including more than 3,500 killed and nearly 12,000 wounded. The 11th Airborne Division suffered 532 casualties, of which 168 were killed, 352 were wounded, and 12 were missing in action.

The total number of Japanese who fought on the island and the casualties they suffered are very difficult to assess. After the war, General Tomochika, the chief of staff of the 35th Army, estimated that 61,800 Japanese had been committed to Leyte and that, by 15 March 1945, 13,010 were alive and 48,790 had been killed. Sixth Army estimated that it had killed 56,263 and captured 389 Japanese and that, as of 26 December 1944, when it relinquished control of the island to Eighth Army, about 5,000 Japanese remained on Leyte and Samar. Eighth Army estimated that for the mop-up period, 26 December 1944 to 8 May 1945, it killed and found dead 24,294 and captured 439.

It is equally impossible to state accurately the number of Japanese killed by the 11th Airborne Division. But from the records available at higher headquarters and from the reports of the units of the 11th Airborne, a conservative estimate of the number of the enemy killed during the Leyte campaign is about 5,760. The division units also captured twelve prisoners of war.

The Allied objective for the Leyte operation had been to secure an entry into the Philippines and to establish a base for further conquest of the islands, particularly the main island, Luzon. The Allies had achieved that objective.

Because General MacArthur felt that the 11th Airborne Division was a "secret weapon," which he could commit rapidly out to the range of the transport aircraft, for many weeks his headquarters failed to mention the presence of the division in the fighting on Leyte. Two men from H Company of the 511th, Privates First Class Feuerisen and Merisieki, had been wounded and sent to the rear area to recover. After they were well enough for light duty, they were put to work loading supplies on C-47s at Tacloban for drops to the units in the mountains. One afternoon, they wandered over to General MacArthur's headquarters near Tacloban. An officer was standing in front of General MacArthur's office. The two Pfc's asked the officer if there was any way they could get to see General MacArthur because they wanted to know why the 11th Airborne had not been mentioned in his dispatches. The officer replied that General MacArthur was very busy and could not see them. But somehow, General MacArthur heard the conversation through an open window and invited the Pfc's to come into his office. Feuerisen and Merisieki once again explained their mission. General MacArthur then showed them the entire situation on his own operations map, pointed out the part played by the 11th Airborne Division, and told them that he wanted to conceal the presence of the 11th from the enemy until the time was "propitious." He asked the two Pfc's to point out on his map the location of the 511th's companies. Then he gave them a message to deliver to General Swing and the men of the 11th. He was aware of their great fight against the Japanese, the elements, and the terrain, he said, and that as soon as he could he would give the division the full credit it deserved.

The two soldiers left with a feeling of great satisfaction and importance. They had proven to themselves that their superb outfit had not been overlooked, that General MacArthur was aware of their presence, and that the only way to get a job done was to go to the top. On their return to the division, they dutifully reported the success of their public affairs mission to General Swing—and to anyone else within earshot.

By 15 January, the entire division had closed back onto Bito Beach for rest, recuperation, reorganization, re-equipping, and retraining. The various units, most especially the infantry, received new men and integrated them into what were now definitely battle-tested squads, platoons, and companies.

To complete the transition from combat, the mud and rain, and the tattered combat fatigues the troops had endured for the past two or so months, General Swing ordered a division review. On 21 January, the division formed on Bito Beach in front of Division Headquarters dressed in khakis, boots, steel helmets, and web belts and carrying personal arms—M-1s, 45s, and carbines. The division lined up with the palm trees behind it and the ocean to its front. It was a fairly unique setting for a division review. The reviewing officer was Lt. Gen. Robert Eichelberger, commanding general of Eighth Army, to which the division had recently been transferred. General Eichelberger pinned medals to the chests of proud airborne soldiers who had earned them in the muck and hills of Leyte and then he made a few remarks to the troops of the 11th. "I expect great things from this division," he said, "because not only had the division fought well and hard on Leyte but also because some of the enterprising troopers of the 11th had been the only ones who had been able to penetrate the WAC's compound at Dobodura, New Guinea."

On a more serious note, he did tell General Swing at lunch that day that he was "elated" when General MacArthur had given him the go-ahead to invade Batangas with the 11th Airborne Division. He also gave General Swing two priorities: One, get to Manila first, and two, free the prisoners at Los Banos as soon as feasible.

General Swing was looking ahead to the battle for Luzon and the capital city, Manila. In a 30 December 1944 letter to General March, he foresaw the tough battles that the American forces would have to fight to retake Luzon.

Had lunch with General Eichelberger the other day and discussed future plans for this division. His army up until now has been largely "dog-robbing" for Krueger. When an island is declared conquered, he has had the unpleasant job of running these rats out of their holes and it's a pretty arduous one. However, before long I prophesy he'll have a role parallel to the Sixth. In my estimation, the Battle of Luzon is going to take everything we've got out here and maybe a little bit more. In the campaigns of the New Guinea coast and contiguous islands, "by-passing" was the word. Cut off from all supply, the Nips were forced to withdraw, break contact and exercise strict economy. There are still thousands of them there whom the Aussies are going to have one h—— of a time killing off before they can start exploiting the place again.

All that is over now. The Japs are reinforcing their garrisons in Luzon to an extent that makes almost every attack a frontal one. The chances of seizing an undefended beach head from which an assault can be launched are nil. We're going to have to fight for every inch. My proposal is to hit at one of the more difficult landing areas once the main attack has gained a foothold. If I can be dropped at one of several places inland where converging roads will allow me to hold off all reinforcements, a secondary landing might turn out to be the quickest way to Manila. Eichelberger sees the possibilities and I believe will push it. Hope so. Anyhow, am busy refitting and spotting aerial equipment so that we'll be ready for anything. My men fought harder than any of them. The high command knows it. As a result, they would like to have their cake and eat it. We can't be pulled out of the fight and launched airborne with the care that one buys an excursion ticket to New York City. . . .

The Air Corps photographers have just finished some stills and movies of our operations in the hills. Believe the stills are promised for *Look* in March and a short film of the aerial resupply is to be released later. The photographers say it is the best story out of the Southwest Pacific. Taken with a grain or two of salt, it still may be of some interest to others besides ourselves.

Sincerely, Joe

The battle for Leyte was over. The Americans had established a base on the island from which medium bombers could strike Luzon, the heart of the Philippine archipelago. Long and hard fighting loomed ahead for the Allies, but even before the invasion of Luzon, the Japanese High Command was not sanguine. General Yamashita, the commander of all the Japanese forces in the Philippines, said after the war: "After the loss of Leyte . . . I realized that decisive battle was impossible. . . ."

For three years the Allies had fought through jungles and over mountains, in torrid temperatures and monsoon rains, at the end of supply lines from which spewed the necessities for battle but few luxuries. Ahead of the forces lay hard battles, more casualties, discouragements, and frustrations, but ultimately victory in the Philippines.

On Bito Beach, the 11th Airborne troopers talked and guessed about their next campaign. Rumors flowed from every conceivable source. The troops knew that Luzon had been invaded on 9 January and that they had not been a part of that operation. Shortly, unit commanders received a supply of handbooks on the terrain and conditions on southern Luzon. Company commanders lectured their troops on the vegetation, climate, and geography of the island. Staffs built sand tables of the area from Nasugbu east to Batangas and north to Manila. Rumors became reality. The 11th Airborne was obviously slated for an operation in southern Luzon.

The debate within the Joint Chiefs of Staff over whether to invade Formosa or Luzon next after the Leyte campaign was finally settled when Admiral King eventually, and at the eleventh hour, accepted Admiral Nimitz's recommendation that Luzon instead of Formosa be the next target for the Allies in the Pacific. With Admiral King's acquiescence, the Joint Chiefs had the unanimity they sought. Even so, they were reluctant to give up the Formosa strategy in favor of Luzon, but the scarcity of logistical and shipping support would have forced the Luzon selection on them in any event. And they could not delay the war in the Pacific until Germany collapsed. On 3 October 1944, therefore, they ordered General MacArthur to launch the invasion of Luzon on or about 20 December, and Admiral Nimitz to execute the Iwo Jima and Okinawa operations on the dates he had recommended—Iwo Jima late in January 1945 and Okinawa on 1 March 1945.

General MacArthur found that he could not meet the Joint Chiefs' 20 December date for the invasion of Luzon for a number of reasons. First, the monsoons and Japanese air attacks had so delayed construction of airfields on Leyte that there was no room on the island for the aircraft to support the invasion of Mindoro and Luzon. Next, sufficient naval air and transport support was not available to meet the 20 December target. In addition, the tidal and moon conditions at Lingayen Gulf would be far more favorable in early January than in late December. Given these problems, General MacArthur reluctantly set 9 January for the date of the Luzon invasion.

General MacArthur wrote later, in *Reminiscences,* about the reasoning he had used to make the major effort on Luzon in the Lingayen area.

With our occupation of Mindoro, General Yamashita became greatly concerned over the prospect of an imminent invasion of the southern area of Luzon. Stationing the Eighth Army off the southern coast of Luzon, I planned to threaten landings at Legaspi, Batangas, and other southern ports, hoping to draw the bulk of the Japanese into the south. Our plans then called for landing the Sixth Army in an amphibious enveloping movement on the exposed northern shore, thus cutting off the enemy's supplies from Japan. This would draw the enemy back to the north, leaving the Eighth Army to land against only weak opposition on the south coast, in another amphibious movement. Both forces ashore, we would then close like a vise on the enemy deprived of supplies and destroy him. No plan ever worked better.

While the 11th Airborne Division was healing its wounds, both human and logistical, on Bito Beach and while the Eighth Army was mopping up Leyte with the forces left behind by Sixth Army, on 9 January 1945, Sixth Army had invaded Luzon with two entirely different corps and four divisions that had not fought on Leyte.

The U.S. invasion proceeded better than the Sixth Army staff had hoped. One report said that the rapid advance "far exceeded the wildest dreams of those who had planned the operation." After the amphibious landings in the Lingayen area, the residents returned to their homes, broke out their long-hidden American flags, and greeted the invading liberators with flag-waving and laughing crowds thrusting chickens, fresh eggs, fruit, and flowers on the soldiers plodding through the barrios. In the first few days after the invasion, the assault troops captured the coastal towns and spread inland to a depth of twenty miles, along dusty roads, a welcome relief from the monsoonally flooded trails of Leyte. The enemy in the area was unusually weak, as exemplified by four Japanese soldiers in San Fabian who failed the test of the Japanese warrior spirit by trying to escape disguised as women.

General Oscar Griswold's XIV Corps on the western side of the beachhead plodded southward through the Luzon Plain against negligible enemy defenses. On the eastern edge of the plain, however, Gen. Ennis Swift's I Corps hit strong enemy resistance along the forward line of General Yamashita's mountain stronghold.

In a week, XIV Corps had pushed inland about twenty-five miles, but far short of General MacArthur's desires and ardent expectations. He urged Generals Krueger and Griswold to move faster and speed up the advance. He vented his exasperations in a 17 January message to General Krueger to "get his forces moving." General Krueger relayed General MacArthur's message to General Griswold, who moved ahead more rapidly until 23 January, when he ran into the forward elements of the 30,000-man force that General Yamashita had ordered to hold Clark Field and the Zambales Mountains in the west.

Meanwhile, General Swift's three divisions, which made up I Corps, had continued to run into extremely stiff opposition in the mountain strongholds to the east of the Luzon Plain, from Lingayen Gulf southeast to the Pampanga River.

The Luzon operation now entered a new phase, and General Mac-Arthur wanted to capture Manila swiftly and with as little damage as possible, for personal as well as political and strategic reasons. One of his main concerns was the release of the soldiers and civilians who had been captured and interned by the Japanese for the past three years.

The closer he got to Cabanatuan, New Bilibid, and Los Banos, the more urgent became his solicitude for the prisoners, and the more impatient he became with the progress of Sixth Army toward the capital of the Philippines. "With every step that our soldiers took toward . . . where these prisoners were held, the Japanese soldiers guarding them had become more and more sadistic. I knew that many of these half-starved and ill-treated people would die unless we rescued them promptly," he wrote. "The thought of their destruction with deliverance so near was deeply repellent to me."

On 22 January 1945, back on Bito Beach, General Swing received Field Order Number 17 from Eighth Army, which alerted the division for an impending operation on Luzon. On 25 January 1945, General Swing wrote another letter to General March in which he explained what had happened:

Dear General:

Well, half a loaf is better than none, I suppose, but, when a whole loaf is sitting right there in the bread box, it makes me d—— mad not to slice it up.

I've won somewhat of a victory over the Air Corps and the Big G-3. We're going in half Airborne and half amphibious. The plan is one I've advocated for four months, only I was to go whole hog by air with another division seaborne. As you can imagine, it's an end run with a forward pass. As a climax, Eichelberger is going in with me to take over as soon as more troops arrive and as there is no love lost between him and Krueger, he's going to give me all the support he can muster from the "leavings" of the Lingayen convoy. If he isn't standing at the bar in the Army Navy Club when Krueger walks in the door, it won't be for lack of trying.

Anyhow, it's going to be a good show and a fast one. We're stripped to the bone due to lack of both air and water transportation, so if we don't get on our roller skates and move, we'll probably have to draw our belts pretty tight before it is over.

The G-2 information on the situation confronting me is absolutely "lousy." I'm going in blind, depending to a large extent on 11th Airborne luck which to date has been OK. These youngsters of mine are raring to go again and I don't believe we'll get our noses bloodied too badly.

Sincerely, Joe

General Swing's annoyance at the "Big G-3" was occasioned by the fact that from 9 January until shortly before 22 January, GHQ had directed General Swing to drop the 511th RCT in two-hundred-man (or reinforced company–sized) units "all over southern Luzon." General Headquarter's reasoning, presumably, was that airborne units scattered all over southern Luzon would confuse the enemy as to the size of the airborne operation and would thus force General Yamashita to keep his forces south of and out of Manila searching for the dispersed paratroopers. General Swing won the argument: The 511th RCT would drop in as a unit in one place, not in small pockets all over southern Luzon.

To an airborne commander, scattering his troops over an area made no sense. He knew that his units could be chewed up piecemeal, that they would have a difficult time assembling at a later date, and that their resupply would be a logistical nightmare. John Conable, the division's assistant quartermaster, wrote recently:

General Swing was livid at the suggestion that we be scattered all over. He was reported to have said to higher headquarters, "If you want to take my Division from me, relieve me of command. But give my men a fighting chance." At the time I thought that the problem was General Eichelberger, but I have since discovered that he was our ally and that the problem was the G-3 of MacArthur's headquarters.

Roy Stout (the Division Quartermaster) discovered that I knew what loads could be put on a plane and that I could figure out what would go on a ship. For a week or ten days I was figuring out how to resupply our two hundred-man units and how they might consolidate after they got in. It was a nasty problem because the first ones in would need resupply before the last ones arrived.

I wasn't getting a great deal of sleep. I think on January 21 Bill Crawford (the division G-4) came back from Eighth Army where he had been with General Swing. He woke me up in an excited state about four in the morning. Everything had changed. He told me the new plan. When I got up at 6 A.M. I could remember everything that had happened except what the new plans were. I realized that when you don't get enough sleep your brain starts to protect you.

Much as I hated to do it, I had to wake Bill up to get the new plans. There were to be enough ships to put in the two glider combat teams amphibiously at a town called Nasugbu on the west coast of Luzon south of Manila. The 511th Combat Team would be flown from Mindoro to Tagaytay Ridge 35 miles inland where they would jump. This would take three round trips by the C-47's. The jump would be made when the Division Commander thought the two groups could link up in twenty-four hours.

The ships were ones that could be found and the plans kept changing daily as to what ships were coming. I later figured that the seven days before embarking I averaged slightly less than three hours sleep a night.

In the formal, military prose of the staff writer, Field Order Number 17 from Eighth Army directed that the "11th A/B will land one regimental combat team on X-Day at H-Hour in the Nasugbu area, seize and defend a beachhead; 511th Parachute Regimental Combat Team will be prepared to move by air from Leyte and Mindoro bases, land by parachute on Tagaytay Ridge, effect a junction with the force of the 11th A/B moving inland from Nasugbu; the 11th A/B Div, reinforced, after assembling on Tagaytay Ridge will be prepared for further action to the north and east as directed by Commanding General, Eighth Army."

The field order galvanized the entire division into action. The staff conferred with the navy to arrange the shipping that would transport the division minus the 511th RCT to Luzon; it conferred with the Air Corps to arrange the aircraft for the drop on Tagaytay Ridge. The 408th Quartermaster Company worked overtime to bring the units up to full Table of Equipment strength. That was a formidable task because 90 percent of the backup supply of individual equipment and clothing and many of the crew-served weapons had been lost in the jungles or destroyed by the Japanese parachute attack in the division supply dumps at Burauen on 6 December. All of the division's vehicles had to be completely overhauled because of their continuous use in Leyte's mud for more than two months. For the amphibious units, the vehicles had to be waterproofed. For the parachute units, their few vehicles had to be loaded with the units landing amphibiously and reclaimed later. All weapons were put through a rigorous and complete inspection.

Many units, including the Division Headquarters, went through staff and command changes as a result of the combat losses and other requirements. In the 187th, for example, Lt. Col. George Pierson took over as executive officer of the regiment from Lt. Col. Bob MacCleave, who had suffered an almost fatal heart attack at Patog, Leyte, and was flown back to Walter Reed Hospital in Washington. Lieutenant Colonel Harry Wilson moved from the 2d Battalion to replace Colonel Pierson, and Lt. Col. Norman Tipton returned from the 511th to take over his old battalion, the 2d of the 187th, from Harry Wilson. The regimental surgeon, both battalion executive officers, and many company officers were also switched.

One of the men in the division wrote later:

From the 22d on, we moved rapidly. Forgotten were our swimmings and sunnings, our extracurricular sack time, our card games in rain-beaten tents. We were getting ready to go back into combat. From all the rumors that floated down, we thought things were going to be rough. And by the time the G-2 information came to us, we knew that we had been thinking correctly. We heard about Nasugbu, Batangas, Mt. Aiming, Tagaytay Ridge, the Genko Line, Nichols Field, Fort McKinley, Cavite, and Manila.

On 24 January, Division Headquarters issued its own directive, Field Order Number 10, which outlined in detail the division's plan for carrying out Eighth Army's order. In addition to telling unit commanders precisely how many days of supplies they would load aboard the ships, it also provided for an amphibious dry run for glider units that were more attuned to entering combat by landing in a field in a glider than they were in wading ashore from a navy amphibian. On 26 January, as ordered, the first three waves loaded, pushed out into Leyte Bay, and then came charging back at Bito Beach. The division commander deemed the dry run a success, and ordered the amphibians to mount their ships.

CHAPTER 12

NASUGBU TO MANILA

Task Group 78.2, under Rear Adm. William M. Fechteler, loaded and landed the assault troops. The task group numbered about one hundred twenty ships and landing craft of all types, with four APDs and six LSTs the largest. There were also thirty-two LCIs and eight LSMs. An additional eight LCIs would carry part of the 511th to Mindoro. Admiral Fechteler was aboard the command ship *Spencer*. Naval fire support for the operation would be provided by Task Unit 77.3.1, which consisted of a light cruiser and two destroyers. Planes of the 310th Bombardment Wing would provide air support. Admiral Fechteler commanded what one of the troopers called "this shoe-string task force and gained the affection and gratitude of the Division through his capable planning and operation of the mission."

The loading of the ships was not totally smooth and without incident. John Conable wrote later:

One night, I was extremely tired and irritable. I was checking the loading between ten and eleven at night. I arrived at one of our LST's which was supposed to have 10 days of expendable supplies of the 127th Engineers and most of the artillery ammunition. The engineer supplies should have taken about one-third of the cargo hold. When I got there, the cargo hold was better than two-thirds full, and the Engineers were still loading their supplies. I found their supply officer, Vic Baccus, who told me that in spite of the Division Order to draw ten days of expendable supplies that Colonel Davis, the Division Engineer, had ordered him to draw thirty days.

About this time Col. Davis arrived at the scene and I confronted him. We were having a rather heated exchange. I knew that the old artilleryman, General Swing, would take a dim view of the situation if his artillery ammunition was on Leyte when his guns were on Luzon. I was mad enough to get into a fist fight with Davis when Roy Stout arrived. He sized the situation up rapidly and told me to go to bed that he would take care of it. I will always be grateful to Roy for getting me out of there before I got into serious trouble.

I don't know whether Roy and Bill Crawford had a ship that they didn't tell me about or whether they rounded one up after they discovered what Col. Davis had done. In any event, another ship arrived. The poor old 457th who were flying to Mindoro had to load the 674th's and 675th's ammunition on it.

General Swing was, of course, deeply concerned about the conditions of the beaches and the enemy defenses in and around the Nasugbu area where his glider units would beach. He had received some intelligence from Eighth Army, but, given his penchant for thoroughness and concern for his men, he felt that he needed one of his own men to reconnoiter the area, a man from one of the units that would be landing there.

On the evening of 14 January, Lt. Robert L. Dickerson was standing in the chow line when a soldier, whom he recognized as a runner from the 188th Regimental Headquarters, came up to him and said, "Colonel Soule would like to see you immediately." Dickerson found Colonel Soule, who told him that he was to report to General Swing at Division Headquarters at 1900.

When Dickerson arrived at the division CP, he found not only General Swing awaiting him, but also General Pierson, Colonel Quandt, and Colonel Muller. General Swing explained to Dickerson that he wanted him to go on an important mission to secure vital information from the southern section of Luzon. He told Dickerson to return to his unit, pick out a noncom to accompany him on the mission, and return to the division war room at 2100. Dickerson walked back to his area, mulling over in his mind the best noncom for the job. He finally decided that S. Sgt. Vernon W. Clark was the man he could rely on in any circumstance.

By 2100, Dickerson was back at the Division Headquarters with

Sergeant Clark. In the war room, Colonels Quandt and Muller went over in great detail the area they wanted reconnoitered. When Dickerson and Clark left the war room, a jeep was waiting to take them to XIV Corps Headquarters at Palo, Leyte, to pick up their orders. The corps order was short and to the point: "Proceed from Tacloban by FS boat to San Jose, Mindoro. Upon arrival, report to BG William C. Dunckel for further orders." No one explained to Dickerson why he had to report to XIV Corps, why he had to report to General Dunckel, or why he and Clark did not fly from Tacloban to Mindoro. Dickerson simply followed his orders and did not reason why.

At about 0300 on 16 January, Dickerson and Clark sailed from Tacloban headed for San Jose, Mindoro, escorted by two PT boats. At one point during the early morning hours of the trip, Sergeant Clark said to Lieutenant Dickerson, "Lieutenant, I've been wondering what we should do if capture by the Japanese is imminent. I'm sure they'll make it a living hell." As Dickerson remembers, "With only the stars of the Southern Cross shining overhead as witness, we made a pact, that should capture become unavoidable, we would reserve our last round of ammunition for each other."

By late afternoon of 16 January, they arrived at San Jose and the next morning reported to General Dunckel. He invited them to his mess hall, and, over coffee, reiterated to them the importance of their mission. On 19 January, they left Mindoro aboard a PT boat accompanied by Lieutenant Angeles, a member of the Hunter ROTC guerrilla unit, who would lead them ashore to his camp on Luzon. At 0200 on 20 January, the PT boat hove to in Loac Cove, north of Nasugbu. The three men inflated a rubber boat and paddled their way to the beach. Above the noise of the surf, they could hear voices ashore. Lieutenant Angeles said, "It is our people who have come to meet us." Once they were on shore, Maj. Calex Gasilao, the guerrilla chief, welcomed them and bedded them down for sleep, which they had not had in more than twenty-four hours.

At about noon, they were awakened and told that it was time to eat. The meal was unique. Dickerson remembers:

The pig, head and all, was on a table, around which handmade rattan stools had been placed. Seated, and with "Thanks" returned, our first course was served: a bowl of fish-head soup, eyes intact, staring up as you looked into the sopa de peces. Around the table, members of the group were attacking the delicacy with mucho gusto. Some were popping out the eyes and eating them as if they were grapes. . . . I don't recall if either of us tried the eyes.

After eating, the guerrillas led Dickerson and Clark to a point where they had a good view of the town of Nasugbu. After more reconnaissance, they returned to the guerrilla camp, where they stood retreat while the guerrillas sang the "Star Spangled Banner." It was quite apparent that there were no Japanese in the immediate vicinity. That evening, Dickerson sent out patrols to reconnoiter the area to determine troop strength and defensive positions, gun emplacements, and the depth of the water at the designated landing site. On the night of 22 January, Dickerson and a patrol of guerrillas made a reconnaissance to the south along the road to Balayan. He located guns in the vicinity of San Diego Point and noted them on his map overlay.

Prior to leaving the PT boat, Dickerson had arranged to be picked up at 2200 on 23 January. When he sighted the ship, he was to flash a Morse code "R" if it was safe to land, or a "Y" if unsafe. At about 2100 that night, Dickerson, Clark, and a guerrilla escort came down from the guerrilla camp in the hills overlooking Nasugbu and started their vigil for the pickup PT boat. Around 0100, they sighted a boat and signaled an "R" but received no reply. Dickerson remembered, "As the vessel sailed from sight, the thought unavoidably crossed my mind—that must have been an enemy ship!"

By 0300, the PT boat had still not arrived and Dickerson was preparing to move back to the guerrilla hideout. Major Marcelo Castillo, one of the leaders of the local guerrillas, suggested that before they leave the beach, they go to the outer edge of the cove by banca and wait for the boat there. "As we approached the outer perimeter," Dickerson wrote later, "we heard and recognized the welcome glub-glub-glub of an idling Liberty engine. Without delay, we were aboard and on our way back to San Jose, Mindoro."

When Dickerson and Clark arrived in San Jose, they were met by Generals Eichelberger, Swing, and Dunckel. Later, Generals Eichelberger and Swing and Dickerson and Clark boarded a C-46 for the trip back to Leyte. Dickerson turned over to General Swing the maps he and Clark had made of the area, with all of the details of enemy positions, water depths, roads, and buildings that he had been able to put on the maps.

The next day Dickerson was summoned to report to General Swing at Division Headquarters. He recalls:

As I entered the General's quarters, he stood looking at one of the maps we had brought back with us. His first question was, "Lieutenant, what about this gun position marked on the map?" "Sir," I replied, "It's a position located south of the Sugar Central, in the vicinity of San Diego Point." The General shook his head and said, "There are no guns there." When I insisted that there were guns at that position, the General roared, "There are no guns there; that position is in defilade and of no value against an amphibious landing." When I persisted, the General said, "Lieutenant, I can read a map."

When the CG of the 11th Airborne spoke in that tone, only one reply was appropriate in order to escape the displeasure of those gun-metal blue eyes. And that was "YES, SIR."[1]

Recently, Gen. Albert Pierson recalled Lieutenant Dickerson's reconnaissance effort. "Dickerson's trip from Leyte by PT boat and meeting with the guerrillas," he wrote, "is one of the outstanding individual exploits of the division. I remember well the night that General Swing, at our CP on Bito Beach, gave Dickerson instructions for his trip to Luzon. We had been told that there were three possible landing beaches in southern Luzon, Nasugbu being one. Dickerson and his NCO were successful in meeting with guerrillas and the information that he brought back had a lot to do with our decision to land at Nasugbu."

In addition to receiving new equipment, on 19 January the 11th also received replacements: 22 officers and 934 men reported in on Leyte. They had originally been scheduled for the 503d, but the division needed them more. Thus, at the start of the Luzon campaign, the strength of the division was about 8,200 men, slightly more than half the size of a standard World War II infantry division. That fact was seemingly lost on the higher headquarters to which the division was attached for combat on Luzon. To higher headquarters, the 11th was a division and given division missions. The proud troopers of the division felt that the odds were about right or even tilted in favor of the standard infantry division.

The amphibious units of the 11th loaded their ships on the 26th and set sail on the 27th. With them, in LCIs, was a part of the 511th

---

[1] As it turned out, there were guns where Dickerson and Clark had plotted them.

RCT, which would be dropped off on Mindoro. The remainder of the 511th, the 457th, and a platoon of the 221st Medics flew by C-46 from Leyte to Mindoro.

The planning staffs at the echelons above the 11th Airborne Division had developed a number of scenarios for the employment of the 11th on Luzon. The 11th was a unique organization: It could enter combat by parachute, glider, or amphibious landing craft; it was lightly equipped and minimally staffed and manned and could therefore be transported overland quite economically once ashore. But its light armament and skeletonized organization, seven small infantry battalions instead of nine large ones, for example, made its staying power dependent on the quality of its soldiers and commanders. This the division would have to prove again in combat.

One of the original scenarios for use of the division on Luzon was an airborne—parachute and glider—attack on Clark Field. This fell through when it became apparent that there were insufficient airplanes, and a surprised staff officer found that all the CG 4A gliders were boxed and stored on an island somewhat removed from the Philippines. Another plan had the 503d Regimental Combat Team attached to the 11th Airborne for operations on Luzon. Both General Swing and Colonel Jones, the commander of the 503d, favored this option. But this possibility evaporated when the GHQ staff began to plan for the recapture of Corregidor and the likely use of the 503d separately for that operation. Another plan, the scattering of reinforced company–sized units by parachute over southern Luzon, collapsed against General Swing's vehement disagreement. Still another possibility had the 188th and the 187th landing on different beaches in southern Luzon—the 188th at Nasugbu and the 187th at Lucena. The latter was such a strong alternative that the 187th staff spent a couple of weeks in January studying the Lucena area.

What finally evolved was Operation Mike VI, the combined amphibious-parachute attack in southern Luzon, essentially a reconnaissance in force, to be exploited at the discretion of the Eighth Army commander. General MacArthur had told General Eichelberger before the attack that he wanted him to "undertake a daring expedition against Manila with a small mobile force using tactics that would have delighted Jeb Stuart."

With those guidelines, Generals Eichelberger and Swing developed Mike VI, an operation that other more traditional military planners might consider unusual and unorthodox. But it was essentially a workable plan. The 188th Glider Infantry Regimental Combat Team would assault Nasugbu beach first and secure a beachhead. The 187th Glider RCT would follow into that beachhead on order and protect the south flank by halting the enemy approaching from the Balayan Bay-Santiago Peninsula area. The 511th Parachute RCT with the 457th Parachute Field Artillery Battalion less D Battery would drop on Tagaytay Ridge when General Swing could assure General Eichelberger that the amphibious elements would be able to link up with the paratroopers in less than twenty-four hours. D Battery of the 457th would land at Nasugbu with the assault units. Eighth Army designated 31 January as X-Day and 0831 as H-Hour. General Eichelberger's staff also arranged for the navy to shell the beaches for one hour prior to the landings. The division would then prepare for further action to the north and east as directed by General Eichelberger. The 13th and 15th Air Forces would provide assault and supporting fires, and the Seventh Fleet would provide both the amphibious and naval gunfire ships.

Butch Muller had assembled all the data that he could gather on the climate and geography of southern Luzon and the enemy situation therein from higher headquarters, guerrillas, Air Corps photos, and Sixth Army's Alamo Scouts. He put it all together in great detail on a sand table in the division war room. He also had available terrain handbooks and maps of the area, which he issued down to include battalion staffs. Major Isaac Hoppenstein, the S-4 of the 187th, remembered that "credit must be given . . . to the excellent G-2 information we had in planning this operation. Much of this credit is due to Lt. Col. Jay D. Vanderpool, who was the GHQ Liaison Officer and had been coordinating guerrilla activities in Batangas and Cavite Provinces of Luzon for approximately four months before our landing. . . . Vanderpool was a volunteer for this job and was landed in Luzon by submarine."

The regiments also made their own sand tables. One of the men of the 187th said that "all platoons were briefed on the terrain from aerial photographs and around sand-table relief mock-ups so realistic that when we reached our destination the area seemed positively familiar."

What the maps, photos, and sand tables pointed out was that the terrain and approaches to Tagaytay Ridge from Nasugbu dictated that the division's advance would be canalized along Highway 17. This road ran east from Nasugbu through valleys, between high mountains, along crests of ridges, and over rolling to flat terrain. Behind Nasugbu were rice and cane fields, which would restrict vehicular traffic to the roads.

Six miles behind the city, the highway began to rise gradually, cross several rivers, and pass through a defile between Mount Cariliao and Mount Batulao. At this point, the road was 700 feet above sea level; the mountains on either side were about 2,500 feet high. The terrain in the area was heavily to slightly wooded and, rather ominously for the attackers, the highway snaked through embankments in most of the area. Beyond the mountains, Highway 17 ran east and up gently rising slopes to the top of Tagaytay Ridge. Here the ridge formed the northern edge of Lake Taal, which filled the blown-out crater of an extinct volcano. The lake had an island in its middle, and there was another lake on that island and still another lake in its center. The northern slope of Tagaytay Ridge was gentle, but the southern slope dropped precipitously to Lake Taal.

Near the eastern edge of Tagaytay Ridge, the road turned north and began a slow descent to a plain area and Bacoor City on Manila Bay. From Bacoor, Highway 17 passed through Las Pinas and Paranaque, and edged past Nichols Field before reaching Manila proper. From Nasugbu to Tagaytay Ridge was about thirty miles; from Tagaytay to Manila was about thirty-seven miles. In the weeks ahead, these names and distances would become vividly familiar to the troopers of the 11th Airborne.

The G-2 estimated that in the Nasugbu-Tagaytay area there were about 8,000 enemy troops, with a regiment of mixed units manning the defenses in southern Luzon. The enemy forces in southern Luzon were the Fuji Heiden, a composite group commanded by Col. Masatoshi Fujishige. The bulk of the enemy troops came from the 17th and 31st Infantry Regiments of the Japanese 8th Infantry Division and other miscellaneous outfits. The G-2 estimate also held that about 500 Japanese defended the shores of Nasugbu Bay, and that the main Japanese force, some 5,000 strong, held Highway 17 at Tagaytay Ridge and a defile west of the ridge, where the highway passed between the peaks of two extinct volcanoes.

The enemy troops were reasonably well equipped, with normal infantry weapons and light and medium artillery pieces. Following his usual tactics in the Philippines, the Japanese commander of the Fuji Heiden concentrated his forces inland in central locations and defended the beaches with light holding forces. The Japanese commander planned to conduct his defense in the first critical terrain feature to the rear of the beaches, probably near Aga, because he did not have enough men and equipment to man the defenses of all possible landing areas. In addition, the hills to the rear of the beaches, heavily overgrown, offered excellent concealment and high ground for dug-in defensive tactics.

The guerrilla reports held that the Japanese were defending the Nasugbu beach area with only two 75mm guns and several machine guns, emplaced on the high ground at Nasugbu Point, Wawa, and San Diego Point.

The enemy air forces posed an insignificant threat. One corps after-action report held that "recent air raids by Admiral Halsey's fleet had reduced the enemy air force [on Luzon] to an estimated nominal figure of 160 fighters and 170 bombers." Other reports held that the serviceable Japanese aircraft were far fewer than those numbers.

Robert R. Smith, writing in *Triumph in the Philippines,* said:

The estimates [of the 11th Airborne Division] were correct in general but wrong in detail. Shimbu Group, responsible for the conduct of operations in southern Luzon, had entrusted the defense of the region to the Fuji Force. . . . Numbering some 8,500 men, the Fuji Force was composed of the 17th Infantry less the 3d Battalion; the 3d Battalion of the 31st Infantry; a battalion of mixed artillery; and combat engineers and service troops of the 8th Division. Cooperating with Colonel Fujishige (and soon to pass to his direct command) were about 5,000 troops of the 2d Surface Raiding Base Force, a Japanese Army unit made up of suicide boat units. . . . The Raiding Squadron . . . each contained 100 suicide boats and a like number of men. . . . Five or six of the Raiding Squadrons, which had lost most of their boats to Allied air and naval action before or shortly after the 11th Airborne Division's landing, ultimately became available to Colonel Fujishige. . . .

With a large area and an extensive coast line to hold, Fujishige originally deployed the bulk of his troops for defense against an Allied attack from the south rather than the west. In the area of immediate interest to the 11th Airborne Division he stationed his West Sector Unit, a nucleus of the 3d Battalion, 31st Infantry. The West Sector's largest concentration—600 infantry with artillery support—held the defile just west of Tagaytay Ridge, while another 400 infantrymen defended a southwestern nose of the ridge. The West Sector Unit had only 100 troops at or near Nasugbu; the remaining men were scattered in small garrisons throughout southwestern Luzon.

Another part of the G-2 estimate had to do with the climate; and the troops of the 11th Airborne, after enduring the rigors of the Leyte weather, were delighted to learn that the climate of Luzon in February was fairly dry with moderate temperatures.

As X-Day drew closer, the pace of activity in the division area increased perceptibly. The division's supply loading plan laid the responsibility for loading the division reserve supplies on the unit commanders. The division G-4, Roy Stout, set up a special section to plan and load the division, an operation run efficiently, if at times justifiably cantankerously, by Maj. John S. Conable.

But, Maj. Isaac Hoppenstein of the 187th wrote:

The catch to the whole plan was the uncertainty of what ships the Navy would send and this was not definite until the ships came in at approximately 2000 hours on 25 January. Most of the supply ships were completely loaded within 24 hours, except for the great bulk of engineer supplies, ammunition and gasoline. The LCI's for the troops arrived at 0700 hours on 27 January and soon thereafter, the troops went aboard. The assault convoy of almost a hundred ships (LSM's, LST's, LCI's, APD's and escort destroyers) pulled out to sea late that afternoon.

The convoy headed south through the Mindanao Sea (rather than risk the narrow passage between Leyte and Samar), then swung north through the Sulu Sea to Mindoro where the 511th Parachute Infantry Combat Team disembarked to prepare for their jump on Tagaytay Ridge. The remaining force proceeded to its assigned mission to arrive on schedule at Nasugbu Bay. Two FS boats carrying a great bulk of the division's ammunition and gasoline did not proceed with the convoy. This affected the division greatly in regard to gasoline, and it became necessary, during the operation, to have gasoline flown in by C-47 planes. . . . The time from 27 January to the morning of the landing on 31 January passed too quickly. The LCI's were crowded. As there were no cooking facilities for the troops, the men ate "10-in-1" rations. There were no "steak and eggs last meals" served these troops as customary prior to landing. . . . Most of the sailing days were spent in map study, planning and orientation. Excess baggage was not carried. The personnel had only that which they could carry on their backs. One half of the kitchen equipment and all T/O and E equipment that the commanders did not believe necessary for the operation were left in Leyte. All gas masks had been inspected, boxed and were held under division control. The lesson learned in Leyte was that men would abandon excess equipment, most especially the gas mask. Personnel carried one K and two D rations and one unit of fire for the assault. We did not see our personal baggage until two months after the landing.

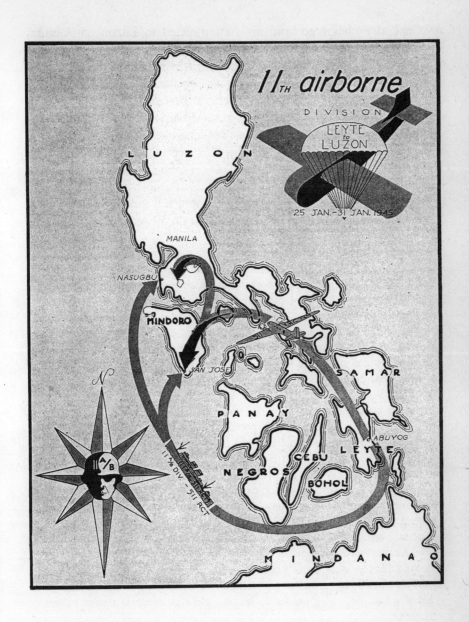

11TH airborne

DIVISION

LEYTE to LUZON

25 JAN.–31 JAN. 1945

General Eichelberger and his staff traveled to Luzon on Admiral Fechteler's command ship, the *Spencer,* along with General Swing and his staff. During the four-day trip, General Eichelberger had ample opportunity to talk to General Swing about the upcoming operation, MacArthur's "reconnaissance in force." General Eichelberger also had a lot of time to write to his wife. At sea in the Philippines on 28 January he wrote: ". . . I understand there are over a hundred ships in the convoy. It is really a beautiful sight and the Navy certainly know their stuff. They run these shows in grand style. . . ." On 29 January he wrote: "I might try a fast drive to Manila. . . . Almost dark. . . . Have been selling Joe [Swing] the idea of a rapid advance—will back him up if he gets his pants shot off. . . ." And on 30 January:

Tomorrow morning about this time we land ourselves. This morning had to laugh at the usual announcement over the loudspeaker: "Sick call— all the sick, lame and lazy report to the Sickbay. . . ." The weather is fine and we now have the pleasure of seeing many good old American planes flying overhead. . . . There are four planes right now flying over my head and circling around. . . . We are not expecting any air attacks but of course one never can tell with people as unpredictable as the Japs. They are just liable to pass up a good target and attack a rowboat.

Joe Swing is grand to deal with. He and Fechteler both seem very glad to have me around. . . . This afternoon I talked to Joe Swing for about an hour and a half. . . . He spent quite a long time in Africa and in the Sicily landing on a very peculiar mission. . . . He saw a great deal of interplay of personalities and from what I judge we get it rather lightly out here. . . . Billie Bowen and I are standing here now talking about what we may run into tomorrow. There is always a big gamble. One always gets surprises. For example, the PT boys at breakfast told me they were cruising in a bay where they had never drawn any fire for a long time and then yesterday they got an awful blast from about twelve places. Fortunately, that is not . . . where we are going to land.

As one travels along like this, I realize how unimportant little things can be. Things that seem important to some people, such as publicity and reputation, mean nothing at a time like this. All we will care about for a while are victories, food, health, and the eventual return to our homes.

At dawn on 31 January, the convoy arrived off the shore of Nasugbu. The sea was calm, the sky was clear, and the visibility was superb. On the LCIs and other landing craft, the troops who could get a glimpse of the shoreline saw the white beaches, the town of Nasugbu, and, beyond that, the green mountains of southern Luzon.

The serenity of the day was broken at 0700 when eighteen A-20s and nine P-38s appeared overhead, roared down on the deck, and strafed the beaches. At 0715, the navy began shelling the landing area, Red Beach, with rockets from LCIs and shells from destroyers. At 0815, the shelling ceased, and the beach party headed for shore. At 0822, the party radioed that they had landed without opposition, and at 0825, the first wave of eight LCVPs chugged toward the shore. When the crafts beached, the men hustled down the ramps, waded through the surf, sometimes up to their waists and chests, and waddled ashore through the soft sand up to their ankles. The first assault troops on land headed immediately for their first objective, Nasugbu, 1,500 yards away. The Japanese responded with light, sporadic machine gun fire and a few scattered artillery rounds from caves on Nasugbu Point to the north and San Diego Point on the south flank. Colonel LaFlamme, the commander of the 1st of the 188th, the first battalion ashore, sent patrols to the flanks to silence the Japanese in the area. Colonel Soule, not wanting to miss any of the action, and his staff had landed at 0830.

General Swing had selected Col. Ernie LaFlamme to lead the first battalion ashore because he knew that Colonel LaFlamme was familiar with the area. Before the war, Colonel LaFlamme, a member of the West Point class of 1937, had been stationed at Fort McKinley, outside Manila, and had spent a number of weekends with his wife at Nasugbu's beach. He knew the area well.

At 0830 on 31 January, General Eichelberger wrote: "Landings going according to schedule—no opposition as far as I can tell from here. . . . Lots of rocket bursts from our rocket ships—air strafing, bombardment, etc. Afraid they have knocked down the building I want to have. Can see Corregidor with the naked eye although it is some distance away."

General Swing was most anxious to get ashore. As was his custom, he formed two skeletonized command groups, which he separated when moving either by glider, as was the case in the Knollwood maneuver, or by ship, as in the invasion of southern Luzon. He wanted to be certain that if he were knocked out, Gen. Al Pierson would be ready to take over. In this case, General Swing and his command group traveled from Leyte aboard the command ship with Admiral Fechteler; General Pierson and his group made the trip aboard an LST.

LINGAYEN GULF

SIXTH ARMY

N

L U Z O N

BATAAN

36TH DIV.

MANILA

MANILA BAY

LAGUNA DE BAY

11TH DIV.

NASUGBU

LAKE TAAL

SHIRET

MARCH
ON
MANILA
31 JAN - 4 FEB 1945

2 1 0   2   4   6   8
MILES

General Pierson remembers the landing at Nasugbu this way:

Each staff transferred to LCVP's to reach the beach and the two landing craft arrived simultaneously, just behind the second wave of the 188th. We had moved only about ten yards when we were taken under fire by a Japanese machine gun to our left. Fortunately the position of the gun in a cave was picked up by gunners on an LCI that had discharged the 188th and was quickly silenced. The only casualty to our group was the compass which was deflected hanging from my belt. It ruined any use it might have had but I did carry it all through the campaign.

The G-2, Henry Muller, was also a part of the division staff landing at about the same time as General Pierson. He remembers: "I was also pinned down for a spell alongside General Swing and Bill Crawford (the G-4). Crawford became exasperated because the naval gunners would not man their guns and return the enemy fire. He announced that he was going to run back across the beach and man the gun of our LCI himself. When he leaped to his feet, Gen. Swing grabbed his boot and tumbled him to the sand again, telling him, 'You keep down. I need a G-4.' "

In a letter to General Pierson, Henry Muller wrote: "I believe it was I who first called your attention to your mangled compass. We had just assembled in the village square in Nasugbu when I noticed it and asked, 'General Pierson, have you seen what happened to your compass?'' General Pierson replied, "I knew that my compass had received a machine gun bullet, for my stomach felt it had received a hit by a baseball bat.' "

While the two command groups were lying in the sand, Colonel Schimmelpfennig, the division chief of staff, retrieved a bullet that had been imbedded in the sand. He immediately dropped the bullet with the comment: "Gee, it's hot." General Swing, lying beside him, remarked rather coldly: "What did you expect?"

The 1st Battalion, 188th, was followed ashore by Lt. Col. Tommy Mann's 2d of the 188th. Colonel Soule ordered Colonel LaFlamme to clear the beach to the north at Nasugbu Point; LaFlamme sent C Company on this mission. Soule ordered Mann to handle the enemy to the south on San Diego Point; he sent E Company.

The calm seas proved to be a hindrance to the landing and unloading of the landing boats carrying the heavier equipment; the absence of swells prevented the boats from getting swept close to shore. One two-and-a-half-ton truck and one tank destroyer foundered in water over their engines about fifty yards from shore. Some Japanese machine gun and artillery fire, from the vicinity of Wawa, was also beginning to fall on some of the landing craft and on the beach. Unfortunately, the artillery supporting the 188th, which could have suppressed some of the Japanese fire, had still not been able to get ashore. By 0930, the advancing troops determined that the fire in Wawa was coming from a red-roofed building. In a few minutes, the naval forward observer with the 188th brought in the fire from two LCIs firing rockets and from the destroyer *Claxton,* which completely destroyed the building and silenced that machine gun.

The navy did not escape without some pesky annoyances from the Japanese. Part of an official navy account of the landing said: "Nasugbu Bay had a nest of Japanese midget explosive boats built of wood. . . . Report of small patrol craft sunk by Japanese. . . . MG fire was silenced by 2 LCIs and Destroyer Claxton. . . . Midgets opened on Claxton which dodged torpedoes—six midgets destroyed—others withdrew. . . . One PT boat destroyed by our Destroyer Escort Lough. . . ."

At 0930, General Eichelberger wrote to Miss Em: "Everything is going forward very nicely so far. There is no opposition and I know Joe Swing will make fast time. I must make the decision after I hear from him whether to put any more troops ashore. The first landing is called a 'reconnaissance in force'. . . . The picture right now is of course very favorable. Lots of friendly planes overhead and lots of power in the harbor. After they all go back, however, there won't be so much, but I like Joe's outfit. They look like they'll fight plenty. . . ."

On the beach, several stalled vehicles just off the landing ships' ramps slowed down the unloading. Later in the morning, the navy directed a couple of destroyers to cruise near enough to the beach to create swells, which helped the landing craft get close enough to unload their vehicles.

As soon as the two battalions of the 188th were organized and ready to move, Colonel Soule ordered them to move rapidly inland and away from the beach. He directed Colonel LaFlamme to push toward Tagaytay Ridge as fast as possible to prevent the enemy from setting up defenses along Highway 17. He ordered Colonel Mann to move to the south across the Lian River, to knock out the enemy position at San Diego Point, and to protect the division's right flank. Later, the 2d of the

188th had also occupied the sprawling Don Pedro Sugar Central. From Filipinos, the troops learned that a seven-man Japanese demolition squad had planted explosives and had been set to blow the Central when a stray round landed nearby from one of the destroyers prepping the beaches. The Japanese, apparently feeling that the naval fire would eventually destroy the building anyway, withdrew without blowing the building.

By 0945, the regiment (less C and E Companies) had moved through Wawa and Nasugbu and its airstrip. Nasugbu had been relatively untouched by the war, and was the first town of any consequence that the troops had seen since they left the U.S. It was complete with village square and bandstand, the site of the first division CP on Luzon.

After the troops had moved into the town, they were greeted not only by the Filipinos but, surprisingly to the troops, by European men and women, refugees from the bombings and strife in Manila, who had taken up residence in Nasugbu. Along with the Filipinos, they were on hand to greet the soldiers with a tumultuous welcome and shouts of "Victoree" and "God bless you" and "Mabuhay" and gifts of bananas, eggs, chickens, and papayas.

Originally, the landing of the glider elements of the 11th had been designed as a strong reconnaissance by one regimental combat team to be exploited only if that unit found little enemy resistance. At about 1000, General Eichelberger, who was aboard the USS *Spencer,* decided from the reports he had received from General Swing and his staff that the time was propitious for the landing of the rest of the amphibious elements. He ordered General Swing to bring in the remainder of his floating force.

At 1030, Col. Harry Wilson led his 1st of the 187th ashore. His battalion, which had been part of the floating division reserve, landed and was attached to the 188th. The battalion quickly assembled and moved up to the Sugar Central to reorganize. After the 2d Battalion of the 188th had taken Lian and the Japanese had been driven back into the hills, the battalion joined the rest of the regiment in the march toward Tagaytay Ridge. The remainder of the 187th landed, relieved C and E Companies of the 188th of their flanking missions, and assumed responsibility for the operation and defense of Nasugbu. One battery of the 674th, when it got ashore, remained to support the 187th in the defense of the port, and Battery A, 102d AAA AW Battalion, attached to the division for the operation, and the 152d AA-AT Battalion landed and set up antiaircraft defense of the beach. By 1300, all combat elements of the two regimental combat teams were clear of the beach. And at about that time, General Eichelberger and a small command group landed and would accompany General Swing and his command group near the head of the column marching and fighting down Highway 17 toward Manila.

The artillery had a very difficult time getting ashore. Captain Lou Burris landed his D Battery of the 457th with the leading elements in support of the 188th. While it was landing, it came under fire from the machine guns and artillery from Wawa. D Battery had to tow its pack 75s by hand because its vehicles stalled in the water after coming down the landing ships' ramps. But D Battery went into position on the beach and countered the enemy fire coming from Wawa. Captain Burris sent D Battery's .50-caliber machine guns to help protect Nasugbu strip, where the division's liaison planes would soon be based. Half of the machine gun crews patrolled the hills north and east of Nasugbu.

The 674th and 675th Glider Field Artillery Battalions had the same difficulties as did D Battery of the 457th. But the artillerymen hauled their pack 75s ashore and moved them by hand until a day later, when they were able to land their jeeps and three-quarter-ton trucks. The Air Section of the 457th winched its disassembled liaison aircraft through 100 yards of surf, and, under some machine gun fire, put together one plane by nightfall and another by the following morning. On 2 February, these planes dropped food and ammunition to the lead elements of the 188th on Highway 17.

The remainder of the division units afloat continued to land—but not without additional difficulty. About a hundred yards offshore of Red Beach, a sandbar blocked some of the landing craft. The LCIs could get to within thirty yards of the shore, but the LSTs carrying the vehicles and other heavy equipment could not get over the bar. Trucks had to be winched ashore by bulldozers on the beach. To solve the problem, the navy waited until midnight, when high tide would permit passage over the sandbar. But even so, some of the vehicles, rolling off the LSTs, sank heavily. One observer said, "Our previous waterproofing had helped but still would not enable two-and-a-half-ton trucks to float."

Captain Albert F. Leister wrote later about the logistics problems and some of the unusual solutions the supply men of the 11th found.

The equipment and supplies brought ashore in the smaller craft were quickly moved inland without a pileup on the beach. A narrow gauge railroad, which paralleled the beach on its course from the Sugar Central to the wharves at Wawa, was utilized in expediting equipment to the dispersal points behind Nasugbu. A spur was laid to the beach by the 127th Engineers, and supplies were loaded directly into the rail cars of the 24-inch gauge railway. The railway also carried personnel landing in the later units to the base of the mountains more than seven miles to the east. Sufficient fuel was found to operate the alcohol-burning engines for an extended period of time.

General MacArthur was becoming more and more impatient with the pace of Sixth Army and its advance toward Manila. General Eichelberger had written to his wife that "the commander in chief is very impatient" and that he had to "speed up your palsy-walsy" and that "Krueger doesn't even radiate courage."

General MacArthur played one commander against another. "Get to Manila," he ordered his field commanders. "Go around the Japs, bounce off the Japs, save your men, but get to Manila. Free the internees at Santo Tomas. Take Malacanan and the legislative buildings."

The encouragement was not lost on General Eichelberger. He reacted with verve, dash, and imagination. He realized that if he could bluff the Japanese into thinking that he commanded a large force moving up Highway 17 across Tagaytay Ridge and heading for Manila, he would have a tactical advantage and a possible rapid and uncontested race to the southern limits of Manila. He ordered General Swing to move both the 187th and the 188th as fast as possible, making as much dust and firing as many weapons and artillery as possible. Eichelberger called the tactic "a monumental bluff."

"Our vehicles were roaring up and down the road," he wrote later, "raising never-ending clouds of dust. By the generous use of what artillery we had, by our heavy and confident assaults, by repeated strikes from the air, we gave the enemy the impression that a force of army proportions—complete with an armored division—was invading southern Luzon. This impression was not lessened by the fact that American radio announced the news that the 'Eighth Army' had landed there."

At 1400, General Swing, satisfied that the navy had accomplished its mission of landing the division, radioed Admiral Fechteler that he was prepared to assume command of the operation and his forces ashore. Few of the division troopers realized that for a brief few hours they had been commanded by an admiral.

Colonel Soule had led the 188th inland at a rapid pace—even though the pace was a walking one. By 1430, the lead elements of the regiment were eight miles from the beach and at the Palico River bridge, a steel-trussed and wooden bridge that spanned a gorge some 85 feet deep and 250 feet wide. The advance had been so swift that the Japanese guarding the bridge were taken by surprise. The lead element of the 188th raced up the road toward the bridge and down a small hill to the west of it, dashed across the bridge, and routed a squad of Japanese who were about to blow the bridge. Six of the enemy were killed, and the rest fled to the east. Destruction of the bridge would have seriously delayed the advance, because the lightly equipped 127th Engineers did not have the material to replace it. Bypassing it would have been difficult because the Palico River flows in a deep, steep-sided canyon. Even so, the Japanese had partially cut some of the wooden stringers and supports. The 127th inactivated the charges and reinforced the weakened sections. By 1530, the 188th had secured the bridge and the surrounding area.

From the Palico River bridge, Highway 17 wound eastward past Tumalin, through the defile between the high peaks of Mount Batulao on the south and Mount Cariliao on the north, through Aga, and up onto the Tagaytay Ridge plateau. On the east end of Tagaytay, it turned north and started gently downhill to Imus, where it turned northeast through Paranaque into the southern outskirts of Manila. The area from Nasugbu to Tagaytay Ridge was mountainous and cut by many deep, heavily wooded gorges. Once off the road, only foot travel was possible and by that mode, fast movement was difficult. Highway 17 itself was suitable for two-way traffic, although the roadbed from Nasugbu to Tagaytay was rough and rocky.

By 1800 on X-Day, 31 January, the 188th was at Tumalin and still moving forward. The 675th and 674th (minus one battery) had moved forward to Palico and had gone into firing positions to support the further advance of the 188th. Captain Lou Burris had his four pack 75s of D Battery of the 457th deployed as assault guns with the leading elements of the 188th. Lieutenant Colonel Davis had used his 127th Engineers to finish removing the demolitions from the Palico River bridge and to strengthen other bridges that the Japanese had weakened along the route. General Swing and his advance command group, following close behind the 188th, set up a CP in the Palico barracks by 1600.

Beyond Tumalin, which was about nine miles from the beach, Highway 17 ascended more steeply, and the 188th shortly found themselves marching cautiously through narrow defiles, perfect spots for Japanese ambushes. The road was bordered by steep wooded banks, which canalized the lead elements of the 188th. The battalion was moving up both sides of the road with A Company, commanded by Capt. Raymond Lee in the lead, followed by Colonel LaFlamme and his command group, then Headquarters Company, followed by B and C Companies. At one point in the march, at the intersection of the Nasugbu road and Highway 17, the advance guard was halted by fire from the right flank. General Pierson arrived at about that time, and Ernie LaFlamme told him that his point men could see enemy activity on the high ground to the right. General Pierson went back to the road junction just as Colonel Soule drove up in his jeep. "He then spread his map on the hood of the jeep when all hell broke loose," General Pierson remembered. "Artillery, machine gun and rifle fire. (I was younger then and my reflexes were quicker.) I jumped into the roadside ditch and Soule jumped in on top of me. He received a piece of shrapnel in his buttocks and commented that he had been hit. He then got out of the ditch and talked to O'Kane (the regimental executive officer). We had answering artillery fire in short order and then the 188th moved in on Shorty Ridge."

At 1900 on 31 January, General Eichelberger wrote:

What a day. About 1000 a flying boat landed near us containing a bunch of newspaper correspondents. . . . They told me that news of the Eighth Army had been definitely released, so I told them how much I appreciated what the Navy had done and how fine I thought Swing's 11th Airborne was going to be. Right after lunch I went ashore where about 25 officers and men of the Eighth Army staff have established an office in the schoolhouse on the plaza at Nasugbu. . . . I do not intend to take command. I am just around speeding things up a bit. . . .

Sometime before morning, Joe may run into more Japs. He had already gone about seven miles and was moving rapidly at 5 P.M. We were very fortunate in capturing a bunch of bridges on Highway 17 before the Japs had a chance to blow them up. I saw a number of big packages of explosives which they never set off.

It is almost dark and apparently some of the Nips are getting fresh because I can see on the north end of the beach that one of our gunboats is pouring in a stream of rockets and the tracers are going across almost on a level.

The normal sunset tactic of most units fighting the Japanese in the Pacific was to halt just before dark, set up a perimeter defense of three-to four-man foxholes about five yards apart all around the perimeter, eat whatever rations were on hand, and bed down for the night, with at least one man in each foxhole or machine gun position awake and on guard. He had a steel helmet ready to drop on a grenade that the enemy might toss into the hole. Every few hours, the guard changed very quietly.

Eichelberger realized that if the 11th kept moving after dark, the Japanese would be kept off balance and would be unable to practice their customary tactic of night probes and attacks. Momentum, he felt, was with the 11th, and he told General Swing to keep pushing. General Swing needed no prodding. One could debate the identity of the more aggressive of the two, but to the men of the 11th, there was no question— General Swing won that debate hands down.

A full moon on the night of 31 January considerably eased the movement of the 188th up Highway 17. Lieutenant Colonel Harry Wilson's 1st of the 187th had been following the 188th. The battalion had had a small skirmish with the enemy in the vicinity of the Sugar Central, killed a few of the enemy, and then moved onto Highway 17 at about 1500. At midnight the battalion moved through the 188th Infantry to lead the attack and kept marching until 0400 on 1 February, when Colonel Wilson halted the march. The men dug in and slept for two hours, and then were off again down Highway 17 at 0600.

At daybreak, the advanced elements of the 1st of the 187th approached the Mount Cariliao-Mount Aiming-Mount Batulao defile. Mount Cariliao rises 2,100 feet on the north side of the road, and Mount Batulao 2,700 feet on the south. At the foot of Mount Cariliao was Mount Aiming, some 1,200 feet high. It was a mound separate and distinct from Cariliao and, like the two higher mountains, was densely wooded. Captain Leister described Mount Aiming ''like a thimble at the base of an overturned tea cup.'' The three peaks afforded the Japanese a perfect defensive position from which to oppose any troops coming up the road. As the lead patrols of the 1st of the 187th found out, the enemy had not failed to utilize and develop the natural defenses of the position. Major Isaac Hoppenstein, the supply officer of the 187th, wrote, ''The enemy, figuratively speaking, were looking down our throats and showed it by their most effective artillery fire from their well dug in and camouflaged positions. Here our troops received their first real casualties of this operation.''

At daybreak on 1 February, the Japanese, from their elevated positions on the peaks around the Cariliao-Batulao defile, saw the point men of

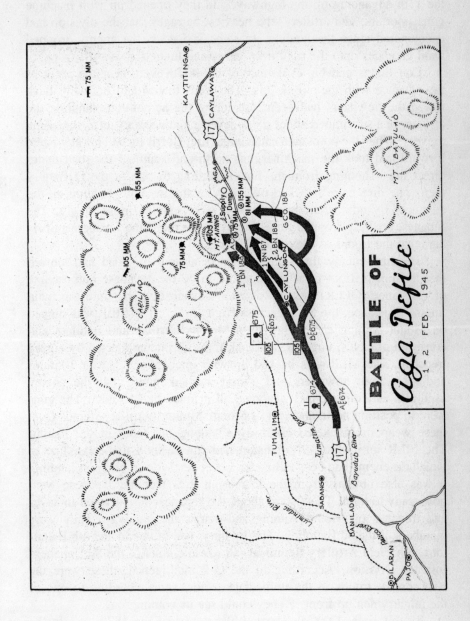

BATTLE OF
Aga Defile
1–2 FEB. 1945

the 11th advancing up the highway, and they opened up with machine guns, mortars, and artillery, the heaviest barrages that the division had encountered since the landing. In some instances, the enemy dropped hand grenades onto the road from caves and tunnels above it.

Lou Burris and his D Battery of the 457th were near the point of the advance with their pack 75s. The jeeps that would normally have towed the howitzers had been lost during the amphibious landing; the artillerymen substituted about six or seven cannoneers to act as the prime movers. When the point men came under fire, Burris moved his howitzers forward and took the machine guns north and south of the road under direct fire—shooting from the hip, according to one of the D Battery men. The direct fire knocked out many of the weapons holding up the advance. By now, the advance troops were moving more slowly. The Japanese artillery dropped some rounds on the road, and Japanese snipers harassed the troops as they moved along.

The first enemy fire from the peaks around the road had slowed the division in front of what appeared to be the Japanese outpost line of resistance (OPLR). As the division advanced, it ran into the main line of resistance, the MLR, across Highway 17. The MLR was hinged on Mount Aiming and anchored on Mounts Cariliao and Batulao, and consisted of caves, dugouts, and tank traps all interconnected by zigzag trenches. The MLR was backed up with one 155mm, seven 105mm, and six 75mm howitzers and 37mm antitank guns, that the enemy used also as antipersonnel weapons, all manned by 250 men. The guns were in position north and east of Mount Aiming. Artillery rounds from these weapons bracketed Highway 17 along the route of the march. The MLR into which the division had run seemed to be the line to which the enemy had been falling back ever since the amphibious landing; it was also obvious from the increasing fires that the Japanese were now ready to fight. There were about 400 Japanese infantrymen in caves and trenches on Mount Aiming and across the highway. They were members of the 3d Battalion, 31st Infantry, and of the 3d and 4th Battalions, 8th Field Artillery Regiment, all organic units of the 8th Japanese Infantry Division. According to the G-2 intelligence, these were the best combat troops in the immediate sector, and, according to one of the infantrymen up front, "They could see us coming."

By this time, Lt. Col. Harry Wilson's 1st of the 187th was in the lead. Colonel Soule was in overall command of the operation to reduce this strong enemy position. He left Wilson's battalion in the center to spearhead the attack; he committed LaFlamme's 1st of the 188th to the left and north of the road; he sent Tommy Mann's 2d of the 188th to the right and south of the road. Lieutenant Colonels Luke Hoska and Mike Massad had brought their 674th and 675th Glider Artillery Battalions into positions to support the attack. The forward air observer with the 188th laid on Air Corps support for the assault.

The attack got under way about 0900 on the morning of 1 February. Air Corps fighters and A-20s attacked, bombed, and strafed the positions on the hills. The artillery fired concentrations on the likely enemy defensive and artillery positions. At about noon, Capt. Raymond Lee led A Company of the 188th up the hill and broke through the Japanese defenses on Mount Aiming using bayonets, rifles, and grenades. In so doing, A Company became separated from the rest of the 1st Battalion. The enemy, well aware of the importance of Mount Aiming in the defensive scheme of things, attacked Lee's men repeatedly all afternoon but failed to dislodge them. One man from the 187th remembered, "We were to learn later that Captain Lee lost but one man from his company because he'd used the Nips' own caves on the west (reverse) slope. . . ." For four hours, however, Lee and his company withstood continuous counterattacks and one banzai attack.

By 1600, the rest of the 1st of the 188th had joined Lee on Mount Aiming. From there they could look down on the Japanese positions, but at the same time the hill reportedly stood out like a sore thumb, and it received more than its share of Japanese incoming artillery rounds.

Seizing Mount Aiming pierced and split the Japanese position. While the 1st Battalion of the 188th held its position on the north flank, the regiment moved into line with three battalions abreast. The 2d Battalion of the 188th moved quickly south of the road, crossed a deep gorge, deployed, and, on the right flank of the regiment, attacked the enemy positions between Mount Batulao and the highway. The 1st of the 187th moved in between the two battalions and, as the center battalion, attacked eastward astride the road.

On the morning of 2 February, the regiment launched an all-out attack to the east. At 0830, P-38s and A-20s and the division's two artillery battalions hit the main enemy positions in the vicinity of Aga between the two mountains. An enemy artillery position at Kaytitinga was finally silenced. The 1st of the 187th and the 2d of the 188th attacked abreast toward the east. They passed the 1st of the 188th on Mount Aiming, which had the mission of protecting the regiment's left flank.

Progress down the road was slow initially, but the pace quickened as the enemy was forced to withdraw. Major Hoppenstein wrote:

> The assault was so vigorous and fast that the enemy was driven back in complete rout. This was verified by the capture of an enemy regimental command post (later found to be the headquarters of the Japanese 31st Infantry Regiment—Colonel Fujishige's CP) at Aga at 1300 hours which showed the haste in which their personnel had departed. Large stores of ammunition, food, clothing, engineer equipment, and cigarettes were captured. Several cases of liquor, many documents, weapons, and a Japanese sabre were also found by the writer. The documents and saber were turned into the division headquarters. Another indication of the hasty retreat of the Japs were the numerous individual soldier packs found containing food and clean clothing.

In the Aga-Caylaway area, the 188th found between seventy-five and one hundred tons of ammunition. In the defense of their regimental CP, the enemy had built three deep tank traps across the highway. The ditches were trapezoidal in shape, twenty feet long across the top, four feet long across the bottom, and twenty-five feet deep. Subsequently, the 127th Engineers built bridges across those ditches that could not be bypassed.

The 1st of the 188th went north through Kaytitinga; the 2d of the 188th continued to attack the Japanese positions in the coconut groves in the northern foothills of Mount Batulao. So far, the division had lost sixteen men killed and forty-one wounded and had killed ninety-one of the enemy. By dusk of 2 February, the division was up against the third and strongest position of the enemy MLR across Highway 17. Throughout the night, the Japanese harassed the forward units with artillery, mortars, and small arms. They located the firing position of the 675th and forced Lieutenant Colonel Massad to order a hasty displacement.

The Division Rear in the meantime was setting up its own supply base at Nasugbu, in the same manner as such installations are usually set up and run by army service troops. Because one such installation at Lingayen was called ASCOM (Army Service Command), Bill Crawford, the division G-4, lumped all the Nasugbu beach troops together and called them DIVSCOM. The troops in the rear had unloaded all the division's supplies except LST 277 by the night of 2 February. One of the division staffers recalled, "LST 277 was such a sitting duck for the pesty Q-boat attacks that it finally had to leave, taking two M-10 infantry self-propelled cannons, a number of trucks, and fifty tons of all classes of supplies. The most important piece of equipment to sail away on 277 was the 511th Signal Company's long-range radio. While the LST ramp was down, the Division personnel tried to salvage drums of gasoline by rolling them into the waves and letting them float into shore. This trick was not very successful.''

As the division advanced to the east, it bypassed a number of Japanese in small and sometimes large unit formations. The task of nullifying these enemy fell to the Filipino guerrillas in the area, who, fortunately, were well organized and would prove to be vital to the division's mission because they permitted the division to advance rapidly without having to take care of the enemy holed up in wooded areas off to the flanks of the division's route of attack. After the division landed, General Swing gave Colonel Hildebrand, the CO of the 187th, the mission of controlling all of the guerrilla units in the area. Captain Leister wrote, "During the later stages of the operation, the Division had the assistance of more than 5,000 guerrillas and they were credited with killing more than 2,300 Japanese."

Meanwhile, the Reconnaissance Platoon under Lt. George Skau moved toward Tagaytay Ridge on a trail north of Mount Cariliao to determine the strength and location of the enemy on the northern flank and to protect the northern side of the 188th as it advanced along Highway 17. The platoon also had the mission of helping to guide the 511th Pathfinders to the drop zone. Throughout the campaign, the Recon Platoon was a vital force in determining the enemy's strengths, weaknesses, and locations. By the time the division reached Manila, the Recon Platoon had spent more time behind the Japanese lines than it did in front of them.

On 2 February, General Eichelberger wrote another letter to his wife.

One of my letters tonight was from Bonner Fellers. . . . He said that the Commander-in-Chief is very impatient and that Bonner hopes that I will get to Manila first. . . . The Big Chief has given me the go-go sign. . . . This morning . . . I went forward where the "Shoestring" task force has been attacking a very powerful Japanese position located on a narrow front between two mountains directly across the road. Thanks to plenty of air support and good artillery work, we were able to push them out this morning. I managed to get in there just as they pulled out of their command post.

I then came to Joe Swing's Command Post where I am going to spend the night. It is on the Palico River about six miles out of Nasugbu. . . . I am fixed up here very nicely in a barracks which was built some years ago for the Philippine Army. If I spend . . . tomorrow night in Tagaytay I shall be looking into Manila, about thirty miles away, with a downhill pull on a concrete road. If I get to Tagaytay tomorrow, I am going to start for Manila the following morning. We have some self-propelled mounts which are like tanks. We obtained these from the 24th Division, but otherwise the men are mostly on foot. They had to walk up that terrific incline. Tagaytay is as high as Asheville. As you can see, I am making a rapid dash with a very small force. We are taking big risks. . . . I am very keen about this 11th Airborne. They are small in number but they are willing to fight.

Unfortunately, the fight at the defile, which was by no means over, had slowed the 11th's advance up to Tagaytay Ridge and had ruined General Eichelberger's hopes that he could bring in the 511th Parachute Regimental Combat Team a day early, on 2 February, instead of the originally planned 3 February. Eichelberger was under a restriction from General MacArthur: He could not drop the 511th unless and until the other elements of the division could link up within twenty-four hours. With the delay of the 188th at the defile, General Eichelberger reluctantly went back to 3 February for the jump of the 511th RCT. By now he knew that the 188th could be on the ridge by 3 February; therefore he ordered General Swing to bring in the 511th RCT on that date. General Eichelberger also ordered a second battalion of the 19th Infantry of the 24th Division to move from Leyte to Nasugbu to operate and protect the port and the main supply route. When this battalion of the 19th arrived, it would free the 2d of the 187th to join the rest of the division.

General Swing wanted to make certain that Colonel Haugen knew precisely his mission and date and time of drop. Therefore, to assure that there would be no misinterpretation through faulty communications, General Swing sent Doug Quandt by Cub plane to Mindoro to issue the necessary orders to Colonel Haugen and to brief him on the current situation facing the division.

Already much had been done by the division in the very short time it had been ashore. It had unloaded all its combat equipment, established a port and an airstrip (the first plane, an L-5 flown by Capt. John H. MacLeod from Leyte to Mindoro to Luzon had landed on the Nasugbu strip on 31 January), advanced on foot a total of nineteen miles and had penetrated the enemy's MLR. By 3 February, the 127th Engineers, in addition to a multitude of other engineering projects, had extended the Nasugbu strip to a length that would permit C-47s to land on its dirt runway. Heavy rains could and did halt air operations on occasion.

Colonel Haugen had designated Lt. David L. C. Hover, who was the Demolitions Platoon leader in Headquarters Company of the 511th, and a portion of his platoon to be the pathfinders for the drop of the RCT on Tagaytay. They had come ashore with the 188th at Nasugbu and had marched forward with the Division Recon Platoon along Highway 17. Now the time had come for them to accomplish their rather hazardous but vital mission: mark the drop zones for the 511th RCT. At dusk on the evening of 2 February, Hover and his men, accompanied by guerrillas and Sgt. Terry Santos of the Recon Platoon, who could speak fluent Tagalog, left the lines of the 188th at Kaytitinga near the base of Tagaytay and moved along a trail to the north of Mount Cariliao. By daybreak of the third, undetected by the Japanese, Hover and his men were on top of the ridge at the 511th's preselected drop zones.

The 511th Infantry had arrived on Mindoro by LCI and C-46. The 457th had loaded its howitzers, paracrates, and ammunition in C-46s and followed the 511th to Mindoro. After the RCT landed, it moved to a bivouac area—a treeless expanse of pebbly ground near the banks of a wide, shallow stream. Each company had one pyramidal tent for a CP; the men slept in pup tents. One of the 457th artillerymen said, "The only way to escape the dry heat of Mindoro was to get in the stream and lie on the bottom of it." The 457th maintenance detail rigged up its planes with the pararacks, checked the electrical systems of the planes, and packed its howitzers, ammunition, and radios, among other gear.

Shortly after the war, Hacksaw Holcombe wrote:

By 30 January 1945, the 511th PIRCT, moving by air and water, had closed in marshalling areas on the island of Mindoro. Here tactical maps (1:50,000) and large scale aerial photographs (1:9,800) of the landing area were made available and preparation of sand tables and "blow-ups" to be used in briefing was begun.

On 1 February the regimental commander, regimental executive officer, the three battalion commanders, the artillery commander and the regimental S-3 together with the commander of the troop carrier aircraft for the operation made an aerial reconnaissance of the drop zone and surrounding area.

The tentative date for the jump was 2 February and briefing and re-equipping went on at a frenzied pace on Mindoro. Meanwhile, information on the progress of the rest of the Division, which had landed at Nasugbu on 31 January, was inconclusive. Rapid progress had been made but determined resistance was encountered around Mount Aiming and Mount Cariliao. The resistance here was such that D-Day for the drop was delayed until 3 February and the final word still was to be given by General Eichelberger only when he felt sure that the entire division could be joined within twenty-four hours of the drop.

The regimental plan was shaped largely by the shortage of troop carrier aircraft. (There were only forty-eight C-47's available.) This short-age of planes made it necessary to plan for three lifts, all planes to be used in each lift. The regimental command group, the 2d Battalion and about half of the 3d were to compose the first lift. The rest of the regiment the second lift and the artillery the third lift the following day. Upon landing of the first lift, the 3d Battalion (minus that half jumping in the second lift) was to secure the western approaches of the drop zone while the 2d Battalion secured the remainder of the drop zone, patrolling to Alfonso and down Highway 17. The 2d Battalion was also to be prepared to move down Highway 17 toward Manila on order.

Because of the shortage of aircraft, the 511th would not have the support of the 457th Field Artillery Battalion until 4 February.

The 2d Battalion of the 187th had moved up Highway 17 after the 19th Infantry had come ashore to protect the base at Nasugbu. Colonel Tipton had his headquarters men dig in the CP on one side of the road; one of his rifle companies dug in on the other. Just before dark, a rifle company from the 19th moved up and relieved the company of the 188th, which moved forward. Colonel Tipton told the new company commander that there did not appear to be many of the enemy in the area and he did not want any unnecessary shooting. Lieutenant Bernheim was Tipton's S-4. He and his platoon had relocated the battalion's supply and ammo dump into the area just before dark but had to leave outside the perimeter a quarter-ton trailer loaded with 81mm white phosphorous rounds and with four loaded flamethrowers lashed to the top. Colonel Tipton very presciently did not want that potential bomb near his troops.

Bernheim remembers that after he had moved the supplies, he was exhausted and, at dark,

I spread a poncho on the ground in the middle of the CP and foolishly did not dig in. I can recall the chattering of a monkey mascot we had acquired as I fell asleep. In the middle of the night I was awakened by bursts of small arms fire from across the highway, and the bullets were snap cracking through our area. Colonel Tipton yelled, "You trigger happy bastards stop that goddam shooting."

No sooner were the words out of his mouth than what sounded like a thousand Japs started yelling and screaming. What turned out to be about twenty Japs were moving down the highway towards Nasugbu, and the 19th Infantry perimeter spotted them first. Our people opened fire and the flame throwers were hit and started burning. The area was lit up like Times Square and you could have read a newspaper. The monkey was up in a tree screaming away. Some of the WP started exploding. I was so scared over my exposed position that I can recall vibrating off the ground. I thought I heard Jap voices coming closer and just as I raised up on my elbows, a 2.36 bazooka round came whizzing end over end and hit me in the left side. I can recall that I saw or sensed it before it hit me. The pin was still in it fortunately because a Jap hand grenade had exploded in a bazooka position and set off the propelling charge. It felt like Ted Williams hitting me with a bat and the wind was knocked completely out of me. Lt. Martyniak lost his cool completely and walked over to where I lay gasping and moaning and, amid considerable fire and exploding shells, stood upright and said: "Quit your pissing, Bernie, you ain't dead yet!" . . . A medical officer, Captain Eastman . . . crawled out of his hole, dragged me into his hole and gave me a shot of morphine. In the morning he strapped my ribs, and some months later X-rays indicated I had five cracked ribs although I was never evacuated. We were resilient when we were young!

By 0700, 3 February, the First Battalion cleared the village of Aga. It was now spearheading the Division's advance toward Tagaytay Ridge with the mission of effecting a junction with the 511th which was to jump at 0800 that morning. The debris left by the air-strike was strewn around and the area was a shambles of dead men and animals. Apparently, the Nips had been shocked into precipitate retirement for we found horses, untouched by the bombing, tethered on a picket-line nearby. These we promptly pre-empted as draft animals.

At 0730 on the morning of 3 February, the 188th, with the 1st of the 187th, attacked the third and final Japanese position in the stubbornly defended Cariliao-Batulao defile. The three battalions advanced rapidly against little resistance until about 1000. Then the lead squads began rounding a bare ridge nose on the north side of a sharp bend in Highway 17 at the western edge of Tagaytay Ridge. The enemy was holding another steep, bare ridge nose south of the bend. When the point of the advance units rounded the curve, the Japanese opened up with heavy artillery, machine gun, and small-arms fire. The southern ridge from which they were firing was the highest ground on Tagaytay Ridge and would be known thereafter by the troops of the 11th as "Shorty Ridge," named after the diminutive but feisty and belligerent Col. "Shorty" Soule.

The accuracy of the Japanese artillery all along the road had confounded and distressed the infantrymen, who noted that, at least in this case, the Japanese did not seem to need to adjust their artillery fire as did the Americans with overs, shorts, and then "fire for effect." The infantrymen soon learned the secret of the Japanese artillery accuracy: Prior to the landing of the 11th at Nasugbu, the Japanese gunners had placed, in the trees along Highway 17, large white crosses. These markings were targets on which they had previously adjusted and had recorded the data. When the Americans reached a certain cross, the Japanese gunners simply set the correct data and fired accurately and demoralizingly.

Not only were the men of the 1st of the 187th and the 188th pinned down by the enemy artillery fire, but so were a number of high-ranking officers who formed the tip part of what the troops called the "spearhead tipped with brass." On the morning of the third, the "brass" contingent consisted of General Eichelberger; General Swing; General Pierson; Gen. Frank Farrell, the 11th Airborne Division Artillery commander; and a number of colonels and lieutenant colonels on their staffs. In one of the barrages that hit the lead elements that morning, among others, Col. Rinaldo Coe, Headquarters commandant of the Eighth Army, and the commander of a supporting tank destroyer unit were killed; Col. Harry Wilson and Capt. William Lyman, of the 187th, were wounded. In all, the barrage killed eight men and wounded another twenty-one.

The artillery barrages forced everyone on the road to take cover. Colonel Soule was with his advanced guard and immediately took over the direction of the ensuing attack. He crawled under the artillery fire some fifty yards to his radio transmitter but was wounded en route. His driver, Pius Corbett, was lying alongside the jeep. Lieutenant Gabe Allen, the communications officer of the 1st of the 188th, remembers that Colonel Soule crawled up to the jeep and said: "Corbett, do you want to hand me that radio?" Corbett replied: "No, Sir, I don't even want to move." But Colonel Soule did get to his radio and to a telephone whose wire had just been strung up to his location and began to direct the attack on Shorty Ridge. He sent orders to his regimental executive officer, Lt. Col. Mortimer J. O'Kane, to send up the lead battalion, Harry Wilson's 1st of the 187th, which was following Colonel Soule and the point.

Colonel Soule then crawled to an exposed position for better observation and directed the attack. Through his command communications net, he adjusted artillery fire on the ridge; his forward air observer brought in a fighter strafing and bomb attack. The two battalions of artillery, the 674th and the 675th, pounded the ridge with their pack 75s and sawed-off 105s (recent acquisitions of the 675th). As in ground battles from the dawn of combat, foot soldiers had to make the final assault over enemy-held terrain and wrest the enemy position by killing the defenders, routing them from the position, and then occupying the objective.

Such was the case on Shorty Ridge. Captain Hanna commanded the lead company of the 1st of the 187th. Colonel Wilson ordered Hanna to swing behind the position and try to take it from the rear. Tommy Mann led his 2d of the 188th off the road to the south and onto Shorty Ridge. By 1300, the attackers, under cover of artillery and mortars and by the use of flamethrowers and hand grenades, wrested Shorty Ridge from the enemy. Colonel Soule had refused evacuation for his wounds, had remained in a forward, exposed position coordinating the attack, and had advanced with the lead elements in overrunning the enemy bastion. For his heroism, he was later awarded the Distinguished Service Cross.

More than three hundred enemy soldiers were killed in and on Shorty Ridge. The position was obviously an important one in the scheme of Japanese defenses: It was honeycombed with enormous supply tunnels, reinforced concrete caves, and strong gun and individual firing positions. With the reduction of Shorty Ridge, the elements of the 11th that had landed amphibiously and fought their way along a difficult uphill route of march were ready to make contact with the paratroopers who, since 0815 on the morning of 3 February, had been landing to their east on Tagaytay Ridge.

Early in the morning of the third, back on Mindoro, the 511th was preparing to mount up for the jump on Tagaytay Ridge. The 2d Battalion of the 511th, Colonel Haugen and his regimental command group, and part of Lieutenant Colonel Lahti's 3d of the 511th were in the first lift.

At 0300, the first lift mounted trucks in their bivouac area and headed for San Jose airstrip. Each truck had been chalk marked with the same number as the chalk number on the plane for which it was headed. Thus there was little confusion in getting the troopers to the correct planes.

In the marshaling area before they left, the unit commanders had briefed each man and issued necessary supplies—ammunition, rations, signal equipment—for the jump. According to Hacksaw Holcombe, the briefing in the marshaling area was hurried but reached every man. ". . . The fact that the briefing was not as thorough as could be desired was brought out by later events."

Just before boarding his plane, Colonel Holcombe had a last-minute check with his company commanders. "It is interesting to note," he wrote later, "that the final precautionary word of the battalion commander was that jump masters of the following planes were to exit only when they observed his [Holcombe's] plane load in the air."

At 0700, the first plane carrying Col. Rock Haugen and part of his regimental command team and piloted by Col. John Lackey, the commander of the 317th Troop Carrier Group, started its takeoff roll. It was followed in rapid succession by the other planes in the flight. By 0715, the planes had formed into a vee of vees formation over the airstrip. The P-61 Night Fighters furnished cover during loading, and P-38s escorted the column during its flight.

The column turned north over Mindoro and headed for Batangas Bay. At that checkpoint, the column headed east for the south shore of Lake Taal, which bordered the southern edge of Tagaytay. At the eastern end of Taal, the column rounded the lake and headed north toward Mount Sungay, where they then turned almost due west on their final run, a route that took the planes along the long axis of Tagaytay Ridge and parallel to Highway 17 along the ridge.

The ridge itself was an excellent drop zone for a mass jump. It was open, about 2,000 yards wide and more than 4,000 yards long, and plowed in some places. Even though it was cut by a number of small streams and dotted with a few scattered nipa huts, there were few major obstacles to the paratroopers. The only danger to a jumper was the possibility of being blown off the ridge, over its steep sides and down into Lake Taal.

Just a few minutes before 0815, Colonel Haugen stood in the door of the lead plane and looked down on the ridge, searching for the smoke signals that would indicate that Lieutenant Hover and his pathfinders had made their way successfully to the drop zone. He had already given the commands to stand up, hook up, check equipment, sound off for equipment check, and close in the door. Sticking his head far out into the plane's slipstream, he saw ahead of him on the ground what he had been looking for—the green smoke of Hover's grenades marking the go point for the jumpers. As a precautionary measure, Col. Doug Quandt was also over the drop zone in a Cub airplane ready to drop smoke grenades if Hover and his team had not been able to get through the Japanese-held area.

Haugen looked back at the stick of men crowding behind him. Then he checked the jump light on the side of the door. It was still red. Haugen shouted: "Are you ready?" Just then John Lackey turned on the green door light. Haugen shouted, "Let's go," and leapt out the door. His stick tumbled out after him as fast as the men could shuffle down the aisle, throw their static line fasteners down the anchor cable to the rear of the plane, make a right turn, and leap. They held their arms across their reserves, legs together, and tucked their chins down as far as possible to reduce the jerk on their necks when they got their opening shocks.

The initial elements of the 511th—345 men in the first eighteen C-47s, consisting of the regimental command group, the 2d Battalion Headquarters and Headquarters Company, D Company and F Company less one platoon—hit the designated drop zone marked by Hover and his men. But the second echelon of the first flight, 570 men in thirty planes composed of the remainder of the 2d Battalion and part of the 3d, were six miles and three minutes behind the lead aircraft. This echelon jumped prematurely about 8,000 yards east of the go point. "Whether this was caused primarily by an airborne or troop carrier error was never definitely determined," according to Hacksaw Holcombe, "but the fact remains that proper jump discipline would have prevented it. This is particularly true in view of the instructions given by the battalion commander that, except in an emergency, no jump master was to allow his troops to jump until the commander, himself, had jumped."

One version of the premature jump holds that a jump master in one of the follow-on planes saw another plane inadvertently drop some equipment bundles, thought that he was over the go point, and jumped. The other planes behind him followed suit. The pilots and the crew chiefs tried to stop the early exits but could not. The cause of the wide jumper dispersion on the ground is a debatable point: Some contend that it was the result of a lack of jump discipline; others attribute it to the inexperience of the troop carrier pilots dropping paratroopers. At any rate, the entire plateau of Tagaytay Ridge was fairly open and gently sloping terrain, so the troopers landed generally without mishap. And the guerrillas in the area had cleared the entire ridge, so there was virtually no enemy opposition to the jump.

At about 1210, the remainder of the 1st Battalion and the remainder of the 3d Battalion of the 511th approached the ridge. Wrote Lt. Col. Henry Burgess, who had recently taken Ernie LaFlamme's place as the commander of 1st Battalion,

I was in the lead plane of the second lift when we came over Tagaytay Ridge. I was appalled to see that since the first lift had jumped, the ridge itself had clouds down to the ground in many areas, making visibility very poor. The clouds were not solid down to the ridge, but in many places were scattered and down to 300 feet to 500 feet above the ground.

As the planes flew north, they made a 90-degree turn at the east end of Tagaytay Ridge and flew over the top of the ridge to areas which had been designated as drop zones and which were to the east of the area where the first lift had dropped.

In making the approach to the ridge, the troop carrier planes seemed to string out with greater intervals between them so that the danger of the planes crashing into one another in a tight formation in the clouds would be reduced. Likewise, in making the 90-degree turn, there was an opportunity for collision, so the planes made a turn farther and farther out over the top of and north of the crest of the ridge, which was a good decision in view of the fact that the wind was blowing and would have carried troopers dropped over the top of the ridge down over the side on the southern side of the ridge, which falls downslope several hundred feet almost vertically.

Many of the pilots, while having flight experience, had very little experience dropping paratroopers. I recall going to the pilots of the plane I was in and discussing the lack of visibility, and they stated that the scattering of the formation was a safety measure, as the lack of visibility in the clouds could result in crashes.

When the planes made the left-hand turn to fly along the crest of the ridge with poor visibility of the ground and between the planes, the flight formation split up and the planes scattered the parachutists for over five miles down the ridge and over a broad area downhill from the crest of the ridge.

Some of the pilots, who had seen through cloud openings paratroopers jumping far ahead of them had given the green light in their planes, which resulted in a string of paratroopers jumping over an area six and seven miles long. With the planes not slowing up below 125 or 135 miles an hour, most of us experienced the hardest physical opening shock in our lives. The result of the shock was that most of us lost helmets, packs broke free from web belts, suspenders broke, and in the wind, which was 20 to 30 miles an hour . . . many had hard landings.

In this second lift, about 425 men landed on the proper DZ; 1,325 landed between four and six miles to the east and northeast. In spite of the scattered landings, the men of the 511th were assembled into unit configurations in about five hours. By 1300 that afternoon, the lead elements of the 188th had moved up the ridge and had made contact with the 511th. There was still some fighting to the west of Tagaytay, but, for all intents and purposes, General Swing had the major portion of his division back together again. (Another echelon, the 457th Parachute Field Artillery Battalion, was still on Mindoro and would not jump onto Tagaytay until the following morning.)

Both General Eichelberger and General Swing were with the forward elements, and at 1330 they contacted Colonel Haugen near the Manila Hotel Annex on the ridge. It was about this time that General Eichelberger told Frank Smith, a reporter for the *Chicago Times,* that the 11th Airborne Division was "the fightingest goddam troops I ever saw."

Once on the ground, Hacksaw Holcombe's 2d of the 511th went rapidly about the task of accomplishing its preassigned, initial missions. His battalion had suffered only two jump casualties; his strength on the DZ was exactly 500 men and officers. E Company set up defensive positions in the vicinity of the junction of Highways 17 and 25B; D Company sent out patrols toward Alfonso, and the remainder of the company occupied positions south of the DZ; F Company went into position north of the DZ.

After Col. Ed Lahti had assembled his 3d of the 511th following the jump, his battalion relieved the 2d of its mission of securing the drop zone. Haugen ordered Holcombe to move his 2d Battalion to the vicinity of the junction of Highways 17 and 25B, to take up defensive positions and to await further orders.

The division CP moved from Palico barracks (actually General Swing and his small command group were usually right behind the lead elements of the 188th throughout the march up Highway 17) to the Manila Hotel Annex on Tagaytay Ridge at 1515 on the afternoon of 3 February. General Eichelberger joined him there, and together they set up a small, joint command post. The annex was a concrete and stone building, perched regally at the top of the precipitous ridge that fell steeply down into the scenic beauty of Lake Taal. Once, in prewar days, it had been opulent, but during the war, it had been neglected and looted, its furniture had been removed, and its surroundings had become overgrown. But its central location made it a convenient command post, control center, and supply dump for the troops moving east and north. And this would not be the last time that the division would use the annex as a CP.

After the 511th and the 188th had linked up on Tagaytay, the 188th continued to clear the enemy from the ridges and slopes to the south of Tagaytay and from the caves and tunnels on Shorty Ridge. Colonel Haugen had his regiment under his control by 1400. In addition to the patrols he sent to the west to contact the 188th, he secured the eastern end of Tagaytay Ridge where Route 17 turned sharply north and downhill toward Manila. He also sent patrols out along roads and trails leading north and south from the ridge crest and, at about 1800, reported to division headquarters that he had found no signs of the Japanese, a situation for which the division could thank, at least partially, the guerrillas in the area.

The division historian summed up the division's advance up Highway 17 this way:

Events moved so rapidly in this attack that the decisive significance of the breakthrough of A Company of the 188th to Mt. Aiming was not fully appreciated, nor apparent, until after the fall of Fort McKinley. It was the decisive battle of the first phase of the division's Luzon campaign. If the 1st Battalion of the 188th had not broken through to secure Mt. Aiming, thus weakening the entire Japanese position, or if the troops had delayed in the forced march from the beachhead, days would have been spent cracking the defenses of the Cariliao-Batulao defile. The restriction placed on the 511th jump would have delayed the jump until the line had been cracked, and the Manila defense would have been warned of and prepared for the subsequent attack of the 511th. The suddenness of the penetration and the power of the regimental attack scattered the Japs in the wooded slopes of Mt. Cariliao on the north and Mt. Batulao on the south. Although several thousand of the defending force still remained in scattered groups, they were so demoralized that they never again attempted aggressive action, remaining in their hideouts to be searched out and killed months later.

From the Manila Hotel Annex, General Eichelberger could see Manila shimmering brightly in the distance and could make out the curved forefinger of Cavite Peninsula hooking into Manila Bay. The "Pearl of the Orient" was aptly named when one viewed from a distance its white buildings laid out around the curve of Manila Bay. It acted like a magnet on General MacArthur moving south and also on General Eichelberger, who was motivated by stimuli different from those that compelled the commander in chief. General Eichelberger very much wanted his Eighth Army (read the 11th Airborne Division) to beat General Krueger's Sixth Army to the prize of the Pacific war.

The road from Nasugbu to Tagaytay was gravel and frequently only one lane; from Tagaytay, Highway 17 was concrete and two lane and sloped gently to the north and Manila. It was a harbinger of good fortune and easy going, thought General Eichelberger—giving him a highly possible shot at getting to Manila before the Sixth Army. The very thought of it, and no doubt the resultant publicity that would accrue to Eighth Army, raised his spirits. He wrote his wife on 3 February: "The guerrilla reports make me laugh. The report tonight is that Manila is being burned by the Japanese, and yet I can look right down into the town and see lights and one little fire . . ." He did not know it yet, but worse, far worse, was yet to come.

At the Nasugbu port, the division quartermaster and the 408th Quartermaster Company had been working long hours to unload ships, establish dumps, and move supplies forward to the division's combat units. By the afternoon of 3 February, seventeen two-and-a-half-ton trucks had been unloaded from landing crafts and moved up the highway to the Manila Hotel Annex. When the seventeen trucks arrived, General Swing immediately assigned them to Colonel Haugen. Both Generals Eichelberger and Swing had hoped that the 511th could move out to the north and Manila on the afternoon or evening of the third; unfortunately, there were simply not enough trucks or sufficient supplies of gasoline readily available to permit a dash to Manila that afternoon. By 4 February, ten C-47s had landed at the dirt strip at Nasugbu with a cargo of gasoline, which the quartermaster rushed forward to Tagaytay Ridge.

In addition to the transportation problem, and in spite of the desire of the two commanders for speed, Generals Eichelberger and Swing realized that the road had not been reconnoitered and that, therefore, it would be prudent to investigate what lay ahead and delay the move of the 511th a few hours. Wrote Robert R. Smith in *Triumph in the Philippines,*

> This plan [the attack north to Manila] constituted a change in mission for the 11th Airborne Division. MacArthur's original instructions to Eichelberger had envisaged that the division's primary duties would be to contain Japanese forces in southern Luzon and patrol to ascertain Japanese dispositions and intentions in its area of responsibility. Manifestly, the division could not carry out these duties if it drove north to Manila. Eichelberger's authority to change the mission apparently derived from personal contact with MacArthur, who had given the Eighth Army commander considerable discretion on the handling of the 11th Airborne Division.

General Swing used the Recon Platoon to check out Highway 17 toward Manila. He cautioned platoon commander Lieutenant George Skau that he was going into an unknown and certainly a hostile area and to report his findings as soon as he ran into Japanese defenses. George Skau, and twenty-two men of his platoon mounted in jeeps, left just after dark.

Meanwhile, at 2100 on the night of 3 February, Hacksaw Holcombe reported to Colonel Haugen, who also had a CP in one of the rooms of the Manila Hotel Annex. Haugen told him that General Swing had ordered the 511th to move out at dawn along Highway 17 to Bacoor, a small barrio about thirty miles to the north and four miles beyond Imus. Haugen told Holcombe that he would move out first with his battalion and set up a defensive position at Bacoor to cover the junction of Highways 17 and 1, thus, according to Holcombe, blocking the road between Manila and the naval base at Cavite. "This move was to be made with all possible speed," Holcombe remembers that Haugen told him. Haugen finished giving Holcombe his orders by telling him that upon reaching Bacoor, or upon meeting resistance that forced the battalion to dismount and fight, he was to return to Tagaytay Ridge all transportation except for four jeeps, two of which were the prime movers for the detachment of pack 75s from the 674th Glider FA Battalion. In addition to those two pack 75s, Holcombe had attached to his battalion two M-8 self-propelled 75mm guns, an engineer bomb-disposal crew of three men, and 17 two-and-a-half-ton trucks and eleven jeeps. Holcombe also took along one SCR-694 and three SCR-300 radios to supplement the organic battalion communications.

At about 2300, George Skau radioed back to Henry Muller in the division CP that he had gone about fifteen miles down Highway 17 and that he had run into no resistance. At 0400 the next morning, he reported that the road was secure as far as Imus, where he had found that the Japanese had blown the bridge and set up a defensive line. But, he reported, he and his men had found a dirt road that bypassed the blown bridge. The dirt road went over a bridge that the enemy had prepared to blow, but he and his men had removed the charges.

During the night of 3 to 4 February, the company and platoon leaders of the 2d of the 511th were busy making preparations to carry out the 511th's plan of attack. About 0200, the commanders were ready. At 0530, the point of the 2d of the 511th moved out in two jeeps. Corporal James T. Wentink, from the S-2 Section of the 2d of the 511th, had the first jeep, and Ward Beaber had the second one. In all, the point squad consisted of eight men including a radio operator with an SCR-300 radio, one man with a BAR, a rifleman, and two drivers. When Wentink asked Colonel Holcombe how far they should go, he said, "Until you get stopped."

About an hour after Wentink and his point left the area, Hacksaw Holcombe and D Company, commanded by Capt. Steve Cavanaugh, mounted in two-and-a-half-ton trucks, followed down Highway 17. As Holcombe and D Company approached the outskirts of Imus, they were met by one of Wentink's men. He told them that the main highway bridge across the Imus River had been destroyed but that there was a second bridge two blocks west of the road. This bridge, however, was dominated by the Japanese in an old Spanish barracks or church of stone construction surrounded by a stone wall four or five feet thick. But, said the point man, he did not think that the Japanese had yet discovered that the Americans were in the town.

Holcombe ordered Steve Cavanaugh to dismount his company and to seize the bridge near the old building, which dated back to the early days of the Spanish occupation. D Company arrived at the building about fifteen minutes after the point had gotten there, according to Wentink. Holcombe told his S-3 to wait for the rest of the battalion and when it arrived to "place it under cover" and to have the executive officer report to him who would be forward with Cavanaugh.

By the time the main body arrived, D Company had set up its

machine guns and mortars. Holcombe told his XO to dismount the battalion and send the trucks back to regiment, and then, with the S-2 as a guide, to move the battalion on foot across a narrow dam east of the highway and await orders. Holcombe also ordered the detachment from Battery A of the 674th to go into firing position, and he attached the two M-8s to D Company.

D Company then launched an attack on the building, initiated by the sound of the first mortar round leaving the tube, and got inside the wall, but it was unable to eliminate the enemy in the building. The fire of the M-8s and the pack 75s was ineffective against the thick stone walls.

When T. Sgt. Robert C. Steele of D Company saw that the pack 75s and the M-8s were having no effect on the thick walls of the building, he ordered his platoon to give him covering fire and then he climbed up on the roof under enemy fire. On the roof, he punched a hole through it with an ax, poured gasoline down into the building, and then ignited the gasoline with a white phosphorous grenade. The Japanese poured out of the building in a rush and were cut down by Cavanaugh's men, who had the building surrounded. Sergeant Steele personally killed two of the enemy who had remained in the building in spite of the fire. Sergeant Steele was awarded the Distinguished Service Cross for his heroism, but unfortunately he did not live to receive it. He was killed on 8 February in the assault on Manila.

After the building was secure, Holcombe told Cavanaugh to leave one platoon to mop up and to secure the bridge while the rest of D Company and F Company moved to rejoin the battalion and continue the advance to Bacoor on foot. When Holcombe arrived back at the highway where he thought the rest of the battalion was under cover, a messenger told him that the rest of the battalion had been gone for about twenty minutes. General Eichelberger had been driving up the highway in his jeep, came across the part of the 2d Battalion not engaged in the fight near the stone building, and told Maj. J. M. Cook, the battalion executive officer, to take the troops who were there and continue the advance. Holcombe remembers then that he "ordered Battery A of the 674th to displace in rear of the battalion and . . . pushed on to overtake Major Cook and his force. Upon arrival at Bacoor, the Battalion was reunited and Major Cook reported that the order (presumably from General Eichelberger who had skipped a few levels in the chain of command) was now to push on to Manila. He also reported that no enemy had been encountered on the way from Imus except one truck load of about twenty who had been surprised and killed.''

While the 2d of the 511th was advancing on foot toward the southern outskirts of Manila, the rest of the 511th was shuttling forward in any vehicles that the division quartermaster could find. John Conable, shortly to become the division quartermaster, wrote, ''We had a supply line 69 miles long and 50 to 200 yards wide.'' Others referred to this supply line as a rather elongated beachhead. In addition to the trucks organic to the 408th Quartermaster, General Swing had assigned all two-and-a-half-ton trucks in the division to the 408th. ''In addition to our own truck drivers,'' Conable recalls, ''we had most of the division band as drivers. Ken Murphy, a lieutenant from Chemical Warfare, came down to help and became wagonmaster particularly during the night runs. He would take a jeep and lead the trucks looking for an ambush. At each end of the run we would check each driver to be sure he was alert enough to make another trip. There was a place at each end for the sleepy drivers to catch a little sleep. A nineteen-hour day was probably average for the drivers.''

On 4 February, the convoy of trucks was moving the 511th forward as fast as the trucks could make the turnaround. After the 2d moved forward, the trucks picked up part of Col. Ed Lahti's 3d Battalion, which was walking up the highway, and carried them as far forward as the road was clear. Lieutenant Colonel Henry Burgess started his 1st battalion from Tagaytay behind the 3d and marched the entire distance, some thirty-six miles, from Tagaytay to the cathedral in Paranaque, on foot. He wrote recently, ''As we made the last few miles, we received many greetings, fresh fruit, and young men offering to help carry our packs and ammunition, which was a godsend. One older woman ran out to a trooper ahead of me, threw her arms around him and said, 'Thank God you are here.' His reply was, 'Lady, I would have been here a year ago if it hadn't been for that damn basic training.' ''

With the Imus River bridge secure, Holcombe led his battalion on another three miles to Zapote, where Highway 17 ended at a juncture with Route 25. This led another half mile northeast across the Zapote River to a junction with Route 1, a mile south of a bridge over the Las Pinas River. The Japanese had prepared the bridge for demolition and were ready to defend it from positions on the north of the river, but Holcombe's men caught the Japanese by surprise. Even so, the 2d Battalion had a tough fight to take the bridge. Holcombe remembers, ''As

Company E, which was now in the lead, approached the bridge at Las Pinas, several Japanese were seen running back across the bridge. E Company deployed and approached the bridge where they were met by heavy fire from a pillbox located at the northwest corner of the bridge and from a school building and school yard on the north bank of the river.''

Holcombe sent F Company up on the left of E Company to add to the firepower directed against the enemy defenses. This additional force was insufficient to drive out the Japanese. One of E Company's mortar crews was wiped out after it fired only one round when it was hit by a large-caliber shell. The Japanese had apparently zeroed in all likely approaches to their positions. Holcombe then pulled E Company off the line and sent it in an enveloping move up the river, where it crossed and entered the town of Las Pinas from the east. A Battery moved to a new position from which it could support E Company's attack as it moved through the barrio.

While the 2d Battalion was attacking the Japanese defenses at the Las Pinas bridge, Henry Burgess and his 1st of the 511th arrived at the end of their foot march at about 1600. Colonel Haugen, who had been forward with Holcombe, came back to Burgess and directed him to move east, bypass the 2d on its right flank, and keep moving until he was stopped either by the Japanese or Haugen. The 1st of the 511th moved out about 1800. Henry Burgess remembers,

> When we came abreast of the 2d Battalion, it was discovered that the school building, being constructed of wood, caught on fire, and that the Japanese were being burned. The few who ran to fight another day were being cut down by the 511th machine gunners, so the 1st Battalion did not stop and continued as fast as it could march in a route parallel to and inland from Manila Bay . . . As we approached the church which housed the bamboo organ, it became obvious that what had promised to be a triumphant entry and warm reception was about to change. No civilians were on the street.

Holcombe remembers, ''Here at Las Pinas, as at Imus, there was no shortage of rank at the scene of the action. The Army commander and division commander were frequently with the leading elements and sometimes overhead in light aircraft. The regimental commander and division chief of staff together with the Army G-3 were present both at Imus and Las Pinas.'' General Swing was frequently over the columns in a Cub plane and, on occasion, when he wanted to see for himself close up what was going on, he would order his pilot to land on the highway, and he would take off on foot for wherever he had an interest. He did not exercise command from the rear.

Neither did Colonel Haugen. While the 2d of the 511th was advancing, Haugen was with them in his jeep. Near Las Pinas, Haugen left his jeep and continued on foot. Bill Abernathy recalls:

General Pierson and Colonel Schimmelpfennig, the division chief of staff, joined him (from where—who knows?). The three of them in the center of the road were moving faster than the troopers on each side of the highway in the approach march formation. The company commander joined them. General Pierson pointed to the trooper just ahead of the four of them and asked who they were. "That's the point, Sir," was the reply. So right behind the division point on the advance to contact was the assistant division commander, the chief of staff, the regimental commander and the company commander. Haugen requested that they get out of the center of the highway and walk with the troopers on the sides. Shortly afterwards, they passed a mansion on the left of the road. General Pierson marked it as the division CP.

The next day, Haugen left his regimental CP in the police station and with Major Frick, his S-3, Major Lyman Faulkner, his S-2, a couple of runners, and an artillery forward observer went forward to observe the fighting. Haugen was not the lead scout, but he stayed close enough to the deployed companies to know where the lead units were and, through channels, to direct the action.

When the troops went through Bacoor, which was short of the Paranaque River, they received a tumultuous welcome. The Filipinos had thrown together a seventeen-piece band, which blared the national anthem and a potpourri of Sousa marches. Nearly three thousand Filipinos crammed the streets, wringing the troops' hands, and giving them bananas, cucumbers, and fried chicken. But they also slowed down the pace of the advance. Shortly, as the fighting intensified, the crowds would no longer present a problem.

"Driving through a densely populated area and following Route 1 up the shore of Manila Bay," wrote Robert R. Smith, "the 1st Battalion ran into increasingly heavy harassing fire from Japanese riflemen and machine gunners. At Paranaque, two miles beyond Las Pinas, the unit found a bridge across the Paranaque River badly damaged, defended by Japanese on the north bank, and covered by Japanese mortar and artillery fire originating from Nichols Field, a mile and a half to the northeast. Here, only four miles south of the Manila city limits, the Japanese stopped the 511th Infantry.'' The 11th Airborne Division was now up against the principal Japanese defenses south of Manila.

Holcombe recalls, ''Darkness had fallen by the time the 2d Battalion entered Paranaque, the last suburb outside Manila proper, and a furious firefight could be heard ahead where E Company and the 1st Battalion were located. At this time the battalion was ordered to halt for the night. Their mission was to protect the rear and seaward flanks of the regiment and to prevent any enemy movement into or out of the positions in Manila. E Company rejoined the battalion and, under intermittent shell fire, the battalion went into positions for the night.'' At about 2300 that night, Holcombe reported to Colonel Haugen and got his orders for the next day: Cross the Paranaque River at 0500 and lead the attack against the enemy in Manila.

Back along Tagaytay Ridge on 4 February, the 188th, having cleaned out the enemy on Shorty Ridge, left one company to secure the area. Colonel Soule led the rest of the regiment on foot toward Manila. At 0815, the third serial of the 511th RCT dropped onto Tagaytay Ridge. This serial consisted in the main of the 457th Parachute Field Artillery Battalion under the command of Lt. Col. Nick Stadtherr. The 457th, with its twelve pack 75s, landed on the ridge opposite the Manila Hotel Annex. The 457th gunners used some ingenuity and persuasiveness to get their howitzers by hand to the road near the Annex. The Filipinos who were standing around watching the jump were soon put to work. They hauled parachutes, containers, and ammunition to assembly points while their carabao and ponies packed the pieces of the howitzers, each weighing about 250 pounds, up the slope. One of the artillerymen remarked that he knew that the 457th had pack howitzers, but he never thought anyone beside himself, let alone carabao and ponies, would ever pack them.

Edward J. Cole made the jump on Tagaytay with the 457th. He remembered:

> I got a good opening, tore a few sections in my chute, which was not unusual when you were loaded up with equipment, reached up to grab my risers and hit the ground. I didn't have a chance to release the jump rope and the 609. We had jumped at about 450 feet with full equipment

and were still alive. I don't think I oscillated even once on the way down. My landing was hard, with all that extra weight. I got rid of my chute as fast as I could. . . . I do not recall anyone shooting at us on the way down but heard from others later that there were shots fired by the Japanese that had evaded the Filipino guerrillas who were waiting for us and who had secured the DZ. We assembled in amazingly good time and secured our area. As usual, the civilian population stole all of the chutes from the drop zone and in the months to follow silk and nylon shirts and dresses were a common sight in the area. I think we helped the local economy by buying some of these handmade items ourselves.

With the division on a new and very tough mission, and with his supply tail strung out over nearly seventy miles, General Swing altered the missions of some of his units. He assigned to Colonel Hildebrand and the 187th the mission of protecting Nasugbu and patrolling the main supply route (MSR). It was a difficult task. Colonel Hildebrand used Filipino guerrillas to assist in carrying out the mission. He was in virtual command of all of the guerrillas in the provinces of Batangas and Cavite. By this time, about 2,000 guerrillas had been assembled. But each guerrilla unit was a separate and distinct entity, commanded by men who were dictatorial in some cases and warlords in others. They controlled their areas in some cases with bloodshed, and they were not above exacting taxes from the civilian Filipinos. Some units, however, were patriotic, well-led, disciplined, well-organized fighting units. But coordinating their activities, supplying them, and sorting out who ran what "turf" was not the same as commanding and operating a U.S. Army outfit.

To assist in the vast task of covering the large area that the rapid advance of the division had liberated, General Eichelberger brought ashore the 19th Infantry, less one battalion, on the night of 5 February and assigned the unit to Colonel Hildebrand. In a few days, both battalions of the 187th would move forward and join the division in its fight against the southern defenses of Manila. The 457th, meanwhile, was in firing positions on Tagaytay Ridge and attached to the 187th to provide fire support for the defense of the MSR.

Colonel Hildebrand accomplished his diverse mission by patrolling the area thoroughly, and by establishing outposts along the entire MSR. His force was not large enough to engage the enemy in large-scale fights, but by active patrolling, the enemy was forced farther and farther back into the hills. One Japanese concentration was centered around

Mount Pico de Loro; another was on Mount Sungay. In future weeks, the 11th would be back in the area to eliminate them.

General MacArthur may have been right in his strategic assessment of the capture of Manila. But the troops had to fight in a tactical situation and suffer heavy losses as they bashed themselves against the interlocking defenses of the Genko Line. And Manila, before its final liberation, had to be subjected to unimaginable devastation of its buildings and people. Manila was far from free and hardly "in our hands" on 4 February.[2]

---

[2] General MacArthur was very much an optimist when he wrote about the capture of Manila.

In the morning hours of February 1st, the 1st Cavalry Division started down toward Manila, its exposed left flank guarded by Marine air units. Simultaneously, the 37th Division from the XIV Corps and the 11th Airborne Division of the Eighth Army closed in on the city. A flying column from the cavalry under Brigadier General William C. Chase entered Manila on February 4th, and relieved the prisoners at Santo Tomas and Bilibid. For all strategic purposes, Manila was now in our hands. A desperate element of the enemy trapped by our encirclement fought for two weeks to the death and caused unnecessary casualties and much destruction of property.

CHAPTER 13

MANILA TO LOS BANOS

By 2130 on the night of 4 February, the 511th had advanced as far as the Paranaque River bridge, the southern boundary of Manila. The Japanese were not caught by surprise. Although the bridge had not been completely destroyed, the Japanese had the north bank studded with machine gun emplacements and pillboxes enclosing other larger caliber automatic weapons. And it was here that the division ran into Japanese naval gunfire for the first time.

In December 1941, the population of Manila was about 625,000; in the fall of 1944, it reached more than 800,000, just before the beginning of the Allied air attacks in September. Then its people began to evacuate the city in droves and move to the countryside.

When the 11th Airborne halted at the Route 1 bridge over the Paranaque River, it was opposed by Southern Force's 3d Naval Battalion, reinforced by a company of the 1st Naval Battalion and artillery units armed with various ground, naval, and antiaircraft weapons. The 3d Naval Battalion's positions were the strongest in the Manila area because they had been there the longest. Reinforced concrete pillboxes dotted the street intersections in the suburbs south of the city limits, and many were covered with dirt, which gave them a natural camouflage. The Japanese had hidden other defensive positions in clumps of trees. North of Paranaque was Nichols Field, from which the Japanese Naval Air

Service operated; it was defended by part of the 3d Naval Battalion. Nichols Field was studded with antiaircraft weapons, which could fire either vertically at planes or horizontally at troops on the ground.

On 4 February, the enemy had few troops at Nielson Field, two miles north-northeast of Nichols, but the 4th Naval Battalion held Fort McKinley, which was just two miles from Nielson. Other Japanese units manned a group of antiaircraft guns midway between Fort McKinley and Nichols. These weapons supported the 3d Naval Battalion. The 11th Airborne Division had come up against the Genko Line.

Rear Admiral Sanji Iwabuchi, who commanded the defenses of Manila, had at his disposal 20,000 men, consisting of 16,000 naval troops and 4,000 soldiers who had been trapped by the American pincers maneuver on Manila from the north and the south. Before the Americans landed, he believed that the main American attack against the city would come from the south and, therefore, he prepared his strongest defenses south of the Pasig River. He integrated into these defenses the reinforced concrete buildings of prewar construction. Iwabuchi also brought in heavy guns from damaged or sunken naval vessels. He intertwined into his defensive line a tremendous number of automatic weapons, mortars, field artillery pieces, and grenades. According to D. Clayton James, "Iwabuchi's defenders were prepared to make the capture of Manila a bloody, time-consuming ordeal for MacArthur's forces."

Iwabuchi's men had also fortified the city with such expedients as overturned trucks and trolleys, and houses converted into machine gun nests, with their entrances sandbagged, stairways barricaded, and walls sliced open for firing ports. Iwabuchi had ordered his men to blow up all of the city's military installations. He meant the port area, the bridges, and the municipal water and electrical supply. His men took him at his word and more. On 5 February, one group dynamited the northern port area and fled south across the Pasig River, blowing up all the bridges behind them. These blasts ignited fires that quickly engulfed a section of bamboo houses near the port. In a short time, much of the northern half of the city was in flames, visible for fifty miles, and hampering the 37th Division as it fought the Japanese from street to street in the northern part of the city.

On 6 February, General Eichelberger wrote to his wife:

The view of Manila last night was a terrible thing as the whole part of one side of the city seems to be on fire. Smoke and flames were going

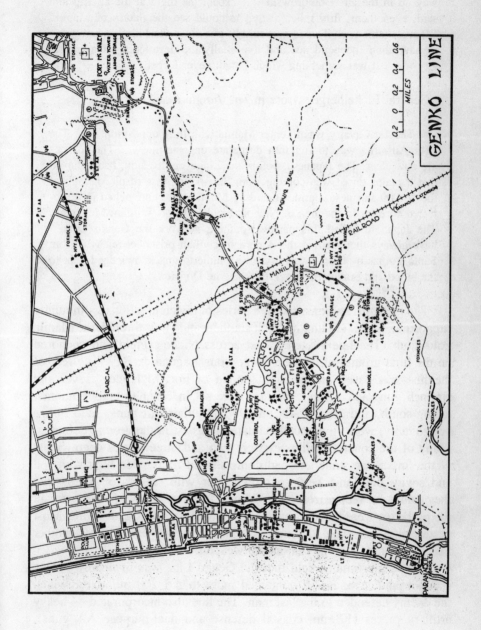

GENKO LINE

MILES
0.2 0 0.2 0.4 0.6

261

way up in the air. Dombrowski . . . spent the night at the airstrip and said, even there, fifty miles away, he could see the flames of Manila. What a shame it is. This is particularly true since the Filipinos are going to have their independence and it is really the destruction of a neutral city. . . . It was something which I shall never forget. . . .

General Eichelberger wrote in *The Jungle Road to Tokyo:*

The 1st Cavalry was to enter Manila with little opposition . . . The 11th Airborne was to run into desperate opposition . . . The reasons are now clear. The Japanese, before the Lingayen invasion, had believed that a major thrust was coming from the south. As a result, 12,500 of the 16,000 Japanese marines guarding Manila were entrenched in a protected corridor in the area of Nichols Field and Fort William McKinley. The Japanese called this narrow southern network the Genko Line. I have always thought that the American civilian prisoners released from Santo Tomas by the 1st Cavalry owe a hitherto unacknowledged debt to the blood and bravery of the 11th Airborne Division.

The Genko Line consisted of a series of concrete pillboxes, mutually supporting, and extending in depth six thousand yards through the Manila Polo Club. The line stretched east across Nichols Field and anchored on the high ground of Mabato Point along Laguna de Bay. The rear of the line was based on the high ground of Fort McKinley. Five- and six-inch guns and 150mm mortars were set in concrete emplacements, facing south, and 20, 30, 40, and 90mm antiaircraft guns, sited to fire horizontally, were strategically situated to assist in the ground defenses. Many of the concrete pillboxes were two and three stories deep. Some of the forts were stone and had dome-shaped roofs piled high with sod and soggy dirt, and were so grown over with tangles of weeds that they could be recognized only from a few feet away. Embrasures in the pillboxes were narrow, but they controlled a wide field of fire. Most of the pillboxes were defended by two men and either a .50-caliber machine gun or a 20mm automatic weapon.

The G-2 estimates held that the Genko Line was manned by some six thousand Japanese. It contained more than 1,200 pillboxes, which the enemy defended to the last man. The line also incorporated 44 heavy artillery pieces (120mm coastal defense and dual-purpose AA guns), 164 antiaircraft 20 to 40mm (single, double, and triple barreled, emplaced for ground defense), and a great number of machine guns, 13mm or smaller, of which the division captured or destroyed 333 during the period 5 to 23 February. This belt of concrete and steel was further reinforced with 245 hundred-pound bombs and 35 antisubmarine depth charges emplaced and rigged as land mines. All roads approaching the line were heavily mined with 500-pound aerial bombs armed with low-pressure detonators.

On the night of 4 February, Henry Burgess was leading his 1st Battalion of the 511th north along a street toward the Paranaque River bridge. As the battalion neared the cathedral in Paranaque, a "wood-pecker" machine gun in the belfry of the cathedral opened up. The troopers took shelter in doorways of the buildings along the street. The men alternated their dashes forward so that the enemy gunner could not get set and aim. It was obvious to Burgess that he was going to have to enter the cathedral and eliminate the Japanese holed up in it. About three blocks from the cathedral, Burgess remembers, Colonel Schimmelpfennig

> came walking through a building from the alley where he had left his jeep. Standing in the entrance to a building with several soldiers and myself, but just off the sidewalk, he had a good view of the action occurring on the avenue as the troopers would run from door to door. Characteristi-cally, he wanted the troops to go faster. I explained what they were doing, where the Japanese machine gunner was, and was pointing out from the doorway the alternate rushes being made on one side of the street from a door to the next door, and within a few moments a similar rush across the street to the next door, and that it took time. To my horror, he stated that he would get the troops moving faster, and walked out of the building onto the sidewalk where he was cut down. It was a sad and unnecessary event. A trooper and I pulled his body back into the doorway. . . .

Burgess's men entered the cathedral and were fired on by several riflemen who were behind the main altar. The paratroopers crawled down the aisles, killed the enemy near the altar, and then started up the steps to the belfry. After surprising and killing a couple of Japanese soldiers in a fight on the steps, they made their way to the tower from which they could see all of Manila. A Japanese gunner from across the river saw them in the tower and took them under fire. There were no casualties, but the men in the belfry, having seen enough of Manila from a church steeple, made haste to get back down to the main floor.

After clearing the cathedral, Burgess and some of his men approached the stone bridge over the Paranaque River. Burgess wrote recently:

It was a beautifully designed and very old stone structure rising from two sides of the river some distance in the air to allow access for fishing boats with tall masts to move from the river into Manila Bay at low tide. As we approached the apex of the bridge from the darkness of the Paranaque side, we noticed for the first time that fires had been started in Manila itself, and the light from the increasing fires provided enough illumination for us to see two Japanese machine gun pillboxes made of stone on the other side of the bridge. . . . The Japanese . . . opened up on us as we approached the apex of the bridge. Too early, it turned out, as we had not reached the apex of the merging lines of fire, and because of the short, narrow firing slits in their pillboxes, the Japanese couldn't traverse the entire bridge. We dropped to the floor of the bridge below the line of fire. . . . We all withdrew, and a second lieutenant replacement . . . was stationed on the road to halt anyone who might attempt to proceed further.

. . . Sometime during the night, a jeep emerged from the dark headed for the bridge. The lieutenant hollered "Halt" and advised that there were Japs on the other side. It was General Swing in the jeep, who said that no goddamned Japs were going to stop him and directed his driver to proceed. As the jeep drove up to the apex of the bridge, the . . . Jap machine gunner sent greetings, causing everyone to desert the jeep for the roadbed. . . . Not wanting to deal with the general at that moment and realizing that facing the general would be harder than facing the machine gunner again, I walked back onto the bridge, found the general's driver, Sgt. DeBaca, and Lt. Col. Douglass Quandt lying prone about where I had been earlier in the evening. It was with great malicious joy that I kicked both in the tail and told them to get up and walk off the bridge, much to Quandt's chagrin. Of course, they didn't realize that they were safe, nor did I tell them.

The 674th and the 675th had by this time moved up into positions from which they could support the advance of the 511th and the attack across the Paranaque River. After General Swing's mishap at the bridge, he set up a temporary CP in the cathedral so recently cleaned out by the 1st of the 511th. Lieutenant Colonel Lukas E. Hoska, Jr., the commander of the 674th, reported to General Swing there and said that he believed that he and his pack 75s could neutralize the heavy enemy fire across the bridge. General Swing gave him permission to try.

Colonel Hoska crawled to the riverbank with his radio, descended to the water's edge, and directed seven hundred rounds of 75mm in precision adjustment (by a single howitzer) between midnight and 0500 on 5 February. He knocked out five machine gun emplacements and two 20mm high-velocity guns embedded in the concrete breakwater wall thirty yards across the Paranaque River from him.

By midnight of 4 February, the division had advanced thirty-two miles and killed a counted total of 413 of the enemy at a cost of 28 troopers killed and 154 wounded.

Ed Lahti had moved his 3d Battalion of the 511th to the Paranaque River on the night of 4 February. According to Capt. John Coulter, the commander of Headquarters Company of the 3d Battalion, 511th, "The night of 4–5 February was spent in huddled groups with walking guard posts to protect the sleeping men. Less than 500 yards to the front, the enemy was strongly defending his position by the light of fires of burning Paranaque. Japanese artillery fired spasmodically. . . ."

At 0500 on the morning of 5 February, the 2d of the 511th attacked across the bridge and started north along Route 1 over a quarter-mile-wide strip of land lying between the river on the east and Manila Bay on the west. At about 0700, according to Coulter, the 3d of the 511th

formed in column with five pace intervals and moved toward the Paranaque River bridge. Enemy artillery was sporadic and ineffective as the air bursts were too high. Engineers were already at work on the stone bridge which had been damaged by shellfire. The column see-sawed back and forth, rushing forward toward the bridge on one order which was countermanded later. At about 1100, contact along the line was broken. Units of the 2d Battalion, who had now been engaged for about 24 hours, became intermingled with the 3d Battalion. Japanese small arms fire was high. The situation was confused since no order had been issued for an attack. The troops formed an inverted "L" with the 2d Battalion in contact to our left front and the 3d Battalion in column stretched to the rear. . . . At about 1300 . . . the column marched again to the right and on line with the 2d Battalion. . . . The Paranaque was crossed and the 3d Battalion established a line across the mud flats and dikes bounding these flats. . . . At 1600, while attempting to move forward, the battalion came in contact with the enemy who had employed his machine guns and small arms to fire the length of the dikes, the only means to traverse the waist deep water and mud.

During the next two days, the 511th fought its way north about 2,000 yards in house-to-house and pillbox-to-pillbox fighting. It was a far cry from the kind of fighting that had been the division's initiation into combat on Leyte. The 511th was supported only by light artillery and had to depend, for the most part, on the infantryman's weapons— flamethrowers, rifles, grenades, demolitions, and mortars. In two days the regiment lost six men killed and thirty-five wounded, and killed about two hundred of the enemy. On 6 February, General Swing called a temporary halt to the advance of the 511th to await the arrival from Tagaytay Ridge of the 188th reinforced by the 2d of the 187th.

For several days after crossing into Manila proper, the 1st of the 511th was held in division reserve, to be committed only by order of General Swing. Henry Burgess had a chance to view the civilians fleeing from the burning city and the savagery of the Japanese, trapped and increasingly ruthless. He recalls:

> With the destruction of the buildings, the civilians in the southern part of the city streamed into our lines in a never-ending column of Filipinos of all ages. Many nursing women had been bayonetted in their breasts, some had the tendons in the back of their necks severed by sabers and could no longer hold their heads up. Small children and babies had been bayonetted. . . . We had been admonished to keep our medical supplies for ourselves, and not to help others. Of course we couldn't, and didn't refuse them assistance. The number of those fleeing increased so that after several days all of our firing was stopped in an attempt to help those who came to us. The whole street became choked with pitiful human beings as thousands moved south to escape the holocaust of Manila.

The 511th's drive into the southern suburbs of Manila was marked by chaos and destruction. Houses and shops, which flanked both sides of the highway leading into the heart of the city, were shattered by both the enemy and American artillery. Tin-roofed houses looked as though a giant can opener had sliced through them. Once pretentious mansions were reduced to piles of rubble around charred chimneys. Nearly every house bore the scars of the heavy fighting. Shrapnel from the continuous barrage of Japanese 90mm antiaircraft shells burst overhead and sprayed fragments of steel over a wide area, pocking roofs and walls. Trees were denuded of limbs and leaves. In one area, a long row of warehouses had been completely flattened. The rusted, corrugated roofs under which the Japanese had once stored their supplies were twisted and crumpled into vast heaps of rubbish. In another sector, a row of apartment houses, their interiors exposed where shell fire had blasted away the walls, lay sagging as if blown apart by a massive typhoon.

By 6 February, Colonel Soule had arrived near Nichols Field with his 188th and with Lt. Col. Norman Tipton's 2d of the 187th attached. General Swing planned to send the 188th against Nichols Field from the south and the southeast while the 511th continued its drive into Manila in the west, on the left flank of the division. The 188th moved up to a line of departure about a mile and a half southeast of Nichols Field under cover of darkness the night of 6 to 7 February.

The 188th's attack on the morning of 7 February gained little ground; it was thwarted by concentrated, accurate, and heavy field artillery, mortars, and machine gun fire from the Japanese defenses in and around the airfield. On the west, the 511th drove north to Libertad Avenue against heavy enemy resistance and rugged house-to-house and street fighting. At one intersection, Capt. Pat Wheeler, commanding G Company of the 511th, was cut down as he tried to cross the machine gun–swept corner.

Private George Canales, E Company of the 511th, was the point man for his company, whose immediate objective was a house in an open field just south of the Polo Club. An unknown number of the enemy had barricaded themselves in the house, which was surrounded by a stone wall, blasted and broken up by artillery and mortar fire. Beyond the wall, in the open, were pillboxes and machine gun emplacements. Canales, acting squad leader at the time, led his men forward, and killed or drove the Japanese from the house and occupied it. The rest of the company was about forty yards away. Outside, another group of Japanese fired on the house with machine guns and mortars and attempted to storm it. Inside, Canales deployed his men to the windows on the first floor and took for himself a window toward the front of the house, the area the Japanese were attacking. In seventy minutes, with his M-1 rifle resting on the windowsill, he picked off twenty-two of the enemy, most of them at a range of about 150 yards. Then he called for mortar and artillery fire around the house and broke the attack.

On the morning of 7 February, the men of the 3d Battalion of the 511th found themselves in a dilemma. The battalion had called for an air strike at 0900 on the sixth, but, for unknown reasons, it never materialized. But at 0700 on the seventh, the A-26s arrived unexpectedly. Coulter writes:

This strike . . . caught the battalion displaced forward. . . . The A-26's were approaching the lines at an angle. . . . Parafrag bombs were dropped very close to friendly units. The enemy comprehended the situation quickly, and while troops were executing a strategic withdrawal to escape . . . friendly aircraft fire, he laid an accurate concentration along the dikes, the only means of retreat. Casualties were heavy from the knee mortars. The mortar concentration ran down the dike along which the main attack had been launched, and after a few extra rounds at the battalion command post, stopped as suddenly as it had begun.

Colonel Lahti decided to abandon positions in that area and attempt to flank the enemy position by moving his men in single file along what he describes as a "tortuous route" bordering the Paranaque River and ending at the Nichols Field service road, which bordered the north side of Nichols Field.

During the night of 7 to 8 February, the Japanese launched an attack in strength against the 3d of the 511th's position, which was repulsed in large part by the machine gun platoon of Headquarters Company under the direction of T. Sgt. (later 2d Lt.) Mills T. Lowe. He had deployed the machine guns along the forward edge of the battalion perimeter, and, because of the accuracy of the fire and the excellent siting of the machine guns, the battalion's casualties were light. During this same night attack, the Japanese tried a unique tactic in which, according to Coulter, "the Japs tried to enter our positions by boat drifting down the Paranaque River past the bridge which marked the front line. Filipinos who had carried the wounded awoke the personnel along the dike and in the command post. Fire was withheld to almost point blank range. A second attack never developed. . . . It was now determined that the enemy with which we were engaged were Japanese marines."

On 10 February, the 11th Airborne passed from Eighth Army control to Sixth Army and, in turn, to General Griswold and XIV Corps. On the tenth, General Griswold radioed General Swing, "Welcome to XIV Corps." General Griswold outlined the new mission for the next day: Continue to exert pressure against the Japanese at Nichols Field but mount no general assault, for the time being; find out the extent and nature of the Japanese defenses at and east of the airfield; prepare to secure Cavite naval base area; await further orders.

On 11 February, the 2d Battalion of the 511th had reached Libertad Avenue. General Griswold halted the battalion's advance, fearing that it might cut across the front of 5th and 8th Cavalry Regiments headed toward Manila Bay from the northeast. General Swing then turned the 511th to the east for the attack on Nichols Field. Eventually, Libertad

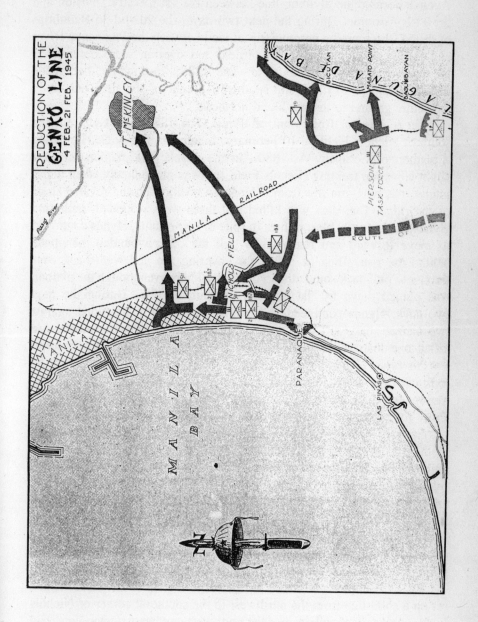

REDUCTION OF THE
GENKO LINE
4 FEB.- 21 FEB. 1945

FT. McKINLEY

Pasig River

MANILA   RAILROAD

NICHOLS FIELD

138

511
187

2
511
187
187

2

ROUTE   OF   TF

PIERSON
TASK FORCE

LAGUNA DE BAY

TAGUIG
BICUTAN
MABATO POINT
DAGUIBAYAN

19

MANILA

PARANAQUE

LAS PINAS

MANILA   BAY

N

Avenue became the dividing line between the 1st Cavalry Division and the 11th Airborne. During the next two days, the 2d and 3d Battalions of the 511th secured a narrow strip of land between the Paranaque River and the western runway of the airfield and overran some defenses at the northwest corner of the field. The 188th, meanwhile, had made contact with the 511th at the southwest corner of the field but could gain little ground to the north and northeast.

But it was not from want of trying. The 188th attacked from the south of Nichols Field on 10 February. Lieutenant Henry G. Hynds led a platoon of Company A, 188th, in the attack. His platoon seized a slight elevation fronting Nichols Field and was immediately taken under intense machine gun fire from a Japanese position on the reverse slope of the ridge. One man was killed and three were wounded, including Hynds, in the initial blast of fire. In spite of his wounds, Hynds continued to move forward and managed to pull the other wounded men back behind the rise. Then he called for covering fire and went back over the rise to pull back some other wounded soldiers even though the platoon was pinned down by flat trajectory antiaircraft fire. During the next two days, Hynds continued to lead his platoon as it defended against two banzai charges. During one of these attacks, Japanese mortar fire killed one man and wounded three others on the platoon's perimeter. By this time, Hynds's wounds had weakened him considerably, but he took over the break in the perimeter and prevented its exploitation by the enemy. Lieutenant Hynds was awarded the Distinguished Service Cross for his intrepidity, aggressiveness, and courage.

Early in February, Maj. Charles P. Loeper had assumed command of the 1st Battalion of the 188th. On 10 February, the leading assault units of his battalion were pinned down by heavy machine gun fire from Japanese pillboxes guarding the southern approaches to Nichols and had suffered many casualties. Major Loeper moved up with the advance elements and personally led an attack on the enemy positions. The battalion moved forward. However, while leading his battalion in the final assault, Major Loeper was killed. He was awarded the Distinguished Service Cross for his gallant, personal leadership.

By 11 February, the division had consolidated its advances. It had set up a solid line from the northwest to the southeast corner of Nichols Field, slicing diagonally across the northwest-southeast runway, and had eliminated the last Japanese resistance on the west side. In the 511th sector, the front lines extended from Dewey Boulevard along Libertad

Avenue and east to Taft Avenue Extension. Division permitted patrols beyond this line, and one patrol made contact on 11 February with a 1st Cavalry Division patrol in the vicinity of the Philippines Racing Club.

The 2d Battalion of the 511th had been engaged in some of the division's heaviest fighting since the Tagaytay Ridge jumps. It had fought hand to hand along the streets leading into Manila; it had been subjected to Japanese timed artillery fire, which burst thirty to forty feet overhead; it had felt the blasts of the large naval guns the Japanese used as artillery; it had fought against the Japanese who were dug in behind thick stone walls around some of the mansions along Dewey Boulevard; it had patrolled to the rear of enemy positions to locate them for artillery and mortar fire; it had fought in buildings going from room to room, eliminating the defenders; it had fought off suicidal banzai charges, one of which, on the night of 5 to 6 February, had penetrated the battalion perimeter and killed about half of a light machine gun squad that was providing local security for the battalion CP. (One survivor of that attack lay beneath the body of a dead fellow soldier until daylight.) The 2d landed on Tagaytay Ridge with 502 officers and men; by 10 February, the battalion numbered 187 officers and enlisted effectives.

By 11 February, the 11th Airborne had not been able to reduce substantially the volume of Japanese fire from the Nichols Field complex of defenses. The A-20s from Mindoro and the light artillery of the division had not destroyed enough of the enemy's weapons to permit the infantry to advance without severe losses. "The Japanese defended Nichols Field," wrote the division historian, "as if the Emperor's Palace itself were sitting on the center runway."

The airfield was the center of the Genko Line. The position was based on a network of concrete pillboxes and gun emplacements connected by underground tunnels. The 100-foot revetments used to protect aircraft were hollowed for defensive positions, and aprons of barbed wire ringed the area. In general, the terrain around Nichols Field was open and provided excellent fields of fire for machine guns and the innumerable dual-purpose ack-ack guns. On the outer rim of the field a number of 5-in. naval guns were embedded in concrete at strategic places. There were so many that one battered company commander sent the following note to the division CP: "Tell Halsey to stop looking for the Jap Fleet. It's dug in on Nichols Field."

One of the most elaborate pillboxes at Nichols Field was found later by the 188th. It was three stories deep and built of reinforced concrete into the side of a hill. The first level, in which the attacking infantrymen found a mahogany bedstead and cushioned chairs, presumably housed Japanese staff officers, while the enlisted men lived on the second level. The third level was used as a storehouse. Given the overall depth and ruggedness, and the number of defensive installations on Nichols, the 11th Airborne obviously needed more and heavier caliber artillery support.

"For some days the division's situation had been a bit anomalous," wrote Robert R. Smith, "especially in regard to coordination of its artillery with that of XIV Corps to the north. Sixth Army had directed XIV Corps not only to seize Manila but also to drive south to an objective line running from Cavite northeast across the Hagonoy Isthmus to Tagig on Laguna de Bay. The 11th Airborne Division had crossed this line as early as 6 February, and every step it took northward toward Manila increased the danger that XIV Corps Artillery might inadvertently shoot it up."

Finally, about 8 February, XIV Corps and the 11th established direct communication. XIV Corps quickly established a no-fire line midway between Nichols Field and the Manila city limits. Under this plan, the XIV Corps artillery had fired sixteen 155mm and 8-in. concentrations in support of the 11th's attack on Nichols Field before the division came under the control of XIV Corps. This arrangement, wherein a division attacking to the north was supported by artillery firing south, was another of the almost routine, unusual situations in which the 11th Airborne found itself.

On 11 February, the 511th was strung out along Manila Bay north to Libertad Avenue and east to the western and northwestern edge of Nichols Field. Eli Bernheim remembers,

At that time, the 2d of the 187th was attached to the 511th. Our battalion CP was in a Spanish style house with a thick wall surrounding it. We were getting harassed by low trajectory 20 mm. AA fire. . . . General Swing, Colonel Haugen, Colonel Tipton and, I believe Captain Dick Barker, the battalion S-3, were in a second floor room discussing the situation. There was a small hexagonal shaped window high on one wall. I was going up the stairs to report to Colonel Tipton when there was a loud explosion that caused me to trip on the stairs. A 20 mm. shell had penetrated the window and exploded in the room. Colonel Haugen received a sucking chest wound. Miraculously no one else was wounded.

Colonel Haugen was immediately evacuated to a field hospital that had been set up by the 221st Medics, according to Dr. R. J. Riley, who was the 511th regimental dental officer but doubled as an assistant battalion surgeon for whichever battalion needed medical help. He remembers, "As soon as arrangements could be made, Colonel Haugen was moved by a C-47 plane with destination Hollandia in New Guinea. Unfortunately, we heard later that Colonel Haugen passed away during the flight. We mourned a truly great leader. Colonel Lahti was given command of the regiment."

During his evacuation, Colonel Haugen's flight stopped at Mindoro for a short layover. While Haugen was there in a hospital, Col. George Jones, the commander of the 503d Parachute Infantry Regiment, visited him. They were old friends from the early days of airborne, a pair of young officers who had been a part of the parachuting business from its infancy. They had grown with it in parachute commands. Colonel Jones told Colonel Haugen that he had his regiment on Mindoro and that they were going to jump on Corregidor on 16 February. Haugen, who had been stationed on Corregidor in prewar days, was astounded that anyone would have conjured up an operation involving dropping a regiment on that small, windswept, rocky, powder keg of an island. George Jones remembers Haugen's reaction. "Orin [Haugen] was very sick, but he had strength enough to look up at me and, looking seriously into my eyes, say, 'George, they can't do that to you.'" But they could and did. The 503d went on to make airborne and military history by its carefully tailored jump onto "The Rock's" two tiny, terrible drop zones, against a fanatical, deeply entrenched, suicidal enemy numbering about seven times more than the prebattle intelligence estimates.

On 12 February, General Griswold authorized General Swing to launch a full-scale attack on Nichols Field. General Swing was well aware of the solidity and depth of the Japanese defenses. His air observer brought in marine SBDs from the Lingayen Gulf fields to soften up the defenses prior to the infantry attack. The 11th's Division Artillery and the infantry's mortars fired hundreds of rounds in preparatory fires. The 2d Battalion of the 187th attacked generally east from the northwest corner of the field; the 188th and the 1st of the 187th drove in from the south and southeast. The artillery and mortar barrages helped to neutralize the defenses, and, under cover of those fires, the infantry could, by leaps and bounds, move forward to assault the various pillboxes and emplacements with rifles, carbines, grenades, and pistols. In hand-to-hand fighting, the infantry made use of their bayonets, knives, and rifle butts. In the afternoon, the Japanese launched a strong counterattack, but it was beaten off. By dusk, the 187th and the 188th had cleared most of the field.

The division continued the attack the next day. The 511th advanced east astride the Manila-Fort McKinley road to come up on line with the remainder of the division along the Laguna Extension of the Manila Railroad. The 187th and 188th continued to fight across Nichols. But the field was by no means ready to accept American planes. The runways and taxiways were bomb-pocked, mined, and rutted, and the Japanese guns at Fort McKinley occasionally dropped artillery rounds at random on the field.

On 11 February, General Eichelberger wrote to his wife:

Sir George [Kenney] thinks I should have dropped the 511th on Nichols Field, but in view of those concrete emplacements I believe they would have been murdered. I do not think I could have gotten a corporal's guard out alive. No one will take a bigger risk than I will if I feel I have a reasonable chance, but I do not believe that would have been a fair show. I would not have minded dropping them in the vicinity of Imus, which is almost down to Manila, because there were practically no Japanese there. My force was so ridiculously small because I only landed with four battalions and one of these . . . had to hold the base, which left me with three battalions; and one had to hold Tagaytay Ridge, which was a very commanding terrain feature, so I would only have had two battalions to march towards Manila if I had not dropped the three battalions from the air on Tagaytay Ridge. There were only seven battalions in the whole division. Personally I think we pulled one of the most daring feats of the war.

In another letter he said, "Joe Swing is going to be very sorry to come under any other unit. I am going to recommend the 11th Airborne Division for a Presidential Citation."

On the morning of 15 February, the division continued its attack across Nichols and toward Fort McKinley. The plan called for the 188th, with the 2d of the 187th attached, to pivot and strike toward Fort McKinley and for the 511th to continue its attack, with all forces converging at the Caribou Gate of Fort McKinley.

The plan of attack for the 2d of the 187th was simple, as there was no choice except to "push straight to the front and keep going," wrote Capt. Harrison Merritt, commander of G Company of the 187th, after the battle. When Colonel Tipton briefed his company commanders on the battle plan, he said: "Don't give the little bastards a chance to get set. I ran a good many problems over this same ground when stationed here as a lieutenant. It is a damned good defensive terrain and so I repeat—hit hard and keep moving. Don't stop for anything. What you by-pass, E Company will take care of."

The line of departure was the south line of the Manila Railroad, which ran north and south at the base of the ridge that the battalion occupied. The bed of the railroad was about six feet above the level of the ground. Just beyond the railroad and running parallel to it was a dry streambed. The terrain to the east rose gradually to form a grass-covered east-west ridge, with its highest point about 1,000 yards east of the line of departure.

At 1215, following an intense artillery and mortar barrage coupled with an air strike, G Company, 187th, jumped off in the attack. Merritt's first platoon scrambled over the railroad tracks in its sector and started moving forward. They found no enemy. The platoon crossed a dry stream-bed and started up the other side, kept moving for a hundred yards, and then two hundred, "and still not a target appeared or a casualty suffered as the platoon crossed the dry streambed and started up the barren slopes," wrote Merritt. The platoon moved forward cautiously but quickly. Still no enemy reaction. Said Meritt,

Something was wrong. Suddenly the unexpected happened again. Machine guns located in the streambed that the platoon had just crossed opened up on the right rear of the first platoon. . . . Every man in G Company was a veteran of the Leyte campaign and was battle-wise. As a result, the platoon was well dispersed. . . . Before any fire could be brought to bear on the general location of the machine guns, a shouting, screaming mass of Japs climbed out of the creek bed and charged toward the platoon. . . . The machine gunners who had been following close behind had their weapons mounted and firing within seconds. Their fire combined with the fire of the BAR's and individual weapons began knocking the Japs over like "ten pins." Still they came on in seemingly endless streams. Soon the leading enemy closed into the first platoon and all semblance of organization vanished. It was every man for himself.

The machine guns, because of their positions, were still in the clear and were pouring a steady stream of fire into the Japs as they came out of the streambed. This fire was very effective as the Japs were very close together as they crawled over the bank.

Merritt knew that he could not use his mortars. He decided to commit his second platoon. He ordered the platoon commander to move into the draw. The platoon leader was ahead of him; he had already led his platoon over the railroad tracks and into the draw on the other side. The second platoon moved down the draw and knocked out several enemy machine guns while suffering only two casualties. Said Merritt,

This had been fairly simple, as the creek bed was empty except for the enemy machine gunners who had ceased firing, because their fire was masked by their own troops, and were engrossed in watching the battle. The platoon leader ordered one squad to continue up the creek for another hundred yards and hold up. Leading the other two squads, he left the creek bed and headed into the melee.

Everything was really confused at this time. The Japs, for some unknown reason, did not attempt to fight it out, but tried to pass through the platoon and reach the shelter of their holes. Screaming like a flock of frightened chickens, they were running right through the first platoon and up the ridge toward their bunkers and pill boxes.

Merritt realized that the enemy in the bunkers would soon start firing even if it meant killing their own men. Merritt tried to move the first platoon up the hill. The second platoon leader and two squads joined Merritt, and together they started up the hill. "The platoon leader of the first platoon was quick to understand what was taking place," said Merritt, "and with the help of his sergeant began pushing his platoon forward. Help now arrived on the scene. F Company on the left flank of G Company had swung to their right and reached the crest of the hill. This put the remaining Japs between the two companies and cut off the route to their positions."

Within a few minutes, firing ceased, and both companies moved to the top of the hill. F Company then moved to the left, back into its own zone. Merritt told a few men to drop grenades into the firing apertures of the position on top of which they stood. Suddenly, and without warning, a muffled explosion shook the area, and "the earth on top of the hill rose and then settled," said Merritt. Most of the men on top of the hill were knocked to the ground, but none was injured. "Preferring death to the disgrace of capture, he had blown his position while the enemy was on top of it,'' Merritt concluded. ''Without doubt, he expected the whole hill to be destroyed, killing everyone on it. Fortunately, the charge was too small or all of it did not explode, and his last attempt turned out to be a failure also.''

The division had now seized two-thirds of the Genko Line. The 511th with the 2d of the 187th attached had pushed through the left end of the line, battering its way through block after block of the crumbled, burning, debris-littered streets of Manila, then turned east to join in the attack on Nichols Field. The 188th and the 1st of the 187th had swung north across defense-heavy Nichols Field and joined with the 511th coming east. The 674th and 675th FA Battalions had been firing incessantly in support of the infantry assault, and brass shells, cases, and fiber covers were piled in high heaps behind the battery positions. Gun crews, of course, worked shifts so that guns were firing twenty-four hours a day; individual guns were given breaks to cool off, get oiled, and sometimes have a barrel replaced.

The artillery, unlike their counterparts in the European war, were often subject to attacks from the Japanese who infiltrated behind the infantry lines to try to knock out the guns that blasted them so incessantly. Around Manila, banzai attacks against artillery positions were commonplace. Each battery set up a perimeter around its gun position to ward off the attacks. The morning after the 675th had beaten off three Japanese charges during the night in a position south of Nichols, Colonel Massad sent a requisition to division for ''12 each, bayonets, for howitzer, 105 mm.''

A steady stream of supplies flowed up Highways 17 and 1 from Nasugbu to Manila and the units deployed along the Nichols Field line. Trucks rolled day and night. The Division Special Troops unloaded supplies and established dumps.

The division hospitals were extremely busy. The 221st Medical Company had set up one hospital in a church close behind the front lines near Paranaque. Others were in various locations close behind the infantry. From the frontline hospitals, the 221st drove the wounded in ambulances to Nasugbu. Early on, some of the more seriously wounded men were flown by Cub planes from strips smoothed out of dry rice paddies to the strip at Nasugbu; later, the 127th Engineers, working at night by the light of jeep headlights, built a strip at Imus that would accommodate C-47s.

Robert R. Smith summed up the division's attacks around Manila and Nichols Field:

With the seizure of Nichols Field, the 11th Airborne Division substantially completed its share in the battle for Manila. Since its landing at Nasugbu the division had suffered over 900 casualties. Of this number the 511th lost approximately 70 men killed and 240 wounded; the 187th and 188th Infantry Regiments had together lost about 100 men killed and 510 wounded, the vast majority in the action at Nichols Field. The division and its air and artillery support had killed perhaps 3,000 Japanese in the metropolitan area, destroying the 3d Naval Battalion and isolating Abe Battalion. From then on the division's activities in the Manila area would be directed toward securing the Cavite region, destroying the Abe Battalion, and, in cooperation with the 1st Cavalry Division, assuring the severance of the Manila Naval Defense Force's route of escape and reinforcement by clearing Fort McKinley and environs. For the latter purpose the airborne division would maintain close contact with the cavalry, already moving to complete the encirclement of the Japanese defenders in the city.

The 1st of the 511th had been the division reserve for a few days after it reached the Paranaque River. On 10 February, Burgess received an order from Colonel Haugen to move his battalion through the 2d and to take the lead on the road leading from Manila east toward Fort McKinley. The terrain east of Manila Bay is open and rolling. On the evening of 12 February, the battalion halted along the road with B Company in front, dug in on both sides of the road, which was about five feet above the surrounding fields. About 400 yards behind B Company was the Battalion Headquarters and Headquarters Company. In the middle was a no-man's-land. Lieutenant John M. Ringler, the B Company commander, had put a light machine gun along the road, sighted toward Fort McKinley. The gunner, a recent replacement to the company, had the supposedly safer evening shift because, the paratroopers had found from expensive experience, the Japanese were less likely to attack in the early evening. The gunner's squad leader had also told him to fire at anyone who moved along the road.

The battalion CP, like the rest of the battalion, had dug in for the night. At dusk, Burgess's telephone operator received a phone call from B Company saying that a man in B Company had been wounded and was being littered to the battalion aid station, in the CP area, by four men. Burgess told the operator to relay the message to the battalion surgeon and to be on the lookout for the litter. The surgeon and two aid men went up to the top of the road to wait for the wounded man.

Shortly after the doctor got up on the road, four men carrying what appeared to be a litter arrived at the perimeter and walked through unchallenged. The doctor turned on his flashlight and knelt down to check the wounded man on the bundle the men were carrying. A large man tapped him on the shoulder, waved him off the road, and pointed to what was obviously another four-man carrying group. The doctor suddenly realized that the man ordering him off the road was a Japanese officer and what had appeared to be a litter was in fact a Japanese machine gun being carried by four men. The doctor hollered "Japs" and jumped off the road into the ditch. The perimeter started firing and set off the ammunition boxes carried by the Japanese at the head of the column. The fires lighted up B Company's perimeter. Men were running around the immediate area, and it was difficult to distinguish the enemy.

One man ran up to the foxhole in which sat Burgess and his battalion executive officer, Maj. Nat Ewing. They thought he was a Japanese, and raised up out of the foxhole and grabbed him. The man was one of Burgess's men who had taken a fragment of a hand grenade through his back and into his chest. Ewing and Burgess pulled him into the foxhole and tried to bandage him but, remembers Burgess, "He was already in his death throes and died within a few minutes."

Following the Japanese machine gunners was a column of infantry four abreast. Wrote Burgess,

As the Japanese realized that they were in an American Army unit, they banzaied us. All of the rest of us by that time were in our holes firing and throwing grenades. Our machine gunners swept the road and established a firing line across the road and our perimeter. B Company realized by this time that the "stretcher" was being followed by a column of what turned out to be a battalion of Japanese Marines entering Manila, and managed to get its machine guns turned around and firing in our direction, taking the Japanese marines from the rear. There really wasn't too much danger of either of our positions being damaged by firing in the direction of one another, so long as everyone stayed down. The fighting went on all night in sporadic firing, grenade throwing, and a lot of "banzai-ing." A small arroyo crossed the edge of the Headquarters position and many of the Japanese tried to escape by crawling through it. The troopers near the arroyo could hear the enemy in the water below them and dropped grenades on them.

After dawn, the battalion continued to mop up the area and found about 160 bodies between Headquarters and B Companies and a number of wounded Japanese who committed hara-kiri when approached. Burgess also found out that the Japanese battalion had been sent from Fort McKinley, only a few miles beyond the U.S. battalion's front line, to assist in the defense of Manila.

Later in the morning, Ringler found out that the replacement who was manning the light machine gun in one of his forward positions had seen the column of Japanese, had lost his nerve, had not fired, and had not alerted his dozing gun crew.

On the morning of 9 February, two days after the 37th Division began crossing the Pasig River, Admiral Iwabuchi decided that he would not be able to defend Manila to the end. He moved his headquarters to Fort McKinley, from where he apparently decided that he could better control the withdrawal of his remaining forces from Manila. He left Colonel Noguchi in charge of all troops remaining in the city. But Noguchi found he could not control the naval elements in Manila, and asked Iwabuchi to return a senior naval officer to the city. Iwabuchi feared that the Americans might take Fort McKinley before Manila fell and decided that he himself would return. He was back in Manila on the morning of 11 February.

Thereafter, the Japanese situation, with orders and counterorders, became confusing. About 13 February, General Yokoyama decided that Manila was untenable and directed Iwabuchi to return to Fort McKinley and to start withdrawing his troops from the city. On 15 February, General Yamashita, from his CP in Baguio, 125 miles north of Manila, took General Yokoyama to task. He demanded to know why Iwabuchi had been permitted to return to the city, and he also ordered all troops out of Manila. Iwabuchi did not receive the two directives until 17 February. By then, XIV Corps and the 11th Airborne had cut all Japanese lines of retreat. Iwabuchi was well aware of this fact and did not try thereafter to evacuate his troops. On 19 February and again on 21 February, Yokoyama ordered Iwabuchi to withdraw his forces. Iwabuchi, from necessity, ignored the order and simply replied to Yokoyama that if he withdrew his forces they would be annihilated by the Americans, but that if they remained, they could cause the Americans heavy losses. Yokoyama then suggested that Iwabuchi withdraw at night, a tactic he said was successful throughout the Pacific. Iwabuchi's reply to this message, if there were one, has been lost. On 23 February, Iwabuchi's and Yokoyama's communications ceased. As Robert R. Smith wrote: "Iwabuchi had made his bed, and he was to die in it."

The fighting within Manila had raged unabated as XIV Corps attacked from the north and continued to compress the defenders into a smaller and smaller circle. The 11th Airborne had cut off the Southern Force's Abe Battalion northwest of Laguna de Bay. Between 14 and 18 February, Maj. Jay D. Vanderpool, commanding a battalion of guerrillas, and working with and under the guidance of General Swing, contained the battalion up against the shore of Laguna de Bay. Later, the 11th Airborne would eliminate it.

Following the fall of Nichols Field, the division regrouped for the assault on the last bastions that had made up the Genko Line: Fort McKinley and Mabato Point, the high ground on Laguna de Bay about 2,000 yards south of Fort McKinley. The tactics used were conventional: Blast the areas with air strikes and artillery; attack from the vulnerable sides; squeeze the enemy tighter and tighter, and, if they tried to escape, attack the escape routes with air or artillery or from previously set ambushes.

On 14 February, General Swing formed a special task force under the command of Gen. Albert Pierson to reduce the Mabato Point stronghold and to attack Fort McKinley from the south. The Pierson Task Force was composed of Harry Wilson's 1st of the 187th, the 3d of the 19th Infantry, A Company of the 44th Tank Battalion, a platoon of C Company of the 121st Engineers, and a platoon from the 221st Medical Company. The 457th Field Artillery Battalion, which had just recently moved up from Tagaytay Ridge, where it had been helping to protect the supply line, was in direct support of the task force. The 188th, the 511th, and the 2d of the 187th, supported by the 674th and 675th FA Battalions, were to attack Fort McKinley from the vicinity of Nichols Field.

On 15 February, the Pierson Task Force advanced north toward McKinley along the east side of the Manila Railroad, which ran parallel to the shore of Laguna de Bay. The 188th, with the 2d Battalion of the 187th attached, and the 511th attacked east in the face of heavy automatic weapons and artillery fire from Fort McKinley, to form a line, facing east, above the left flank of the Pierson Task Force. General Swing received permission to launch his attack on Fort McKinley on 17 February.

In preparation for the attack, the unit commanders consolidated their positions, made and passed their plans down the line, and resupplied their troops.

The 1st of the 511th, in the lead and moving in from the west, came onto open rolling hills leading toward Fort McKinley. The battalion ran head on into numerous concrete pillboxes, heavy artillery, and a number of rapid-firing 120mm AA guns. All of the positions along the road were protected by machine gun nests and were mutually supporting.

Private First Class Manuel Perez was in Lt. Ted Baughn's 3d platoon of A Company of the 511th. The company approached Fort McKinley along the heavily defended Nichols Field-McKinley road and had succeeded in knocking out eleven of twelve emplacements along the route of march. Perez had already killed five Japanese in the open on the way forward and had blasted others in dugouts with grenades. He realized that the twelfth and final position had to be reduced if the company were to advance. Perez circled around the emplacement, which held two twin-mount .50-caliber dual-purpose machine guns and got up to within twenty yards, killing four of the enemy on the way. Then he lobbed a grenade into the position, and, as the crew started to withdraw through a tunnel just to the rear of the emplacement, shot and killed four more Japanese before his rifle clip ran out. He reloaded and killed four more when one of the escaping Japanese, in desperation, javelined his bayoneted rifle at Perez, which knocked his own rifle out of his hands. But then Perez picked up the Japanese rifle, bayoneted the man with his own bayonet, and continued his one-man assault. He killed two more of the enemy with the Japanese rifle. He rushed the remaining Japanese, killed three more with the butt of the rifle, and then went into the pillbox, where he bayoneted the one survivor. Single-handedly Perez had killed eighteen enemy soldiers and knocked out the pillbox that had been holding up the company. He was awarded the Medal of Honor, but he was killed in another action at Fort McKinley before he learned of it.

Staff Sergeant Richard Sibio was in the 3d platoon of A Company on the day Perez made his assault on the pillbox on the road to McKinley. He remembers:

Lt. Baughn, S/Sgt. Marvin Lewis, and S/Sgt. Max Polick were within a few yards of him [Perez] when he did his crazy assault on those pillboxes. I can remember the Jap with his fixed bayonet charge Perez, and we saw him beat the Jap and bayonet him with his fixed bayonet—besides grenading the pillbox. (In training at Camp Mackall and Fort Polk, Perez was not a very good shot. Lt. Baughn and Lt. Hojanaki and Lt. Cavanaugh brought him along until he qualified.)

During this skirmish at Ft. McKinley and after Perez did his thing, Pat Berardi came into still another pillbox where S/Sgt. Max Polick and I had just used up a full box of mortar shells we found inside the pillbox. Pat Berardi came in and said he was hit. We looked and he surely was (in the behind). We dressed the wound as best as possible and he returned to his mortar squad. I regret to say a few weeks later Perez was killed and still later, in the skirmish near Lipa where I was wounded severely (through the stomach and spine), Pat Berardi tried to help me and he was also fatally wounded. Pat . . . was awarded the Distinguished Service Cross for his brave attempt to help.

The combined assault on Fort McKinley got under way on 17 February. In the west, Burgess's battalion was in the lead. "The closer we got to Fort McKinley the more artillery, ack-ack fire, small-arms fire and mortar fire from emplacements and pillboxes were encountered," Burgess wrote. "At one time in the open rolling country one could see seven infantry battalions attacking on a line supported by tanks and self-propelled guns . . . just like they do it in the movies!"

One of the gallant actions in A Company, 511th's attack, involved Sgt. Ted McGourty, a squad leader in the 1st Platoon. Moving up the road to McKinley, McGourty noticed that a machine gun squad was badly hit by machine gun fire. He was wounded four times as he crawled forward in the face of "murderous" fire, but continued his lone attack. McGourty flipped grenades into the ports of one of the emplacements and, read his citation, he "knocked out two of the gun emplacements, killing more than five Japs. In spite of his wounds, McGourty refused medical treatment until he had organized details which safely evacuated the wounded men, and had reorganized his squad."

Burgess continued,

As we approached Fort McKinley, its presence became more ominous. Built of brick, the buildings were beautiful, and the fort dominated the surrounding terrain for hundreds of yards. Streets were paved and the grounds were immaculate. Approach routes to the fort itself were open and devoid of any cover. The 1st Battalion of the 511th had been designated as the lead battalion in taking Fort McKinley, an assignment which was going to be expensive in troopers.

That morning, as we came closer to McKinley, Lt. Col. Tipton, CO of the 2d of the 187th, was on our right. Colonel Tipton's first assignment had been at Fort McKinley upon graduation from West Point. He came to see me and told me of his love for McKinley, the good years he had spent there, and that he would deem it a great achievement to retake his first post. I couldn't believe my ears! Here was a tough nut to crack, and he was wanting the assignment. We had telephone wire from battalion to Division Headquarters through the intermediate switch boards, and in a few minutes Colonel Quandt, the G-3, authorized Colonel Tipton and his battalion to take McKinley. It immediately deployed and commenced the approach on the fort.

A short time after Burgess had had his conversation with Tipton, Colonel Lahti, who had taken over the 511th after Colonel Haugen's fatal wound on 11 February, had come up from his CP on a motor scooter and was talking to Burgess and Holcombe, the CO of the 2d of the 511th, on the outskirts of McKinley. With both hands, Lahti held up a map in front of his body of the area around Fort McKinley. Tipton's battalion had just entered Fort McKinley. Burgess remembers:

No one knew that in the grass lawn of the Fort between the curb on the streets and the sidewalk there had been buried large depth charges from Naval stores with detonating wires leading back into the Fort to places of observation. When the first company of the 188th was well within the Fort, the Japanese detonated the enormous charges. Even though the troopers were strung out with space between them, there were many casualties. A large fragment of a Japanese artillery shell flew hundreds of yards from the Fort upon detonation, passed between Holcombe and me, hit Colonel Lahti in the right upper arm, and landed several feet beyond him. Slowly Lahti, with an odd expression on his face, dropped the map and held his arm with his free hand. I looked down and saw the shell fragment which Lahti had seen and wanted me to pick up for him. Of course, the metal was hot, burning my hand, and I dropped it. At that point . . . Lahti finally commented, "I think I have been hit," and slowly sat down on the ground. Large bandages were tied on his arm, he rose to his feet, mounted his motor scooter, kicked the starter, and took off for an aid station, where twenty-one stitches were taken. In a few hours he was back with the regiment (with his arm in a sling) as if nothing had happened, although his complexion was somewhat pasty. He was then, and still is, indestructible.

Doctor R. J. Riley was also with Colonel Lahti when he was wounded. He put a compress on the wound. "It was an ugly looking wound," he recalls, "and I wanted Colonel Lahti to be evacuated for further medical attention. He adamantly refused, and never missed a minute of the ensuing action. History records, and I humbly confirm, that Colonel Lahti did an excellent job in leading the regiment in our part of the ultimate victory."

By 18 February, the 188th was inside the fort, and, with the 511th and elements of the 1st Cavalry Division, spent the next few days mopping up. The battle for the fort cost the enemy 961 counted dead within its confines. However, the bulk of the enemy who had been within the fort had escaped to the east. The 4th Naval Battalion and remnants of the 3d Naval Battalion from Nichols Field withdrew eastward toward the Shimbu Group's main defenses during the night of 17 to 18 February. About 300 survivors of the 3d Naval Battalion and 1,000 men of the 4th managed to get out of the fort. The original strength of the 4th had been about 1,400 men.

Sunday, 18 February, was to be a memorable day for Henry Burgess; the experience that he was about to begin would be etched indelibly on his mind for the rest of his life. Colonel Lahti came up to Burgess's CP in the field near McKinley and told him that he was to withdraw his battalion from the line right away, turn it over to his executive officer, Maj. Nat Ewing, and that he, Burgess, was to report to General Swing at the division CP at once. Ewing, meanwhile, was to march the battalion back to the division rear area for a "rest." Burgess remembered thinking that a "rest" in the minds of everyone in the battalion was a "duplicitous word which sparked rumors and trepidation, for no one had had a rest since the landing on Tagaytay Ridge, and the battle for Manila was still raging unabated."

Burgess and two soldiers went back to Division Headquarters, which was in one of the abandoned mansions along Dewey Boulevard South. Before Burgess reported to General Swing, he and the two soldiers went on a private reconnaissance of the street along the beach north of Division Headquarters. The area was lined with mansions that faced Manila Bay. The houses were set amid extensive and formerly beautifully tended gardens. Several blocks from the division CP, Burgess recalls, he and the two men

quietly entered the yard of a large, two-story opulent house and entered through the open door. To our, and their, surprise, in an adjoining room from where we entered were three Japanese men in white bathrobes talking to one another and drinking tea. They had not heard us enter. As we walked into the room to join them for tea, they suddenly became aware of us, took one look, and ran right out through the front French windows into the yard without bothering to open the door and into the yard, where they fell to our fire.

In going back through the house and searching it thoroughly, we found golf bags and a number of papers. A pocket of one of the golf bags yielded a membership card identifying the Japanese owner. The owner of the bag had been a member of the Princeton University golf team. Two more Japanese were encountered in reconnoitering the area and killed. How division headquarters had operated without discovering the Japs several blocks away and without the Japanese discovering division headquarters has always mystified me. On the other hand, one could hardly expect a graduate of Princeton to be much of a soldier, and certainly not a match for a Harvard graduate.[1]

The 1st Battalion soon closed at the beach in the new area, was served a hot meal, their first in days, and told it was being "rested." Actually, it had just taken the first steps of its march to liberate Los Banos.

Shortly after General Swing formed the Pierson Task Force, General Pierson moved his force on line to the right of the 188th on Nichols Field. General Pierson wrote:

Glenn McGowan was the executive officer, Major Arthur L. Moseley was the S-3, Major Widmyer was the S-2. Stadtherr [the Commander of the 457th FA Battalion] and I were watching the advance up a slight hill, both of us with field glasses, when a Japanese anti-tank gun opened fire with only one round. McGowan, Moseley, and Widmyer were on my left rear, sitting on the ground. The round exploded and a large piece of shrapnel penetrated Moseley's helmet, killing him immediately. Widmyer was wounded and evacuated; McGowan's escape was a miracle. Moseley was known on Leyte for his daily "Milk Run."

A few days later, General Pierson turned the task force over to Lt. Col. George Pearson, who was the executive officer of the 187th Glider Infantry Regiment. General Pierson said he "went back to my regular tasks of visiting the different units and making myself available to mem-

[1] As was Burgess.

bers of the general and special staffs.'' On 18 February, the task force had attacked northwest beyond Mabato Point and then turned east to the shore of Laguna de Bay south of Fort McKinley, isolating a Japanese stronghold occupied by the Abe Battalion of the Southern Force, on the high ground at Mabato Point on the northwest shore of Laguna de Bay. The terrain in the area was rolling and open, and, from the high ground at Mabato Point, which was the eastern anchor of the Genko Line, the Japanese had perfect observation and fields of fire. Like the rest of the Genko Line, the Japanese had been preparing the defenses of the area since 1942.

They had burrowed and dug into the hills around Mabato like giant moles. Tunnels wound for hundreds of yards underground, occasionally opening into large rooms for living quarters, supply rooms, communications centers, hospitals, and shrines. The entire maze of subways was interconnected, and the Japanese could move from one location to another hundreds of yards away and on the other side of a hill without ever surfacing. All key terrain features dominating the avenues of approach to the catacomb position were guarded by machine gun nests and covered with mortar and artillery fire.

To crack such a formidable redoubt, the task force first surrounded it; then blasted it with artillery, tanks, mortars, and air strikes, including 1,000-pound bombs from P-38s, P-51s, and Marine Corps SBDs; and then assaulted it with infantrymen. The 3d Battalion of the 19th attacked from the north; the 1st of the 187th attacked from the west; and the 3d of the 511th,[2] now commanded by Lt. Col. John L. Strong, and Major Vanderpool's guerrillas held a line across the south road. The ground around the Japanese defensive position was so hard that aerial bombs merely chipped off pieces of the defensive works; the artillery was somewhat less destructive. Finally, the attackers called for napalm, which did two things: It burned the camouflage off the cave and tunnel entrances and, when a firebomb landed in or near the openings of the position, it burned up so much oxygen so rapidly that the enemy soldiers were suffocated inside.

By 21 February, the Pearson Task Force had surrounded the Japanese and cut off all routes of escape; boats patrolled Laguna de Bay to block escape routes over water. That morning, a group of guerrillas and a young girl appeared near the task force command group in the field

---

[2] The 3d Battalion of the 511th joined the task force on 20 February 1945.

west of Mabato Point. According to one description, the girl, a "comely Filipino phone girl from the barrio of Hagonoy, was ushered into Colonel Pearson's presence where she asked if it were possible for a Japanese medical officer to surrender. Colonel Pearson asked the whereabouts of the officer and she pointed to one of the 'guerrillas,' a nondescript little individual in white shorts and blue sweat shirt." The man promptly surrendered, and, through a Nisei interpreter, indicated that there were perhaps four hundred more Japanese in the Mabato Point area who would surrender unconditionally if given the opportunity. Colonel Pearson thought that it would be worth a trial and ordered the task force to cease fire.

The girl's brother volunteered to take a message to the Japanese and shortly set off on a scrawny horse with a white flag and a message, which stated that at 1200 that day all American fires would be halted for half an hour and that any Japanese who wished to surrender should walk out with their hands over their heads and proceed to the American lines.

There is some controversy about what happened next. One version holds that the artillery started firing at some Japanese in the open near the Mabato Point fortification. The other version holds that the Japanese commander of the Abe Battalion rejected the proposal out of hand. At any rate, his men killed the Filipino's horse and sent the messenger scurrying back to the task force lines.

At 1230, the attack resumed after a series of air strikes and artillery concentrations and tanks' and tank destroyers' direct fire on the position. Captain Schick, and his C Company of the 187th, led the assault. The task force and all supporting weapons and planes blasted the position with as much force as they could muster. The Japanese retaliated with deadly accurate 150mm mortars. Finally, the infantry assaulted the position and, with rifles, grenades, flamethrowers, and bayonets, killed off a number of the enemy.

That night, all fifteen surviving officers of the Abe Force marched, on the commander's order, to Mabato Point and committed hara-kiri. Later that night, a group of the enemy tried to escape down the road to the south, apparently unaware of the 511th and guerrilla ambushes set up along the road. The Japanese were marching in a close column, a perfect target for the machine guns in the ambush sites. The result was a slaughter.

But not all of the Japanese who tried to escape from Mabato Point were that unmilitary and careless. Near Bagumbayan, just south of Haganoy, T. Sgt. Mills T. Lowe, chief of a machine gun section of twenty-four men of Headquarters Company of the 3d of the 511th, had established a position along the shore of Laguna de Bay about three hundred yards from any supporting troops. A Japanese force of some three hundred men made repeated banzai attacks on the position. Sergeant Lowe personally manned one of the machine guns and directed the fires of the others. The section managed to fight off four attacks. After the fourth attack, the ammunition supply was low. Lowe led a raiding party outside his perimeter and captured seven Japanese machine guns, two mortars, and an ample supply of ammunition. With the captured weapons back inside the perimeter, Lowe and his men broke up the fifth attack. Then the remaining enemy troops attacked Lowe's position from both the front and the rear. Lowe, constantly exposing himself to the enemy fire, coordinated the fire of his section and personally killed eight Japanese in hand-to-hand combat. After the sixth attack was beaten off, the Japanese retreated, dragging their wounded and leaving a large number of dead around Lowe's position. During this fight, Lowe personally accounted for fifty of the enemy killed in action. For his extraordinary performance, Sergeant Lowe received a battlefield commission and the Distinguished Service Cross.

According to Robert R. Smith, "In this final action [at Mabato Point] the Japanese unit lost about 750 men killed; the 11th Airborne Division lost less than 10 men killed and 50 wounded. . . . The Abe Battalion's final stand made no tactical sense, and at least until 14 February the unit could have escaped northeastward practically unmolested."

By 21 February all organized Japanese resistance in the areas of Mabato Point, Nichols Field, and Fort McKinley had ceased. The division had killed hundreds of Japanese at Mabato Point alone. The fight for McKinley went on apace with the battle for Mabato Point. The fort was a series of stone and brick administrative buildings, barracks, and officer and NCO quarters, with the addition of sandbagged pillboxes covering all the roads on the post. Reducing the pre–WW II U.S. Army post was somewhat reminiscent of the fighting in southern Manila. But by 21 February, the infantry had overrun Fort McKinley.

The Cavite Naval Base was on the northeast end of a short, narrow peninsula that jutted to the northeast into Manila Bay about four miles to the west of Paranaque. Before the war, it had been a large U.S. Navy installation. During the war, the Japanese had installed antiaircraft and artillery weapons on it, posing a serious threat to Allied ships entering Manila Bay. On 16 February, GHQ, through Sixth Army and XIV Corps, ordered General Swing to neutralize Cavite.

On the afternoon of 16 February, Doug Quandt and Henry Muller called a small staff meeting in the Division Headquarters at Paranaque and decided that, since every unit of the division was committed to the fight at Nichols and McKinley, they would have to form a small, impromptu task force to accomplish the mission. Available were the Recon Platoon, the defense platoon around Division Headquarters, and some guerrillas. Quandt called in Glenn McGowan from the Pearson Task Force and told him that he was the commander of the task force. Lieutenant Skau, commander of the Recon Platoon, and Lieutenant Reed, from Division Headquarters, were two other officers in the force. Quandt and Muller briefed McGowan, Skau, and Reed on the plan. XIV Corps furnished Major Burns, a civil affairs officer, and two men. Two men from the 511th Signal Company handled the communications.

Under cover of darkness, a PT boat beached on shore near the Division Headquarters; the fifty men of the task force loaded their weapons and ammunition on board and bedded down for the night on the beach adjacent to the boat. At 0200, the task force loaded aboard the PT boat and took off under quarter power toward Cavite. At 0300, the force went ashore and deployed to the outskirts of the naval base. Lieutenant Skau took one recon patrol and Lieutenant Reed another and moved out in search of Japanese guns that were still active. About 0400, Skau returned to the boat and reported to Colonel McGowan that he had located a gun position around which an enemy gun crew of twelve or more men sat at a fire preparing breakfast. Skau and his patrol moved to within 100 yards of the group. McGowan told Skau to move his patrol within range to attack at first light. At 0500 Skau and his patrol wiped out the enemy gun crew. The gun was an 88mm antiaircraft weapon with about twelve rounds lying near it.

Major Burns rounded up a group of Filipinos on the base to bury the dead Japanese. The task force dismantled the gun, took out the firing pin, and returned to Division Headquarters at about 1100—"tired, wet and hungry," according to Colonel McGowan. "No casualties."

It was not until 3 March that General Griswold finally decided that all organized resistance in Manila had ceased. He so reported to General Krueger, who relayed the information to General MacArthur the next day. The battle for Manila had been bloody and almost totally destructive of many of the sections of the city. In their desperation, the Japanese had raped, murdered, and committed the most uncivilized of atrocities on the Filipinos in the city. The inner city of Intramuros, surrounded by stone walls forty feet thick and twenty-five feet high, resisted the heaviest artillery pieces that the American forces could bring to bear. Intramuros after the battle was a scene of total devastation.

With Manila, the Genko Line, Fort McKinley, Nichols Field, and Mabato Point behind them, the 11th Airborne Division was now about to undertake a new mission with a specially tailored task force—the rescue of civilian internees forty miles behind the Japanese lines at a place few in the division had heard of until about 16 February. And it was to be a mission whose objective was not the usual destruction and killing of the enemy but the salvation of innocent, incarcerated Allied civilians.

CHAPTER 14

LOS BANOS

Shortly after the 11th Airborne Division landed in southern Luzon, General MacArthur's headquarters alerted General Eichelberger to the pressing need to rescue POWs and interned civilians in the various camps throughout the Eighth Army's area of operations. MacArthur gave Eichelberger no set timetable for the release of the prisoners. MacArthur made it clear that the first priority was the defeat of the main Japanese forces on Luzon; he did indicate that the release of prisoners, for whom he felt a deep responsibility, was a very close second priority. In his *Reminiscences* he said: "There was no fixed timetable [to reconquer Luzon]. I hoped to proceed as rapidly as possible, especially as time was an element connected with the release of our prisoners. . . . I knew that many of these half-starved and ill-treated people would die unless we rescued them promptly."

On 3 February, General Eichelberger passed on to General Swing the mission of rescuing the civilian internees in Los Banos, a place that would eventually fall into the 11th's zone of operations. On 5 February in his CP in Paranaque, General Swing alerted Doug Quandt and Henry Muller to the Los Banos mission and directed them to start planning.

By February 1945, morale in Los Banos had sunk to its lowest depth; the internees felt that relief and release from their captivity was still remote. Some internees had hidden radios and knew that the Americans had invaded Luzon, but they were not aware that the Americans were moving in their direction. They had no idea that deliverance was close at hand.

To piece together a complete picture of the then-unknown (at least to the 11th Airborne planners) Los Banos camp, Henry Muller used every agency at his disposal: the division reconnaissance platoon, Air Corps photo reconnaissance, organized guerrilla units in the area, Filipino civilians, and a source with which he was not familiar at the time— escaped internees. Doug Quandt knew that when the time came for the raid, which clearly would have to be after the reduction of the Genko Line, he would have at his disposal the various units of the division. But he was also aware that there were guerrilla units in the area of Los Banos that could provide operational as well as intelligence assistance.

Major Jay D. Vanderpool was the guerrilla "coordinator" in the Cavite, Batangas, and western Laguna areas, a region in which the 11th Airborne was also operating. To insure close coordination between the 11th and the guerrillas, Major Vanderpool located his headquarters across the street from the 11th's in Paranaque. Major Vanderpool was well aware of the capabilities and limitations of the guerrillas. He had infiltrated into Luzon from a submarine in the fall of 1944 and had worked with the guerrillas since that time. He organized the General Guerrilla Command (GGC) for southern Luzon and through that headquarters, staffed by guerrilla officers, he attempted to coordinate the activities of the several guerrilla bands in his area.

Through them and the civilians in the area around Los Banos, Major Vanderpool was well aware of the plight of the internees. He was so concerned with their deteriorating condition that as early as 10 February he called a conference of his guerrilla staff to seek a solution to the problem. At the end of the conference, he and his staff concluded that the guerrillas, acting alone and without help from the 11th, might be able to free the prisoners. Vanderpool issued a letter order to Lt. Col. Gustavo C. Ingles, a member of his staff and a highly respected, hard-working officer, to lay the groundwork for a guerrilla-only attack on Los Banos by making a detailed reconnaissance of the area, determining enemy strengths in and around the camp, ascertaining the condition of the internees (how many could walk out, how many had to be carried), sketching the layout of the camp and the condition of the roads and bridges in the area, and verifying the number and combat readiness of the guerrillas who might be available for the raid. Vanderpool even authorized Ingles to "order an attack with available forces or to await reinforcements."

But by 14 February, Colonel Ingles was having some second thoughts about the rescue attempt.[1] He reported to Major Vanderpool that although he had enough men, arms, and ammunition to subdue the guards at the camp, he was not certain that he could hold the camp long enough to evacuate the sick and nonambulatory internees to any point of safety. He also pointed out that the Japanese had a relatively large force at Lalakay, only six kilometers from the camp. That report reinforced Major Vanderpool's belief that guerrilla units alone could not make a successful rescue.

Vanderpool remembers that on that day he recommended to General Eichelberger "that U.S. Forces should be the controlling and most visible elements in the raid, supported by guerrillas in the scouting party and in diversionary attacks to delay counterattacking Japanese elements until the internees could get out."

During this time, the 11th Airborne staff was also putting together the basics of a plan to liberate Los Banos. Liaison between Vanderpool's guerrillas and the 11th commander and staff was fairly direct and easy, because the 11th Division Headquarters at Paranaque had a rudimentary officers' mess (airborne units were not given to luxurious trappings), where General Eichelberger (until he left Luzon on 9 February and returned to his Eighth Army Headquarters on Leyte) and his staff, General Swing and his principal staff officers, and Major Vanderpool and some of his guerrilla staff officers ate together. At least once a day, Major Vanderpool and his staff could brief the 11th staff on the situation around Los Banos. Vanderpool's G-2 was Col. Marcelo Castillo, a 1938 graduate of the U.S. Naval Academy; his G-3 was Col. Bert Atienza, who had military experience with the U.S. forces before the war and spoke fluent English. Thus Henry Muller could keep up with the latest intelligence from the guerrillas, and Doug Quandt could keep abreast of their operational planning and continue to work on a plan of his own. It was perfectly clear to Doug Quandt after Ingles's report of 14 February that the rescue mission would fall almost totally on the U.S. forces and their resources.

The 11th staff got information not only from Vanderpool and his staff but also directly from the guerrilla headquarters in and around Nanhaya by way of Sgt. John Fulton, a member of the division's 511th

---

[1] See *The Los Banos Raid,* E. M. Flanagan, Presidio Press, Novato, CA 1986.

Signal Company. Against all the soldierly lore with which he had been indoctrinated, Sergeant Fulton volunteered for a mission to join the guerrillas on the south shore of Laguna de Bay. On the night of 10 February, he and two guerrilla guides and an American soldier who had escaped from the Japanese and was living with the guerrillas sailed across Laguna de Bay in a Filipino fisherman's *banca* during the dark of the night. Fulton took a radio, a hand generator, code and decoder equipment, a carbine, and as many grenades as he could stuff into his jacket pockets. During the trip, Fulton lay covered up in the false bottom of the banca to escape detection by any Japanese patrol boats that might intercept them. Finally, at dawn on 11 February, Fulton and his guides landed on the east shore of the lake near Nanhaya. Guerrillas met them there and escorted them to the headquarters of the Red Lion unit in Tranca. For the next few weeks, Fulton ate and slept with the guerrillas, transmitted messages back and forth, and played a large role in the eventual release of the internees.

The internees were not idle. The younger and stronger of the men frequently left the camp at night to contact the local Filipinos for food and information. Freddy Zervoulakos, nineteen years old, son of a Greek and a Filipino, was fluent in Tagalog. On the night of 12 February, Freddy slipped under the barbed wire around the camp near a hidden gully and made his way to Mrs. Espino's home. There he met Ingles, who told him about the guerrilla rescue plan. Freddy made his way back to the camp and told Pete Miles and Ben Edwards about the planned raid. They immediately contacted the camp committee secretary, George Gray, who called a meeting of the camp committee to discuss the guerrilla plan. Most of the committee was reluctant to pursue the matter; Gray, Miles, and Edwards were not. On the night of 14 February, Gray and Freddy left camp again and met Ingles at Mrs. Espino's home. Gray briefed Ingles on the camp's guard posts, the guards' routines, and the condition of the internees. Gray and Ingles agreed that without transportation for the sick and infirm internees, the guerrilla plan would undoubtedly fail.

Gray again called a meeting of the committee, who decided that they could do nothing and that their rescue should be left in the hands of the U.S. forces. Gray did not accept that restriction. He talked it over with Freddy, Pete Miles, and Ben Edwards, who decided that Pete, Ben, and Freddy would go out again and meet with Ingles on the night of 18 February.

About 2100 on the eighteenth, the trio made their way through camp carrying a lantern, with Pete Miles feigning illness so that they could get to the hospital hut without arousing the suspicions of Japanese who had established a 1900 curfew. The men went past the hospital, then crawled under the two barbed-wire fences and dropped down into a deep gully. Under the black and difficult conditions, the trio arrived at Tranca about 2300. There they met Colonel Price and his party, among whom was the peripatetic John Fulton. Miles and Edwards briefed Price on conditions in the camp and discussed their next move. They decided that Miles should go to the headquarters of the 11th at Paranaque and Freddy and Ben should go to Nanhaya. In the event that Miles could not reach the 11th headquarters, then Ben should make the attempt.

About 0130 on 19 February, the party left Tranca escorted by about eight young guerrillas and headed north toward the shore of the lake. It was a hard trip because the night was dark and moonless and their path was along the slippery sides of rice paddies. In a short time, though, they arrived at the beach and procured two bancas, one for Miles and one for Edwards and his party. Here the group split, with three guerrillas escorting Miles to Paranaque and the others going toward Nanhaya. Miles made it to Paranaque by about 1100 that night; Edwards and Freddy arrived in Nanhaya at about the same time. By 20 February, they learned from a Filipino boatman that Miles had made it safely to the 11th headquarters.

Shortly after his arrival at Paranaque, Miles met with Henry Muller and gave him information about the camp, which no other source could do. Miles had an encyclopedic memory and plotted out on a diagram of the camp the guards' barracks, the various guard posts and pillboxes, the location of camouflaged machine gun nests and their fields of fire, and the location of the guards' rifle racks in a short, connecting room between the two guards' barracks. But most important of all, Miles was able to tell Muller the routine of the guards and that the off-duty guards rose just before dawn and took calisthenics in an open area away from their weapons. This information proved vital to the timing and thrust of the 11th's raid on the camp.

By mid-February, the pieces of the Los Banos puzzle had begun to fit together, and between them, Doug Quandt and Henry Muller had developed a plan of attack. From his various sources, Muller had an excellent description of the camp and the number and condition of the internees; he knew the condition of the roads and the bridges surrounding the camp and the approaches to it; he knew that there were ten guard posts surrounding the camp and that the guard contingent consisted of between 200 and 250 Japanese guards; he knew the location of defenses at the camp other than the guard posts; he knew that at the Dampalit River quarry about two miles to the east of the camp there was a Japanese infantry company of about 200 men armed with two 105mm guns and four machine guns; he knew that there were twenty soldiers and a machine gun at Mayondon Point, two 3-in. guns on the Los Banos wharf, an understrength company of about 80 men just south of the San Juan River west of Calamba, and most troubling of all, the Japanese 8th Division, the Tiger Division, with about 9,000 battle-hardened troops was located just south of the Santo Tomas-Alaminos-San Pablo area, about an hour-and-a-half march for a Tiger Division battalion.

Based on that intelligence, Doug Quandt's operational plan evolved. Essentially, it was this: The Division Recon Platoon would precede the main force by two days; cross Laguna de Bay in bancas; contact the guerrillas; coordinate their participation in the raid; form teams with the guerrillas, which would infiltrate and surround the camp during the hours before dawn on D-Day; and, at H-Hour, attack the guards, race to the arms rack, and then eliminate the guards at calisthenics. At H-Hour, an infantry company would jump two hundred meters to the northeast of the camp on a drop zone marked by the Recon Platoon and guarded by guerrillas, fight its way into the camp, and begin to round up the internees for evacuation. A parachute infantry battalion, less the company that was parachuting in, and supported by pack 75mm howitzers, would sail from Mamatid across Laguna de Bay in amphibious tractors, land near Mayondon Point at H-Hour at a point marked and guarded by the Recon Platoon and guerrillas, and then move rapidly to the camp either on foot if they had to fight their way in or in the amtracs if the area were clear of the Japanese. Another battalion of infantry, reinforced by two battalions of artillery and a company of tank destroyers, would travel by truck south from Manila along Highway 1, dismount and attack across the San Juan River near Calamba, block the Japanese forces known to be in the area of Santo Tomas, and then move to the camp to reinforce the parachute company and the battalion in the amtracs.

Lieutenant George Skau was still in command of the 11th's Recon Platoon. After Skau received his assignment from Quandt and Muller, he and Lieutenant Haggerty from the division's 127th Airborne Engineer Battalion left Division Headquarters on the night of 20 February and traveled by banca across the lake. Once on shore, they made their way on foot to Nanhaya. There they met Ben Edwards and Freddy Zervoulakos, who were most agreeable to leading the two lieutenants back to the camp even though they had just escaped for what they thought was the last time.

The quartet and a few guerrillas left Nanhaya during the dark of the evening of 20 February and, after a few hours, arrived in the vicinity of Los Banos. Skau checked the drop zone, which Doug Quandt had selected tentatively from maps, and decided that Lt. John Ringler's B Company of the 511th Parachute Infantry could drop on it with no problem in spite of a railroad and a power line that bordered the DZ on the east. Then they moved very cautiously toward the camp itself, checking the route that the paratroopers would take from the DZ to the camp and two guard posts that secured that part of the camp. Next, they moved stealthily around the perimeter of the camp, checking the guard posts. After Skau had satisfied himself that he had seen all he could in the dark, the group went back toward the beach, checking the roads and bridges over which the amtracs would travel. At the beach, a banca awaited Skau and Haggerty, who took off immediately for Paranaque; Ben and Freddy had to wait for their guerrillas to scrounge up another banca to take them back to Nanhaya.

With Skau's and Haggerty's report, the division staff had enough intelligence to fine-tune the plan it had been developing. Now, what Quandt needed to do was call in the selected unit commanders and brief them on the plan. The paths so carefully followed by the 11th Airborne, the guerrillas, and the internees were now beginning to converge: D-Day was 23 February 1945; H-Hour was 0700, the time when the off-duty Japanese guards were away from their arms doing their daily calisthenics.

When Henry Burgess arrived at the Division Headquarters on Sunday, 18 February, after having left his battalion with Nat Ewing, his XO, Burgess met first with Doug Quandt, who gave him his mission—liberate more than 2,000 civilian internees from Los Banos. This was the first time that Burgess had heard of Los Banos and his new mission. Then he met with Muller, who filled him in on every bit of intelligence he had been able to gather. For the next few days, Burgess absorbed every detail he could find and, after Pete Miles arrived in the headquarters, talked to him at great length. Burgess was beginning to see the difficulty of his mission but also some solutions.

John Ringler was the commander of B Company of the 511th and the man selected to lead the parachute attack on the camp. Ringler was "an experienced and excellent troop commander," according to Burgess, and well suited to lead the jump element. On 19 February, Lahti personally took Ringler in to see General Swing in the division Paranaque CP, who, according to Ringler, "informed me that my mission was to take my company and drop on Los Banos prison camp, release all internees, and organize the people so we could start to march them to the point where they were to be evacuated."

In the few days before the raid, the unit commanders briefed their troops, issued ammunition, and began to move into position for the attack. Skau and his thirty-one-man platoon left Paranaque on the night of 21 February, crossed the lake in bancas, and met the guerrilla chiefs the next day. Skau broke his platoon into various teams, assigned guerrillas to each team, and during the night of 22 to 23 February moved to his attack positions so that he would be ready to attack at H-Hour. He had some difficulty in moving to the camp, but he was essentially ready on time.

On 22 February, Burgess moved his battalion to a bivouac area near Mamatid to await the arrival later that day of the fifty-four amtracs of the 672d Amphibious Tractor Battalion; at dusk, the amtracs waddled out of the lake and moved in with the 1st Battalion, 511th. Colonel Shorty Soule, the commander of the 188th Glider Infantry Regiment, and the designated commander of the Soule Task Force, which was to move overland, closed in to the north side of the San Juan River just before dark on 22 February. That afternoon, John Ringler had moved his company to Nichols Field; met with Maj. Don Anderson, the CO of the ten C-47s that were to drop Ringler and company the next day; issued parachutes, ammunition, and rations; and bedded his troops down under the wings of the C-47s. John Ringler must have felt some trepidation, because he knew that the opening of his parachute at 0700 the next day was the signal for the attack to begin.

At 0659 on 23 February, John Ringler stood in the door of the lead C-47 of the ten-ship formation, which were in vees in trail. His plane was 400 feet above the DZ, with the rest of the planes echeloned higher to the rear. Ringler looked at the ground, spotted a green smoke grenade thrown out by one of Skau's recon men, turned to the stick of men behind him, and shouted, "Close in the door." Then at 0700, when he was directly over the green smoke, Ringler yelled, "Let's go," and jumped out the door.

On the ground, some of Skau's teams of recon men and guerrillas were in place around the camp, but others were not. Nonetheless, when the team leaders who were in position saw Ringler's chute open, they started firing at the guards; those not in position gave up any pretense of stealth and raced to their assigned positions. Sergeant Town and his team approached the camp from the southwest corner. As his team was moving up to the camp, Carroll, Sergeant Town's BAR man, spotted four Japanese streaking across an open field. Carroll emptied a full clip into the fleeing enemy and killed all four. Sergeant Angus and his team approached the camp from the rear gate. The pillbox guarding that gate was empty, but Angus and his men killed two Japanese who were hiding just inside the gate. Sergeant Call and his men scrambled out of a deep ravine on the northeast side of the camp near the hospital and came under heavy fire from a previously unreported machine gun. Sergeant Call was hit in the shoulder, and one of his men, Botkin, had his nose bloodied from a grenade exploding nearby. Sergeant Call contacted Ringler's company, who knocked out the gun with five or six 60mm mortar rounds. The recon men and the guerrillas continued their attack on the perimeter, the pillboxes, and the bunkers along the fence line for the next fifteen or twenty minutes with grenades, rifles, BARs, and occasionally with bolos by the guerrillas. Skau and his team assaulted the main gate, knocked out the pillbox guarding it, and then raced the off-duty guards at calisthenics to the weapons rack and won. They made short order of the unarmed guards, either killing them or sending them racing to various places of shelter in and around the camp.

By 0715, Ringler had assembled his company and was leading it to the camp from the northeast. One of the men who jumped with Ringler was Capt. Nick Boosalis, a surgeon with one of the other battalions of the 511th who was handpicked by Maj. W. L. Chambers, the 511th Regimental surgeon, to make the jump. Doctor Chambers wrote, "We determined that he was the best qualified medical officer in the regiment for this mission." His medical expertise would become useful as the day wore on.

In short order, B Company killed a few of the guards who were trying to escape. Then Ringler led his company through the perimeter of the camp, cutting the wire with the cutters they had brought along. Once they were inside the camp, only a few of the Japanese remained at large. Ringler's company and the recon teams hunted them down.

Burgess, meanwhile, in the lead amtrac, hit the beach at Mayondon

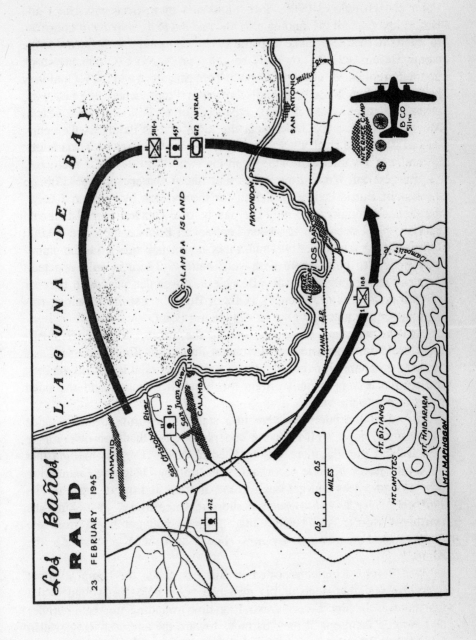

Los Baños
RAID
23 FEBRUARY 1945

Point on schedule at 0700. Two of Skau's men, Sergeants Hahn and Bruce, had marked the landing area and had led in a company of guerrillas to guard it. Burgess picked up the two recon men and headed for the camp. Before he left, however, he saw that A and C Companies took up their preplanned missions. Captain Tom Mesereau and his C Company had moved out immediately to Mayondon Point, where the company proceeded to eliminate a small Japanese force. Following this action, Mesereau set up a roadblock near the town of Los Banos. A Company moved down the road toward the barrio of Bay and set up a roadblock to intercept any enemy moving from the east.

Burgess left Capt. Lou Burris and his D Battery of the 457th on the beach. Burris had been alerted for the mission by General Farrell, the division commander, only the day before. General Farrell had told Burris: "This operation has been kept secret because there are 10,000 Japanese troops within a two-and-a-half-hour truck ride from the camp. Your job is to block them with your battery. There is only one pass they can use through the hills. Be able to cover that pass with all four of your howitzers at all times." One of Burris's first fire missions was on some active machine guns at Mayondon Point.

On the way into the camp, one of the amtracs took some small-arms fire from the enemy at Mayondon Point, but Burgess pressed on. He led the column into the camp, past Baker Memorial Hall, and directed the amtrac drivers to pull off on the baseball diamond and the open fields opposite the hall.

By now, the internees were in a state of rapturous bedlam. Once they saw the huge, well-fed paratroopers, they felt that their deliverance was at hand and that there was no need for haste. Burgess thought that he would never be able to organize the milling, laughing, wandering crowd of internees and get them to the amtracs and out of danger. The Japanese Tiger Division, such a short distance away, gave him just cause for worry. And besides that, Burgess had not heard from the Soule Task Force, which by now should have been getting near the camp.

When John Ringler reported to Burgess inside the camp at about 0745, he said that none of his men had been killed or wounded and that he was having a very frustrating time rounding up the internees and moving them out of their barracks toward the amtracs. Ringler also told Burgess that the guard barracks were on fire and that the internees in that area were moving ahead of the fire toward the parked amtracs.

Burgess seized on the burning barracks as the answer to his problem. He told Ringler to go to the south side of the camp, upwind, and torch the other barracks.

"The results were spectacular," Burgess remembers. "Internees poured out and into the loading area. Troops started clearing the barracks in advance of the fire and carried out to the loading area over 130 people who were too weak or too sick to walk."

By 0830, Burgess saw some progress, although the situation was still chaotic. "Little seems to have been accomplished," he recalls. "Troops, internees, and amtracs were jammed into a small area, and there was great confusion."

But there was progress. Burgess loaded the amtracs as fast as possible and sent them to the beach at San Antonio. Burgess had, of course, used part of his battalion to form a security perimeter around the camp and to set up defensive positions in the event that the Tiger Division made a move in his direction. With the rest of the battalion, he made certain that all of the internees had left the barracks and were on their way to the beach, either on foot or in amtracs. Burgess had no control over the guerrillas and, after the initial raid and attack on the perimeter, the guerrillas faded into the area around the camp and presumably made their way back to their units.

By about 1130, the evacuation of the camp was almost complete. Burgess formed a rear guard of B Company and the Recon Platoon and followed the tail of the marching internees, who were guarded along the road by the rest of the battalion who had moved slowly back from their roadblock positions.

Burgess's problems were far from over. Even though he knew that the camp had been cleared of the internees, that the Japanese garrison had been killed or dispersed, that his troops and the Recon Platoon had suffered no fatalities and only two wounded, that there had been only two guerrillas killed and four wounded, that all of the internees had been rescued with no loss of life so far, that only a few of the 2,122 internees had suffered only minor injuries, and that the amtracs up ahead were already afloat on Laguna de Bay starting to shuttle the internees to the safety of Mamatid, he still did not know what had happened to the Soule Task Force or if the Japanese were forming for an attack on his straggly, undisciplined column of internees.

The Soule Task Force had attacked across the San Juan River early on the morning of 23 February and had run into some opposition near the Lecheria Hills, where one man was killed by Japanese fire. The commander of the 637th Tank Destroyer unit was also killed when he attempted to inspect a gun emplacement at a road junction that was still manned by a Japanese soldier. By midmorning, the task force had cleared the area and was marching down the road toward Los Banos. By this time, Colonel Soule could see the amtracs on the lake moving back to Mamatid. He ordered his task force to reestablish a bridgehead near the San Juan River. John Ringler credits the Soule Task Force with a great contribution to the success of the raid because it engaged and diverted the enemy in the Lecheria Hills-Rock Quarry area and blocked the road from Santo Tomas to Los Banos. Without this help, it is very possible that the Tiger Division could have sent a force to attack the internee column. It would have been a disaster if the Japanese had made such a move.

The first shuttle run of the amtracs left San Antonio about 1000, each carrying thirty to thirty-five internees, their baggage, and a few paratroopers to guard them. The amtracs returned from Mamatid to San Antonio at about 1300 for the remainder of the internees and the rest of Burgess's troops. As the perimeter at the beachhead at San Antonio grew smaller, the Japanese became bolder and stronger. By the time Burgess and the last six amtracs were getting ready to pull out of San Antonio at 1500, the Japanese were dropping artillery into the beachhead and spraying it with machine gun fire from positions around the Rock Quarry. Even when Burgess and the rear guard of his battalion were afloat on the lake, the Japanese managed to bracket a couple of the zigzagging amtracs but were not able to hit any of them.

At Mamatid, the internees were behind our own lines, they were in one large group in a small, constricted area, and they carried a minimum of baggage. Thus Burgess had somewhat better control. The internees wandered about looking for close friends, hugging one another, and embarrassing the paratroopers of the 511th with the warmth of their gratitude and congratulations. But in about an hour, the internees loaded up into trucks and ambulances and moved out on Highway 1 for the fifteen-mile ride to Muntinlupa and the New Bilibid prison, which would be their home for the next few weeks before their evacuation to the U.S. At New Bilibid, they ate heartily but carefully. One of the rescued nuns, Sister Maria, remembers: "When we landed here [at New Bilibid] they took our names and checked us off as 'released' from the Los Banos Internment Camp. Then, a smiling soldier boy handed us each

four Hershey bars. How good they were! Went to the kitchen and got
bean soup. Oy, bean soup, real bean soup!''

Doctor Boosalis remembers:

> There were not more than a couple of aid men with me on that mission.
> . . . I wonder what the hell I was supposed to do—probably to advise
> in an emergency. I did look at some of the youngest tots. And I did
> suture up one man (without anesthesia) for a rather nasty laceration. . . .
> The most striking feature of the mission which will always remain in
> my perception is the memory of the conspicuously drawn features of
> fatigue on those gallant troopers, as I viewed them in the "Ducks," as
> we departed Los Banos. There was a quietude—each seemingly enveloped
> within himself . . . very quiet . . . no complaints . . . no levity . . .
> just quiet.

On the day after the raid, 24 February 1945, General MacArthur
sent a special communique to the men of the 11th Airborne Division.
It read: "Nothing could be more satisfying to a soldier's heart than
this rescue. I am deeply grateful. God was certainly with us today."

And for once, the 11th Airborne could count a victory in the number
of people saved rather than the number of men killed or miles of ground
gained.

CHAPTER 15

SOUTHERN LUZON

General Krueger's plans for Sixth Army to clear southern Luzon called for XIV Corps to strike into the area in early March, driving rapidly south and east to include the Lipa Corridor. The corps would clear the northern side of the Visayan Passages east as far as Batangas Bay, while at the same time securing the shores of Batangas and Balayan Bays. Then XIV Corps would strike to the east, clear the remainder of southern Luzon, and secure the north side of the Visayan Passages east to the Bondoc Isthmus.

To accomplish this mission, General Griswold had at his disposal only the 7,000 men of the 11th Airborne, still engaged in combat to the north, and the 158th Regimental Combat Team, under the command of Brig. Gen. Hanford MacNider. The 158th, also understrength, had had about two weeks' rest after its tough campaign in the Rosario-Damortis area at Lingayen Gulf. General Griswold attached the 158th to the 11th Airborne for the operation.

Through guerrillas, other intelligence sources from Sixth Army, aerial photos, and the constantly roving Division Recon Platoon, Muller's G-2 staff was beginning to put together a picture of the enemy locations and installations in southern Luzon. General Yokoyama had given command of the southern Luzon defenses to Colonel Fujishige. He commanded the Fuji Force, composed of two battalions of the 17th Infantry, one reinforced battalion of the 31st Infantry, a provisional infantry battalion, a battalion and a half of various calibers of artillery, and elements of the 8th Division Service Forces. Fujishige also controlled two or more Gyoro (suicide boat) squadrons and an unknown number of naval troops who had escaped south from Manila. In all, he had about 13,000 men, of whom about 3,000 were trained infantry combat soldiers, scattered about southern Luzon. Southwest of Manila was the Shimbu Shudan force, composed of remnants of the 31st Infantry; two artillery battalions; and other army, navy, and air force personnel numbering some 15,380 troops.

One Japanese force formed a line from Laguna de Bay to Lake Taal along the line Mount Bijang-Mount Maquiling-Hill 580-Hill 660-Mount Sungay. Another occupied the Ternate-Pico de Loro sector, to which the enemy, scattered by the initial drive of the 11th up from Nasugbu, had fled. There was also a strong defensive position along the Mount Macolod-Lipa Hill-Mount Malepunyo hill masses, and considerable enemy strength in the Bicol Peninsula north of Legaspi. Colonel Fujishige's mission was to prevent American forces from rounding the eastern shore of Laguna de Bay to outflank Yokoyama's Shimbu group's main defenses. Colonel Fujishige had a great deal of leeway in his operations because, after 1 March, the communications between Yokoyama and Fujishige had completely broken down.

General Griswold told General Swing that his first mission was to open the Manila-Santo Tomas-Lipa-Batangas highway so that the port of Batangas could be used to mount further amphibious operations, particularly an attack on Legaspi by the 158th to clear the Bicol Peninsula. Because of that pending operation, General Griswold specified that the 158th Bushmasters had to be employed on the right flank of the division attack into southern Luzon, specifically around the west side of Lake Taal, with a route of advance through Balayan, Lemery, and Batangas, the area in which the G-2 estimated that the fighting was expected to be much easier. General Swing also had the mission of opening the southern shores of Manila Bay by eliminating the Japanese concentration in Ternate.

To accomplish these missions, the division staff came up with a plan that sent the 187th down the steep southern slopes of Tagaytay Ridge to the northern shore of Lake Taal in order to attack the strong enemy positions at Tanauan; Colonel Lahti and the 511th were to move south through the Lipa Corridor toward Santo Tomas; and Colonel Soule (less the 2d Battalion of the 188th) was ordered to attack the enemy entrenched in Ternate and in the Pico de Loro hills on the southern shore of Manila Bay. The 2d of the 188th was to complete mopping up in the area south of Manila after which it was to move to Tagaytay Ridge to protect the three division supply lines from Nasugbu—one to Ternate, one to Balayan, and one to the 511th at Calamba. General Farrell put the 675th in direct support of the 187th; the 674th in direct support of the 511th; and the 457th, reinforced by the 472d (105mm howitzers), in direct support of the 188th at Ternate. The XIV Corps artillery provided additional artillery support.

To accomplish these missions, the division staff came up with the following plan:

Unit	Mission
187th	Attack and seize Tanauan
511th	Attack toward Santo Tomas
188th (minus 2d Battalion)	Reduce Ternate
2d Bn 188th	Protect division supply lines
675th FA Bn	Direct support 187th
674th FA Bn	Direct support 511th
457th FA Bn	Direct support 188th at Ternate
472d FA Bn	Reinforce fires of 457th
XIV Corps Artillery	Reinforce 674th and 158th RCT

One of the first and most important tasks was to shorten the supply lines over the vast area assigned to the 11th Airborne. In the initial disposition, the supply route to the 511th, for example, ran from Nasugbu to Tagaytay Ridge to Manila and thence across to Laguna de Bay and down the west shore to Calamba—a distance of some 125 miles. The 127th shortened the lines with three new roads, construction of any one of which was a remarkable feat.

The 158th met no resistance until it reached Lemery. In order to cut the long, roundabout trip from Division Headquarters, the engineers carved a road along the edge of a cliff that is the western edge of Lake Taal. From the western end of Tagaytay Ridge road, down the crest of Shorty Ridge, the 127th hacked out a dusty, twisting, narrow road that debouched from the foothills of Mount Batulao just west of Lemery. The road came to be known as the Shorty Ridge road, and it shortened the supply line to the 158th by one-fourth.

The second pressing need of the 127th was to shorten the route to the 511th, away on the division's left flank. Halfway from Tagaytay Ridge to Manila there is a small town named Silang. Here the 127th found a narrow dirt road that led to the western shore of Laguna de Bay, emerging just south of Muntinlupa. The engineers widened this trail, bridging and bypassing ravines and streams, and opened it as a temporary supply line. It cut the original route by seventy miles.

The third road that the engineers constructed was the most astounding. It came to be known as the Stilwell Road, after the Ledo Road in Burma. The steep, sheer cliff on the north side of Lake Taal is vertical, except for razorlike noses that corrugate its surface. The top of the ridge is 2,400 feet above sea level. General Swing felt that if the 187th could move down this cliff, it would, by this surprise flanking movement, facilitate the advance of the 511th south toward Santo Tomas. With some difficulty and ingenuity, the 127th Engineers carved a road out of the face of this sheer cliff so that the 187th could get down to the northern shore of Lake Taal.

By 25 February, the two battalions of the 187th had closed into a "rest area" on Tagaytay Ridge, according to the 187th historian.

> The Ridge was ideal with plenty of water available, the area secure and the sleeping excellent, for the altitude insured cool nights. The scenery was lush and beautiful and the natives were eager to sell us fresh tomatoes to augment our 10-in-1 rations. Patrols, however, were necessary, for the enemy was still free to move along the Laguna de Bay and along the west shore of Lake Taal. By night we could see the burning villages to our west indicating that the Nips were pursuing their usual ruthless treatment of the natives.

Until this time, the 187th had not operated as a regiment on Luzon; its two battalions were habitually attached to one of the other regiments, partially because the other two regiments were critically short of effective fighting strength. But early in March, Colonel Pearson received from division an order that would employ the 187th as a regiment. The order directed the 187th to attack to the east to link up with the 511th moving south. On 7 March, the 187th, less C Company, descended the steep southern slopes of Tagaytay Ridge to the northern shore of Lake Taal. Turning east, the regiment met little opposition until, on the afternoon of 8 March, it ran into the Fuji Force defenses on Hill 660, two miles west of Tanauan. The 675th Field Artillery Battalion, in direct support of the 187th, was in firing positions on the old golf course of the Manila Hotel Annex.

Company C of the 187th, with a company of guerrillas attached, attacked down the Mount Sungay road. The 187th historian recorded,

We used the guerrillas first to make a double envelopment of the Mt. Sungay position while Company C moved up the knife-like ridge in a frontal attack. As expected, the swarms of Filipinos in their white shirts and shorts drew heavy fire as they advanced over the open ground and rice paddies to the west of the ridge. Meanwhile, however, the artillery was subjecting the Nips' outpost to severe fire and, under its cover, Company C was able to close with the position without being discovered by the Japs. A very brief gun-fight at close range followed, but, when tracer bullets set fire to the kugan grass, the Japs fled. Company C chalked up thirty-eight dead Nips as its score and held the position as an observation post. From this position patrols were sent out which gained contact with the 511th moving . . . along the shore of Laguna de Bay.

On 24 February, the 511th was in position south of Calamba to commence its attack south toward Santo Tomas. Henry Burgess's 1st of the 511th, just a day after its successful raid on the Los Banos internment camp, went back down Highway 1 toward Los Banos from the New Bilibid prison, where they had left the internees in the hands of the medics and civil affairs people. On the afternoon of 24 February, the 1st Battalion went into the position occupied by the 1st of the 188th when it was supporting the raid. After dark, however, Burgess pulled his battalion back about 600 yards to terrain that was more favorable for defense. Burgess had his companies booby-trap their forward positions with hand grenades before they pulled back. Previously he had the artillery calculate data for shelling the abandoned position.

As Burgess had expected, the Japanese came down from the Lecheria Hills and elsewhere after dark on the evening of the twenty-fourth and banzaied the old position. When the forward observer heard the grenades explode in the old position, he called in the artillery concentrations. The 511th infantrymen in the forward foxholes swept the area with machine guns, and the mortar men dropped in rounds on the old position. The next morning, the 1st of the 511th counted forty-odd Japanese bodies in the old position; the battalion's loss, according to Burgess, was "a couple of hours' sleep."

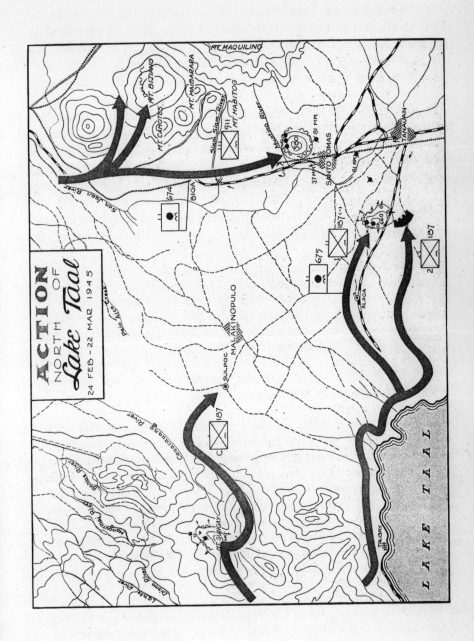

ACTION NORTH OF *Lake Taal*
24 FEB - 22 MAR 1945

MT. MAQUILING

MT. BIJIANG

MT. CAROTES

MT. MALGAZARA

MT. MABITOG

Siam-Siam River

511

674

San Juan River

BIGA

Madilo River

37 MM

81 MM

81 MM

SANTO TOMAS

TANAUAN

187(-)

675

240

ALAGA

187

2

Pule Alay Creek

675

MALAINGPULO

SULPOC

Caguduang River

Banga River

MT. SUNGAY

TALISAY

Manumala River

Lakte River

Diano River

187

C

LAKE TAAL

The troops of the 1/511th practiced the same tactics the entire time they fought in the area near the Lecheria Hills. They never stayed in the same position two nights in a row. They dug new foxholes and machine-gun pits every day and occupied them after dark each night. Thus, their casualties were extremely low during that part of the campaign.

One loss, however, was Lt. Raymond Younghans of the 674th FA Battalion. Ordinarily he was the liaison officer from the artillery battalion to the 1st of the 511th. He and his team joined Burgess at Calamba just after the Los Banos raid. Because there was a shortage of artillery forward observers, Younghans and his team, Staff Sergeant Wilder, Corporal McCoy, and Pvt. Charles Mahan, joined Capt. Tom Mesereau's C Company as a forward observer party. On one occasion, the 1st of the 511th was preparing to attack southward on the main highway toward the barrio of Santo Tomas. C Company was in the lead. Mahan remembers:

Prior to darkness, one platoon of C Company was sent to the railroad tracks (near Santo Tomas) and the FO Team accompanied this platoon. We dug in on the south side of the railroad tracks. Lt. Younghans conferred with the platoon leader and they decided that the Japs were watching our every move from the railroad station about 400 yards from our position. Lt. Younghans stated he would register his artillery past the railroad station. . . . He also suggested to the platoon leader that we continue to dig on the south side of the tracks, but after dark we should move to the north of the tracks and dig in again. The platoon leader concurred and this was accomplished. . . .

. . . About midnight we could hear the Japs breaking their saki bottles and getting drunk and working themselves into a frenzy. Presently, all the noise ceased and one voice could be heard, ostensibly the Jap commander issuing his orders in the form of a pep talk, just as a football coach would deliver during halftime.

Shouts and screams filled the midnight air and approximately one hundred pairs of running feet could be heard pounding the ground, heading toward our abandoned holes on the south side of the tracks. The platoon leader previously issued orders that he would fire the first shot—for everyone to sit tight until he did. The Japs charged the vacant holes and the platoon leader fired his carbine. We started throwing grenades and firing our rifles in the vicinity of the vacant holes. It was pitch dark and we couldn't see anything, but we heard the screams of banzai change to screams of confusion and one designated infantryman started firing flares. The flares illuminated the whole area from the railroad station to our vacant holes and Japs were running back towards the railroad station in a confused and disorganized manner. That is, those that could still motor. Many had fallen from our onslaught of rifle fire and grenades.

When the first flare illuminated the area, Lt. Younghans gave the artillery the command to fire. Artillery rounds came screaming in and he walked the rounds up and down the railroad tracks between our position and the railroad station, inflicting many enemy casualties. We had beaten off the banzai attack and had suffered no casualties whatsoever. We continued to fire flares and send harassing artillery fire for the remainder of the night.

The following morning the platoon was ordered to rejoin C Company on the main highway. When the platoon reached the C Company position, we immediately dug foxholes. Lt. Younghans decided that it was not necessary to register the artillery again. We had not gotten any sleep the night before so we sacked out in our holes as soon as it was practicable.

No sooner had we closed our eyes, the mortar rounds began falling—hundreds of them. One round landed on Lt. Younghans's back as he lay face down in the slit trench. He died instantly. . . . Lt. Younghans was a fine artilleryman and I was proud to have served with him. He was an inspiration to me and to this day, I maintain that he was instrumental in saving the lives of all of us in the platoon that participated in the banzai attack at Santo Tomas.

Finally, early in March, the Japanese withdrew from the area back toward Los Banos. The 1/511th followed them and only then discovered the heinous massacre of the Filipino civilians around Los Banos and the college, a war crime of the most immoral proportions. Burgess estimated that 1,500 Filipinos around Los Banos had died in the massacre. He is of the opinion that the Japanese 8th Division assumed the Filipinos around Los Banos had assisted in the raid: "Its elements arrived in the afternoon [of the raid] and proceeded to wreak vengeance on the civilian population."

While the 1st of the 511th was moving toward and into Los Banos, Ed Lahti moved the rest of the regiment down the highway to the Siam River and across it almost to the Muntino River against sporadic resistance. Initially, Lahti set up his CP near Binyan; however, the battalions were assigned missions that separated them from regimental installations—supply, medical, communications—by several thousand yards. As the situation developed, Lahti moved his command post on 11 March to the Sugar Central, a commercial installation near Highway 1 and about 7,000 yards north of Mount Bijang, a round, bald knob whose bare slopes offered the Japanese, hidden in the usual array of carefully camouflaged caves, unrestricted fields of fire.

Major Lyman S. Faulkner was the S-2 of the 511th. From information he received from division and from the reports of reconnaissance patrols, he estimated that the Japanese occupied Mount Bijang with at least a reinforced company. He guessed that the enemy was also capable of reinforcing the position by boat across Laguna de Bay. The 511th had captured several inboard motorboats from the Japanese Gyoro units. Hacksaw Holcombe's battalion used them to patrol Laguna de Bay. The Division Air Section also patrolled the area looking for enemy infiltrators. But even with this surveillance, the Japanese were able to reinforce the Mount Bijang position at night.

On 11 March, I Company of the 511th attempted to reach the crest of Mount Bijang but was repulsed. The 674th FA Battalion pounded the area for the next two days until a new attack could get under way. Air strikes by six P-38s with 100-pound bombs struck the hill on the afternoon of the twelfth and again on the morning of the thirteenth. On the afternoon of the twelfth, Steve Cavanaugh went to the 511th CP at the Sugar Central and was briefed on the situation by Maj. William F. Frick, the 511th S-3. Then Colonel Lahti took over and gave Cavanaugh a fragmentary order for the attack the next morning. Lahti had taken Cavanaugh to the roof of the Sugar Central from where they could see the major approaches to Bijang; Lahti pointed out the routes of advance for both D and I Companies. After the meeting with the regimental CO, Cavanaugh sent for his XO and two platoon leaders to brief them on the situation. Essentially the attack involved I Company moving up the north slope of Bijang and D Company attacking from the west, with the top of the mountain the objective. Colonel Lahti had made it clear to Captain Cavanaugh that he was to be back within the regimental perimeter before dark.

At 0715 on 13 March, I Company had cleared the regimental perimeter, followed by D Company, ninety-five men strong. The air strikes had pounded the mountain, and the artillery continued to fire concentrations on the suspected enemy positions ahead of the infantry companies. Each company moved in a column of platoons, with one file on each side of the road. The companies moved up the mountain for a couple of hours against little opposition. Near the crest, however, rifle and automatic fire brought D Company to a halt. The platoons maneuvered around the fire, and the 1st Platoon made its way to the top of the mountain. Shortly, crawling and climbing over the blasted face of the mountain, scrambling from one covered point to another, all of D Company was on the objective.

By midday, the Japanese began to react. Wrote Maj. John M. Cook, the executive officer of the 2d of the 511th, who accompanied D and I Companies on the attack,

> Fire was beginning to fall on the troops on the objective. At first small arms fire from those Japanese returning from the fight with Company I was directed into the 3d Platoon of D Company. Very little return fire was heard from Company D the first few minutes. Then, as the enemy came into view, the two machine guns of the entire 3d Platoon opened fire. Its effect was murderous. When no more movement could be seen, the fire lifted. For a moment the only sound was a squad leader in the 3d Platoon calmly calling for the aidman.

Two men had been wounded.

Then mortar rounds at the rate of twenty to thirty rounds a minute began to fall within D Company's position. The fire was accurate, but so many rounds were duds that they were relatively ineffective. "Small arms fire was equally accurate but more effective," wrote Cook. "The infantry communications sergeant, kneeling in his 'covered position,' was shot through the mouth. At 1330, six wounded and two dead had been evacuated to the 2d Platoon position by members of the 3d Platoon."

At 1400, Cavanaugh received a message from the regimental CP that I Company was moving up to assist him on the top of the hill. The enemy continued to drop mortar rounds into the position and cover it with automatic weapons fire. Then the Japanese started to move up. D Company and the enemy threw grenades, but the range was too great to be effective. The Japanese continued to crawl forward under their own fire and came within range of D Company's grenades. One of the Japanese shot the leader of the 1st Platoon through the head. He was in turn killed by a hand grenade from one of the platoon's riflemen.

At about 1600, Cook told Cavanaugh to withdraw his company from the objective by the same route he had taken to get up the hill. According to Cook, "It had been anticipated that the withdrawal would be difficult. It was completed during daylight hours and contact with the enemy was rather close; however, the enemy did not pursue the company . . . and allowed the company to complete the move to cover. . . .

Company D was joined by Company I [at the foot of the mountain]."

Cook, with the two company commanders, reported to Colonel Lahti, who had come up with the supply party at the base of the mountain. "The company commanders were instructed to bring their companies to a bridge at the foot of the mountain and await trucks that would haul them back to the regimental perimeter," Cook wrote. "Informal reports on casualties and other information regarding the day of fighting was given at this time. Company D had suffered four men killed in action and twenty-four wounded. There were seventy-five known enemy dead.

"In addition to the twenty-four wounded who were evacuated, the commanding officer of Company D had been painfully wounded. He was hit in the shoulder and two bullet holes in his helmet attested to the fact that he had been shot at and missed as well as shot at and hit."

On a Friday afternoon in mid-March, the 1st of the 511th also turned south and stopped near the small town of Santa Rosa, about thirty miles southeast of Manila. Steve M. Hegedus, of A Company of the 511th, noted, "The whole town turned out to see their first Americans in four years. The occupying Japanese soldiers had left about a week ago; hail the Liberators! the euphoria of new freedom, and the promise of a better life was in the air. We were the symbol of better days ahead. We were showered with bananas, papayas, and booze."

Hegedus and a six-man patrol were camped out in the inner, walled-in courtyard of an old Catholic church. The sergeant in command of the small detachment made certain that guards were posted at night and patrols made during the day. Hegedus remembers looking into the town jail:

There were some people in the jail cells. They were dirty (which was very unlike the majority of Filipinos); some had bandages on their heads, or their arms in slings; their hair was unkempt, and they looked scared. There were about six of them; they were "Makipili." We also learned why they were in jail: not only did they curry favor with the Japanese during the four years of occupation, but last week they participated in something worse. About 70 male villagers were marched out of town on their regular, daily work detail, but this day they were massacred by the Japanese. . . . These six collaborators were caught and were awaiting trial. We heard that there was also an old woman, called a witch by some, who was one of them, but we didn't see her in jail; but we would see her later that day.

That evening, after the parish priest had left the church, the people of the barrio began to file into the courtyard, which was as big as a baseball diamond infield. There were men and women milling about, but no children. Thirty American soldiers were among the crowd. Hegedus continues:

Finally, through the arch of the courtyard, came the first of the Makipili, surrounded by some very angry citizens. His hands were tied in front of him. He had a bloody towel-bandage on his head. At the sight of him, the people hissed and booed and spat in his direction . . . several men kicked and beat the traitor with their fists and with clubs. He fell to the ground face down. More kicks, spit, epithets. Finally, someone produced a . . . bolo knife. The prisoner was stabbed deeply in the lower back; it must have hurt, because he arched his back, lifting his feet and face off the dirt. That blood squirted out of him a foot high, straight up. . . . In a minute, the spurt ebbed to a gentle flow; the ground around him was a puddle of blood. He slumped into stillness. . . .

Now another prisoner appeared on a bicycle. Although he was sitting on the seat, he was blindfolded, and his hands were tied behind his back. Four or five men were guiding the bike to a spot right under the arch, where a hangman's noose was dangling from some kind of hook. After some derisive remarks from the crowd, the noose was placed over his head, tightened around his neck, and the bicycle removed. . . . His feet were barely a foot off the ground. . . . He writhed and kicked and jerked a few minutes, but he never lived to see the setting sun. . . .

With the last light of day, the main event unfolded. Thru the arch came "the witch." Indeed she looked like one; her long, gray hair hung below her shoulders, uncombed. She was tiny and wiry, and her face was wrinkled, but she was not handcuffed. She walked freely, and you must admit, she was brave. . . . She walked a complete circle around the entire inner part of the crowd. . . . Without assistance, she stepped over the bundles of twigs and branches that had been piled around the upright pole, and she put her hands behind herself, put her back to the pole, and stared straight ahead, awaiting her fate.

Here came a man with a canful of gas. . . . He poured it all around on the twigs; then a last few splashes on her dress, and finally, tipping the can upside down, he dropped the last few drops on her head. . . . The first and only match did the trick; the flammable liquid caught, the twigs caught: a good fire was starting, and poof!—her hair burst into flames, from those last few drops. Now, in a matter of seconds, the fire was roaring, and she was right in the middle of it—part of it—her silence a final mockery to her judges. . . .

The next morning was a bright, sunny, warm Philippine Sunday.

While we were eating our self-made C-ration breakfast, the churchbells, almost over our heads, rang out. I guess it was first call. Soon, people started to appear; some families, several groups of 2 and 3 women— barefoot—clean dresses; a handkerchief or a piece of starched lace on their heads. No market today. This is the first Sunday of Liberation. Give thanks to those wonderful Americans.

CHAPTER 16

MACOLOD & MALEPUNYO

On 4 March, General Swing wrote another letter to General March, which summed up the division's situation to date.

> Thank goodness, all I have left in Manila is a platoon guarding the Pasay telephone exchange and a platoon in Cavite waiting for the Navy to take over.
>
> Have "about faced" and am starting to clean up the remainder of Batangas Province, southern part of Laguna and Tayabas. Have the 158th RCT under Gen. MacNider attached to me but no replacements of my own—the stuffy Army staff doesn't like airborne and won't do anything about getting me any. I think it will get to Gen. MacArthur's ears before long and probably some fur will fly. A new Table of Organization gives me 12,000 men and of course am way below that now.
>
> Have my command post at the Manila Hotel Annex on Tagaytay Ridge where I spent one night on the way to Manila. Until we have conquered the territory between Lake Taal and Laguna de Bay and that on the other side of the lake down to Balayan Bay, I'm really in somewhat of a fix with my front extending completely across the peninsula some 35 miles and my rear 50 miles back on the outskirts of Manila. General Krueger comes down about every other day telling me not to stick my neck out when it's been sticking out a mile ever since we landed. The only thing that keeps my lines open and allows me to spread so thin is

the fact that we have organized 5,000 guerrillas and have them attached to all the infantry, artillery and engineer units. We let them wear the 11th A/B shoulder patch over their left breasts. They are proud as punch and really fight. Put artillery forward observers with them, give them all the captured Jap machine guns and mortars, and they keep on pushing. . . .

It is amazing how despite all training maneuvers, movies, lectures, and what not, the doughboy will never realize until he has seen it what artillery can do for them. Have had two battalions attached to me from other outfits and they both say that they fired more ammunition in the first two days with me than they had fired since they landed at Lingayen five weeks ago. All my regimental and battalion commanders know that it's just too bad if I hear the report that supporting artillery would not be used because the enemy machine gun was too close to our lines. These young forward observers have more nerve—one sang back over the radio the other day that he wasn't quite sure of his orientation, but he thought his own position was so and so—said drop a round about that point—it ought to be close enough for me to get a sensing!

Hope we get this island cleaned up shortly—the men want a new invasion. Am hoping for the China coast.

In the other sector for which the division was responsible, the area southwest of Manila, the 188th attacked the town of Ternate on 2 March and met heavy resistance. During February, General Swing had ordered his guerrilla command to make a reconnaissance in force of the town, and, if possible, to seize it. The Japanese forcibly threw them back. Though the town itself had been battered by air strikes, its rubble made an artificial barricade for the Japanese defenders amid the wrecked stone buildings. In addition, the Japanese had heavily mined the streets with aerial bombs.

On 2 March, the 1st of the 188th captured the town of Ternate, with the loss of one man killed and one wounded. But that action was only the beginning of its operations in and around the area extending from Ternate southwest to Pico de Loro. The Japanese who had not been killed in Ternate withdrew across the Maragondon River into the bamboo and heavily wooded ridges, where they had previously prepared extensive defensive positions. The terrain was extremely difficult for the attacker, consisting as it did of a series of knifelike bamboo- and tree-covered noses leading from the top of Mount Pico de Loro down to the shoreline of Manila Bay. Between the ridges were deep gorges, and in the sides of these gorges the Japanese had dug the usual cave

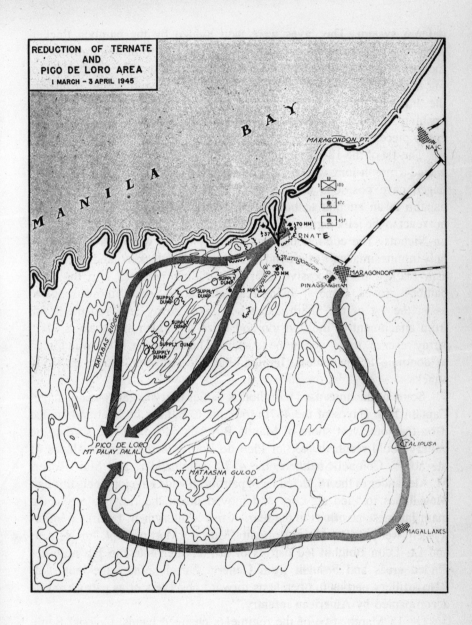

REDUCTION OF TERNATE
AND
PICO DE LORO AREA
1 MARCH – 3 APRIL 1945

MANILA BAY

MARAGONDON PT.

NAIC

TERNATE

MARAGONDON

PINAGSANHAN

SUPPLY DUMP
SUPPLY DUMP
SUPPLY DUMP
SUPPLY DUMP
SUPPLY DUMP
SUPPLY DUMP

BATABAS RIDGE

PICO DE LORO
MT PALAY PALAI

MT MATAASNA GULOD

TALIPUSA

MAGALLANES

defense system. The caves were well hidden by the bamboo thickets and brush and, even when located, were difficult to hit with artillery or mortars because of the depressed and masked location. The enemy defending in the Ternate area employed suicidal tactics and would wait until the attacking troops were within a few feet of a hidden cave before opening fire with murderous "woodpeckers." Lead scouts were often cut to pieces before the Japanese gunner could be killed.

The 1st of the 188th, supported by the 457th and 472d FA Battalions, waged a month-long war of attrition against the innumerable well-camouflaged cave positions that dotted the sector. Fighter aircraft dropped napalm in an attempt to burn off the camouflage, but the bamboo did not react to the jellied gas as favorably as had the grass and leaf camouflage on Nichols. The continuous, day-after-day attack with loss of men and only infinitesimal gain of ground discouraged the attackers, and no enthusiasm marked the successive and never-ending ventures into the thick bamboo groves. General Swing realized that he needed more troops to assist the 1st of the 188th, but when Sixth Army removed the 158th from attachment to the division and froze the 511th at Bauan as Sixth Army reserve, there were none to spare. The 1st of the 188th was forced to continue its piecemeal, limited-objective, irksome, and exhausting attacks.

Some of the units used unorthodox tactics to try to gain an advantage. Captain Jack Hayes of the 457th took his C Battery by boat and landed it on the southwest shore of Manila Bay behind Loac Cove so that the battery could reach the top of Pico de Loro and the western slopes of the noses. Colonel Stadtherr, the 457th commander, and Maj. Robert M. Alexander of the 188th led large patrols on wide envelopments through Magallanes to Pico de Loro and moved down the ridge to strike the main Japanese positions in the rear. A few artillerymen, frustrated infantrymen, went too far. Major Norman "Mortar" Martin, Capt. Jim Nelson, and Lt. Leon Botchin led patrols of artillerymen into the Japanese-defended areas and brought from General Farrell a message that said: "No artillery parties to operate as forward observers or as patrols unless accompanied by American infantry."

On 15 March, two of the regiments changed hands: Colonel Soule was replaced as 188th commander by Lieutenant Colonel Tipton, who had commanded the 2d of the 187th; Colonel Soule was promoted to brigadier general and became the assistant division commander of the 38th Division. Colonel George Pearson replaced Colonel Hildebrand as commander of the 187th.

During the month-long fight in the Ternate-Pico de Loro sector, the 188th had captured forty Japanese suicide Q-boats used by the enemy to ram American ships. The 188th used the boats to ferry troops across the Maragondon River to get behind what was left of the enemy in the area. By 3 April, only isolated mopping up remained for the battle-weary troops of the 188th. The 1st Battalion had suffered heavily in the protracted campaign: It lost 40 men killed, including Capt. Raymond Lee, commander of A Company, and 103 men wounded in action. During the period from 4 to 23 March, the 11th Airborne, including the 158th RCT, had 90 men killed in action, 300 wounded, and killed some 1,490 Japanese.

About 21 March, General Krueger alerted General Swing to a change in disposition of major forces in southern Luzon. The 1st Cavalry Division would relieve the 11th Airborne in the Calamba-Tanauan area and the 158th would be relieved from attachment to the 11th for a possible amphibious landing on the Bicol Peninsula; the 511th (less the 3d Battalion) would move to Bauan and would remain there as Sixth Army reserve for a possible airborne operation on the Bicol Peninsula to reinforce the 158th, if necessary. On 23 March, the 1st Cavalry relieved the 11th Airborne in the Santo Tomas-Tanauan area at the northern end of the Lipa Corridor. On the same day, in a truck movement, the 187th moved from Tanauan by way of Tagaytay and Shorty Ridges around the south end of Lake Taal to relieve the 158th.

In the accomplishment of its mission, the 158th had moved swiftly against light resistance along the route Tuy-Balayan-Lemery. At Lemery, resistance grew heavier, and the Japanese bombed the 158th with rounds from one of the heaviest field pieces in existence—the 300mm howitzer/mortar, firing from the southwestern slopes of Mount Macolod overlooking Lemery. At night, the rumbling of the great shells could be heard in Division Headquarters on Tagaytay Ridge, across the lake. (After the war, the division used the 300mm brass shell cases as very much prized wastepaper baskets.)

While the 158th was still attached to the 11th, General Swing had told General MacNider to capture Mount Macolod. To accomplish that mission, General MacNider knew that he would need his entire RCT. Accordingly, General Swing ordered the 2d of the 188th to Bauan to relieve the elements of the 158th who were there clearing the Calumpan Peninsula to the south. The 158th then moved to the northeast and attacked and seized two small satellites of Mount Macolod—San Jose and Santa Rosa hills. Meanwhile, the other elements of the 158th, in a frontal attack, overran the town of Cuenca. But before the 158th could take on the formidable task of taking Mount Macolod, General Krueger had ordered the 158th out of action to prepare for the Bicol Peninsula landing at Legaspi. The 187th, moving down by truck from Tanauan, after having been relieved by the 1st Cavalry, relieved the 158th in place and took over the Mount Macolod mission. The 2d of the 188th moved to Batangas, seized it, and secured the airstrip there for use by the 511th if committed to a jump in the Legaspi invasion. The XIV Corps divided southern Luzon between the 1st Cavalry and the 11th Airborne, with Lipa, Mount Macolod, and Mount Malepunyo in the 11th's sector in the south and the sector to the north to the 1st Cavalry Division.

More specifically, General Griswold ordered General Swing to complete the reduction of Japanese defenses at Macolod, seize Lipa, and clear Route 19, the main road through the Lipa Corridor, for five miles north of Lipa. He ordered the 1st Cavalry to seize Santo Tomas and Tanauan and advance south along Route 19 to gain contact with the 11th.

General Swing was still faced with the prospects of a large area of operations and a very small force to accomplish his mission. He had, in fact, only four infantry battalions on hand because two of the 511th's were in Sixth Army reserve and the 1st of the 188th was still mopping up south of Ternate. General Swing then set up two regimental task forces organized around two infantry battalions to accomplish the missions assigned by General Griswold. Colonel George Pearson's 187th, reinforced with tanks, guerrillas, and artillery, was to seize Mount Macolod; Colonel Tipton's 188th, less the 1st Battalion but with the 3d of the 511th attached, would strike toward Lipa up the roads lying east of Mount Macolod. Colonel Tipton also had some tank destroyers and guerrillas to supplement his two battalions of infantry.

In preparation for the final clearing of southern Luzon, the headquarters of the senior commanders moved: 11th Airborne Division Headquarters moved from the Manila Hotel Annex to a schoolhouse at Alitagtag, and XIV Corps Headquarters moved from Grace Park in northern Manila to the Sugar Central in Calamba. The division was now disposed to continue fighting eastward, join hands with the 1st Cavalry north of Lipa, and head for the east coast of Luzon at Antimonan. Two massive obstacles stood in the way: Mount Macolod and Mount Malepunyo. A third possible impediment to free movement in the area was Lipa Hill, from where the Japanese would shoot down two A-20s in the last week of March.

On 24 March, Colonel Tipton's task force left the town of Batangas and met no serious resistance until, on the evening of 26 March, it reached hill defenses two-and-a-half miles southeast of Lipa held by the Fuji Force's 86th Airfield Battalion. The next day the task force overran the positions. During the night of 27 March, the Japanese remaining in the Lipa area withdrew eastward to Mount Malepunyo. The Americans following the Japanese into Lipa thought that the enemy had set fire to the town, given the totally gutted ruins that they found. In reality, American air and artillery had already almost completely destroyed the town. What the Americans saw when they walked into Lipa looked to them like the ruins of ancient Rome—a vista of roofless, stone-walled buildings with empty windows.

On 22 March, the 187th had completed its move from Tanauan to Cuenca and had moved into the positions left by the departed 158th. The 187th now had supporting it, in addition to the 674th and 675th FA Battalions of the 11th, two 155mm howitzer battalions in position in the flatland south of Cuenca. A platoon of Sherman tanks from the 44th Tank Battalion and Company B of the 127th Engineers were also attached.

On the night of 23 March, the Japanese banzaied A Company's outpost on San Jose Hill. The outpost repulsed the attack, but Company A lost its commander, Captain Hanna, who was killed instantly by a machine gun burst. Hanna was in the forward outpost position rather than in the relative safety of his company position at Cuenca. On that same night, a guerrilla patrol had probed east of Dita, where it lost six men. The artillery forward observer with the guerrillas had been able to call in artillery fire on the enemy locations. The next morning, Colonel Pearson dispatched G and F Companies to clean out the area. In the attack, tanks battered down houses, and the engineers deactivated land mines as the assault moved through the village outskirts. But northwest of the village, the enemy, firing from concealed caves, stopped the attack, wounding six men and killing Private First Class Baier. At dark, the force withdrew to a perimeter 200 yards south of Dita.

That night, the Japanese reentered the village of Dita. On 24 March, the four battalions of artillery and a squadron of P-47s made several strikes with bombs and strafed the village. F and G Companies followed up the attack with house-to-house fighting through the streets. The intensity of the enemy machine gun and mortar fire again halted the attack. Lieutenant Massey and Staff Sergeant Echols were mortally wounded, and Privates Zronchak and Lundt were killed. On 27 March, the 1st

Battalion, following a 4.2-in. mortar barrage from the 85th Chemical Battalion and air strikes using napalm, swept around the village to positions north of Dita. The 1st Battalion continued its attack and, after air strikes and artillery concentrated fire, seized and dug in on Bukel Hill; the 2d Battalion held the pivotal position near Dita.

Thus began for the 187th the bloodiest and toughest battle of its short military history. It was now face to face with Mount Macolod, which dominates the southeastern shore of Lake Taal. The peak is 2,700 feet above sea level and 2,100 feet above the water of Lake Taal. Its north and west slopes rise nearly vertically from the water. On the east and south sides, the drop from the peak is also vertical from about 1,200 feet; then three ridges descend gradually to the bottom of the mountain. Two of these ridges are bare noses leading into the highway that runs through Cuenca and Dita. The north-south nose was known as Brownie Ridge and the one on the east as Bashore, after the commanders whose companies assaulted them. The third ridge was heavily wooded and was actually a saddle connecting Mount Macolod with Bukel Hill, a lesser eminence some 500 yards due east of Macolod.

In this saddle, the Japanese had constructed another of their diabolically contrived defensive positions. They had used Filipino laborers to construct the underground installations and had slain them when the work was finished, to insure the secrecy of the position. From the air, only dummy positions were visible, but the mountain bristled with artillery and automatic weapons carefully laid to cover all approaches with interlocking fields of fire.

By 1 April, the 187th had encircled the landward sides of Mount Macolod and had concentrated its entire strength against the Japanese defenses in and around Macolod. It had not been easy. At midnight of 28 March, in a perimeter south of the Dita schoolhouse, G Company had repulsed yet another banzai attack. At 0500, about fifty Japanese had attacked F Company and its attached guerrillas, killing eleven and wounding ten of the guerrillas. Private First Class McCoy had been killed and Lieutenant Roberts and seven other soldiers seriously wounded. In spite of the shelling and the air strikes, the enemy had been able to continue nightly banzai attacks. The 187th historian reported, "The Nips took a much heavier toll of the attached guerrillas who had the old-fashioned idea that tropical nights were made for sleeping."

On the night of 1 to 2 April, Staff Sergeant Ellis of C Company was outposting Bukel Hill with his platoon. At about 0115, the sergeant had to relieve himself outside his slit trench. He took the required three steps away and, in the kunai grass around the position, found himself face to face with a Japanese officer about to attack him with his samurai sword. Ellis beat him to the draw and killed the enemy officer with his .45 pistol. The remainder of the Japanese patrol left the area.

During the period 3 to 17 April, there was a hiatus in the operations to reduce Mount Macolod. The 1st of the 187th continued its probe of the ravines and gullies that wrinkled the surface of the mountain. On 8 April, the battalion mounted another attack, preceded by heavy artillery fire. A Company went up Brownie Ridge, C Company on the north side of the Cuenca Ravine and B Company on the right of C. The companies would converge at the head of the ravine. There was little opposition until the companies met. When they did, they were assaulted with machine gun, sniper, and mortar fire from camouflaged spider holes, which were impossible to see. The enemy fire killed Capt. Paul G. Bashore, B Company's commander, Staff Sergeant Hawkins, and Private Pelfrey. Captain Bashore had been noted for his aggressiveness ever since B Company's first combat action around Buri on Leyte.

On the night of 17 April, Private Harkink of F Company, "a bustling lad of 22," had a premonition. He was a veteran of all of the combat of F Company, but somehow felt that his luck had run out. According to the historian,

> Private Harkink and four of his pals from F Company returned from a well-deserved, but unauthorized, "rest" period and cheerfully received, as a "reward," the precarious honor of acting as lead scouts for Company A to which they had attached themselves. . . . Harkink solemnly inventoried his possessions and asked his pals to mail them and several sizeable money-orders to his sister. "Tomorrow I am going to get it," he predicted.

On the morning of 18 April, Harkink was killed near the head of A Company as the company moved up a ravine to the right side of Bashore Ridge.

During this general period, the 188th less the 1st Battalion, but with the 3d of the 511th attached, protected the division's right flank by making a series of rapid moves, which carried them to the area around Lipa Hill, Rosario, and Tiaong. The force first cleared the Batangas area and reconnoitered the road net north of the town. A portion of the 511th then moved to Batangas to remain there as inactive Sixth Army reserve and secure the city. The 188th moved north and occupied Ibaan and San Jose. The 3d of the 511th pushed ahead and established a roadblock 2,000 yards south of Lipa; the 2d of the 188th, meanwhile, seized Lipa Hill. The 3d of the 511th took Tambol Hill near Old Rosario and made a juncture with the 1st Cavalry at Lipa. In this entire area, the G-2 made the estimate that the Japanese had withdrawn hastily, and, with the exception of the Mount Macolod position, resistance along the Tanauan-Lipa-Batangas road had crumbled. It was equally apparent that the enemy had withdrawn into the foothills of Mount Malepunyo, due east of the battered town of Lipa.

With the seizure of Lipa, the entire highway from Manila through Calamba, Tanauan, and Lipa to Batangas was in the American forces' hands. Mount Macolod was still undefeated. In addition to that complex, a thorn in the side of the 11th Airborne, two other missions assumed great importance. The first was to drive the enemy out of the foothills and back into Mount Malepunyo and therefore free the highway of Japanese artillery fire from the foothills. The second was to move to the east coast of Luzon with utmost speed and, if possible, seal off the top of the Bicol Peninsula so that the Japanese would be caught between the division at the north end and the 158th at the south end. The 511th, less the 3d Battalion, was still in Batangas and Bauan in Sixth Army reserve and not available for these missions. Then General Griswold ordered General Swing to add a third priority mission: Reduce Mount Macolod but not at the cost of delaying the other two missions.

General Swing redeployed the division's elements to facilitate the accomplishment of these three missions. He moved Colonel Pearson's headquarters and the 2d of the 187th from the Macolod battle to the foot of Brownie Ridge. In this action, Major Loewus, fresh from the States and a replacement for Colonel Tipton as the 2d of the 188th commander, was wounded through his shoulder by a sniper. He was replaced by Maj. Buck Ewing. General Swing filled in the void around Macolod left by the departure of the 2d with guerrillas who had orders to hold the position and prevent the escape of the Japanese from the hill mass. Major Davy Carnahan, the operator of the Biscuit Bombers and Burauen airfields on Leyte, had assumed command of the 1st of the 187th when Harry Wilson moved up to become Colonel Pearson's XO. Davy Carnahan and the 1st of the 187th stayed in the Macolod area. General Swing gave Colonel Pearson the mission to attack from a position east of Lipa, pushing the Japanese back into Malepunyo so they could not shell the highway, and to begin the development of the Malepunyo position.

General Swing also ordered the 188th, by now with the 1st Battalion, which had rejoined the regiment on 1 April after the termination of the Ternate-Pico de Loro battle, to attack to the east. On the basis of Muller's intelligence estimate that the enemy had largely withdrawn from the coastal area into the two mountains of Malepunyo and Banahao, General Swing put the northern boundary of the regiment below these two mountains in the expectation that the regiment would thus meet slight resistance and proceed rapidly to the neck of the Bicol Peninsula. This proved to be the case, and on 2 April, the 2d of the 188th skirted around the southern edge of Mount Malepunyo and occupied the barrio of Tiaong east of the mountain. The regiment patrolled the southeastern slopes of Malepunyo and located only scattered Japanese resistance.

Meanwhile, General Swing had flown in a Cub plane over to Antimonan on the east coast in a preliminary, fairly high-level reconnaissance of the area still to be traversed by the 11th. On his return flight, he had his pilot circle the grass-covered airstrip at Lucena, some twenty-five miles beyond the 188th at Tiaong. The strip appeared deserted, so General Swing had his pilot land. He was greeted by a Filipino guerrilla who reported that the Japanese had deserted the city the day before and that there were sufficient guerrillas in the city to hold it if they only had arms and ammunition. General Swing gave the guerrilla his pistol and returned to the division CP. There he told Muller to mount up the Division Recon Platoon in the eleven Cubs of the artillery air fleet and fly them in shuttles to Lucena with orders to initiate patrols back to the 188th at Tiaong and to organize the guerrillas at Lucena to hold the town until the arrival of the 188th. Doug Quandt, on orders from General Swing, organized another small force consisting of B Company of the 188th, B Battery of the 457th, and ninety guerrillas, and sent them by LCM from Batangas around to Tayabas Bay and landed them across the beach at Lucena. On 7 April, the force at Lucena and the force at Tiaong joined hands at Candelaria, halfway between the two towns. Captain Fitch and his B Company of the 188th and Lieutenant Skau and the Division Recon Platoon moved north and seized Tayabas, and the 1st Battalion of the 188th moved to Lucena. Then Fitch and Skau and their troops moved to Antimonan through one roadblock, occupied the town, and sealed off the northern exit of the Bicol Peninsula.

During the next few days, patrols scoured the coastal plain of Luzon, and, except for a few scattered pockets of Japanese, found no other opposition. General Swing reported to General Griswold that south of a line drawn around the southern edges of Mounts Macolod, Malepunyo, and Banahao, the area was free of the enemy. F Company of the 188th, on the right flank of the regiment in its move to the east, entered and liberated the town of San Juan on the western shore of Tayabas Bay.

During this time, when the 188th and part of the 187th was attacking to the east, the division command post had moved from Alitagtag to Rosario.

The remainder of the division's attacks did not move as smoothly as the fast-paced move of the 188th to the east coast of Luzon. The 2d of the 187th had moved from Macolod eastward to Lipa and then toward Mount Malepunyo and the town of Sulac at its base. As the battalion crossed the first low ridge east of Lipa, it was hit by a prolonged artillery concentration and heavy mortar and automatic weapons fire.

Eli Bernheim remembers Colonel Pearson's reaction to the loss of two of his officers. "We were in the Sulac area, and I was in Col. Pearson's presence when the word came that Lt. Siegel and Lt. Solecki had been killed in a fire fight. Solecki was a former Sergeant who had received a field promotion. Colonel Pearson sat down on a stump, took off his helmet and began to weep softly. I suppose no one but a former combat infantryman can understand that kind of compassion in such a huge man. Ever since that event, I've had warm feelings about George Pearson. . . ."

The 187th was somewhat weary from its fierce battles on Brownie Ridge during the preceding week and needed reinforcements for the attack on Malepunyo. General Swing ordered John Strong and the 3d of the 511th from Rosario, where they had gone into a short, twelve-hour R and R. On 6 April, the 3d of the 511th and the 2d of the 187th, following an air strike and heavy artillery support, overran the barrios of Sulac, Sapac, and Talisay, towns nestled against the western foothills of Malepunyo. On 7 April, in a brilliant attack, the 3d of the 511th swarmed up Malaraya Hill, a cone-shaped hill square in the entrance of, and dominating, the canyon that led to the top of Mount Malepunyo. The battalion held this key position against repeated enemy attacks.

When the Japanese artillery was pounding the 2d of the 187th near Sulac, an artillery air observer spotted a muzzle flash among the dense trees and brought in a heavy counterbattery concentration. When the 3d Battalion took Malaraya Hill, Colonel Strong found that Colonel

Fujishige had massed all of his artillery in this one position; all of the guns had been knocked out by the counterbattery fire.

On 12 April, General Krueger released the other two battalions of the 511th from Sixth Army reserve; General Swing moved Lahti and the two battalions of the 511th to "probe" the Malepunyo area and sent George Pearson, the 187th Headquarters, and the 2d of the 187th back to reduce Macolod.

The 511th was supported by the 674th FA Battalion and one platoon of the 85th Chemical Mortar (4.2-in.) Battalion. Major Lyman S. Faulkner was the 511th's S-2. To him, and the 511th battle-hardened veterans of the Leyte campaign, the order "to probe" meant that they would "move along the ridges, establish supply routes, occupy high ground, set up booby-trapped positions at night, and in daylight dispatch strong patrols to kill stragglers and locate the main Jap positions." To implement the probe, Faulkner reported, "Battalion sectors were assigned and tentative patrol routes were selected from map and aerial reconnaissance. Arrangements were made for the commanders of the initial company-size patrols to examine their routes from a liaison plane."

While the 511th was "probing" Mount Malepunyo, the 187th was preparing to attack Macolod. General Griswold had assigned to the division the 760th and 756th Field Artillery Battalions, which were armed with 155mm howitzers, large cannon to the troops of the 11th, who were used to the pack 75s and the "sawed-off" 105s of the division's organic artillery. Griswold also attached a company of 4.2-in. mortars, a company of medium tanks, and a company of tank destroyers. All of these units, plus the 675th FA Battalion, General Swing assigned to George Pearson and the 187th.

After the 2d of the 187th pulled out of the Lipa area and assembled southeast of Macolod, Capt. Buzz Miley, formerly of the 511th and now the commander of G Company of the 187th, received some personal instructions from General Swing on the details of the Macolod attack. Two days before the attack got under way, Buzz Miley got a message to report to Major Ewing, the battalion commander. Ewing escorted Buzz to General Swing and two of his staff officers, who were near the 2d of the 187th's CP. Buzz Miley recalls,

We were situated approximately a thousand yards south of the mountain, but with a good view of the south side and the west water side. I was told by General Swing that the new plan to clear the mountain was to send a unit up the water side at night to sweep the Japanese down the west side into a killing zone at the bottom and I was selected as the unit to go to the top. A staff officer and an engineer officer briefed me, said I would move out the next afternoon and asked for my requirements as soon as possible. After a meeting with my platoon sergeants, I sent a list of ammunition and an overabundance of hand grenades through the Battalion S-4, and I requested one infantry platoon be attached and at least forty Filipino laborers to carry explosives for the seven Engineer EM who had reported to me to blow caves shut as the attack moved down the mountain.

That night, Lt. Wally Brooks reported to me with a platoon of E Company 187th for attachment.

The following morning I took Lt. Brooks and my platoon sergeants on a recon to view the south and southwest slopes. I had been told earlier that recon and aerial photos had found no Japanese positions on those sides. About noon we had a dry run of the anticipated sweep down the mountain with the Co. E platoon on the right of the two G Company platoons (3d platoon front), the machine gun section, with weapons, to move down the two major draws and the mortar section (without weapons) to be in reserve for use as required.

On 18 April, the 187th launched a coordinated attack with two battalions abreast, the 1st on the right, in a semicircle around the south and east slopes of the mountain. The 1st Battalion seized Bukel Hill and retained it as a departure point. Advance was slow, particularly on the left flank, where it was necessary for troops to proceed across the bare face of Brownie Ridge, swept by mortar and machine gun fire. Tank destroyers went into position along the highway just west of Dita, from where they could fire directly at the mouths of caves in the side of the mountain, and 155mm howitzers moved up to the front lines, where they could lay directly on the caves with armor-piercing shells. At night, howitzers and tanks stayed up front, surrounded by well-gunned perimeters in an attempt to lure the Japanese to banzai them. The troops had found that when the Japanese attacked in mass they were profitable targets, and, to the infantryman, it meant just that many fewer of the enemy he had to dig out of caves and tunnels.

For a couple of days, the 187th and its reinforcements blasted the Japanese positions on Macolod with a constant stream of fire—mortars, artillery, and machine guns. Meanwhile, the 127th Engineers filled a deep ravine that separated the base of the mountain from the highway,

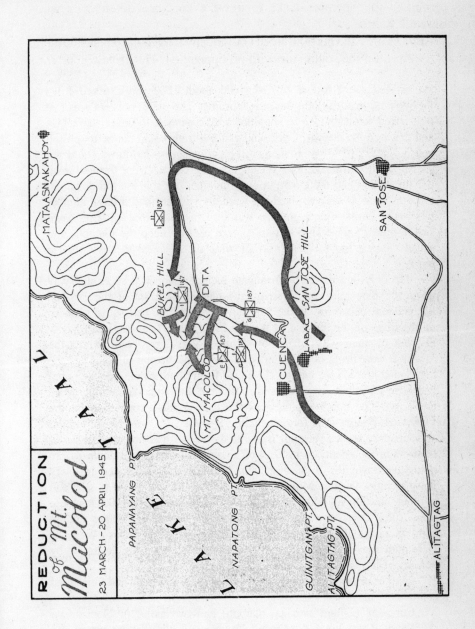

REDUCTION
of Mt.
Macolod
23 MARCH - 20 APRIL 1945

MATAASNAKAHOY

T A A L

BUKEL HILL

DITA

187

I 187

187

G 187

CUENCA

ABAC

SAN JOSE HILL

SAN JOSE

MT. MACOLOD

E 187

C 187

PAPANAYANG PT.

NAPATONG PT.

GUINITGAN PT.

ALITAGTAG PT.

ALITAGTAG

L A K E

333

permitting the Sherman tanks to move even closer to the targets on Brownie Ridge.

Buzz Miley and his reinforced G Company moved out on the afternoon of 19 April up the south side with no opposition. He wrote recently,

We arrived at the top of Mt. Macolod about 1500 and attacked down the west slope at daylight the next morning. The major concern was that we moved out shoulder to shoulder and expanded to cover the ridges and draws to the bottom. Caves and gun positions could not be by-passed and progress had to be slow since the personnel in the draws could not see those in the next draw. An excess of grenades were thrown down the slopes and into the caves. A large number of Japanese ran down the slope as soon as they realized we were above them and a large number ran out of caves after a grenade was thrown in. Each cave was blown shut by the Engineers—536 radios were used to keep the platoons and squads abreast and to keep from allowing the Japanese to criss-cross to our rear.

The only unusual and unfortunate incident happened about half-way down the mountain. Sgt. Gerrity, the platoon sergeant of the extreme left platoon, called me on the 536 radio and said the half squad (4 men) on the ridge on the left end of the front line had a Japanese in a foxhole in front of them with what looked like a very large bomb which the Japanese were firing over. I alerted the adjacent platoon to hold, and the half-squad fired on the bomb. The squad leader notified me that the bomb had been hit numerous times and must be a dud and was moving down the ridge. The bomb exploded as the four soldiers converged on the foxhole and bomb. The four, including Sgt. Gerrity, were blown to bits.

Japanese bodies were all over the draws—it was not unusual for at least 30 of the enemy to run out of a cave and be mowed down before going far downhill. A machine gun or BAR was positioned in every draw and most ridges. Movement was slow and I was called to stop and hold in position at 1600 hrs. I was told approximately 400 Japanese were killed but I am sure that I saw twice that many bodies and in addition no count could be made of those buried in caves. Weapons were numerous and I saw two large caliber guns that were destroyed by our engineers.

Our G Company casualties were two slightly wounded and four killed and/or missing.

Company G [and attached platoon] had two major problem areas: (1) Water. It was hot and no resupply was available or programmed and (2) Ammunition was getting critical late in the operation and I had to warn the troops to fire only on sure targets. The minor problem was not enough time to plan in more detail—but when Gen. Swing said "Go," that was it!

On one occasion in the fight down the hill, Sgt. Morris of G Company tossed a grenade into a cave opening; one of the occupants threw it back out. Sgt. Morris held the next grenade a little longer after he pulled the pin; this time it exploded inside the cave. He heard Japanese walking inside the cave on its boardwalk. Shortly, 18 Japanese wearing gas masks dashed out and ran down the ravine. Harrison, a BAR man in G Company, killed them all. Lt. Anzerone with his platoon, now numbering only eleven men, picked off a number of snipers with his M-1 before he fell with his second wound of the campaign. Private Campbell, the last of three brothers to die in combat in World War II, was killed coming down the ridge.

On 19 April, the 1st Battalion of the 187th held its ground and blew up and sealed all the caves in its area. C Company experimented by rolling drums of gasoline into its section of Cuenca Ravine and then igniting them with grenades. The resulting fires burned off the vegetation and prevented the Japanese from infiltrating between B and C Companies.

On 20 April, the 187th had succeeded in overrunning Macolod. When some of the troops emerged at the bottom of the mountain, they saw an unusual sight: Sitting on the ground on a small rise near what had been the 1st of the 187th's line of departure was General Griswold, his chin cupped in his hands. He had come to see the finale of the formerly formidable Japanese bastion.

Up to this time, General Griswold had planned to reduce the Malepunyo position with two divisions, the 11th Airborne and the 1st Cavalry. But late on the night of 22 April, General Swing received a phone call from General Griswold. The XIV Corps commander told General Swing that he would have to do the job alone. The 8th Cavalry Regiment of the 1st Cavalry Division would remain in place attached to the 11th Airborne, but the rest of the 1st Cavalry would relieve the 11th east of Sariaya. The new mission of the 11th Airborne was clear and concise: "Capture Mt. Malepunyo and destroy all the Japanese thereon."

Mount Malepunyo was a welter of conical hills covered with tangled rain forest and bamboo thickets, surrounded by precipitous slopes and interlaced with sharp ridges. The highest peak rose 3,160 feet above the plains of southern Luzon. There were no roads and only poorly kept jungle trails within the thirty-odd-square-mile area of the mountain.

All loads would have to be hand carried; resupply and evacuation would be by Filipino bearers, with emergency supplies dropped from liaison planes.

General Swing's plan of attack deployed the 187th, weary from its hard-won battle of Macolod, to Tiaong to relieve the 188th and to prevent the retreat of the Japanese out of Malepunyo to the east; it moved the 188th, when relieved by the 187th, to Alaminos to attack due south; it held the 8th Cavalry in position at the mouth of what was known as the Grand Canyon, a gorge on the northeast slope of the mountain. It assigned the main effort to the 511th, which was on the right flank of the 8th Cavalry, an effort that involved attacking east along the Malaraya Hill canyon, and then north to join the 188th and a special task force composed of C Company of the 511th, Troop F of the 7th Cavalry, and a platoon of D Battery of the 457th, with two pack 75s for assault guns. This latter force was called the Ciceri Task Force after its commander, Maj. John Ciceri, of the 511th.

The main Japanese position was south of the Onipa River and north of the Malaraya Hill canyon. The position was extensive in scope and included vast supply dumps; a hospital; artillery positions; and widespread underground caves, tunnels, and passageways. It was the headquarters of Lieutenant General Fujishige, commander of all Japanese forces on Luzon south of Manila. The rough terrain forced the engineers to cut, grade, and fill supply roads throughout the area of operations of the various forces. The fill across the Torac River on the southern outskirts of Alaminos was 110 feet deep.

General Farrell deployed his seven battalions of artillery (five light and two medium) around the mountain so that no area was masked from fire. The 675th, the 61st (from the 1st Cavalry), and a medium battalion, the 756th, were on the north and northwest. Colonel Johnson, the new commander of the 674th, and Colonel Bienvenu's 472d, now an organic part of the 11th Airborne, were on the west and southwest. The 457th was well around to the east. In addition, B Company of the 637th Tank Destroyer Battalion and A Company of the 44th Medium Tank Battalion supported the 188th from the north, and Company C of the 85th Chemical Mortar (4.2-in.) Battalion supported the attack from positions west of the mountain. D Battery of the 457th broke down its two pack 75s into pack loads and carried them up the side of the mountain, then emplaced them and fired at the caves above, not in front of, the infantry.

A coordinated attack was launched against the Japanese mountain bastion on 27 April. Fighter-bombers, directed by an Air Corps lieutenant named Hatfield, who had been the forward air observer with the division since the Nasugbu landings, pounded the enemy in front of the infantrymen, so close at times that blood sprang from the noses and ears of men in the 511th. The proximity of the 511th's troops to the bursting aerial bombs was caused by the fact that the troops noticed that the enemy went underground at the approach of the fighter-bombers and, immediately after the bombing, broke out of their caves and tunnels to man their outer defenses. Thus, the 511th men moved closer and closer to the bursting aerial bombs, and caught many of the Japanese as they came out of their caves.

On 26 April, Colonel Lahti had gathered his commanders and laid out the plan for the attack the next day. He ordered John Strong's 3d Battalion, in reserve, to establish ambushes covering the draws to the west; he ordered Hacksaw Holcombe's 2d Battalion to guard the supply trail, give fire support on call, and protect the pack 75s of the 457th in position on the Dalaga Ridge and Hill 2362. The 1st Battalion, with Lt. Col. Fred Wright now commanding, in conjunction with the Ciceri Task Force was to make the main assault after the massed artillery and all the air strikes that Lieutenant Hatfield could gather had been laid on. This effort was to focus three columns against Hill 2380—B Company advancing eastward from the draw between Dalaga and Hill 2362, A Company driving north, and Ciceri Task Force clearing Mount Mataasna Bundac westward.

On 25 April, the air strikes were relatively ineffective; Capt. Steve Cavanaugh moved up to Hill 2362 and talked the planes into the targets by relaying directions to them through the air forward observer. The strikes on 26 April were on target.

The artillery plan called for 5,000 rounds of mixed caliber from six battalions to fall on Hills 2375, 2380, 2218, Davis Ridge, and Ringler Ridge. The heavy concentrations would start when John Ringler, commanding B Company, signaled that he had arrived at the base of Ringler Ridge. During the night, four battalions of artillery fired time-on-target missions into the draws and suspected water points.

At dawn on the morning of 27 April, the 511th attack got under way. A Company moved forward under a smoke screen and behind 81mm mortars walking up the trail ahead, and seized Hill 2218 without opposition. While A Company prepared to continue north, artillery plastered

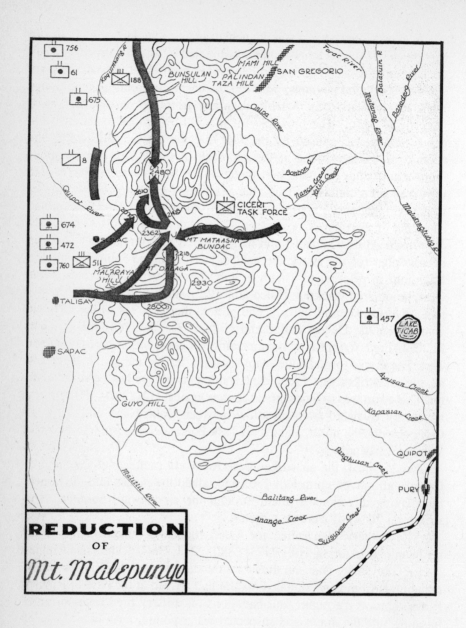

756
61
188
675

8

Kaguimitang R.

BUNSULAN
HILL

MAMI HILL
PALINDAN
TAZA HILL

SAN GREGORIO

Terac River

Matang River

Banadero River

Onloa River

Bonbon C.

Nanca Creek

Yatin Creek

2480

2610

Quipot River

801

2418

CICERI
TASK FORCE

674

472

511

760

2362

MT MATAASNA
BUNDAC

2218

Malungarubie R.

SOPAC

MALARAYA
HILL

T DALAGA

2930

TALISAY

2800

457

LAKE
TICAB

SAPAC

GUYO HILL

Ayusan Creek

Kapaniar Creek

Panghuian Creek

QUIPOT

Malitlit River

Balitang River

Anange Creek

Suisuyen Creek

PURY

REDUCTION
OF
Mt. Malepunyo

Hill 2380 and, on signal, lifted to the higher hills as the infantry labored up the slopes. A Company received some sniper fire from Hill 2375; the assault howitzers on Hill 2362 silenced the snipers. At 1300, eighteen A-20 attack aircraft worked over Hill 2610, and an hour later a second flight struck effectively at Hill 2418. A Company sent a platoon to cover Hill 2375.

Ringler and B Company continued to move through the thick jungle most of the day. The company uncovered and searched out numerous Japanese supply caves along their route, but these depots were guarded only by dead men. By midafternoon, Ringler had occupied his objective, Ringler Ridge, just short of Hill 2380 and dug in for the night.

Once in position, A Company's commander sent a patrol along the saddle to the east to establish contact with the Ciceri Task Force. En route, the patrol met heavy resistance, and several of the patrol members were wounded. Sergeant Pat Berardi of A Company took two men from the company and started down the saddle to assist the patrol. Japanese snipers killed Berardi's two men and wounded him. Berardi rushed the thicket hiding the snipers, and attacked and killed them with hand grenades and his rifle. He then moved to the isolated patrol, assumed command, and supervised evacuation of the wounded men of the patrol. Then and only then did he permit himself to be carried to the company position, where he died of his wounds. For his heroism, Sergeant Berardi was awarded the Distinguished Service Cross.

In its attempt to capture Mount Mataasna Bundac, Ciceri Task Force ran into a strongly fortified enemy defensive position. Sergeant Edward Reed, Jr., was the commander of the lead squad of Tom Mesereau's C Company of the 511th as it attacked the fortification. As the squad moved up the steep slope of the mountain, two enemy machine guns opened up from the direct front. The two lead scouts were wounded, and C Company held up. Sergeant Reed crawled forward over fifty yards of fire-swept terrain and, by himself, attacked the first machine gun emplacement. He threw one of his hand grenades into the nest, and killed three of the four Japanese there. He then closed in and killed the fourth with his rifle. During his one-man attack, he received a painful wound, but he moved around to the left flank and crawled forty more yards under fire to the second machine gun position. This time he was even more accurate with his grenade, and killed all four of the enemy in the hole. Then, still under fire, he moved to the two wounded scouts and removed them, one by one, to safety. For this action, Sergeant

Reed received the Distinguished Service Cross. The remainder of the task force moved on and captured its objective.

In the evening of 27 April, the 511th dug in for the night. A supply column of Filipino bearers moved on to all positions with C rations, water, and ammunition. The 511th had suffered eight men killed and twelve men wounded in action. The artillery and the mortars fired harassing fires in the draws around the battalions' positions all night.

On the morning of 28 April, an air strike by nine P-38s at low level dropped parachute demolition bombs and napalm in front of B Company. Major Faulkner later reported the attack:

At 1006 hours, as the artillery preparation neared its close, B Company was ordered forward. At 1010, the artillery lifted to Hills 2070 and 2610, and the 4.2's ceased fire. B Company, moving along a narrow trail on the slope of Hill 2418, bypassed A Company and pushed up the sides of Hill 2418, killing the few remaining Japs without receiving a single casualty. Jap fire from a mountain gun was ineffective. After a short rest, B Company was ordered to advance on the final objective, Hill 2610. Captain Ringler soon discovered that the only feasible route, staying on the ridge lines, was via Hill 2070, which I Company had been ordered to take. The regimental commander diverted I Company and ordered it to relieve A Company on Hill 2418, since he decided to let the 1st Battalion carry the attack until they asked for help. While this relief was under way, the artillery checked its registration on Hill 2070 and then laid in a 675-round concentration. He ordered the final assault on Hill 2610 for the next morning.

On the morning of 29 April, B Company launched its final attack on Hill 2610. Lyman Faulkner reported,

The day broke bright and clear, and the artillery fired early to check their registrations. By 0800 the P-38's, with 1,000 pound bombs aboard, were searching for their target. Red smoke grenades popped on the occupied hills; white phosphorus shells burst on Hill 2610; and A and B companies snuggled a little closer to the ground. The first flight roared in, following their leader in column, strafing, then loosing their bombs. The mountain shook but the peak of Hill 2610 still loomed untouched between the bracketing hits. The second flight had a clear view of the target and their leader scored on the crest of the hill. One by one they followed, each bomb starting a small landslide. The third flight circled, awaiting instructions. Ringler radioed, "Call off the planes, one man wounded, several with bloody noses."

The battalion commander replied, "Last flight cancelled. Coordinate artillery concentrations, using at least 500 rounds, including smoke. Shift fires to the north slope of Hill 2610. Let me know when you move out." B Company moved. They had climbed halfway up the precipitous slope when strange shells started dropping in. While a radio check determined that the shells were from the tank destroyers firing for the 188th to the north, the regimental commander, in a liaison plane, guided B Company away from the target area and encouraged them upward. At 1045 hours, B Company reached the top of Hill 2610.

But not without some difficulty. On top of their objective, Ringler's troopers were surprised by machine gun bursts coming out of the ground. Japanese, under the top of the hill, were firing their machine guns through apertures in the roof of the underground CP. Ringler's men quickly found the apertures and, with a flamethrower dropped to them by Colonel Lahti from his liaison plane, shot blasts of fire through the openings. The tactic was successful and drove the enemy out of the cave, burning and screaming. But the enemy had one last shot. Before they were mowed down, they threw large satchel charges into the air, where they burst, wounding eighteen men of B Company.

Across a saddle from Hill 2610, which had been the 511th's objective, was Hill 2480, the objective of the 188th advancing from the north. Colonel Lahti requested permission to seize Hill 2480, and because the 188th was still some distance from it, General Swing gave his okay. On 30 April, G Company of the 511th moved northward down the ridge to Hill 2480, from where the company's patrols were able to contact the 188th.

The 188th, advancing southward from the Onipa River, ran into much the same kind of defensive fortifications as had the 511th. The 188th found the heaviest resistance in the coconut grove gullies leading up to the base of the mountain. Once the regiment had destroyed the coconut log pillboxes at the base of the mountain, its troops moved more easily up the razorlike ridge and met the 511th on the top of Hill 2480 on 30 April.

Wrote the division historian just after the war;

While moving up the ridge, they [the 188th] experienced one glorious interlude. To the left of the ridge as they ascended, a vertical cliff fell some three hundred feet to a small stream, surrounded by coconut trees. Here, in this stream, they saw fifty or sixty Japs start to bathe—even though a terrific battle was raging in the hilltops above them. Quick as a flash the 4.2 mortar observer called for six volleys from his company. To the delight of the 188th, and the Division Commander who was sitting with his legs dangling over the cliff watching, the concentration landed and broke up the swimming party.

The 511th possessed the high ground of Malepunyo on 30 April. Colonel Lahti ordered all of his battalions to patrol the draws and hill slopes to flush out the last remnants of the Japanese Fuji Heiden. Artillery concentrations pounded the areas where the patrols suspected the Japanese were still hiding. The 1st Battalion moved their guerrillas up to Davis Ridge, named after Lt. Norvin L. Davis, of Company E of the 511th, who was killed leading his platoon up that ridge.

The patrols found large caves connected by wire communications and stocked with large amounts of ammunition and supplies on both the east and west slopes of Hill 2380. Hill 2610 hid a mountain gun with seventeen rounds of usable ammunition and a honeycomb of trenches and caves. In the largest cave, a patrol found high-powered radio equipment and many Japanese bodies. On 2 May, after the 511th patrols had completed a thorough search of all draws and caves, the 511th turned the mountain over to the guerrillas and marched out of the hills. The subjugation of Mount Malepunyo was complete. Since 6 April, Fujishige (variously referred to as a colonel, a major, and a lieutenant general) had lost almost 2,500 men in his futile defense of the Malepunyo hill mass.

Captured maps and documents confirmed Colonel Muller's contention that the mountain fortress was the last stronghold of General Fujishige's Southern Luzon Defensive Force, the Fuji Heiden. With the collapse of Malepunyo, all organized Japanese resistance in southern Luzon ceased, and the only task remaining to the 11th Airborne Division was clearing out the stragglers. On the eastern slopes of the mountain, the 187th formed a block that stopped a great many but not all of the enemy trying to escape. Colonel Muller notified his counterpart at XIV Corps that, in all probability, many of the enemy had escaped to Mount Banahao. The 1st Cavalry Division organized an all-inclusive scouting patrol of Mount Banahao by dividing it into pie segments and assigning each segment to a subordinate unit. These patrols reported no large elements of Japanese units in the area of Banahao.

The condition of the enemy soldiers who were on Mount Malepunyo is described graphically by one Japanese enlisted man whose diary was found on his body near Tiaong on 1 May by a patrol from the 187th. The diary describes the last two weeks before his death.

14 April 45: My suffering surpasses even that of death. I finally arrived at Mt. Malepunyo. I have just one ball of rice to eat. The enemy air and artillery bombardment is fierce.

15 April: The enemy has concentrated great numbers of troops in Tanauan, San Pablo, and Lipa, and is approaching our front—the enemy artillery bombardment is terrific. We, who are ready to die, are preparing for the enemy attack. My great crisis is approaching. This morning the enemy approached to within 100 meters in front of us. Their rifle and artillery fire is increasing.

Day after day the enemy drop propaganda leaflets which request us to surrender. To hell with them; I'll never surrender even if I must die. No food and no water, only grass and wood. The suffering is great, and there is no communication with Headquarters. Perhaps death is finally upon me.

16 April: I'm hungry. I want to eat rice, fish, and vegetables. I want to eat everything. My bowels are growling. If I go down the mountain, I will be able to drink sweet coconut juice, but there are many troops.

Why don't friendly troops come quickly from Manila? There are no friendly planes. Day after day, there are only enemy airplanes. I want to take a bath.

Today again I survived. I wonder when they will attack again. The friends who promised to die together have died, but I am still wandering around the fighting zone. At present only seven men under Sgt. Okamura are left from the squad.

17 April 45: I'm still alive. This morning another hopeless day has come. I finally started to eat grass. Enemy aerial bombardment is fierce. Corporal Sugihie and two others went to headquarters for a message. I pray that they got through safely and will accomplish their mission. My hope is that friendly troops will come from Manila and help us. Mt. Malepunyo is cold in the morning and night. Every night I'm thinking of home.

18 April 45: Hunger woke me. About 1500 hours the enemy approached our rear. The crisis is great now. Artillery shells drop like drops of rain. The end has come, I'm going to die bravely, I pray for the country's everlasting good fortune. I'm completely surrounded. I am going to attempt to cross the enemy lines under cover of darkness. I anticipated going towards Manila. Passing through mountains and ravines I penetrated the enemy front lines.

19 April 45: Manila is still far away. Today I was assigned as a supply man.

20 April 45: The enemy is all around. Three men killed and three wounded. The annihilation of the unit is imminent.

21 April 45: Danger is approaching this ravine. Last night an enemy patrol entered the ravine, but we repulsed them. Enemy bombardment comes closer and closer.

24 April 45: Another day and no food. At 0800 I started to penetrate the enemy lines with seven other men as a raiding unit. By 1830 I accomplished my mission.

25 April: I'm still alive, the danger is increasing. I heard that headquarters is fighting fiercely, despite being surrounded by the enemy. The enemy seems to have stopped our supplies.

Today three men came under my command.

26 April 45: The enemy is fierce but the morale of my men is high. Three messages from headquarters came through the enemy lines.

27 April 45: Preparation to move was completed by 0400, and at 0800 we departed towards Mt. Banahao via Tiaong. I wonder if we can get through safely—the enemy line is dangerous.

29 April 45: Arrived east of Mt. Malepunyo. I sent out a patrol. Arrived near Tiaong and hid in the ravine.

30 April 45: Day has come, and because of the enemy we cannot talk. No food. I hope the enemy will not find us.

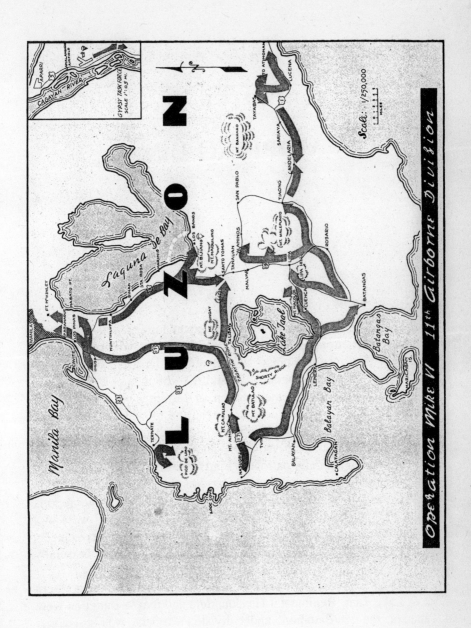

Operation *Mike VI* 11th *Airborne Division*

CHAPTER 17

MOPPING UP

After the fall of Mount Malepunyo, there were no longer enough Japanese units cohesive or strong enough to form a significant defense or a valid objective for the division's units. Neither did the Japanese attempt even a small-scale raid or a desperate, last-shot banzai charge. Nonetheless, the 11th Airborne still had the mission of ferreting out those enemy soldiers who did remain in hideouts, caves, and tunnels throughout the division's mountainous sector of operations. Each regiment, supported by the fires of the Division Artillery, and reinforced by some 5,000 guerrillas, maintained daily patrols to search for and destroy the isolated enemy pockets. The units paid particular attention to the bridges along the major roads in their areas. They also responded to various reports from the Filipino civilians that "large numbers of Japanese" were in a given area. Patrols, sent to investigate, found most of the reports exaggerated; where hundreds of the enemy had been reported, patrols usually found only tens.

The 187th's zone of responsibility was a large arc around the northern shore of Lake Taal. Regimental Headquarters and the 2d Battalion were at Tanauan; the 1st Battalion, under division's orders, was at Tiaong, to cut off the retreat of the enemy from the Mount Malepunyo stronghold.

Major David Carnahan was the commander of the 1st of the 187th. He remembers,

We laid ambushes up and down the river for a distance of some ten miles, endeavoring to cover every possible crossing. In those ambushes we accounted for some four hundred Japanese captured and killed. Our most successful ambush was just above the little town of Rosario, where there were three crossings about fifty yards apart. We used three light machine gun sections, reinforced by fifty guerrillas. Each section zeroed in on its respective bridge.

About 2400 hours one night, movement across the bridges was noticed. The ambushers were alerted, and the Japs started across all three bridges simultaneously. In the uncertain light the men noticed some strange looking objects among the column of Japs, but couldn't identify them. When the first Japs had almost reached our bank, the three sections opened up together, supported by the small arms of the guerrillas. The surprise was complete and deadly, some 100 Japs being killed and wounded, including quite a few high ranking officers. One of our captives told us that we had just missed capturing General Fujishige, commander of all forces in Southern Luzon, by a matter of seconds.

The strange looking objects that had so startled and bewildered the men turned out to be sedan chairs, that all the ranking Jap officers were being carried in.

During May, the first replacements since the Leyte campaign began to arrive. General Swing fully expected that the entire division would be employed in an airborne capacity in the last, ultimate objective of World War II—the invasion of the home islands of Japan. Even though Germany had surrendered officially and unconditionally to the Allies on 8 May 1945, the commanders in the Pacific, and the Joint Chiefs of Staff, believed without a doubt that the war in the Pacific would be won only when Japan itself had been invaded and subjugated.

In anticipation of that final battle, which would climax the long and arduous fight from New Guinea and through the Pacific Ocean islands, General Swing wanted all of his men—especially the replacements—to be combat ready. Therefore, he instructed his commanders to work the new men gradually into combat readiness by assigning them in small numbers to the mopping up patrols.

On 1 May, the Division Recon Platoon had reported contact with a group of 50 to 100 Japanese in the vicinity of Aya and Calaway on Tagaytay Ridge. Major Bud Ewing, CO of the 2d of the 187th, assigned F Company, reinforced with a section of 81mm mortars and a section of light machine guns (LMGs), to attack and destroy the enemy concentration. F Company moved out of the battalion area at dawn on 2 May. Shortly, the company found the stronghold, from which the enemy poured forth a heavy volume of rifle and automatic weapons fire. F Company deployed and attacked the position from three sides. One of the squads, which included a high percentage of new men, was led by a veteran of Leyte and Luzon, Pfc Joe R. Siedenberg. He deployed his squad, led them in an assault, overran the Japanese in his area, and killed twenty-seven, with no loss of any of his men. The total kill for the company that day was ninety-two enemy dead; that evening, the company had one man missing.

The next day, Siedenberg's squad was not as fortunate. As the squad stalked up a wooded draw late in the afternoon, it was pinned down by heavy fire. The opening burst wounded one of the new men. He fell, exposed to additional fire from the Japanese guns. Siedenberg crawled across the open area to the wounded man. On the way, Siedenberg was wounded in his chest, but he continued on, gathered up the wounded soldier, and turned back to cover. He was hit twice more by Japanese small arms, but he continued withdrawing his wounded squad member to relative safety. Then Private First Class Siedenberg died of his wounds. He was later awarded the Distinguished Service Cross.

By 10 May, the division had regrouped and had established a base camp on the outskirts of the devastated city of Lipa. The patrolling and the manning of outposts continued. But that portion of the division not on outpost duty or patrolling spent the first two weeks of May building camps in the coconut groves and around the airstrip near Lipa and in the area between Mount Macolod and Mount Malepunyo. In short order, rows of the ever-present pyramidal tents sprung up and, because the rainy season was due to start at the end of May, the troops floored their tents with bamboo strips or steel matting about a foot off the ground. Division Special Services built an amphitheater in a natural bowl near Mataasnakahoy for the traveling USO shows, division boxing matches, and movies. Large crowds of off-duty troopers watched such USO shows as *Oklahoma*; Joe E. Brown repeating his famous pitching scene from *Elmer the Great*; Kay Kyser shouting "Stoooodents!"; Al Schacht and his animated baseball comic strips; and the movies *Three Men on a Horse* and *This is the Army,* among others.

But training went on apace. As General Swing put it to General March on 20 May: "We are building a rehabilitation camp in the vicinity of Lipa. Must train about 6,000 replacements before the next operation—

so have started a jump school and glider classes. Hope the next time we go in it's completely airborne. . . . The service troops are arriving in numbers and I understand Manila has gotten to be quite a gay place what with the WACs and mestizos. It appears that the black market with its nightclubs, etc. are going full blast.''

Another milestone in the history of the 11th Airborne Division was marked on 11 May 1945. It was the first day since 31 January—a total of 101 consecutive days—that men of the division had not killed an enemy soldier. In the preceding days on Luzon, the division's soldiers had killed an average of 93.8 Japanese per day. These were the enemy who could be counted; numberless other Japanese had been sealed in caves and tunnels, uncounted, throughout the division's broad sector of responsibility, so vast that the division was committed in its entirety during the 105 days from the landings at Nasugbu to the end of the Malepunyo battle. The division commander could never afford to have even a company of infantry in reserve; the one time he tried it, with the 3d of the 511th in reserve at Rosario, he had to commit the battalion within twenty-four hours.

The month of May was an odd period for the 11th Airborne Division. As the division historian put it on hearing that Germany had surrendered, ''We were happy for the men who had been fighting the battles from Africa to the Elbe, and we felt that perhaps our days of fighting on a shoe-string were almost over, but we knew that the Japs were still plenty strong, we hadn't made much of a dent in China, and we hadn't set foot on the home islands of Japan. With the certain knowledge that our scheduled landings on the Japanese homeland were going to be rough, we went about our work and play, shooting straggling Japs in the mornings and playing softball in the afternoons.''

On 9 June, Gen. Joseph W. Stilwell—Vinegar Joe of Burma fame— visited the division at Lipa. General Swing ordered a full division review in General Stilwell's honor. The division lined up on the Lipa strip dressed in khakis, steel helmets, boots, and web belts. At the command ''pass in review,'' nine double jump door C-46s, new to the theater, flew over the field and dropped 324 paratroopers directly behind the troops. Then the paratroopers assembled and passed in review behind the division. The air fleet of Division Artillery, nine L-4s and two L-5s, not to be outdone, followed the C-46s and each dropped one paratrooper. Then six CG 4A gliders were cut loose over the reviewing stand, landed, skidded to a halt on the east side of the runway, and spewed forth a battery of artillery, which assembled and passed in review after the paratroopers.

On 25 May, the Joint Chiefs of Staff published the directive for Operation Olympic against Kyushu, with General MacArthur's recommended target day of 1 November. The JCS directive gave General MacArthur primary responsibility for the conduct of the entire operation. With this mission in hand, General MacArthur wrote, "It was possible to quickly make final detailed strategy for the invasion of Japan. Code designation of the entire operation was 'Downfall'; the first phase, 'Olympic,' was to be followed by 'Coronet,' the landing on Honshu—the heart of Japan. The Sixth Army would be employed for 'Olympic,' the Eighth, and the First Army from Europe, for 'Coronet.' The XXIV Corps of the Tenth Army was to be used in Korea when opportunity permitted."

General MacArthur charged General Krueger and his Sixth Army with the mission of planning for and executing Olympic. Sixth Army would have a total of eleven army and three marine divisions—about 650,000 troops, some of whom would stage for the operation from as far away as Hawaii. Three corps of three divisions each would land at three separate points in southern Kyushu while the XIth Corps would make a diversionary landing on Shikoku. General MacArthur planned to occupy only the southern half of Kyushu, giving him enough room to build the airfields and staging areas necessary for the final assault on Honshu, scheduled for March 1946.

For Olympic, the 11th Airborne Division was scheduled to be a reserve for GHQ, to be committed when needed but not slated for the initial assault. The division would travel to Kyushu on the first turnaround shipping that returned from the Kyushu landings. By this time, John Conable was the division G-4. He wrote later that, because the division would load on the turnaround ships,

I would not know what types of ships I would have until about twenty-four hours before loading began. All I could do was give the tonnage and cubic footage needed. . . . While we were doing this, we also were working on plans for Coronet. This was to be an operation against Tokyo, Yokohama. We were to be the lead Division of the XVIII Airborne Corps under General Ridgway. Our division and the 13th Airborne Division were to parachute on the peninsula forming the east side of Tokyo Bay and establish a beachhead for a couple of armored divisions. . . . I can remember pouring over aerial photographs of the area, trying to find some decent jump fields. We didn't find any. I was unsuccessfully trying to figure out what to do with 5 to 10 percent casualties instead of our usual one to two percent. . . . I had to get them evacuated somehow somewhere.

Meanwhile, the war on Luzon was drawing to a slow and bloody close in other sectors of the island. General Yamashita had concentrated his 14th Area Army of some 150,000 men in three separate defensive areas of northern Luzon. He had realized, as early as December 1944, that the most he could accomplish with his forces was to delay the Allied progress toward Japan by tying up in battle as many of the American divisions as possible. He also realized that the conditions of the roads, his limited supplies, and the preponderance of American air power would not permit him to launch a counterattack. Yamashita concentrated his best force, the Shobu group, in the north because that area provided him the best opportunity for delaying action. His plan was initially successful. Sixth Army was finally forced to commit four reinforced infantry divisions, an armored group, a large force of guerrillas, and a separate RCT against the Shobu group.

Sixth Army's plan had been first to contain the Shobu group and then to destroy it. In that mission, General Kruger's forces were successful. But the Shobu group in turn tied up about one-third of Sixth Army's strength for an extended period.

By mid-June, General Krueger estimated that if the 37th Division, attacking up the Cagayan Valley toward Aparri, could continue its fast drive north, the 37th might be able to end the Luzon campaign then and there. On 17 June, the 37th continued its advance up Route 5 in the Cagayan Valley. On the nineteenth, the 37th ran into elements of the Yuguchi Force, which was still trying to move south along Route 5. Over the next four days, the 37th killed more than 600 Japanese, captured 285 more, and destroyed fifteen light tanks in a fifteen-mile stretch along the highway. By 25 June, the remnants of the Yuguchi Force were in full flight toward the untracked wilds of the Sierra Madre, which separated the Cagayan Valley from the east coast of Luzon.

Nonetheless, General Krueger still felt that it was necessary to assist the 37th Division in its drive north and that an airborne force, landed near Aparri on the northern tip of Luzon and then attacking south, could seal off the Cagayan Valley and assist the 37th in this way. General

Krueger may also have been motivated by a desire to clean up northern Luzon before Eighth Army took over operations, scheduled for 1 July. Sixth Army's report on Luzon stated that "in order to complete the annihilation of the enemy forces fleeing north, it was decided to make a vertical envelopment of airborne troops to close the trap and prevent the enemy from all possibility of escaping from Aparri." On 21 June, General Krueger ordered General Swing to drop a battalion combat team near Aparri on 25 June.

On 23 June, Maj. Robert V. Connolly and his truck-mounted Connolly Task Force (800 men including a reinforced company from the 33d Division, a Ranger Company, and a battery of artillery) entered Aparri from the west; the next day, elements of the task force and the 2d Battalion of Col. Russell W. Volckmann's 11th Infantry of the Philippine Army were ten miles south of Aparri along Route 5 and had secured the Camalaniugan Airfield, three miles from Aparri. Despite the success of the Connolly Task Force and the 2d of the 11th Infantry, General Krueger decided to go ahead with the airborne operation. He concluded, "The seizure of Aparri, without opposition by elements of the Connolly Task Force on 21 June 1945, together with the almost unopposed advance of the 37th Division, indicated clearly that the time had come for mounting the airborne troops to block the enemy's retreat in the Cagayan Valley."

Because of the rapid advance of the 37th Division, General Krueger moved up the target date of the airborne operation to 23 June. This meant that thirty-six hours after Sixth Army had alerted the 11th Airborne for the operation, the task force would be in action. General Swing formed the Gypsy Task Force to accomplish the Aparri mission and assigned the command of the force to the executive officer of the 511th, Lt. Col. Henry Burgess. The task force of 1,030 men consisted of the 1st Battalion and Companies G and I of the 511th; Battery C of the 457th; a composite platoon of C Company, 127th Engineers, and all "Camp Mackall veterans," according to Jake Swindler, who was the first man from the 127th selected for the operation; the 2d Platoon, 221st Medical Company; and teams from the 511th Signal Company, the Language Detachment, the CIC, and the 11th Parachute Maintenance Company.

On the afternoon of 22 June, General Krueger arrived at Lipa to inspect the preparations for the next day's drop. As Generals Krueger and Swing walked through the men who were loading their gear on the planes and checking parachutes, Colonel Burgess reported to General

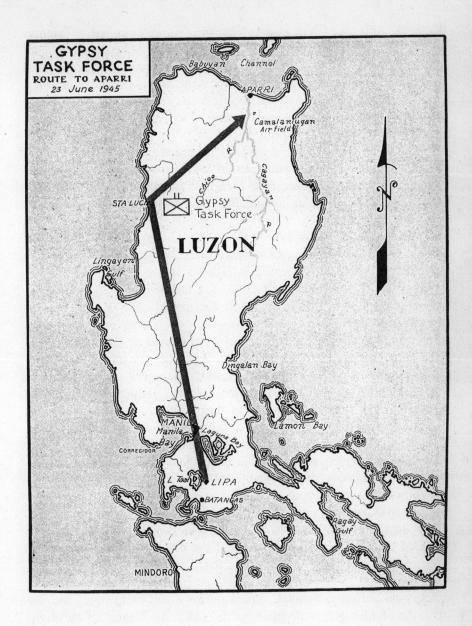

GYPSY
TASK FORCE
ROUTE TO APARRI
23 June 1945

Babuyan Channel

APARRI

Camalaniugan
Air field

Chico R.

Cagayan R.

STA LUCIA

Gypsy
Task Force

LUZON

Lingayen
Gulf

N

Dingalan Bay

MANILA
Manila
Bay

Laguna Bay

Lamon Bay

CORREGIDOR

L. Taal

LIPA

BATANGAS

Ragay
Gulf

MINDORO

353

Krueger, who asked him how old he was. Burgess replied, "Twenty-six." Then General Krueger asked General Swing if he didn't have an older officer to command the force. General Swing said, "Yes, Colonel Lahti, who is thirty-one, but in the event the Gypsy Force has trouble, Lahti would take the rest of the regiment and reinforce the troops." At that time, Colonel Lahti was the oldest officer in the 511th and older than all of the enlisted men except two.

The departure strip for the Aparri operation was the concrete Lipa airfield, built by Japanese engineers in 1942. It is somewhat ironic that when the Japanese launched their parachute attack on the 11th Airborne units around the airfields at San Pablo on Leyte, they used Lipa as their departure airfield.

For the Gypsy Task Force, Col. John Lackey, CO of the 317th Troop Carrier Group, assembled fifty-four C-47s and thirteen C-46s. And for their first use in the Pacific Theater, he also rounded up seven gliders—six CG 4As and one CG 13. The task force began loading the aircraft at 0430 on 23 June. Generals Krueger and Swing were present for the 0600 takeoff.

The first plane off the strip was a C-46 piloted by Colonel Lackey. One after another, the other transports followed, assembled in the air, and went on course in a vee of vees, with the seven gliders and their tug ships bringing up the rear of the column. Fighter aircraft circled overhead. The flight course was to the northwest to a checkpoint at Santa Lucia on the west coast of Luzon above the Lingayen Gulf, then to the northeast directly to the Camalaniugan Airfield, the drop zone. Bombers and fighters of the 5th Air Force flew cover, and other planes laid smoke screens to the east and the south of Camalaniugan to conceal the drop from the Japanese in the hills to the east.

On 21 June, two days before the drop, the 11th's Pathfinders had flown up to the area, contacted Colonel Volckmann's unit on the west bank of the Cagayan River, and then, the night before the drop, had slipped across the river and moved to the Camalaniugan drop zone.

At 0900 on 23 June, the Pathfinders popped colored smoke. Colonel Lackey picked up the signal, turned on his green jump light, and the first vee of nine planes dropped on the field. As the rest of the flight flew over the go point in succession, the pilots turned on their green lights. The jumpers landed in the proper area, but the jump casualties were high: Two men were killed when their parachutes malfunctioned, and seventy men—a very high rate of about 7 percent—were injured.

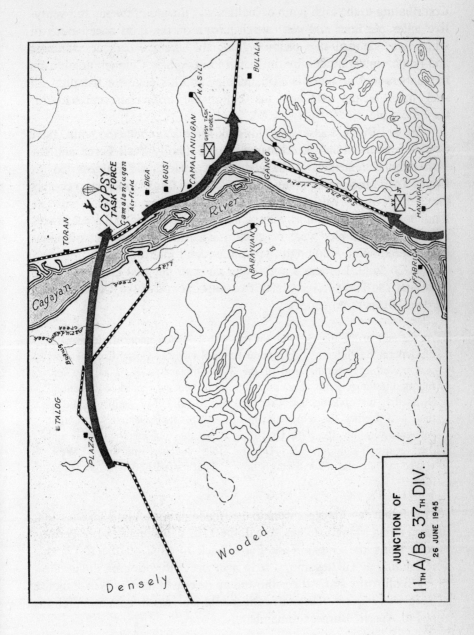

Densely Wooded

Cagayan

Cagayan River

TORAN

GYPSY TASK FORCE

Camalaniugan Airfield

BIGA

AGUSI

CAMALANIUGAN

KASILI

BULALA

GYPSY TASK FORCE

GANGO

Saprang Esteto

MAXINGAL

XX 37

FABRICA

BABAYUAN

Creek

Baracatan Creek

Banaus Creek

TALOG

PLAZA

JUNCTION OF
11TH A/B & 37TH DIV.
26 JUNE 1945

355

Contributing to the high jump casualties was a wind of twenty to twenty-five miles per hour and very rough terrain on the drop zone, much of which was flooded rice paddies along the airstrip, carabao wallows, and bomb craters hidden by thick, tall kunai grass. Colonel Volckmann remembers that he had his 11th Infantry and his engineer battalion fill shell holes on the strip and, just before the drop, chase carabaos off the drop zone.

Colonel Burgess assembled his task force and contacted both Major Connolly and Colonel Volckmann. The Connolly Task Force and the 11th Infantry remained in the vicinity of Aparri, and Burgess led his Gypsy Task Force south along Route 5 and the Cagayan River to contact the 37th Division. Burgess wrote later, "The Aparri operation was one long, hot march, but militarily it was not difficult. A drop of flamethrowers and Lt. Ken Murphy were of great assistance in taking out pillboxes encountered and continuing the march without interruption."

On 26 June, Burgess's point men ran into the lead elements of the 37th near the Paret River, thirty-five miles south of the Camalaniugan Airfield. Burgess remembers,

At the end of the march, we met the 37th Division under the command of General Beightler. . . . General Ennis Swift, the Corps Commander, was travelling with the lead of the 37th Division. . . . I saluted and reported to the generals. General Beightler turned and remarked to General Swift that his division had "rescued the 511th." My temper flared at that, as I deemed the remark an insult, and pointed out that we thought we were rescuing the 37th Division, as we had out-marched them and their armored column. . . . General Swift laughed and said, "Well, you sound like one of Joe Swing's boys." That remark ended the conversation.

Later that day, Burgess went to the Headquarters of the 37th Division, situated along a small stream, to call the 11th's Headquarters for permission to bring the Gypsy Task Force back to Lipa on the C-47s that were landing at Tuguegarao, a strip near the 37th, bringing in supplies.

A Sixth Army staff officer showed up on one of the C-47s in response to Burgess's request. The staff officer told Burgess to countermarch his troops to Aparri. Burgess remembers,

[There] we would be picked up by Naval shipping which would take us to Manila, some 80 miles from . . . Lipa, which would mean a truck ride and a week or more delay in returning to the division. There was no way that I was going to march that battalion back up the valley some 55 miles in midday heat of 120 degrees in the shade for three . . . days if we could ride those airplanes. . . . So I talked to the pilots as they came in, and they began flying men ''home'' to Lipa in exchange for some mementos . . . Japanese guns, uniforms, helmets, etc. . . . Within two days we were all back at Lipa. . . . I landed in the last plane.

John Conable, the division G-4, also had a part to play in the return of Gypsy Task Force to Lipa. He had intended to jump from an L-5 near Jack Hayes's C battery of the 457th to help arrange the return of the task force. But General Swing found out about the ''combat jump'' scheme and told Conable that he would land on the highway, not jump from the L-5. He remembers, ''I landed properly on the highway and got everyone back to Lipa safely.''

For Sixth Army, the meeting of the 11th Airborne and the 37th Division marked the strategic end of the campaign in northern Luzon. But there was still much fighting for the Eighth Army when it took over responsibility from Sixth Army for northern Luzon.

On 3 July, General Swing wrote to General March.

Well, the Sixth Army had declared the end of the Luzon campaign (June 30th). The Eighth was scheduled to take over on that date. In order to call it a complete job, they had to send for the 11th Airborne at the last minute. On 36 hours notice, I dropped a combat team just south of Aparri. They ran the Japs out of the hills and made 75 miles [sic] to contact the 37th Division and open Cagayan Valley. I pleaded with the 6th Army staff to drop the whole division up here two months ago when they were having such a helluva time in Balete Pass. Had they done so we would have been on the Japs' tail and cleaned out the valley six weeks ago and saved a lot of casualties the other divisions had in making their frontal attack. As it was, they let the Japs withdraw the greater part of their garrison at the northern end of the valley and, unmolested, take them down to reinforce the defenders of the pass. Do you wonder that sometimes I think I'll lose my mind?

During June and July, the division was totally involved in its retraining, R and R, and reorganization phases. In May, the division had shifted to a new TO and E, which in effect gave three battalions to the glider regiments, made the 188th and 674th parachute units, made the 472d Field Artillery Battalion organic to the division, upped the two-

and-a-half-ton trucks from 100 to 250, and increased the strength of the division from 8,600 to more than 12,000 men. In late June, Col. Ducat McEntee arrived in the Philippines with his 541st Parachute Infantry Regiment aboard the USS *Johnson*. Colonel McEntee had organized the 541st from scratch in 1943 but had seen it depleted time after time to provide replacements for the European airborne divisions. This time, he thought that his regiment would remain an entity and become a regiment of the 11th. But that was not to be. As soon as he debarked in Manila, Colonel McEntee received orders deactivating his regiment and assigning his men to the 11th Airborne as replacements.

At Lipa, the division instituted training for the troop carrier pilots who, because they had spent so much time delivering supplies in single ship runs, were not accustomed to dropping paratroopers in formation. Colonel John Lackey sent one squadron every ten days to Lipa for training in the fundamentals of airborne operations, from flying alone and dropping dummies on panels to flying in squadron formation and dropping full sticks of paratroopers on selected DZs. The pilots also practiced tugging gliders in tight formations and even practiced "snatch pickups," a procedure whereby a C-47, flying about fifteen feet above the ground with a hook—on the end of a cable wrapped on a drum in the plane—protruding from the door, would hook onto a glider's tow rope, that had been looped and erected on a vertical frame next to the glider. To the men in the C-47, it was not much of a challenge; to the men in the glider, it was an interesting phenomenon to be sitting still one moment and be airborne at 120 miles an hour a few seconds later.

Somehow the division found the time and the equipment to field a football team. On 4 July, the division team played the Navy at Rizal stadium in Manila on a field of thick mud in a heavy rain. In spite of the fact that Admiral Spruance had somehow brought in a Chicago Bear running back, the division held the Navy to a zero-zero tie.

The intensity of the Air Corps Troop Carrier Groups' training and the establishment of the division's third parachute school at Lipa started many rumors floating about the division area. The more practical savants had the division jumping ahead of the forces invading Japan; others thought China a more obvious choice; and still other amateur strategists thought that Formosa would make a fine DZ. But, of course, none of these courses of action was to be.

About 20 July, General Swing called John Conable into his makeshift office in a schoolhouse outside Lipa. General Swing introduced Conable to an Air Corps major. The major asked Conable how many planes it would take to move the division about 800 air miles. Conable remembers,

> I asked General Swing how many units of fire he wanted. He said figure on a quarter of a unit. To say that I was surprised is a major understatement. The Old Man never wanted to go anywhere without at least two units of fire. Then the General added: "Be sure to bring the band in one of the early serials." The major and I went back to my desk. I got out the plans I had for Olympic. While he was looking at them, I excused myself and went to the map room. It was just 800 miles from Okinawa to Tokyo! Both the major and I were worried about gasoline. A C-46 or 47 didn't have enough fuel capacity to make a 1,600 mile round trip. He left with the number of men, weight, and volume of mortars, jeeps, etc. No more was said.

But the incident caused Major Conable to consider that there was definitely "something different in the wind." And indeed there was. On 6 August, the *Enola Gay* dropped an atomic bomb over Hiroshima; on 9 August, *Bock's Car* dropped a second atomic bomb on Nagasaki; on 10 August, Japan decided to surrender. After a few days of negotiations, on 14 August, Emperor Hirohito took the unprecedented step of addressing the nation on radio to inform his people that Japan had accepted the Allied surrender terms.

On 15 August, Washington received Japan's acceptance of the surrender terms, President Truman announced the end of the war in the Pacific, and General MacArthur was appointed supreme commander for the Allied powers.

At 0430 on the morning of 11 August, the 11th Airborne duty officer awoke Generals Swing and Pierson with a long top secret message that alerted the division to be prepared to move all combat elements and equipment by air on forty-eight hours' notice to a staging area on Okinawa for the occupation of Japan. The message in short meant that General MacArthur had selected the 11th Airborne Division to lead the Allied forces in occupying Japan. The division G-3 Air, Maj. E. M. Flanagan, Jr., flew up to FEAF Headquarters at 0530 that Saturday morning, 11 August. When he first arrived about midmorning, the FEAF operations officer, Col. Francis C. Gideon, confirmed that the planes would start arriving in forty-eight hours; a few minutes later, Colonel Gideon (West

Point, class of 1940) told Major Flanagan to get back to his headquarters because the planes were already on the way to Lipa and some would be arriving that afternoon.

Thus began for the 11th Airborne Division another chapter in its relatively short but action-packed history.

CHAPTER 18

LIPA TO OKINAWA TO JAPAN

Saturday, 11 August 1945, was a day of feverish activity for all the troopers of the 11th Airborne Division.

Early in the morning, General Swing sent General Pierson to Manila "to check in with the different staff sections of GHQ for necessary details," General Pierson wrote later. "Colonel George Rehm in the Operations Division gave me what information he had and I then saw Major General Frank Heileman in Logistics." General Pierson then made a quick trip to Far East Air Force Headquarters at Fort McKinley, where he also learned that the forty-eight-hour alert had evaporated and that aircraft for the move would start arriving at Lipa at 1600 that afternoon.

When General Pierson phoned General Swing from Fort McKinley, General Swing was already aware of the change in his alert status. General Swing told General Pierson to return to Lipa at once, that he had told General Pierson's orderly to pack "a musette bag, a bedding roll and other equipment," and that he would take an advance party to Okinawa by C-46 as soon as he could return to Lipa. When General Pierson arrived back at Lipa, he found the advance party of representatives of the various staff sections and division units waiting at the strip. They loaded into a C-46 and cleared the Lipa runway before the start of the arrival of the planes to lift the division.

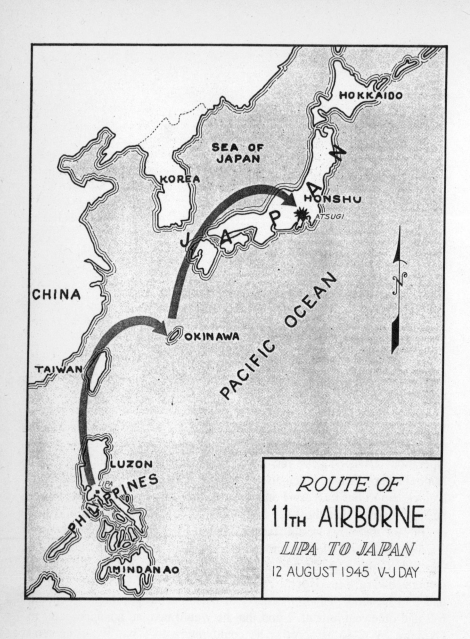

KOREA

SEA OF
JAPAN

HOKKAIDO

HONSHU

ATSUGI

J A P A N

CHINA

PACIFIC OCEAN

OKINAWA

TAIWAN

LUZON

LIPA

PHILIPPINES

MINDANAO

ROUTE OF

11TH AIRBORNE

LIPA TO JAPAN

12 AUGUST 1945 V-J DAY

General Pierson and his party spent the night at Clark Field and left the next morning for Okinawa. General Pierson remembers,

> Major General Fred L. Walker of the Okinawa Command had members of his staff meet the plane and escort us to a close-in bivouac area. After allocating specific areas to the division organizations, I saw General Walker who told me that his command was prepared to assist the division by replacing worn-out equipment, providing necessary paint and painting, etc., so that the troops would present a first-class appearance on arrival in Japan. All steel helmets would bear the stencil "11 A/B" after being painted; all jeeps would be painted and properly stenciled "11 A/B Division. . . ." We had splendid cooperation from the Okinawa Command.

Back at Lipa, the division staff had moved into action on the double. Major Flanagan selected four captains from the G-3 Section and sent them as liaison officers to the four fields from which the division would depart: Lipa, Nichols, Nielson, and Clark Airfields, the last three of which were, respectively, forty-five, fifty, and seventy-five miles from Lipa.

General Swing personally alerted the 511th. Lieutenant Colonel Henry Burgess, the 511th XO, was leaving the regimental mess at noon on 11 August when he heard the phone ring in the 511th Headquarters tent. Burgess answered the phone and General Swing said, "Hank, tell Lahti to get the 511th to the runway at Lipa, combat loaded, within two hours. We are leaving for Okinawa." Burgess hung up the phone and then remembers,

> I began to wonder if he had lost his mind, which I ruled out in about fifty seconds. So I called him back and asked him to repeat what he had just told me. He laughed, said it was proper to confirm the message, and that time was wasting.
>
> I found the bugler and he played "Call to Arms." I sent a messenger by jeep down to the truck stop about a mile away and told all the men to come back at once, as we were going somewhere that afternoon. There was a lot of excitement, enthusiasm, speculation, and busy soldiers getting their weapons and gear together. Two hours later the 511th was on the airdrome ready for a trip to who knew where.

The G-3 Section alerted the rest of the units to the move. The unit commanders in turn called all men back from the rest camps and weekend passes. By the afternoon of 11 August, all units were on alert, standing by in their areas, and were sorting out which men and equipment would fly to Okinawa and Japan and which rear-echelon men and equipment would follow by LST.

The basic problem in the move from Luzon to Okinawa, besides the need for speed, was that the G-3 Air Section did not know what type of aircraft—C-46s, C-47s, or B-24s—were arriving until they landed. Therefore, they could not make up plane loads in advance. The plan, however, was relatively simple: Whenever runway and taxiway space became available at the Lipa strip, the G-3 liaison officer, working closely at the strip with a staff officer of Brig. Gen. Warren Carter's 54th Troop Carrier Wing, who controlled all of the aircraft in the lift, would contact the Wing Headquarters and inform that staff of the number of planes needed and the time schedule to be followed; at the other fields, the A-3 staff officer would inform the G-3 Air liaison officer of the number and type of planes available. The G-3 Air liaison officer would then calculate the number of men and equipment to fit into the planes and inform the G-3 Air at Lipa. He would work with the G-4 staff and the unit commanders to send men and equipment to fill the planes. The G-3 liaison officers and the unit staff officers would direct the loading and dispatch of the planes. On 11 August, there were more planes available than the 11th Airborne could load; by 12 August, units were moving rapidly to the departure fields and had short waits before takeoff.

The shuttle of the 11th Airborne from Luzon to Okinawa was not without its calamities. On Sunday afternoon, 12 August, B-24s, with twenty men crammed into their bomb bays, were hauling troops from the Lipa strip. The first twelve took off successfully. The thirteenth, however, was still not airborne when it rumbled and bumped across the pierced-steel planking that had been used to extend the concrete strip. The plane raced out of control across the road at the far end of the strip, bounced off an embankment, and burst into flames on the other side. Eleven men from the 511th, veterans of all of the division's battles, died in the flaming wreck. If it had not been for the courageous work of Lt. Headley G. Ryan of the 511th, more men would have died. He was injured in the crash, but he carried one man out with him and then returned to the burning plane, carried out two more, and dragged them to safety away from the plane that might have exploded at any time.

John Conable remembers the crash of the B-24 at Lipa. "That plane had been equipped with a radar snooperscope which weighed 1,500 pounds and had been overlooked. My air loading officer went to pieces when he realized what had happened and blamed himself for not asking the capacity of the plane. I had to send Bill Roberts to replace him. Bill did his usual excellent job.''

The second crash occurred at Laoag, Luzon, when a C-47 crashed on takeoff after landing to refuel. The third and most disastrous accident was at Naha on Okinawa. The pilot of a C-46, carrying men from the Headquarters of the division and part of an attached language detachment team, had tried twice to land on the Naha strip, which was on the top of a cliff bordering the ocean. At the time he was trying to land, kamikazes were attacking shipping in the harbor, and the ships put up smoke screens to hide them from the attacking planes. By the time the C-46 pilot made his third attempt, it was early evening and quite dark. The airfield was blacked out and the smoke from the harbor obscured the end of the field on the cliff. In trying to pull up over the ships in the harbor, the pilot dropped one wing, crashed into the cliff, and fell to the beach below. All thirty-one men on the plane were killed, including Lt. George E. Skau, who had led the Division Recon Platoon on so many hazardous and daring missions behind the Japanese lines. At Lipa, George Skau, wanting to be on Okinawa early on with his platoon, had bumped Martin Squires, a member of his Recon Platoon, from the airplane. And Major Flanagan told Lt. Jim Adamson to get off that same plane just as it was about to take off because he needed him at the strip. Lieutenant Adamson retired from the army in 1974 as a major general.

At 2300 on 12 August, the G-3 alerted Colonel Pearson to move the 187th by truck at 0630 the next morning to Nichols and Nielson Fields. The first plane carrying the men of the 187th took off from Nichols at 1053 and landed at Naha on Okinawa at 1645 that afternoon. Succeeding flights took off as planes became available and landed at Naha, Kadina, and Yontan Fields.

One problem faced by the unit commanders of the 187th and other division units was that some of the young Filipino lads who had attached themselves to various soldiers during combat ended up on Okinawa with their heroes. They were sent back, very reluctantly, to the Philippines as soon as unit commanders discovered them and return transportation was available.

By 15 August, the bulk of the forward echelon of the division had closed on Okinawa. For the aerial movement, the 54th Troop Carrier

Wing had rounded up 99 B-24s, 351 C-46s, and 151 C-47s to airlift 11,100 men, 1,161,000 pounds of equipment, and 120 special-purpose jeeps for communications, command, and supply. Lieutenant Colonel Robert Conine, the division's adjutant general, was once again in command of the rear echelon on Luzon. He gathered the units' rear-echelon elements, the troops' baggage, and the division's major items of equipment, loaded them on LSTs, and took off for Okinawa and Japan by sea. And on Monday night, 13 August, Major Flanagan and his four liaison officers were back in Lipa, and headed for bed for the first time since 0530 on Saturday, 11 August.

The division was sequestered on Okinawa for the next two weeks. The weather was a mixture of New Guinea and Leyte—blindingly hot one day and soakingly wet the next. At least one typhoon roared across the island. Because the men were combat loaded, they had only pup tents in which to live and Cs, 10-in-1's, and K rations to eat. Most of the desirable campsites had been commandeered by units already on the island, so the 11th ended up on the sides of hills, several of which were Ryukuan cemeteries dotted with small tombs. General Pierson remembers, "The opening into the tombs which had been dug into the hillside was in the shape of a heart, each hill having dozens of these hearts." On the hillsides, the heavy rains formed rivulets through the pup tent camps. "Strong, hot winds sprang up," reported one frustrated trooper, "and the pup tents blossomed out like parachutes and took off."

Henry Burgess remembers the bivouac area slightly differently.

The Division bivouaced in an area on Okinawa that had many tombs dug into the earth. The tombs had been shaped symbolically to represent the womb of a woman. Each had considerable room, with the ashes from cremation being stored in small jugs. Entry into the tomb was by a small entrance several yards long into a large room, or rooms, many of which were capable of holding twelve to fifteen men. A few days after arrival on Okinawa, a typhoon hit the island, and many soldiers in the Division found the tombs were great shelters. . . . It was into one of these tombs that those of us who had brought our water cans (loaded with whiskey somehow fleeced from the newly arrived 541st officers) with us enjoyed the contents for the several days we remained out of the wind and rain.

Nonetheless, the division had much work and training to do. Because the staff of Maj. Gen. William O. Ryan, the commander of the Air

Transport Command-Pacific, which was running the Okinawa to Japan leg of the move, could still not tell the division staff what type and number of planes would be available, the G-3 and G-4 Sections developed eight separate and distinct plans for the flight. Besides not knowing the number and types of planes that might be available, the capacity of Atsugi—the target airdrome outside Yokohama—to handle incoming planes and turn them around for the return flight to Okinawa was also unknown. The plans were detailed down to and including where each man and each piece of equipment would be carried.

The ultimate, overall plan for the occupation of Japan was still not firm by mid-August 1945. On 24 August, General Swing wrote to General March, "As you know, we have been sitting here prepared to drop on Tokyo on five hours' notice ever since the twelfth." Because the 11th staff thought that the parachute elements might still jump into Japan (one fairly well-founded rumor had a parachute force jumping into a park in Tokyo), the staff tested the B-24 as a possible jump ship because the C-46 could not make the trip from Okinawa to Japan and back with enough of a safety factor. The jumpers, one of whom was the G-3, Doug Quandt, decided that the B-24 was not a plane one would jump from voluntarily, not only because it could not slow down to a safe jumping speed but mostly because the small exit door and the cramped interior permitted only two or three jumpers to get out on each pass over a reasonably long drop zone. ATC-Pacific did not use the B-24 on the flight from Okinawa to Japan after all.

The plane that did fit prominently in the move to Japan was the four-engined C-54, which the 11th Airborne troops had only rarely seen. Compared to the C-47 and C-46, the C-54 was gigantic. ATC-Pacific began assembling them from all over the world, and the 11th practiced loading and unloading them with forklifts and placing the cargo in the right places: The C-54 had a tricycle landing gear and had to be loaded with 4,000 pounds in the nose and 8,000 pounds in the main fuselage, spread out evenly. Speed in unloading was essential; the ATC staff told the division that the C-54s had to be unloaded in three minutes, and they trained the division troops to slide down ropes from the front door and then run to the rear to help the unloading.

The troops were subjected to many lectures and orientations on the Japanese people, their country, and their customs. The troops were warned that no one knew exactly how the Japanese Army and people would react to the occupation; that, however remote, the whole scheme might be a gigantic plot to "suck in" the American Army and then annihilate it in Japan, and that the Japanese Army in Japan greatly outnumbered the occupiers. General Headquarters ordered the 11th to go into Japan combat loaded.

At the international level, negotiations proceeded toward the second momentous event of 1945—the signing of the peace treaty on the *Missouri* anchored in Tokyo Bay. But before that event could transpire, there were a number of meetings with a Japanese delegation to smooth the way for the initial occupation. General MacArthur did not take part in the original negotiations for the surrender, but he was responsible for the implementation of the surrender. "Over the radio," he wrote later, "I directed the Imperial government to send a delegation to Manila to receive instructions concerning the surrender ceremonies. This delegation was charged with the removal of all propellers from all Japanese aircraft on Yokohama's Atsugi Airfield, with providing transportation for the Allies from Atsugi to Yokohama, and to reserve the New Grand Hotel for Allied use. Yokohama would be my temporary headquarters, the battleship *Missouri* the scene of formal surrender ceremonies."

On 19 August, a Japanese delegation of sixteen men, headed by Gen. Torashiro Kawabe, the deputy army chief of staff, landed at Nichols Field, outside of Manila, in an American C-54 that they had boarded on Ie-Jima. They had traveled from Japan to Ie-Jima in two Japanese Betty bombers, painted white with two large green crosses painted on their sides. The delegation was to receive instructions and to work out surrender arrangements with an American team headed by General Sutherland, General MacArthur's tough and crusty chief of staff. ("Someone's got to be the bastard around here," he'd been heard to say.) General MacArthur refused to see the Japanese until the moment of the formal surrender. General Charles Willoughby met the delegation at the field and escorted them to the Rosario Apartments, down the street from the gutted Manila Hotel.

That evening, Willoughby led the Japanese delegation to Manila's City Hall for their first meeting with General Sutherland and his party. The Japanese left their swords at the entrance and were escorted to a second-floor conference room.

For the first order of business, General Sutherland read, in a strong and clear voice, General Order Number 1: "Japanese forces in Manchuria and northern Korea would capitulate to the Russians, while units in

Indochina, Formosa and China would surrender to the Chinese. All other Japanese combatants would surrender to the Americans and the British.''

Then General Sutherland got down to the details of the occupation. Among other things, General Sutherland instructed the Japanese delegation to have four hundred trucks and one hundred sedans on Atsugi Airfield ready for the Americans who would start arriving on 23 August. The Japanese were concerned about only one thing in the American plans—the decision to use Atsugi for the arrival airfield and the date of arrival. The Japanese pointed out that Atsugi was the training base for kamikaze pilots, and a large number of them who refused to surrender lived in the vicinity of the field.

The Japanese fear was not without foundation. Before 14 August, when Emperor Hirohito had broadcast to the Japanese people his unprecedented, recorded, five-minute radio speech announcing the surrender, two fiery, undaunted, and unrepentant Japanese officers, Maj. Kemji Hatanaka and Col. Masataka Ida, mutinied and tried to prevent the radio station from playing the record that Hirohito had previously made. Hatanaka and Ida, with a rebel company led by Capt. Takeo Sasaki, torched the house of the prime minister, Kantaro Suzuki, when they found that he had escaped, invaded the palace grounds, and killed Gen. Takeshi Mori, the commander of the Imperial Guard Division. The palace guard sealed the palace grounds. The rebellion fell apart when Gen. Shizuicki Tanaka, the commander of the Eastern District Army, refused to go along with the mutineers. Ida went to the home of General Anami, the war minister, and tried to persuade him to join the coup. Anami refused and the next day committed *seppuku,* a painful death by dagger thrusts across and into the abdomen. On the morning of 15 August, with the mutiny a failure, Hatanaka put a bullet through his head with the same weapon he used to kill General Mori; Ida performed the rite of *seppuku* and then shot himself.

General MacArthur's staff was also opposed to landing at Atsugi, calling it "a gamble." The staff pointed out to General MacArthur that on the Kanto Plain of Tokyo alone there were twenty-two Japanese divisions made up of 300,000 well-trained fighting troops. General MacArthur, of course, had the final word. Later he wrote, somewhat grandiosely, "Years of overseas duty had schooled me well in the lessons of the Orient and, what was probably more important, had taught the Far East that I was its friend." General Sutherland did, however, agree to postpone the landings on Atsugi until 28 August.

On Okinawa, General Swing, as ordered by GHQ, formed an honor guard for General MacArthur. Each 11th Airborne infantry regiment furnished a double-sized platoon of soldiers with the proviso that each man had to be taller than five feet eleven inches. Captain Carter of the 187th was in charge of the company that was attached to the 3d Battalion of the 188th, commanded by Maj. Thomas Mesereau, six feet three inches tall, and an all-American tackle from West Point. Captain Leo Crawford commanded the sixty-six-man platoon from the 188th.

On 24 August, the 11th Airborne Division published Field Order Number 34. Paragraph 2a stated:

11th Airborne Division (Major General J. M. Swing, U.S. Army, Commanding) will:

(1) Land by airborne movement on Atsugi Airdrome and immediately seize and secure the field for additional airborne operations.

(2) Evict all Japanese from the area surrounding the airfield to a distance of three miles and secure the airfield.

(3) Furnish security for advance echelon, General Headquarters, U.S. Army Forces Pacific, Eighth Army and other subordinate units as directed.

(4) Occupy the initial area of evacuation to include the city of Yokohama.

(5) Prepare for further occupation operations in Northern Honshu.

(5) b. Target date: Z Day: 28 August 1945; H-Hour: to be announced.

By 28 August, General Ryan's command had assembled on Okinawa almost every C-54 from around the world, enough so that no other military type of plane was needed. He had also obtained some airplanes from the civilian airlines. "From the heights above Kadena Strip, the silver four-engined transports seemed to stretch endlessly in all directions," wrote one of the 11th's troopers. For the division's planners, the use of only the C-54, in cargo and passenger configurations, made the planning simpler. The plan called for both cargo and personnel planes to depart Okinawa at the rate of fifteen planes per hour for eleven hours per day. The timetable called for one takeoff every three minutes for the first forty-two minutes in each hour and land in the same order, flying to Atsugi singly, not in formation. The last eighteen minutes of each hour were used for takeoffs at Atsugi. Initially, the plan called for no night landings or takeoffs because the Japanese lights and control devices on Atsugi were inadequate.

The target date for the start of the airlift had to be postponed for two days because of additional typhoons. But on 28 August, an advanced party headed up by Col. Charles Trench of General MacArthur's staff landed at Atsugi. Thus was Japan's soil touched for the first time by the boots of an enemy soldier. The party included Air Corps communications, control, and ground crews and staff representatives from the 11th Airborne—headed up by Maj. Paul Ellis of the G-3 Section. On about 20 August, Doug Quandt, the G-3, had been evacuated to a hospital in the States with an unknown ailment, and Lt. Col. Henry Burgess became the acting G-3.

On 29 August, the first echelon of the division started to load its aircraft for takeoff at 0100 the next morning. General Swing, Col. Alex Williams, the division chief of staff, and the principal staff officers would be on the first plane to land. General Swing had procured a large American flag from the Okinawa Command and loaded it on the first plane. He also had painted in large letters, "CP 11th Airborne Division," on a large, ten-foot-high piece of white canvas that also went on the first plane. General Pierson and the alternate division staff would be on the second plane to land.

At 0600 on 30 August, General Swing's C-54 touched down on Atsugi, the first plane in a seemingly endless string of transport aircraft ferrying the 11th Airborne Division into Japan for the start of the peaceful occupation of that country, an event that the troops of the 11th thought impossible just days ago. The next phase in the division's chronicle was underway.

CHAPTER 19

OCCUPATION BEGINS

After General Swing's plane touched down and taxied to a stop at Atsugi, he was the first man down its steps. He was dressed in battle fatigues, jump boots, and a steel helmet with "11 AB" stenciled on its front; he carried a .38 pistol on his belt and wore a bandolier of .38-caliber rounds diagonally across his chest. Combat readiness—not diplomacy—was obviously uppermost in his mind.

General Pierson's plane was next to land. "I rode in style on the last leg of our airlift to Japan," he said. "The plane which I boarded shortly after midnight was a United Airlines plush job, complete with a UAL crew including stewards. We were even served an in-flight breakfast and were given box lunches to take with us. It was a stateside breakfast—I had not seen a California navel orange for over a year. . . . It was daylight when we could see the outline of Honshu and then we could pick up Mount Fuji looming in the distance—a most welcome sight. The shooting war was over."

By the time General Pierson's plane pulled up abreast of a hangar that would become the 11th Airborne's first CP on Japanese soil, men who had debarked from General Swing's plane were already on the roof of a hangar on the east end of the runway erecting a crude iron pipe to serve as a flagpole. Hanging from it was the large American flag that General Swing had brought with him. The huge white sign indicating the location of the 11th Airborne CP was hanging on a wall of the hangar. The infantrymen who had been on General Swing's plane had already moved out to predesignated positions around the airfield; they were joined shortly by the contingent from General Pierson's plane. The 511th Signal Company also had on board the second plane a team with radio equipment strong enough to reach back to Okinawa.

Hundreds of trucks were parked at the end of the runway. "Nearby was a 'battalion' of Korean laborers also for our use as needed," General Pierson recalled. "The trucks were a sorry sight—many of them had charcoal burners attached to the rear which furnished fuel. The drivers were Japanese soldiers who didn't stay with us very long."

About twenty minutes after General Swing stepped on the Atsugi Airport tarmac, he had established his CP in the hangar. The entire CP consisted of one small folding table and a chair. Shortly thereafter, Colonel Tench and a small Japanese delegation, headed by a lieutenant general, arrived. The Japanese general and his interpreter, a captain "with an Oxford accent," according to Henry Burgess, were in a long black Packard limousine. After the Japanese senior officer got out, he bowed and extended his hand for the traditional handshake, but General Swing ignored the gesture. General Swing noted immediately that the Japanese officers were wearing short daggers on their belts. He told Colonel Tench to have the Japanese take off those "frog stickers" and that he would talk to them only after they had done so. The Japanese, through an interpreter, told General Swing that the daggers were "signs of authority." General Swing replied that from now on, he was the authority and the daggers would come off. They did.

The leader of the Japanese delegation told General Swing that there were still two regiments of kamikazes who had as yet not laid down their arms, and he asked General Swing to keep his troops within the specified area and within the time schedule previously agreed upon by the delegation that had gone to Manila. General Pierson remembered, "Although we were combat ready, our advance element was quite small and the best we could do was to have about a regimental combat team on the ground by the time of General MacArthur's arrival which was scheduled at 2:00 P.M. We were told before noon that the kamikazes had laid down their arms and were being returned to their homes."

The Japanese delegation wanted to take an American senior officer to Yokohama to make arrangements for General MacArthur's arrival.

General Swing told Burgess to go with the group. Burgess got into the Packard with the Japanese general and the interpreter. The old Packard, recalls Burgess,

> had been beautifully maintained. It "purred" slowly through thousands of Japanese troops who were surrendering their arms and leaving the barracks of the Japanese Army to go home. We proceeded to a large, well-appointed building and into a beautifully furnished meeting room with long tables, highly polished, at which sat about fifteen officers representing the Navy, Army and Air Force. All were sitting erect, obviously disappointed and humiliated to be discussing the surrender of their country with such a young lieutenant colonel, a lowly rank, dressed in a much-laundered and faded cotton khaki uniform.
>
> Discussion was had about the time of arrival of General MacArthur—he was to enter Japan and be driven in a limousine escorted by American troops in trucks into Yokohama. The entire route from the airport to the New Grand Hotel in Yokohama would be guarded by Japanese troops standing 50 yards between soldiers on both sides of the road. Trucks would be available for our soldiers to precede MacArthur as a bodyguard and to follow him and establish a perimeter around the area of the New Grand Hotel where General MacArthur would be establishing his headquarters. It took about an hour to complete the details and the arrangements. . . .

After an altercation in which Burgess and a Japanese general had a shoving standoff, the interpreter and the senior general drove Burgess back to the 11th's hangar CP. Burgess debriefed General Swing about the arrangements for the arrival of General MacArthur and the areas the division would occupy. The staff began making detailed plans to deploy troops between Atsugi and Yokohama and around the New Grand Hotel.

The troopers of the 11th continued to pour into the airfield in the rapidly landing C-54s. In the second serial came Maj. Tom Mesereau's 3d Battalion of the 188th and the Honor Guard Company. Shortly thereafter the band landed.

General Swing sent Major Mesereau, his battalion, and the Honor Guard to the Grand Hotel in Yokohama, the site of General MacArthur's Headquarters for the next few days. Earlier, General MacArthur's Headquarters had asked Swing, as he later recorded, to designate "a colorful young officer to be present at the signing of the historic document and to depart for Washington with the document, pictures, movies, and sound recordings immediately after the event. Have selected a youngster by the name of Tom Mesereau, recently received a combat promotion to major and the command of an infantry battalion. Is 6 ft 3, weight 210, was all-American tackle, class of January 1943 at the Point. He should make the brass hats appear rather colorless in comparison."

General Pierson followed the battalion into Yokohama about an hour after it had left Atsugi. He remembers,

It was an eerie ride as we went through the several deserted villages that were between Atsugi and Yokohama. The houses appeared to be unoccupied but in one village a small boy came out to look at our jeep. His mother dashed behind him and snatched him up carrying him back into the house. Hundreds of Japanese soldiers lined the entire length of the road making it a point to face away from us as we went by. I learned several years later from Iwatana Uchiyama, the Governor of Kanagawa Prefecture, that his office had been charged with preventing any outward occurrence marring the landing of the Occupation Forces. The prefecture stationed 20,000 policemen and 30,000 auxiliary policemen in the Atsugi Airfield area and along the road to Yokohama and to patrol the occupied districts of Yokohama and Yokosuka cities. Yokosuka was the landing place for our naval forces.

Many square blocks in Yokohama had been devastated by the B-29 bombings although most of the rubble had been cleared away. The port area with its docks and business buildings remained unscathed along with a number of sections in the city. The Grand Hotel had no battle scars and, when I arrived there, Mesereau's battalion was already in place. The combat veteran troops presented a splendid appearance, proud that they were part of the division that had been selected by General MacArthur to spearhead the arrival of the Occupation Forces and that they in turn had been designated as his "Palace Guard" in Yokohama.

Major John Conable, the division G-4, was also in the first plane to land. He started immediately to make arrangements for troop movements, ration distribution, and supply dumps. He wrote later:

One of the surrender terms required the Japanese to furnish us with a number of motor vehicles. I went down to look them over. There was a 1939 Cadillac in good condition for General MacArthur's use. I couldn't believe the trucks. There were alcohol burners, charcoal burners, steamers, and even a few still operating on gasoline. The tires were bald with

many of them showing fabric. After one look, I was on the radio telling
Okinawa to send me the best truck mechanics from the 711th Ordnance
Company as fast as possible no matter who had to be bumped.

About ten that morning, I went to get some trucks to move some
supplies. All the Japanese drivers had disappeared. I asked my shadowing
Japanese officer what was going on. He was very apologetic. The soldiers
had been told that as soon as the Americans arrived they could leave the
Army and go home. They were all anxious to go home. If true, a most
encouraging sign. I began to feel better.

About an hour after Burgess had debriefed General Swing in the
Atsugi hangar, the Japanese limousine and its two passengers, the Japanese
general and his interpreter, appeared once again near the CP. The Japanese
general dismounted and walked about a hundred yards from the car.
According to Burgess,

Swing told me to "come on," and headed for the limousine. Arriving
first, Swing jerked open the door and we got in. In his Oxford accent,
the interpreter told Swing that he couldn't use the car, as it was reserved
for the Chief of Staff of the Imperial Army. Swing roared, "Goddamn
it, we won the war, drive me down the strip." The driver drove us
down the strip. Swing wanted to see the troops arriving, assembling,
and expanding over the area. As Swing stepped out of the vehicle, the
Japanese captain with the British accent commented to me, "Well, Sir,
Generals are alike in all armies."

The shuttle from Okinawa continued to bring in the 11th Airborne
troops throughout the day. The troops immediately moved out and
strengthened the perimeter around the Atsugi Airfield. General Eichelberger and a small Eighth Army staff arrived about noon. General Eichelberger moved to the 11th Airborne's CP to check on the details for General
MacArthur's arrival. By 1400, Generals Eichelberger and Swing, members of their staffs, and the 11th Airborne Band were assembled for
the arrival of the supreme commander himself. Among those on the
ground and in General MacArthur's circling plane, there was still some
concern that a single fanatic or small groups of kamikazes might wish
to make the supreme sacrifice and attack General MacArthur. Fortunately,
things went smoothly.

"At two o'clock in the afternoon," General MacArthur wrote, "my
C-54, *Bataan* emblazoned on its nose, soared above Kamakura's giant

bronze Buddha, past beautiful Mt. Fuji, and swung down toward Atsugi.''

General Whitney, who was acting as General MacArthur's secretary, wrote later of his emotions at this significant occasion in the history of both Japan and the U.S.

We circled the field at little more than treetop height, and as I looked out at the field and the flat stretches of Kanto Plain, I could see numerous anti-aircraft emplacements. It was difficult not to let my mind dwell on Japan's recent performances. The war had been started without a formal declaration; nearly everywhere Japanese soldiers had refused to give up until killed; the usual laws of war had not been complied with; deadly traps had frequently been set. Here was the greatest opportunity for a final and climactic act. The anti-aircraft guns could not possibly miss at this range. Had death, the insatiable monster of the battle, passed MacArthur by on a thousand fields only to murder him at the end? I held my breath. I think the whole world was holding its breath. But as usual, he had been right. He knew the Orient. He knew the basic Japanese character too well to have thus gambled blindly with death. He knew and trusted that national spirit of traditional chivalry called ''Bushido.''

The stage was set for the arrival of the supreme commander. General MacArthur had rarely been upstaged by anyone and, on this occasion, he was not going to be. *Bataan* taxied up to the waiting American group and stopped. The door of the plane opened and the ramp was lowered to the ground. General MacArthur appeared at the door of the plane and stopped. He was dressed in ribbonless khakis with his shirt open at the throat and trousers with pleats (probably the only officer in the U.S. Army who wore pleated khaki trousers) and wearing his customary summer khaki garrison hat with the gold-encrusted visor and crown. His corncob pipe stuck out of his mouth at a jaunty angle. Obviously, he savored the historic and histrionic moment. More than any other event, his arrival signaled the defeat of Japan.

The 11th Airborne band played the ruffles and flourishes appropriate for a five-star general and then launched into the ''General's March.'' General Eichelberger strode forward to welcome General MacArthur. They shook hands and General MacArthur said in a quiet voice: ''Bob, from Melbourne to Tokyo is a long way, but this seems to be the end of the road. This is the payoff.''

Behind the band, the Japanese had assembled a number of vehicles for General MacArthur and his staff to move to Yokohama. General Whitney wrote,

MacArthur climbed into an American Lincoln of uncertain vintage. The other officers found their places in a ramshackle motorcade. A fire engine that resembled the Toonerville Trolley started with an explosion that made some of us jump; then it led the way as the procession headed for Yokohama. That was when I saw the first armed troops in Japan proper.

All along the roadway the fifteen miles to Yokohama they stood in a long line on each side, their backs to MacArthur in a gesture of respect. They were guarding the American Supreme Commander in the exact fashion that they guarded their Emperor.

The fact that the Japanese police and soldiers along the route to Yokohama turned their backs on the American convoys upset and confused some of the Americans initially. Some men felt that the Japanese were scorning them; others felt that "They could not bear to look upon the face of their conqueror." Still others, including General Whitney, thought that they were paying MacArthur the same respect they paid their emperor.

Ralph E. Ermatinger was the commander of the 511th contingent of the honor guard for General MacArthur. He reports a different reason for the "backs to the road." He wrote about the trip of the honor guard and Mesereau's battalion this way:

Fact: Each Japanese soldier turned away from the road because he was commanded to do so by a civilian interpreter standing in the lead truck of the convoy. The interpreter was ordered to do this by a U.S. Army captain who also stood in the lead truck.

As commander of the 511th contingent of the Honor Guard for General MacArthur, I, too, stood in the lead truck and witnessed the shouted commands to "about face" and saw the look of uncertainty and confusion on the faces of the Japanese soldiers who appeared to have been given other orders.

John Conable reports yet another version. He had a seventeen-year-old interpreter who had been born in Hawaii, spent twelve years there, and then, because of the possibility of war, was sent back to Japan by his parents to live with his grandparents. Conable wrote:

I commented to him [his interpreter] that we were amazed that there had been no incidents.

He replied, "Of course, there have been no incidents. You know the Emperor made a speech on the radio asking all his subjects to cooperate with you. You know the Emperor had never spoken to us on the radio before. Wasn't that a wonderful thing for him to do?"

I was astounded that a man who had spent his first twelve years in America would have that attitude but it explained why we had had no trouble. It also explained the soldiers who charged a machine gun armed with bamboo spears. In 1945 the Japanese would do anything for their Emperor—even cooperate with the Americans.

Leo Crawford, the CO of the 188th's Honor Guard Platoon, noted that when they drove into Tokyo, they did not see "any females between the ages of 8 and 70. Even those had baggy clothes on to hide any feminine identification. Evidently the Japs expected us to come in raping and looting as they always did." He also reported that as a member of the honor guard he spent part of his first night in Yokohama in the Grand Hotel until he was ranked out of his room by a general officer. He also pointed out that, although the 1st Cavalry was to be the first U.S. division to occupy Tokyo, he and some other officers from the honor guard went into Tokyo and had dinner at the Imperial Hotel a few days before the arrival of the 1st Cavalry. The officers signed chits for the meals, which, Crawford supposes, were never redeemed.

General MacArthur and his party arrived at the New Grand Hotel in Yokohama late in the afternoon of 30 August. The first Grand Hotel had been destroyed by the earthquake of 1923; its successor, the New Grand, "a magnificent establishment," according to General Whitney, survived WW II intact. He added,

> The manager and his staff all but prostrated themselves as they greeted us and showed us to the suite selected for General MacArthur. We were tired and hungry, and we lost no time in going to the dining room, where amid the other American officers and almost surrounded by solicitous hotel officials, we were seated and served a steak dinner.
>
> I found it difficult to resist the impulse to snatch MacArthur's plate away from him that first night and make sure that his food had not been poisoned. When I voiced my misgivings to him, he merely laughed and said: "No one can live forever."

By the end of the day on 30 August 1945, 123 C-54s had landed at Atsugi, bringing in 4,200 troopers of the division and other units. The first serials brought in no large vehicles or heavy equipment because General Swing wanted the maximum number of men, lightly equipped, to land initially, given the unknown enemy situation on the ground. What equipment that was brought in was essential: two jeeps and one water trailer per regiment, a five-day supply of 10-in-1 rations, and squad rolls. The 188th landed first with 1,096 men; then came the 187th with 1,257 men. The 511th landed next with 1,165 troopers. Mixed in with the division's serials were GHQ personnel, Eighth Army staffers, Air Corps equipment and men to operate Atsugi, and correspondents and photographers. The Division 511th Signal Company and the 127th Engineers brought in skeleton crews.

By the evening of 30 August, Colonel Lahti's 511th was in Yokohama and posted the Yokohama-Tokyo road to a point about eight miles beyond Yokohama. Colonel Tipton's 188th had fanned out from Atsugi toward Fujisawa; Colonel Pearson's 187th remained in the Atsugi area; and the division CP had moved to the Sun Oil Compound in Yokohama. The compound contained about fifteen American-style homes complete with furniture, dishes, silver, and linens. Other more senior staffs (Eighth Army, for example) were not as fortunate and ended up with their command posts in warehouses, without central heat, on the docks. The troops of the 11th were initially quartered and fed in the nearby Yokohama race track. One company moved into an exclusive businessmen's club there—"the lap of luxury," General Pierson called it.

On 1 September, the 1st Cavalry Division's ships docked at piers in Yokohama. The 11th Airborne's band was on hand to greet the debarking cavalrymen. One of the numbers the band played was "The Old Gray Mare," which many of the troops in the 11th thought was quite appropriate.

Eli Bernheim and Dick Barker had established the 187th's S-4 office in one of the hangars at Atsugi. Bernheim remembers,

Outside of our hangar were parked numerous aircraft that belonged to Generals etc., who were there for the surrender ceremonies. One was a B-17 belonging to General Stilwell, remodeled with several cots and a desk and chairs. One night there was a knock on the door. I opened the door and there stood Gen. Stilwell in his campaign hat with 4 stars. He was accompanied by BG Merrill of Merrill's Marauders. Gen. Stilwell said, "All of those people are down in Yokohama patting themselves on the back and telling each other how they won the war. We came back to sleep on my plane, and I smelled some coffee and thought we might bum a cup." That turned out to be a memorable evening for a first lieutenant.

W. C. Kitchen of the 511th Signal Company was walking down the street in Yokohama when a Japanese officer stopped him and asked:

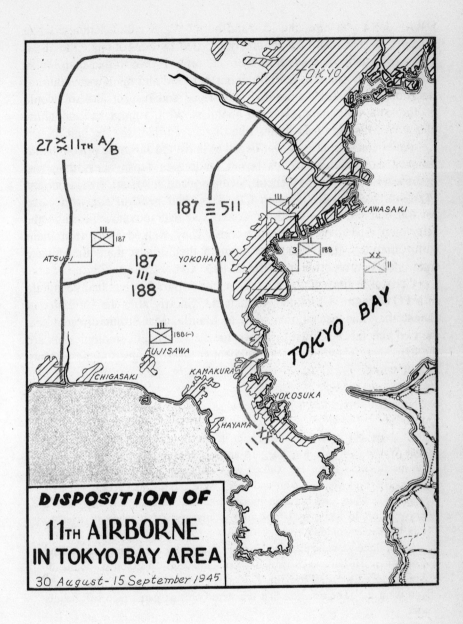

27 ⊠⊠ 11TH A/B

187 ☰ 511

187 ||| 188

187

188(—)

TOKYO

KAWASAKI

ATSUGI

YOKOHAMA

3 ⊠ 188

XX 11

FUJISAWA

CHIGASAKI

KAMAKURA

TOKYO BAY

YOKOSUKA

HAYAMA ||| XX

DISPOSITION OF
11TH AIRBORNE
IN TOKYO BAY AREA
30 August – 15 September 1945

"Why don't you rape and loot and burn? We would." Kitchen wrote recently, "That man was genuinely puzzled by our actions. . . . I am ashamed to tell you what an inadequate reply I gave to that man. What an opportunity I had to tell him about our God and his laws, about our traditions. . . . All we wanted was peace and respect and we would do the same for others, even our enemies. Well, I mumbled something about 'We just don't do things like that.' And that was the end of it."

American prisoners of war began to leave the Japanese prison camps as soon as American troops began landing in Japan. Less than two hours after the arrival of General Swing's plane at Atsugi, two American POWs arrived at the division CP. They had been in a prison camp several hundred miles south of Tokyo and had somehow heard of the scheduled arrival of American troops. They walked away from their camp after the guards had left them to themselves; then they rode a train north and reported in to the division CP.

General Wainwright and Lt. Gen. Sir Arthur Percival had been held in a POW camp in Mukden, Manchuria. Shortly after the surrender of Japan, they had been flown back to Manila. MacArthur directed that the two generals be flown to Tokyo for the surrender ceremonies aboard the *Missouri*. They arrived in Yokohama on 31 August. General Mac-Arthur wrote:

> I was just sitting down to dinner when my aide brought me the word that they [Wainwright and Percival] had arrived. I rose and started for the lobby, but before I could reach it, the door swung open and there was Wainwright. He was haggard and aged. His uniform hung in folds on his fleshless form. He walked with difficulty and with the help of a cane. His eyes were sunken and there were pits in his cheeks. His hair was snow white and his skin looked like old shoe leather. He made a brave effort to smile as I took him in my arms, but when he tried to talk his voice wouldn't come.
>
> For three years he imagined himself in disgrace for having surrendered Corregidor. He believed he would never again be given an active command. This shocked me. "Why, Jim," I said, "your old corps is yours when you want it." The emotion that registered on that gaunt face still haunts me.

The morning of 2 September (3 September in Japan) was yet another momentous and significant date in the annals of the world's history. On that morning, the U.S. battleships *Missouri* and *South Dakota* and the British battleship *Duke of York* and hundreds of other warships were at anchor in Tokyo Bay. The *Missouri* would be the site for the surrender. President Truman, at Navy Secretary Forrestal's suggestion, selected the *Missouri* as the surrender site to soothe the feelings of Admiral Nimitz, who was annoyed that MacArthur would oversee the surrender ceremonies and that the army would take the spotlight in a war that Nimitz felt had been a navy show.

At 0500 on the morning of 2 September, the Japanese delegation of eleven men left Tokyo by auto. General Yoshijiro Umezu, the army chief of staff, represented the supreme command, and Mamoru Shigemitsu, the one-legged foreign minister, represented the government. General Umezu had threatened to commit hara-kiri rather than be a member of the delegation, but the emperor personally persuaded him to take part. An hour later, the delegation boarded the destroyer *Lansdown* at the Yokohama dock. The *Lansdown* was one of four destroyers ferrying observers and officials out to the *Missouri*. Colonel Sidney F. Mashbir of MacArthur's staff, a master intelligence officer well versed in the Japanese language, was the escort officer. Toshikazu Kase, a graduate of Amherst and Harvard and a member of the Japanese party, wrote later: "As the destroyer pushed out of the harbor, we saw in the offing lines on lines of gray warships, both heavy and light, anchored in majestic array. This was the mighty pageant of the Allied navies that so lately belched forth their crashing battle, now holding in the swift thunder and floating like calm sea birds on the subjugated waters."

After an eighteen-mile trip, taking about an hour, the *Lansdown* pulled alongside the *Missouri*. The Japanese probably did not know it, but the flag flying from the mainmast of the *Missouri* was the same flag that had been flying above the Capitol in Washington on 7 December 1941. Mounted on the ship was another flag with only thirty-four stars. It was the banner flown by Admiral Perry on his flagship *Powhatan* when he entered Tokyo Bay in 1854. Admiral Halsey had had the Naval Academy rush the flag from its museum in time for the ceremony.

A little after 0800, a barge from the *South Dakota* pulled alongside the *Missouri* and Admiral Nimitz climbed aboard. Shortly thereafter, the *Nichols* arrived at the *Missouri,* and General MacArthur debarked. On board, MacArthur looked over the assembled brass, shook hands with Admirals Nimitz and Halsey, and said, "It's grand to have so many of my colleagues from the shoestring days here at the end of the road." After MacArthur was aboard, at 0815 the Japanese delegation climbed with some difficulty up the gangway of the *Missouri*. Shigemitsu led the way, leaning heavily on his cane. General Umezu followed him.

Kase recalled the scene.

> There were row upon row of American admirals and generals in somber khaki; but what added to the festive gaiety of the occasion was the sight of war correspondents who, monkeylike, hung on to every clifflike point of vantage in most precarious postures. . . . Then there was a gallery of spectators who seemed numberless, overcrowding every bit of available space on the great ship, on the mast, on the chimneys, on the gun turrets— on everything and everywhere. . . . As we appeared on the scene we were, I felt, being subjected to the torture of the pillory. There were a million eyes beating on us in the million shafts of a rattling storm of arrows barbed with fire. . . . Never have I realized that the glance of glaring eyes could hurt so much.

After the Japanese delegates were in place in two rows in front of a mess table covered with green felt, MacArthur walked from the interior of the *Missouri* and took his place behind the table, faced the Japanese, and began to speak:

> We are gathered here, representatives of the major warring parties, to conclude a solemn agreement whereby peace may be restored. The issues, involving divergent ideals and ideologies, have been determined on the battlefields of the world and hence are not for our discussion or debate. . . .
>
> It is my earnest hope and indeed the hope of all mankind that from this solemn occasion a better world shall emerge out of the blood and carnage of the past. . . . As Supreme Commander for the Allied Powers, I announce it my firm purpose, in the tradition of the country I represent, to proceed in the discharge of my responsibilities with justice and tolerance, while taking all necessary dispositions to insure that the terms of surrender are fully, promptly and faithfully complied with.

After the speech, MacArthur stepped back from the table and motioned to Shigemitsu to come forward and sign the surrender document. The Japanese foreign minister limped forward and took a seat at the table. He took off his yellow gloves and silk top hat, put them on the table, and then stared at the document for a few moments. "Show him where to sign," MacArthur said to General Sutherland, who stepped forward and showed Shigemitsu the line for his signature. General Umezu was next. He marched forward, refused to sit, signed almost with a slash, and strode, ramrod straight, back to his place.

Next it was General MacArthur's turn. He picked up three pens, and with one wrote his signature a few letters at a time. He gave the second pen to General Wainwright and the third to General Percival; he pocketed the first, a bright red one, for his wife and son. Admiral Nimitz then signed for the United States, and representatives of other Allied nations signed for their countries. When all the representatives had finished, MacArthur said: "Let us pray that peace be now restored to the world and that God will preserve it always. These proceedings are closed."

General MacArthur walked over to Admiral Halsey, put an arm around his shoulder, and said to him: "Bill, where in the hell are those airplanes?" According to Kase, at that moment, "the skies parted and the sun shone brightly through the layers of clouds. There was a steady drone above and now it became a deafening roar and an armada of airplanes paraded into sight, sweeping over the warships. Four hundred B-29's and 1,500 carrier planes joined in the aerial pageant in a final salute. It was over."

And with the signing of the surrender documents on the *Missouri,* the greatest disaster in the recorded history of man was over. After six years of war; the loss of 55 million civilians and soldiers; the destruction of untold and uncounted cities, factories, transportation facilities, and ports; and the loss of countless millions of dollars worth of minerals and materials; the guns, grenades, bombs, rockets, and rifles were finally silent. "Fix bayonets" became a command reserved for the parade grounds. The truly global World War II was over.

CHAPTER 20

JAPAN

From 30 August until 7 September, the C-54s and civilian transports continued to ferry the troopers of the 11th from Kadena on Okinawa to Atsugi. The first serials on 30 August departed Kadena in an orderly fashion because, for the first lift, the 11th Airborne staff knew exactly where the planes were parked on the field, could make specific assignments of aircraft by number to each unit, and knew the types of loads—passenger and cargo—that the planes could carry. After the initial serials took off, however, the plans fell apart. The G-3 Air Section of the division would call units to the field only to discover that the weather had closed in and flights were not possible. Then the unit, which had already closed out of its bivouac area, could only sit under the planes' wings and wait. In other situations, some returning planes would need repairs, which would throw off the schedule. In addition, the units had a difficult time finding their planes on the taxiways because, after the planes returned from their first flights, they parked wherever they could find space on the ramps and taxiways. In spite of these problems, however, the division closed at Atsugi on 7 September. In the previous nine days, the ATC–Far East, under the command of Maj. Gen. William O. Ryan and his assistant commander Brigadier General Alexander, moved 11,708 men, 640 tons of supplies, and more than 600 jeeps and trailers of the 11th

Airborne Division. It was the longest (1,600 miles) and largest air-transported troop movement ever attempted and completed.

Initially, the division staff broke down its zone of responsibility in the Tokyo Bay area into regimental-sized areas. The 187th CP stayed at Atsugi. The 511th set up its CP in Yokohama on Tokyo Bay and patrolled as far north as the Tama Gawa, the river separating Yokohama from Tokyo. The 188th RCT, with its CP at Fujisawa, was responsible for the southern sector of the division zone. The Fleet Landing Force, the 4th Marine RCT, was responsible for the Yokosuka Naval Base area. And the 27th Division, which followed right behind the 11th into Atsugi and which had been helped in its air move by a detail from the 11th, occupied an area to the west and north of Atsugi.

After the signing of the surrender documents on 2 September, troops and equipment continued to land steadily. The G-4 and the quartermaster established supply dumps in the hangars at Atsugi using, for the most part, Japanese labor to unload planes, drive their makeshift trucks, and work in the supply depots.

On 8 September, General MacArthur left the Grand Hotel in Yokohama and traveled the twenty-two miles to the American Embassy in Tokyo, destined to be his home throughout his days as the supreme commander in Japan. He wrote that the trip was "22 miles of devastation and vast piles of charred rubble." His headquarters would be in the Dai Ichi Building in downtown Tokyo, across the moat surrounding the emperor's palace.

In their zones of responsibility, the 11th and the other divisions of Eighth Army occupying Japan carried out, to some degree, the tasks outlined by General MacArthur. One of them was to assist in the demobilization of the Japanese armed forces. On 2 September, those forces numbered 6,983,000 troops in some 154 army divisions. On the home islands there were 2,576,000 troops making up fifty-seven divisions, fourteen brigades, and forty-five regiments. The rest of the armed forces were scattered along a huge arc from Manchuria to the Solomons and on the islands in the Central and Southwest Pacific. The responsibility for the demobilization of this huge force fell to the Japanese army and navy ministers. But, according to General MacArthur, "Eighth Army and the U.S. Navy supervised and coordinated this complicated and top-priority operation, but it was the Japanese themselves who performed the task."

The U.S. forces were impressed from the beginning of the occupation with the total surrender of the Japanese people, a surrender amounting almost to subservience. There were no incidents of revolt against the U.S. forces. The entire structure of the Japanese military and civilian establishments reversed themselves from wartime belligerency to peacetime acquiescence. General MacArthur wrote:

> Let there be no mistake about the extent of Japan's defeat in the war. It was completely crushed. Part of the defeat was physical, with factories, homes, and whole cities destroyed. But another part of that defeat was spiritual. For almost four years the Japanese people had expected nothing but victory. Every bulletin blared success. Not only that; the people had been told that they were fighting a kind of holy crusade against barbarians who had no respect for anything. The war must be won to prevent rape, murder, and other unspeakable crimes. . . . From the very beginning, I tried to erase this false conception. . . . I was determined that our principles during the occupation would be the same principles for which our soldiers had fought on the battlefield.

What made the occupation a relatively easy task for the supreme commander and his forces was the extent to which the civil government, taking its cue from the emperor, was able to instruct, even dominate the mass of the people and force them into complete cooperation with the occupying forces. As one of the 11th Airborne soldiers wrote after the war,

> We were amazed to find that the government which had produced the cunning, wily, almost beast-like men we had fought, could, in a few short days, impress on its vast population the need for conducting itself as a beaten race. Undoubtedly our extensive bombings had served to make known to the Japs at home that they were a defeated populace. But their country had not been invaded; the people were not aware of the complete extent of our victories on land, sea, and in the air; their towns and cities had not been overrun by a conquering enemy. Nevertheless, it was apparent that the Japanese, from the highest officials in the land down to the lowest classes of workers and farmers, were prepared actually, and seemingly mentally, to do our bidding.

On 14 September, the Americal Division relieved the 11th Airborne Division of its zone of responsibility in the Tokyo-Yokohama area; on 15 September, the 11th began its move by truck and rail to previously assigned sectors in northern Honshu. The motor convoy had been organized and headed by Brig. Gen. Frank Dorn, who had relieved Gen. Frank Farrell as commanding general of the 11th's Division Artillery in July, after General Farrell had become ill and left for the United States. General Dorn, a Chinese language student, had been with General Stilwell in China and made the trek with General Stilwell out of Burma. Thereafter, he stayed in the China theater with General Chiang Kai-shek until he went with General Stilwell to the Tenth Army on Okinawa. When General Stilwell visited the division at Lipa, General Swing asked General Stilwell to release General Dorn to the 11th. Stilwell agreed.

According to General Pierson, "General Dorn did very well in making billeting arrangements for the division in the Sendai area." Division Headquarters, the 127th Engineers, 408th Quartermaster, 711th Ordnance, 511th Signal, 221st Medical, Parachute Maintenance, and the 187th and the 188th were housed in a Japanese Army arsenal in the Sendai area (it would shortly be named Camp Schimmelpfennig, after the chief of staff who was killed in action). The 511th moved to a camp in Morioka, soon to be named Camp Haugen after the valiant leader of the 511th who was mortally wounded south of Manila. The 457th and the 152d moved to Akita; the 472d went to Yamagata; the 674th went to Jimmachi and Camp Younghans; and the 675th went to Yonezawa. In the Sendai area, the Japanese authorities turned over several small hotels in the beautiful Matsushima area for officers' quarters, with one set aside for the three general officers and Col. Alexander N. Williams, the chief of staff.

The movement of the troops by rail was a remarkable operation. The division G-4 Section ordered the Japanese to have trains at certain stations on a definite time schedule. Given the pounding that the railroads and trains had taken during the war, it was almost a miracle of management and improvisation that the Japanese railroad system met the schedule— on time. The cars were old and reminded one trooper of the pictures he had seen of the 40-and 8-cars from World War I. But by 17 September, the division had closed into its new areas of responsibility.

The movement of supplies north from Tokyo was not without its frustrations, difficulties, and even comic relief. Eli Bernheim, in the S-4 Section of the 187th, had the mission of moving a convoy of forty Japanese trucks loaded with supplies from Tokyo to Sendai. He wrote,

The trucks had charcoal burner devices and broke down constantly. Some had to be abandoned. I had a jeep with a siren and a Jap interpreter. I

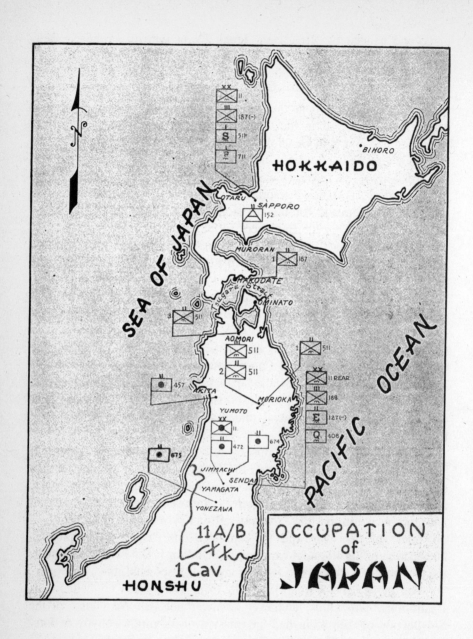

had another jeep with my platoon sergeant in the rear and the balance of my platoon with the Jap truck drivers. I can't recall how long it took to get to Sendai, but wherever we went the Jap village inhabitants fled in panic. Eventually the word got out that we were not doing any harm. We got lost and stopped at a village square that was paved with some type of stones. The interpreter and I spread the map on the stones and while trying to figure out where we were, I looked up and saw that we were surrounded by a crowd of curious Japs. I nervously shifted my carbine on my shoulder, and they scattered like rabbits. The interpreter suggested I lay my carbine down on the street beside the map, and the crowd came close enough to touch me and even touch my hair out of curiosity. It became apparent that they had never seen an American. From that time on we had it made. We were greeted at every town by the Mayor, etc., and given or offered all kinds of food and drink and thinking back it amazes me that we ever got to Sendai.

Once the division's units were in their respective areas, their immediate problem was to make the various camps livable. By the standards of Camp Polk, the Japanese barracks buildings that housed the elements of the division were primitive. The plumbing was almost medieval; the sewage was deposited in reservoirs and then collected by carts to be used as fertilizer on the Japanese farms and gardens. The division historian records that of all the traffic accidents within the division area, no 11th Airborne trooper was ever guilty of hitting a "honey-cart."

The barracks' heating systems were also crude and antiquated. Most buildings were heated by potbelly stoves, and numerous barracks fires attested to the fact that in the cold weather of northern Honshu, the 11th troopers tried to heat more of their barracks than the stoves would safely permit.

General Swing assigned General Pierson to command a newly organized Miyagi Task Force composed of the 187th and 188th Regiments. The task force set up headquarters in Sendai in a multistory building that had been built by a large insurance company. General Pierson assigned each regiment its own area of occupation responsibility.

Throughout the fall months of 1945, the troops spent more time on housing and patrolling than on anything else. John Conable summed up the division's tasks this way: "Our principal job was to collect and destroy all arms, munitions, and armament factories. We were also charged with seeing that General MacArthur's edicts were carried out."

General Pierson wrote:

We had lists of military installations in our zone. There were several arsenals listed and I visited them in turn. I spent a number of hours going through a large plant which was underground. Two long tunnels had been dug in a mountainside, each containing hundreds of machine tools of varying descriptions. Each tunnel had been cleaned of any debris but the machine tools had started to rust. I am certain that most of the tools, such as the lathes and drill presses, would eventually be converted to civilian use. . . . We sent word to the Governor's office that the disarmament applied to sporting shotguns and samurai swords. The people turned these in to the Japanese police, and I visited police stations to see that these items were properly secured. Many of the shotguns were handsomely tooled and must have cost a fortune. There was some anguish when it came to losing samurai swords that had been in families for generations. Some of the swords were ''appropriated'' as war mementoes and officers from Eighth Army Headquarters came to Sendai to select what they wanted.

For their own areas, the commanders of the units of the division had been furnished lists and locations of the Japanese military installations and the arms and equipment therein, which had to be demilitarized and destroyed. The task was more difficult because, at the installations, the commanders found that most of the Japanese soldiers had been demobilized. Colonel Tipton had in his area a submarine base for two-man subs. The naval commander complained that he had been left with only a handful of men and that he had been ordered to assemble all weapons and equipment and to guard them. He, too, he said, wanted to go home. General Swing said he decided that his troops ''were not about to take over a submarine base.''

By this time, early fall of 1945, many of the combat soldiers of the division had returned or were in the process of returning to the States and discharge based on the number of ''points'' they had accrued in their overseas service. Even General Pierson, who had been with the division since its activation, was transferred to Washington as the deputy G-4 of the Army Ground Forces in October 1945. He was replaced by Gen. Shorty Soule, who had commanded the 188th in training and in combat and had then been promoted to assistant division commander of the 38th Division.

Replacements—officers and enlisted men alike—were arriving by the hundreds. Many of them were not jump qualified. So for the fourth time in its history, the division established a jump school, this one at a former Japanese Air Corps installation near Yanome, about fifteen miles from Sendai.

After the rigors of combat, the troops in the occupation of Japan found life more than bearable. General Swing did everything possible to make the life of the soldier pleasant. Athletics, as usual, was high on General Swing's list of off-duty recreation for the troops. In the Sendai area, the main mecca for sports was the 11th Airborne Coliseum. It was formerly a Japanese auditorium so large that there was ample space for four basketball courts, a theater seating 2,500, and a boxing arena for 4,000 spectators. It had six bowling alleys imported from the States. It had a poolroom with one hundred pool tables. It also housed a Red Cross office, a snack bar, a library, a training room, and Special Services offices.

In the fall of 1945, an Olympiad of all sports was held in the Tokyo area for troops from Japan and Korea. In the major sports, football was the highlight. The division team, coached by Lt. Eugene Bruce of the 188th, won the Japan-Korea championship. Then the team took on the Hawaiian All-Stars in Mejii Stadium in Tokyo and won, 18–0, thereby winning the All Pacific Championship. The division became so successful in sports that, when the division won the finals of the boxing tournament of the Olympics at Sendai, the headline in the *Stars and Stripes* sports section read: "Ho-Hum, It's the Angels Again."

In the months after the surrender, the division moved its major elements a number of times. In February 1946, the War Department inactivated the 77th Division, and Eighth Army, still commanded by General Eichelberger, assigned the area of northern Honshu and the entire island of Hokkaido to the 11th Airborne as its zone of responsibility. The Division Headquarters and the 187th moved to the unbombed city of Sapporo. The 187th set up in the old Japanese Army barracks outside Sapporo, and the Division Headquarters moved into a bank building. The Grand Hotel became the bachelor officers' quarters. Sapporo was a city that had been partially laid out by American engineers. Wide streets, American-style buildings, and the ivy-covered walls of the University of Hokkaido reflected the American influence.

By June 1946, the division was located in four major areas: Division Headquarters and the 187th were in Sapporo and its outskirts; the 511th was at Hachinoe; Division Artillery was at Jimmachi; and the 188th and the bulk of Special Troops were at Sendai. At these four locations, the division built semipermanent camps with all stateside facilities.

The 11th Airborne's reputation for mission accomplishment, even though through somewhat unorthodox means, carried over into its occupation and housekeeping duties. For example, before dependents arrived, General Swing had a Japanese factory turning out American-style furniture for the quarters of the officers and enlisted men. General Headquarters was not happy with General Swing's initiative, because they were also working to have the Japanese build furniture for the entire command. But General Swing was impatient with the delays. On one of General Eichelberger's visits to Sapporo, and after he and his staff had had a chance to inspect the activities of the division, including the furniture factory and the better-than-GHQ-standard brick barracks under construction, General Eichelberger said to General Swing: "Joe, I don't know whether to court-martial you or commend you." He commended him later.

By the summer of 1946, wives and children of men who were interested in staying in the Occupation Forces for a year began to arrive. The first group docked in Yokohama on 24 June. Thereafter, a steady flow of dependents came on the scene and changed the entire complexion of the occupation. At first, the units took over Japanese homes for families, but later Japanese contractors built homes at the four major division locations. And to provide family cars, GHQ authorized the sale of surplus jeeps to officers and men with dependents in the theater. The GHQ quartermaster divided the surplus jeeps into three cost categories, depending upon their condition. Even the second-rated batch at $275 was a bargain. (All mine needed was a battery. The Japanese craftsmen in Sapporo upholstered it with fabric from a downed C-47 and made a body of plywood. It traversed with ease the Sapporo snow and ice and made its way frequently to the ski slopes on the site of the scheduled but unheld Winter Olympics of 1940.)

Training in the field and in division schools continued apace. The jump school qualified 3,376 jumpers between March and June 1946. The division flying school, on a former Japanese air base outside Sendai, and using the talents of the division's Cub pilots, qualified 25 officers and 75 enlisted men by June 1946. In the summer of 1946, the War Department decreed that all airborne soldiers be qualified as both paratroopers and glidermen, thus echoing an old policy of General Swing's. The division opened an airborne school at Yamoto and named it Carolus Field in honor of Corp. Charles H. Carolus, who was killed in a glider crash in Manila Bay on 22 July 1945. The airborne school trained one battalion at a time for a two-week period. The jump school moved to Carolus Field in July 1946.

The 11th Airborne Division was a lot of things to a lot of men. It was a crucible in which, in a very short time, boys "just off the farm" became highly trained soldiers with a will to fight. It was a unit in which men, inured to the hardships of training and then combat, became closer to one another than brothers and fought the hard and good fight, not so much because of discipline and fear of punishment but because they did not want to let their buddies down. As Leo Crawford put it: "Although I have been retired from the Army for 29 years and it has been 35 years since I left the 11th, I still feel an attachment for men I served with like Gamble, Lussier, Ringler and dozens of others that I feel for no others."

It was a small division, half the size of a standard infantry division in men and firepower, which, nonetheless, took on the missions of a full-sized division and proved that heart and courage and training and camaraderie and esprit and loyalty, not only up but down, engender self-confidence and invincibility, making giants of ordinary men. Then they become extraordinary. It was a combat division, a unified group of men cemented together with soul and pride, perhaps even arrogance and swagger. No matter. They were troopers of the 11th Airborne, a division tested on the most awesome of proving grounds, the bloody field of prolonged battle under abominable conditions of weather and hunger, which stretched men's durability beyond expectancy, against a cunning and ruthless enemy who fought under no rules of "civilized" land warfare. The 11th Airborne Division graduated magna cum laude.

EPILOGUE

ANGELS: The derivation of the nickname for the troopers of the 11th Airborne Division is somewhat obscure to many of the 11th's original members. Some attribute it to the Los Banos Raid, and the alleged comment of one of the nuns in the camp who said, on seeing John Ringler and B Company of the 511th jumping just a few hundred yards from the perimeter of the camp: "They are like angels from Heaven come to deliver us." But that is not the origin of the nickname.

The use of the word "Angels" in reference to the troopers of the division was probably initiated by Doug Quandt, then the CO of the 457th Parachute FA Battalion. John Conable was the Battery Commander of Service Battery of the 457th. He remembers a 457th Battery Commanders' meeting on a Monday morning in the summer of 1943 in which the conversation went something like this:

Quandt: "Martin, was everything all right in Hqs Battery over the weekend?"
Martin: "Yes, Sir."
Quandt: "Conable, any of your angels in jail?"
Conable: "No, Sir, not this weekend."
Quandt: "Utter, how about yours?"
Joe Utter: "Everything was all right."
Quandt: "Godsman, how many of your angels are in jail?"
And so the conversation went.

Later, through Doug Quandt's use of the term around the Division staff and General Swing, the nickname came into general use especially in and

396

around Camp Polk, where the men of the 11th resented the tankers' blatant and unauthorized wear of paratrooper boots, and in New Guinea, where the commanders of the various ports, having used the troopers of the 11th on unloading and stevedoring details, came to refer to the men of the 11th as "Joe Swing and his 8,000 thieves." General Swing is alleged to have said: "My angels wouldn't possibly be involved in such shenanigans."

DISTINGUISHED UNIT CITATIONS: In February 1945, the Commanding General of the Eighth Army, Lt. Gen. Robert L. Eichelberger, cited the entire division in an Eighth Army General Order for the division's bold and rapid move from Nasugbu and Tagaytay Ridge to Manila. He also recommended to the War Department that the entire division receive a Distinguished Unit Citation for that operation. The War Department, however, disapproved the DUC for the entire division but awarded the Distinguished Unit Citation to the following units:

Headquarters and Headquarters Company, 11th Airborne Division
1st Battalion, 187th Glider Infantry Regiment
Headquarters and Headquarters Company, 188th Glider Infantry Regiment
1st Battalion, 188th Glider Infantry Regiment
2d Battalion, 188th Glider Infantry Regiment
Headquarters and Headquarters Company, 511th Parachute Infantry Regiment
The Provisional Reconnaissance Platoon, 11th Airborne Division and Company B, 511th Parachute Infantry Regiment (for the Los Banos Operation)
1st Battalion, 511th Parachute Infantry Regiment
2d Battalion, 511th Parachute Infantry Regiment
3d Battalion, 511th Parachute Infantry Regiment
Air Section, 457th Parachute Field Artillery Battalion
D Battery, 457th Parachute Field Artillery Battalion
674th Glider Field Artillery Battalion
675th Glider Field Artillery Battalion
511th Airborne Signal Company

11TH AIRBORNE DIVISION POST-WORLD WAR II HISTORY. General Swing continued to command the division in Japan until January of 1948. He was succeeded by Gen. William M. Miley who commanded the division until 23 March 1949 when he was relieved by BG Lemuel Mathewson, the division artillery commander who became the acting division commander.

In May of 1949, the division was relieved of occupation duties in Japan and moved to Fort Campbell, Kentucky. Following the move, the 188th AIR was inactivated. In May of 1950, the division participated in Exercise Swarmer at Camp Mackall, NC.

On 1 September 1950, the 187th AIR and the 674th AFA Battalion were broken out of the division as a separate airborne regimental combat team and were ordered to Korea. The 187th was replaced by the reactivated 188th.

During the period September 1950 until December 1950, the division trained, processed, and prepared 13,000 recalled enlisted reservists for overseas shipment to Korea. In December 1950, Maj. Gen. Lyman L. Lemnitzer took over command of the division. On 2 March 1951, the 503d Air was reactivated and became an organic unit of the 11th at Fort Campbell. The Division now consisted of the 188th, the 511th, and the 503d airborne infantry regiments; the 544th, 89th, 457th, and 675th FA Battalions; the 88th AAA Battalion; the 127th Abn Engineer Battalion; the 76th and the 710th Tank Battalions; the 11th Medical Battalion; other special troop units.

On 15 October 1951, the division was transferred from Second to Third Army because Department of the Army had decided to combine all airborne training activities under Third Army. In November of 1951, General Lemnitzer was succeeded by BG Wayne C. Smith. On 15 January 1952, BG Ridgely Gaither succeeded General Smith; in April of 1953, MG Wayne C. Smith succeeded General Gaither in command. In 1954, the division participated in the atomic tests at Camp Desert Rock, Nevada. In May of 1955, MG Derrill McC.Daniel succeeded General Smith. In 1955, the 188th jumped into the jungle of Panama on a training exercise.

On 4 March 1956, the division left Fort Campbell on Operation Gyroscope and joined Seventh Army in Europe to replace the 5th Infantry Division in the Augsburg-Munich area of Germany. In October 1956, MG Hugh P. Harris succeeded General Daniel in command of the division in Germany. While in Germany the Division went "pentomic," i.e., five small battle groups instead of three larger regiments. In April 1958, General Harris was succeeded by MG Ralph C. Cooper who commanded the division until its inactivation, 1 July 1958. General Cooper was thus the last commander of the original 11th Airborne Division.

Department of the Army reactivated the division on 7 February 1963 as the 11th Air Assault Division (Test) at Fort Benning, Georgia. As a test division, the 11th was not deployable. MG Harry W. O. Kinnard, Jr., commanded the division during its test phase. On 30 June 1965, the division was again inactivated. The next day, the 1st Cavalry Division (Airmobile) was officially activated pursuant to GO 185, Headquarters Third Army and was formed from the resources of the 11th Air Assault Division (Test) and the 2d Infantry Division at Fort Benning, Ga.

MEN OF THE 11TH AIRBORNE. A follow-up of some of the distinguished men of the division. Note that Generals Gavin and Yarborough though not specifically attached to the division have been so close to it, and so involved with the airborne concept, that they are also included here.

Bernheim, Eli D. Jr. Joined the Army Reserve after the war. Called to active duty during the Korean War, he served with the 187th Abn RCT in Korea. Returned to civilian life in 1953 and joined the Pennsylvania National Guard. Promoted to colonel in 1969. Currently works with the IRS. Lives in Wyncote, PA.

Burgess, Henry A. Joined the Wyoming National Guard in 1937. Graduated from Harvard in 1940. Entered University of Michigan Law School, September 1940. Came on active duty when the Guard was activated in February 1941. Originally a platoon leader in Troop E of the 115th Cavalry (Armored Cars), which was designated the recon company for the 11th Philippine Infantry Division being activated in the Philippines. Troop E left San Francisco in November 1941 on the Army Transport *Tasker H. Bliss*; on 7 December 1941, the War Department ordered the transport to return to San Francisco. In 1943 Burgess joined the 11th Airborne Division. Shortly after the war, he married Mary, finished law school, returned to Sheridan, Wyoming, served in the Wyoming House of Representatives and Senate, and as County Prosecuting Attorney closed down gambling which had been wide-spread in the county for many years. Today he is a prominent lawyer and rancher (his spread covers some 40,000 acres) in Sheridan. Currently is president of the 11th Airborne Division Association.

Carnahan, David. Served as Deputy Commissioner of the Immigration Department 1955–1961. Died in 1984.

Conable, John S. After the war, returned to Warsaw, NY and started a law practice and began farming. In 1951, elected Wyoming County Judge and Surrogate and held the job until retirement on 1 January 1984. Member of the Bennett Commission (1965–68), which made recommendations to the New York legislature for the modernization of laws relating to estates. Would like to think that his greatest accomplishment is passing on "to future generations the qualities of mind, personality and character necessary to be a good paratrooper." Currently farming in Warsaw.

Crawford, Leo E. Served with the 11th Airborne after the war at Fort Campbell as XO of the reactivated 3d Battalion of the 188th, at the time an all-black battalion. Retired from the Army in 1958. Now resides in La Mesa, CA.

Ewing, Bud. Served as a Deputy Commissioner of the Immigration Department, 1955–61. Died 1984.

Gavin, James M. USMA 1929. Promoted to major general in 1944 at age 37. Commanded the 82d Airborne Division from 1944 until 1948. Commanded VII Corps in Europe 1952–54. Served as Chief of the Army's Research and Development Office. Retired in 1958 as a lieutenant general. U.S. Ambassador to France 1961–62. Chairman of the Board of Arthur Little Company. Now a consultant. Lives in Winter Park, Florida.

Kennington, Robert E. After the war, served in Sapporo as the 11th Airborne

Division JAG but spent most of the rest of his Army career in infantry units, including the 2d Battle Group of the 504th in the 11th Airborne in Germany and Commander of the 4th Battle Group at Fort Ord, CA. Retired from the Army in 1961 as a colonel and worked for a number of years as a claims representative for an insurance group. Retired again in October 1976 and lives in Sonoma, CA. Travels and researches steamship history.

LaFlamme, Ernest H. USMA 1937. Retired as a colonel in 1962. Died in Manchester, NH, on 6 August 1980.

Lahti, Edward H. USMA 1939. After the war, continued to command the 511th until September 1947 when he returned to Fort Bragg and assumed command of the 504th Parachute Infantry Regiment of the 82d Airborne Division. June 1949, assigned to the Office of the Chief of Staff, U.S. Army. In 1952–53, attended the Army War College. Later commanded the Pacific Atomic Proving Grounds and served successively as the Inspector of Infantry for the Army Field Forces, Special Assistant to the Secretary of Defense, and Senior Advisor to MAAG Viet Nam. Retired as a colonel in 1962. Currently lives in Herndon, VA.

Lombardi, Arthur P. Received a battlefield commission during the war. After the war, received a regular army commission and served in a number of airborne artillery positions. Last assignment was post commander of Fort Campbell, KY. Retired in the rank of colonel. Currently serves as President of the local chapter of the 11th Airborne Association and is the Honorary Colonel of the 320th FA Battalion. Lives in Clarksville, TN.

McGowan, Glenn J. During the occupation commanded a battalion of the 187th and was executive officer of the 187th when the unit moved from Japan to Ft. Campbell; commanded the 508th RCT at Forts Benning and Campbell, 1953–55; commanded the 188th AIR at Campbell 1956; served as military attache in Rangoon; attended the Army War College; served as deputy chief of staff of Seventh Army; deputy J-3 of EUCOM in Paris; and commander of Fort McNair, Wash, DC. Over the years, among other things, played golf with Gen. Ne Win of Burma, the Duke of Windsor and Henry Ford; walked with President Truman on his morning "constitutional"; supplied cigars to Winston Churchill; and dined with Vice President Alben Barkley in his home in Paducah, Ky. Retired from the Army as a colonel, 31 July 1961; later taught school and coached Riverside City College golf team; retired from teaching in 1971; resides in San Diego, CA.

Mesereau, Thomas A. USMA January 1943. Immediately after the signing of the surrender document in Tokyo Bay, he hand-carried the document back to Washington. Served in the 11th after the war. Coached the division's theater championship football team, Fall of 1946. Resigned from the Army in 1953. Worked in the restaurant business as an owner and consultant. Died in Irvine, CA, 16 March 1986.

Miley, William M., Jr. Returned from Japan in April 1947 and then headed the A and B Stages at Benning's Jump School until 1950. Then rejoined the 11th Airborne Division at Fort Campbell. Joined the 187th as acting battalion commander and regt'l S-3 during the Korean War, 1951–53. Returned to duty at the Infantry School until 1955. Served in Berlin, 1956–58. Joined the Green Berets in 1960 and served in Viet Nam, 1964. Returned to Fort Bragg as XO of the 3d Special Forces Group, 1965–66. Headed UW department of the Special Warfare School and then commandant of the School until retirement as a colonel in 1973. Currently lives in Starkville, MS.

Miley, William M. USMA November 1918. CG 17th Airborne Division, ETO 1945. CG U.S. Army Alaska 1952–55. Retired as a MG 1965. Currently living in Starkville, MS.

Muller, Henry J. After the war, became Assistant G-2, Eighth Army. Next served as aide to General Courtney Hodges and General Walter Bedell Smith and as special assistant to General Smith when he directed the CIA. Attache in El Salvador, 1953–56. Commander of 503d PIR, Fort Bragg, NC, 1960–61. Commandant of US Army School of the Americas in the Canal Zone, 1963–64. Promoted to BG and served as deputy director in DCSOPS in the Pentagon and then as chief of U.S. Military Group in Argentina. Moved to Viet Nam as ADC of the 101st Airborne Division. Returned to States as CG of the Infantry Training Center Fort Polk. Retired in July 1971. Owns and operates a garden supply company in Santa Barbara, CA.

Pearson, George O. Left the 187th in fall of 1945, returned to the States, became a member of the Engineer Corps, returned to Manila in 1946 as Area Engineer to assist in the rehabilitation of Manila and the Luzon railroads. June 1947, at the request of General Eichelberger, returned to command the 187th on Hokkaido. Left the 187th again in 1948. Attended the Industrial College, Class '51. Served with the DCSOPS, Pentagon. 1952, commanded the 508th AIR at Benning. 1953, assigned to Berlin. Retired as a colonel in November 1958. Joined the National Guard of Wyoming and from 1962 to 1967 served as the adjutant general of Wyoming as a major general. From 1967 to 1970, was in Viet Nam as operations officer of PA and E and as manager of Cam Rahn Bay. Retired again in 1970. Currently, associated with Husman General Contractors in Sheridan, Wyoming.

Pierson, Albert E. In October of 1945, left the 11th for assignment to Hqs. Army Ground Forces as the Deputy G-4. Served successively as Deputy Administrator for Administrative Services and Special Assistant to the Administrator of the War Assets Administration; CG of South Sector Command, Hawaii; Deputy Director of the Joint Staff for Logistics Plans; promoted to MG in 1950; Chief of Joint Military Advisory Group and Advisor to the President of the Philippines; President of the Joint Airborne Troop Board, Fort Bragg; Chief of Staff, Army Forces Far East in Japan; Inspector General of the Army; 1959, retired for age at 60. After retirement, became a student and received BA and MBA degrees from George Washington University; currently resides in Washington, D.C.

Quandt, Douglass P. USMA 1937. Served in the Korean War as Assistant Artillery Officer of X Corps. In 1960–61 served in SHAPE. Commanding General of the 4th Armored Division Artillery, 1961–62. Commanded 16th Corps, 1962–64. Retired from the Army in 1966 with the rank of major general. Lifelong bachelor. Died in San Francisco, 30 March 1973.

Ringler, John M. Colonel U.S. Army, retired. Served in the Army for thirty years, twenty-four of which were with airborne units—a near record. After World War II, served with the 11th Airborne in Japan and Fort Campbell, KY. Served as an advisor in Viet Nam 1957–1958 and with the Green Berets at Fort Bragg from 1966 until his retirement on 30 June 1970. In 1971, joined the State Department as an advisor to the Vietnamese National Police and served again in Viet Nam until the summer of 1973. Now fully retired and lives in Fayetteville, NC.

Ryder, William T. USMA 1936. Retired from the army as a brigadier general in 1966 after serving with X Corps in the Korean War, as attache to Japan, later with NATO, and with the Department of Army Research and Development Office. Currently resides in Pinehurst, NC.

Santos, Terry R. Discharged from the Army on 8 October 1945. Returned to college and received a BS/ME and a BA in English (Humanities). Retired on 31 December 1986 after 30 years as a teacher of English composition, both oral and written, to mid- and top-level executives. In retirement spends time on charity work and finding former recon platoon members (24 to date).

Skau, George. Killed when the C-46 in which he was riding from Lipa, Luzon to Okinawa crashed into a cliff above the Naha harbor obscured by smoke from ships in the harbor protecting themselves from kamikaze aircraft over the harbor.

Soule, Robert H. Returned to the division and served as assistant division commander of the 11th Airborne during the occupation of Japan. Promoted to major general and served as Military Attache to China during the reign of Chiang Kai Shek. Retired to San Francisco from the Army as a major general and died some years ago.

Swing, Joseph M. USMA 1915. Left the 11th Airborne Division on 2 February 1948, thus completing a continuous, record-establishing, five-year tour as the commander of the same division in training, combat and occupational duties to assume command of I Corps in Kyoto, Japan; on 12 April 1949, moved to Fort Sill as the Artillery School commandant; on 1 April 1950 he became the commandant of the Army War College at Fort Leavenworth, Kansas and on 1 July 1951, moved the War College to Carlisle Barracks, PA. He was promoted to lieutenant general on 9 February 1951 and assumed command of Sixth Army at the Presidio of San Francisco on 1 August 1951. On 28 February 1954, on his sixtieth birthday, General Swing retired from the Army. In May 1954, President Eisenhower appointed him U.S. Commissioner of Immigration and Naturalization, a post he held until 1961. He died in San Francisco on 9 December 1984 at age ninety.

Vanderpool, Jay D. Completed thirty years service while in Viet Nam and retired from the Army in 1976 as a colonel. Currently lives in Sarasoto, FL and serves occasionally as a consultant to the Defense Department.

Yarborough, William P. USMA 1937. Retired in 1971 as a lieutenant general after an outstanding career including command of the Special Warfare Center at Fort Bragg, commanding general of I Corps in Korea, and deputy commander and chief of staff of USARPAC in Hawaii. Currently resides in Southern Pines, NC.

BIBLIOGRAPHY

Abernathy, Col. William C. Four letters to author, 1988.

Allen, Gabe E. Letter to author, 2 May 1988.

Ammerman, Mort. Letter to author, 24 April 1988.

Annex Number 2 to Ltr Orders, Hqs. 11th Airborne Division, 29 December 1943.

Barnes, 1st Lt. Richard V. Monograph, "Opn of 3d Bn 511th PIR—Leyte," The Infantry School, 1949.

Becker, Carl M. Unpublished manuscript re Headquarters Battery, 866th AAA AW Bn., Leyte.

Belanger, Richard J. Letter to author, 22 June 1988.

Bernheim, Col. Eli D. Jr. Letters to author, March 1988, including an unpublished, detailed history of the 187th in combat—author unknown.

Blair, Clay. *Ridgway's Paratroopers*. N.Y.: Dial Press, 1985.

Bollman, Benjamin E. "Liberation, Free at Last," 25 October 1979.

Bolner, Merrill H. Letter to author, 3 July 1982.

Boosalis, Nicholas A., MD. Two letters to author, 1988.

Bostick, Deane E. "The 11th," *Gent* magazine.

Brezae, Arthur J. Letter to author, 12 June 1988.

Burgess, Henry A. Fifteen monographs, undated; ten letters to author, 1988.

Burris, Lt. Col. Lou. Two letters to author and monograph re D Battery 457th PFA Bn, 1988.

Cannon, M. Hamlin. *Leyte, The Return to the Philippines*. Washington, DC: U.S. Government Printing Office, 1954.

Cavanaugh, Col. Stephen E. Jr. "Let's Attack at Night," The Infantry School Quarterly, October 1953.

Chambers, W. L., MD. Letter to author, 23 May 1988.

Chiesa, John. Letter to author, 11 June 1988.

Childers, Paul S. Two letters to author, enclosing clippings and reminiscences.

Cole, Edward J. Autobiographical monograph, 25 February 1988.

Conable, John S. Superb personal reminiscences: "A Mouldy Civilian Becomes a Soldier," 1988, and letters to author.

Conley, Lt. Col. Manuel. "Silent Squadrons," American History, June 1983.

Cook, Maj. John M. Monograph, "Opn of Co. D 511th PIR near Lipa," The Infantry School, 1949.

Coulter, Capt. John A. Monograph, "Opn of H Co. 3/511th PIR-Manila," The Infantry School, 1947.

Crawford, Leo E. Two letters to author, undated, probably July 1988.

DA, Chief of Military History. Letter to author verifying award of battle star to 11th Airborne Division for New Guinea campaign.

Department of the Army Publication #20-260, "The German Campaign in the Balkans," 1953.

Devlin, Gerard M. Paratrooper! New York: St. Martin's Press, 1979.

Dickerson, Robert L. Monograph re Hqs Co 1st Bn 188th GIR and invasion of Luzon, undated.

Doherty, George. Four monographs, undated.

E Company 511th PIR Passenger List, Shipment 1855-D, May 1944.

Eichelberger, Lt. Gen. Robert L. "Our Jungle Road to Tokyo," Saturday Evening Post, 10 September 1949, and "Dear Miss Em," 1945.

11th Airborne Weekly newspaper, "The Quick Release," Augsburg, 22 February 1957.

Ermatinger, Ralph E. Letter to author, 2 August 1988.

Fant, Lindsay B. Letter to author, November 1988.

Farnsworth, Clayton B. Letter to author.

Faulkner, Col. Lyman S. Monograph, "511th PIR in Malepunyo," TIS, 1949; letter to author with clippings, 22 February 1988.

Fish, David B. Many clippings and photos of 1/188th AIR during nuclear tests in Nevada, 1951; letter to author, 16 June 1988.

Flanagan, Lt. Gen. Edward M., Jr. The Los Banos Raid. Novato, CA: Presidio Press, 1986.

Flanagan, Maj. Edward M., Jr. The Angels. Washington: The Infantry Journal Press, 1948.

Fullilove, Mrs. C. W. (nee Mary Anne Swing). Letter to author, 24 February 1988, including 17 letters from General Swing to Gen. Peyton C. March, his father-in-law; letters cover the period 9 October 1945 to 4 October 1947.

General Order Number 26, Hqs. USAFFE, 11 February 1945 (battle honors for 11th Airborne Division for New Guinea campaign).

Gensiejewski, A. A. Photos, clippings from 511th newspaper, 8 June 1946, and *Stars and Stripes*, 19 May 1947.

Gideon, Lt. Gen. Francis C. Letter to author, 10 December 1988.

Giordano, Maj. Joseph B. Monograph, "Opn of G Co 187th GIR—Ormoc," The Infantry School, 1948.

Grace, Thomas G. Letter to author, 14 July 1988.

Grigg, Maj. Martin C. "The Operations of the 1st Bn, 149th Infantry in the Battle of Buri Airstrip."

Halsema, James J. Letter to author, 23 February 1988.

Hammrich, Edward A. Two letters to author, 1988.

Hart, B. H. Liddell. *History of the Second World War*. New York: E. P. Putnam's Sons, 1970.

Hausen, Arnold C. Two letters to author, 1988.

Hayward, Maj. Gen. Harold I. Letter to author, 11 January 1988.

Hegedus, Steve M. Monograph, March 1988, and undated manuscript, "A Story about A Co 511th PIR at Camp Mackall, NC."

Hembree, James E. Monograph and log of 711th Abn Ord Maintenance Company and Battalion, 12 December 1942 to 1 July 1958, and letter to author, March 1988.

Hendry, Col. James B. Letter to author, 29 March 1988.

Holcombe, Lt. Col. Frank S. Monograph, "Opn 2/511th PIR Tagaytay Ridge and Advance on Manila," The Infantry School, 1950.

Hoppenstein, Maj. Isaac. Monograph, "Opn of 187th GIR Nasugbu," The Infantry School, 1948.

Hoska, Col. Lukas E., Jr. Letter to Arnold C. Hansen, 7 March 1988.

Jablonsky, Maj. Gen. Harvey J. Monograph, undated.

James, D. Clayton. *The Years of MacArthur 1941–45*. Boston: Houghton Mifflin Co., 1975.

Jansen, Dorothy. Monograph and two letters to author, 1988.

Jeffress, Capt. Edwin B. Monograph, "Opn of 2d Bn 511th PIR in Southern Manila," The Infantry School, 1949.

Johansen, Maj. Herbert O. "Banzai at Burauen."

Julien, priest of "The Missionaries of Our Lady of La Salette." Excellent undated autobiography.

Kalamas, Michael J. Unpublished autobiographical manuscript re Japanese parachute attack near San Pablo.

Keegan, John. *Six Armies in Normandy*. New York: The Viking Press, 1982.

Kennington, Col. Robert E. Clippings, four letters to author, 1988; four letters to Rev. Franklin D. Haas, 1988; and monograph, "Opn of Los Banos Force," The Infantry School, 1948.

Kitchen, W. C. Two letters to author, 1988.

Kornbluh, Jacob. Letter to author, 22 August 1988.

Kozlowski, Chester J. Clippings and three letters to author, 1988.

Krueger, Gen. Walter. *From Down Under to Nippon*. Washington, DC: Combat Forces Press, 1953.

Kusmierszyk, Henry. Letter to author, 14 February 1988.

Lahti, Col. Edward H. Letter to author, 5 December 1985.

Leister, Capt. Albert F. Monograph, "Opn of 11th Abn Div Nasugbu to Manila," The Infantry School, 1950.

LeRoy, Rev. Bob Powell. Letter to author and numerous clippings and monograph, 1988.

Lewis, Frank J. Reminiscences and letter to author, 30 January 1988.

Litherland, Robert N. Letter to author, 30 January 1988.

Log of the 1st Bn 188th GIR at Ternate, 26 February 1945 to 31 March 1945.

Lombardi, Col. Arthur P. Many letters to author, including documents and his World War II service record.

Lorio, James W., Ed. *Winds Aloft*. New Jersey: 511th PIR Association, 1988.

MacArthur, Gen. Douglas A. *Reminiscences*. New York: Da Capo Press, 1964.

Mahan, Charles. Letter to author, 20 June 1988.

Manchester, William. *American Caesar*. Boston: Little, Brown and Co., 1978.

Marks, Dean E. Monograph, "The Day the Tank Blew Up," 1988; letter to author, 23 June 1988.

Marshall, Bert W. Autobiographical monograph, August 1988.

Maurus, Roy A. Letter to author, 4 May 1988.

McCullough, Thomas J. Letter to Henry Burgess with monograph, 3 February 1988.

McGourtys, Ted J. Letter to author with clippings, 8 June 1988.

McGowan, Col. Glen J. Many photos and thirteen letters to author, 1988.

Merritt, Capt. Harrison John. Monograph, "Opn of G Co 187th GIR in attack on Nichols Field," The Infantry School, 1948.

Miley, Col. William M., Jr. (Buzz). Two letters to author, 1988.

Miller, Mrs. Kenneth G. Letter to author, 14 July 1988, enclosing illustrated, autobiographical manuscript of Pfc K. G. Miller with pertinent newspaper clippings of World War II.

Muller, Brig. Gen. Henry J. Four letters to author, 1988.

Natkiel, Richard. *Atlas of World War II*. New York: The Military Press, 1985.

Nestor, Dr. Thomas. Letter to author, 15 January 1988.

Newill, William C. Letter to author, 5 February 1988.

187th informal, unpublished, and undated history.

Parsons, Otis, Jr. Letter to Henry Burgess, 6 February 1988.

Patane, Sam V. Letter to author, 25 April 1988.

Pearson, Maj. Gen. George O. Letter to author, 18 January 1988.

Piaseczny, J. J. Letter to author, 30 January 1988.

Pierson, Maj. Gen. Albert E. Thirty letters to author, 1988.

Polka, Jim. Letter to author, undated—probably October 1988.

Poole, C. Smith. Two monographs dated 29 February 1988, and letter to author, 21 March 1988.

Prange, Gordon W. *Miracle at Midway.* New York: Penguin Books, 1982.

Richmond, Col. R. T. Letter to author, 5 February 1988.

Riley, Lt. Col. E. F. Letter to Henry Burgess, 10 March 1988.

Riley, Dr. R. J., Dental Officer, 511th PIR. Letter to author, 3 February 1988.

Rivers, William R. Letter to author, 2 February 1988.

Roberts, Bill P. Letter to Henry Burgess, 10 June 1988.

Ross, K. E. Three letters to author, 1988.

Santos, Terry R. Five letters to author, 1988.

Scheer, Maj. Gen. Frederick J. Letter to author, 12 September 1988.

Shaw, Col. Donald P. Letter to General Swing, 30 September 1982.

Sibio, Richard. Letter to author, 12 March 1988.

Smith, Robert Ross. *Triumph in the Philippines.* Washington, DC: U.S. Government Printing Office, 1973.

Special Orders Number 1, Hqs., 11th Airborne Division, Camp Mackall, NC, 25 February 1943; Special Orders Number 1, 188th GIR, Camp Mackall, NC, 25 February 1943.

Special Orders Number 149, Hqs., 75th Infantry Division, Fort Meade, MD, 11 December 1942; Special Order Number 2, Hqs., 188th GIR, Camp Polk, LA, 10 January 1944.

Spector, Ronald H. *Eagle Against the Sun,* New York: The Free Press, 1985.

Steinberg, Rafael. *Return to the Philippines.* Alexandria, VA: Time-Life Books, 1983.

Stilz, Wallace P. Clippings from "Voice of the Angels," 1982, and letter to author, 4 April 1988.

Svrcek, Edward M. Letter to author, 1 February 1988.

Swindler, H. R. (Jake). Letter to Henry Burgess, 12 May 1988.

Swing, Joseph M. "Dear General: World War II Letters, 1944–45." San Francisco, CA, 1987.

Vail, Brig. Gen. Nathan C. Letter to Henry Burgess, 22 March 1988.

Vignola, James. Letter to author, including photos and personal sketches made during WW II, and memoirs, 31 August 1988.

Walker, Maj. Wayvren K. (Ripcord). "I Came Here to Jump for Joe" (song), 1946.

Wallace, Leonard. Letter to author, 4 March 1988.

Wallace, Robert. *The Italian Campaign.* Alexandria, VA: Time-Life Books, 1978.

Wentink, James T. Three letters to author, 1988.

West, William W. Monograph, "My Best Bargain Ever," undated, and letter to author, 8 May 1988.

Wheeler, Keith. *The Fall of Japan.* Alexandria, VA: Time-Life Books, 1983.

"U.S. Occupies Japan," *Life*, 10 September 1945.

Yarborough, Lt. Gen. William P. *Bailout Over North Africa,* Williamstown, NJ: Philips Publications, 1979; three letters to author, 1988.

INDEX